# THE

# PREMA-SAGARA

# THE

# PREMA-SAGARA

## *OR* OCEAN OF LOVE

**BEING A LITERAL TRANSLATION OF THE HINDI TEXT OF LALLU LAL KAVI AS EDITED BY THE LATE PROFESSOR EASTWICK, FULLY ANNOTATED AND EXPLAINED GRAMMATICALLY, IDIOMATICALLY AND EXEGETICALLY BY FREDERIC PINCOTT ( MEMBER OF THE ROYAL ASIATIC SOCIETY), THE SAKUNTALA IN HINDI, TRANSLATOR OF THE SANSKRIT HITOPADESA ETC.**

**AUTHOR: LALLU LAL KAVI**

**EDITOR: PROFESSOR EASTWICK**

GYAN

*Published by*

GYAN

Gyan Publishing House
5, Ansari Road
Daryaganj, New Delhi-110002
Phone: 011-47034999, 9811692060
E-mail: books@gyanbooks.com

*Distribution Network*
gyanbooks.com
India, USA, Canada, UK, Australia, France



ISBN: 978-81-212-9084-5 (PB)
First Published, 1897

2nd Impression 2023

*Printed at:* Gyan Press, Delhi.



**THE PREMA-SAGARA**
AUTHOR: LALLU LAL KAVI

THE

# PREMA-SÂGARA

*OR OCEAN OF LOVE*

BEING A LITERAL TRANSLATION OF THE HINDÎ TEXT OF LALLÛ LÂL KAVI AS EDITED BY THE LATE PROFESSOR EASTWICK, FULLY ANNOTATED AND EXPLAINED GRAMMATICALLY, IDIOMATICALLY AND EXEGETICALLY BY FREDERIC PINCOTT (MEMBER OF THE ROYAL ASIATIC SOCIETY), AUTHOR OF THE HINDÎ MANUAL, THE S'AKUNTALÂ IN HINDÎ, TRANSLATOR OF THE SANSKRIT HITOPADES'A, ETC., ETC.

WESTMINSTER
ARCHIBALD CONSTABLE & CO.
2, WHITEHALL GARDENS, S.W.
1897

# TRANSLATOR'S PREFACE

It is well known to all who have given thought to the languages of India that the Hindî, or Bhâshâ as the people themselves call it, is the most widely diffused and most important language of India. There are, of course, the great provincial languages—the Bengâlî, Marâṭhi, Panjâbî, Gujarâtî, Telugu, and Tamil—which are spoken by immense numbers of people, and a knowledge of which is essential to those whose lot is cast in the districts where they are spoken; but the Bhâshâ of northern India towers high above them all, both on account of the number of its speakers and the important administrative and commercial interests which attach to the vast stretch of territory in which it is the current form of speech. The various forms of this great Bhâshâ constitute the mother-tongue of about eighty-six millions of people, that is, a population almost as great as those of the French and German empires combined; and they cover the important region stretching from the Râjmahal hills on the east to Sindh on the west; and from Kashmîr on the north to the borders of the Nizam's territory on the south. Necessarily there are differences, both verbal and grammatical, over a district of this vast extent; but these differences arrange themselves under two great divisions, which have been called respectively the Eastern and the Western Hindî. Of these the Western Hindî is now the more important of the two, on account of the extensive literature which it has produced, and is yearly expanding; and because of political, commercial, and social considerations. One of the pioneers in the modern literature of this Western Hindî was S'rî Lallû Lâl Kavi, Bhâshâ Munshî in the College of Fort William at the beginning of this century. He was the author of several volumes, the most famed of which are the *Râja-nîti*, written in the dialect of Braj, and the *Prema-Sâgara*, composed in what is now termed the classical form of Hindî. This latter book has always been treated as the first reading-book placed in the hands of Hindî students, and it will long remain a book of primary value to every European resident in northern India. It is a book perfect familiarity with the contents of which is absolutely essential to the missionary; for it contains the life-work of that revelation of Deity which commands the most absorbing interest among the people of India. The two great objects of worship in modern India, whose influence extends to every act of life, are Râma and Krishṇa; the former being the exemplar of heroism and fidelity, and the latter the type of supreme love. The incidents in the lives of these adored beings are familiar to every Hindû throughout the length and breadth of India, and no Western person can understand the people, and no missionary can address himself advantageously to the work of his calling, until he has made himself master of the facts, the philosophy, and the spiritual import of the records enshrined in the *Râmâyaṇa* of *Tulsî Dâs*, and the story of Krishṇa's life as related in the *Bhagavad-Gîtâ*. It is the latter work which was presented to his countrymen in their great vernacular by Lallû Lâl in the *Prema-Sâgara*, a translation of which into English is given in the present volume. The passionate adoration which Hindûs feel for S'rî Krishṇa is conveyed in the following words, quoted from an Indian newspaper of December 27th, 1892:—

"We cannot but place him in the front rank of those who are regarded by the unanimous voice of all mankind as the spiritual lights which lead men to salvation. All his actions were Nishkâma [without desire], and he left his body while in Samâdhi [holy meditation]. He is regarded by the greatest Rishis of this land as the Pûrṇa Brahma [perfect God], the incarnation of the Absolute. If one desires to see the very embodiment of the Vedânta philosophy, he will not be satisfied with Buddha or S'ankara, with Râma or Christ, with Muhammad or Chaitanya; the spiritual grandeur of S'rî Krishṇa alone will shine before him like the absolute space from whose standpoint the million-fold curtain of Mâyâ is non-existent."

Such being the esteem in which S'rî Krishṇa is held, it is clear that no book could be better suited to the missionary, the teacher, and others who are called upon to mix among the people, in order to learn the great vernacular of India, than the *Prema-Sâgara* of Lallû Lâl. This, in fact, has been the chief use to which the book has been put by Europeans, and it must long continue to fulfil that office.

The first edition of the text, containing only half of the story, was published in 1805; and it was not until 1810 that Lallû Lâl completed the text, and reprinted the whole in a single volume. In 1825 the third edition appeared, with the addition of a vocabulary; and in 1831 another edition followed. Eleven years after this last, in 1842, a carefully revised edition by Pandit Yoga Dhyân Miśra was published under the patronage of the Government in India. Then in 1851 followed the standard text of Professor Eastwick, which was printed at Hertford under the liberal patronage of the Honourable Court of Directors; and this has remained the text-book to the present day. There have been two translations into English of this popular and useful work; one by Captain W. Hollings, of the 47th Regiment Bengal Native Infantry, and the other by Professor Eastwick himself. Captain Hollings's translation from one of the early editions is original and valuable, and the translator's intimate relations with Indians, and familiarity with colloquial Hindî and the ideas current among the people, enabled him to catch the meaning of phrases that would have proved obscure, or even unintelligible, to others less specially qualified. Unfortunately the Captain was a busy man rather than a scholar, and cannot have given sustained attention to the whole of his task. The result is a work of uneven merit, which cannot meet the requirements of a student of Hindî.

Professor Eastwick made his translation expressly for the use of learners, and states in his Preface that "every endeavour has been used to make it as literal as possible, without rendering it altogether unintelligible." A comparison between translation and text, however, fails to support this claim; for the Professor constantly departs from the form of his text for the purpose of imparting a quaintness to his English rendering, and sometimes apparently for no other object than that of presenting the ideas in a manner differing from that of Captain Hollings. Here and there, however, perhaps accidentally, he agrees with the Captain in omitting entire sentences, which are nevertheless found in his own Hindî text. Professor Eastwick also occasionally alters ideas which may have been deemed inelegant, such as changing "an umbrella" into "a canopy," and "a cuckoo" into "a bird," because in England people do not consider a cuckoo to be a sweet songster. He omits the phrase "with gait like an elephant" when applied to a lady for similar reasons; and changes "a young man" into "a man of extremely youthful appearance." His translation is furthermore, in many places, at variance with his own text, which is the one he is supposed to be rendering, and he even changes interrogations into affirmations. In fact, the Professor's translation is very far from literal, even to the extent of furnishing equivalents for all the sentences as they occur. Poetic effect seems also to have been studied, and words are introduced for which no equivalents are to be found in the original, while points of idiom elsewhere are passed over untranslated. The defects here indicated must have greatly detracted from the utility of the Professor's work.

The translation of Professor Eastwick has, however, long been out of print, and the high price obtained for such copies as occasionally change hands is a sufficient indication that a translation of the *Prema-Sâgara* is still in demand. Unfortunately for India, Hindî has not received the encouragement which its importance deserves, and it is, therefore, only the trader, teacher, and missionary, who, impelled by necessity, give attention to its study. The consequence is that those desirous of learning this rich, expressive, and useful language are left very much to their own resources. It is to meet this state of things that the present translation of Professor Eastwick's text has been prepared. It has been brought to the level of a beginner who, having acquired the elements of the language from a Grammar, takes up the *Prema-Sâgara* as a text-book without any instructor to guide his first attempts at reading, translating, and acquiring Hindî style. No attempt has, therefore, been made to offer anything else than a faithful translation, sentence by sentence, for the practically useful purpose of teaching the learner the exact meaning of each phrase, and the explanation of every idiomatic turn as it occurs. It is a book of instruction, and it keeps to that useful purpose throughout. Any attempt to render the literal translation of such a book pleasant reading is worse than useless; for, in works like the present, where both the ideas and the idioms of the languages concerned are so violently in contrast with each other, accuracy must inevitably be sacrificed to style, and even to secure the humbler object of well-rounded sentences.

Those who use this translation must remember that its sole object is to teach the language by giving an accurate rendering of each phrase, and by explaining every idiom in a book the contents of which ought to be known by every European residing in India.

The method of translation here adopted has, therefore, been one suited to the progress of the learner. The first chapter is as closely literal as the English language permits, preserving, as far as possible, the very structure of the Hindî sentences, so that the student may realize the logical sequence of ideas in the Indian mind. All words needed to complete the sense are carefully marked by brackets, and all unusual idiomatic constructions are explained. In the second chapter the translation is still quite literal, and all supplementary words are indicated, but a choice of expression has been allowed, showing the adverbial character of the Conjunctive Participle, &c., &c. In the third chapter the structure of the Hindî sentence is less rigidly adhered to; for by this time the student may be supposed to have acquired some familiarity with Indian methods of thought. In this way, while still translating literally sentence by sentence, a little more play is allowed to the English language, and in the latter half of the book the brackets have been omitted.

Throughout the entire book the literalness of the translation is consistently maintained; but the notes on idioms, &c., necessarily diminish as the book proceeds. It is a mistake to suppose that the study of a language is facilitated by placing obstacles in the path of a student under the fallacious idea that it makes him think. The too common result is that it disheartens him, and gives him wrong notions at the beginning of his course, thereby rendering subsequent progress needlessly difficult. The object of this translation is to facilitate progress, and to make the path more easy, so that the student may be encouraged by rapid and real progress, and may acquire a correct idea of the structure of the language he is endeavouring to learn. This help is especially needful in the case of Hindî, because, in most cases, it has to be acquired without tutorial assistance.

It has already been stated that this is a translation of Professor Eastwick's text of the *Prema-Sâgara*, because that has long been the standard text, and is the only version generally available. The text is, however, disfigured by a plentiful crop of misprints, and by eccentric and inconsistent spelling. In my notes I have directed attention only to such of these blemishes as affect the sense, or might confuse the learner. It is to be regretted that the transpositions of words indulged in by Lallû Lâl from the childish desire to create assonances, were not put right by the Editor. All these should have been swept out of the prose, and a consistent method of spelling should have been introduced. An entirely fresh Vocabulary is needed, giving all the words occurring in the text, and arranging them in alphabetical order, besides introducing the many very needful corrections. The subject is only alluded to here, lest the student might be occasionally puzzled by the differences between the renderings of this translation and some of the statements in that Vocabulary.

FREDERIC PINCOTT.

# CONTENTS

## CHAPTER I.



## CHAPTER II.



## CHAPTER III.



## CHAPTER IV.



## CHAPTER V.



## CHAPTER VI.



## CHAPTER VII.

## CHAPTER XVIII.



## CHAPTER XIX.



## CHAPTER XX.



## CHAPTER XXI.



## CHAPTER XXII.



## CHAPTER XXIII.



## CHAPTER XXIV.



## CHAPTER XXV.



## CHAPTER XXVI.



## CHAPTER XXVII.



## CHAPTER XXVIII.

CHAPTER XL.



CHAPTER XLI.



CHAPTER XLII.



CHAPTER XLIII.



CHAPTER XLIV.



CHAPTER XLV.



CHAPTER XLVI.



CHAPTER XLVII.



CHAPTER XLVIII.



CHAPTER XLIX.



CHAPTER L.

## CHAPTER LI.



## CHAPTER LII.



## CHAPTER LIII.



## CHAPTER LIV.



## CHAPTER LV.



## CHAPTER LVI.



## CHAPTER LVII.



## CHAPTER LVIII.

---

Page 164, note [3], *for* p. 49 *read* p. 149.

---

# PREM-SÂGAR;

OR,

## *OCEAN OF LOVE*

### REVERENCE TO THE HOLY GANES'A.[1]

Obstacle-cleaving, most famous, elephant-faced, resplendent,
Grant the boon [that] much advanced may be pure[2] speech
[and] intellectual delight.
Thee, [whose] two feet the world is gazing on, and meditating
on day and night;
Mother of the Universe, Saraswati![3] grant aptness and
eloquence to me, remembering [thee].

[At] one time the story of the Tenth Section of the holy Bhâgavata [Purâna]; composed by Vyâsadev, Chaturbhuj Miśra converted into couplets and quatrains [in] Braj-Bhâshâ, that, for [the use] of the College, in the reign of the revered king of kings, the repository of all [good] qualities, the virtuous, profoundly

[1] *Ganeśa*, = *gana*, "company," and *íśa*, "lord"; "the leader of the troop" [of subordinate deities]. He is the Hindû god of sagacity, with a human body and an elephant's head, having, however, only one tusk. The head is, no doubt, complimentary to the well-known sagacity of the elephant; but the Brahmâvaivarta-Purâṇa asserts that it was due to the first glance which the planet Saturn gave to the new-born son of S'iva and Pârvati. No sooner had that ill-omened glance fallen on the infant than his head flew off, and re-united with Krishṇa in the realms of bliss; hereupon Vishṇu, hastily finding a sleeping elephant, cut off the head and clapped it on the child's shoulders. Ganeśa both causes and removes obstacles, and his name is, therefore, cited at the commencement of all undertakings, whether literary or practical.

[2] For *vishad* read *viśad*, i.e. "pure," not "poisonous."

[3] *Sarasvati* means "the watery," and is the name of a stream in the Punjab which watered the holy region of the Hindûs in Vedic times. On the banks of this stream the solemn sacrifices were performed; and the flow of these purifying waters was compared, and afterwards identified, with the flow of purifying speech, prayers, and sacred texts. Thus she came to be regarded as the goddess of speech, the inventress of the Devanâgarî alphabet, the patroness of wisdom and the sciences, the mother of the Vedas, and the wife of Brahmâ. This explains her invocation at the beginning of a literary composition.

intelligent, and illustrious Governor-General the Marquis of Wellesley,—

[He] adorned poets [and] scholars, clothing [them in] jewels
[and] ornaments ;
Having repeatedly investigated knowledge, he [to] the
delight [of his] heart made all subject [to himself];
[By] the fame [of his] munificence, all around, the hearts of
poets were elevated,
They are coming [and] they are receiving rubies, jewels,
horses, elephants, and much wealth.

And by order of the revered patron, the gifted conferrer of happiness, Mr. John Gilchrist, in the year [of Vikramâditya] 1860,[1] S'rî Lallû Jî Lâl, the poet, a Gujarâtî Brâhman, [of the] Sahasra Avadîch [family], an inhabitant of Agra, taking the gist of it, rejecting foreign vocables, [and] relating [it] in the pure language of Dehli [and] Agra, has named [the book] *Prema-Sâgara.* But, by the departure of the revered John Gilchrist, it remained half-done and half-printed.[2] That same [book] now, under the rule of the famous ruler of kings, the most compassionate, beneficent, renowned, and glorious Gilbert Lord Minto ; by order of the famous, the abode of happiness, liberality, and kindness, the fortunate and powerful, Captain John William Taylor ; and by aid of the revered, profoundly intelligent ocean of kindness, the benevolent and fortunate, Dr. William Hunter ; and with the suggestions of the revered, most accomplished, kind, and fortunate, Lieutenant Abraham Lockett ; that [aforesaid] poet, in the year [of Vikramâditya] 1866, completed [and] printed [the book], for the instruction of the students of the College.[3]

[1] The era of Vikramâditya began fifty-six years before Christ ; and, therefore, by deducting that number the date of the corresponding Christian year can always be ascertained.

[2] *Lit.*, "formed and half-formed, printed and half-printed" ; but the phrase means simply "half-done."

[3] The gentlemen here spoken of were :—Richard Colley, Earl of Mornington, brother of the great Duke of Wellington. He was Governor-General of India from 17th May, 1798, to 30th July, 1805 ; and, in consequence of the success of his administration, was created Marquis Wellesley. The Earl of Minto was Governor-General from 31st July, 1807, to 4th October, 1813. Dr. Gilchrist was a medical officer in the employ of the East India Company, at the beginning of this century, who devoted his attention to the cultivation of the *patois* which formed the medium of communication between the Persian rulers of northern India and the inhabitants. He caused a whole literature to be written in this mongrel dialect, and by copiously enriching it with Persian words, may be said to have created what Europeans call the Hindustani language. This artificial form of speech having been adopted for public business in 1830, has spread since then at a prodigious rate, and has had the unfortunate result of greatly obstructing communication between the rulers and the ruled. Capt. Taylor and Lieut. Lockett were officers of the East India Company's Bengal Army, who, with Dr. Hunter, of the Medical Service, were the active collaborateurs of John Gilchrist in the creation of Urdû.

## CHAPTER I.

Parîkshit becomes King in Hastinâpura—He insults the Rishi Lomas—Is cursed by the son of the Rishi—He repents of his sin, retires to the Ganges to die—He is there visited by the saintly S'ukadev, who recounts the surprising history of S'rî Krishṇa; the hearing of which confers salvation on King Parîkshit—The birth of Kañs—His efforts to suppress the worship of Vishṇu—The birth of Krishṇa announced.

Now [is] the story's beginning.[1] At the end of the great Bhârata [war],[2] when S'rî Krishṇa had disappeared,[3] the Pâṇḍavas,[4] having become deeply grieved [and] having given the dominion of Hastinâpur to Parîkshit, went to the Himâlayas for [final] dissolution; and King Parîkshit, having subdued all countries, began to reign justly. After some time,[5] one day, King Parîkshit went to the chase, [and][6] there saw a cow and a bull running along towards [him],[7] behind them a S'ûdra, with[8] a club [in his] hand, was [also] coming, beating [them]. When they drew near, the King [having become] grieved and enraged,[9] called to the S'ûdra [and] said, "Hi! who art thou? Explain thyself, that thou art beating a cow and a bull, knowingly.[10] Hast thou supposed Arjun

[1] This should be *atha kathârambhaḥ*. It is a Sanskrit phrase.

[2] After *Mahâbhârat* the word *yuddh* is understood, as is frequently the case. It means "the great war of the descendants of Bharata," in which the sons of Dhṛitarâshṭra and Pâṇḍu, who were descended from Kuru and Bharata, contended for mastery in the neighbourhood of Hastinâpur, near Dehli. Bharata was the son of Dushyant and S'akuntalâ, and the story of his birth is told in Kâlidâsa's well-known drama, bearing his mother's name.

[3] For *antaradhân* read *antardhân*.

[4] The Pâṇḍavas are the five brothers, the reputed sons of Pâṇḍu, who formed one of the contending parties in the great war. Their renunciation of hard-won sovereignty is related in the Mahâprasthânika section of the Mahâbhârata.

[5] *kitne ek* is indefinite; *din* = "time."

[6] *to* is here the correlative of *ek din*.

[7] *chalâ ânâ*, "to advance towards"; *dauṛe chalâ ânâ*, "to approach in a running condition." Colloquially, *dauṛe chale â,o* is the equivalent of "Hurry up!" or "Look sharp!"

[8] The Past Participle thus inflected implies concurrency as to time; *lit.* "a club [being] held [in] the hand," i.e. "with a club in his hand."

[9] For *bhumbhulâ,e* read *jhunjhulâ,e*. The *kar* is the termination of the Conjunctive Participle, applicable to all three of the verbs.

[10] The Conjunctive Participle may often be thus translated adverbially. This disjointed sentence is the first instance of the rhyming prose with which Lallû Lâl has filled this book. The jingle of sound is revealed by printing the words thus—

Are! tû kaun hai? apnâ *bakhân kar*,
Jo mârtâ hai gâ,e au bail ko *jânkar*.

The next two sentences are also rhyming couplets. Attention will not again be called to this; but whenever the student meets with an awkwardly constructed sentence, he may find the explanation in some transposition of words to produce a rhyme.

gone afar, and hence hast disregarded[1] his law? Hear [me]! in the family of Pâṇḍu[2] thou wilt not find any such person in whose[3] presence anyone shall oppress the humble." Saying this much, the King took [his] sword in [his] hand; [the other] perceiving that [action], stood still from fear.[4] Then the King, having called the cow and bull near [him], asked, "Who are you? Tell me clearly;[5] gods are you or Brâhmaṇs? and why are you fleeing away?[6] Tell [me] this fearlessly; while I am here[7] no one has so much power as to afflict you."[8]

This much was heard; *then*[9] the bull, having inclined[10] [his] head, said, "Mahârâj! this form of evil, [this] black-coloured, frightful figure, which is standing in your presence, is the Kali-yug;[11] because of his coming I am fleeing away. This cow-formed [one][12] is the Earth; she also is fleeing from fear of this same [Kali-yug]. My name is Dharma;[13] I have four feet—penance, truth, compassion, and meditation. In the Satyayug my feet were twenty-twentieths,[14] in the Tretâ-yug [they were] sixteen, in the Dwâpara [they were] twelve, now in the Kali-yug four-twentieths remain; hence during the Kali-[yug] I am unable to move about."[15] The Earth said, "O incarnation of justice! I also cannot remain in this Age [of the world],[16] because S'ûdras

1 *Lit.*, "not recognized."
2 For *Panḍu* read *Pâṇḍu* throughout.
3 This untranslatable *ki* is quite idiomatic as a pivot linking two clauses, one of which illustrates as well as complements the other.
4 *Lit.*, "became erect through fear."
5 *bujhâkar* = "instructingly."
6 *bhâgâ jânâ* is continuative, on the model of *chalâ jânâ.*
7 *mere rahte*, "my remaining," i.e. "while I am remaining here."
8 *itnî* and *jo* are correlative.
9 The *to* simply emphasizes *tab*.
10 For *bhukâ* read *jhukâ*.
11 The Kali-yug is the last of the four ages into which the life of every cosmical creation is divided. The names of the four ages are Krita or Satya, Tretâ, Dwâpara, and Kali; the first endures for 4000 divine years, with a period of 400 divine years both before and after as a kind of twilight; the second age lasts for 3000 divine years, with two periods of twilight of 300 years each; the third age endures for 2000 divine years, having 200 years of twilight both before and after; and the fourth age will consist of 1000 divine years, with two twilights of 100 years each. The divine years are each as long as 360 years of men, and therefore the duration of a creation is a tolerably protracted period. It may tranquillize the nervous to know that the present, or Kali, age is to endure for 432 000 years of men, of which only about 5000 years are as yet expired.
12 *swarûp* is an affix; for *pirthî* read *prithwî* throughout.
13 Dharma is Justice personified (based on *dri*, "to hold, fix, restrain"), and hence also applied to Virtue and Religion. In Manu's Code (i. 98) it is asserted that the birth of every Brâhmaṇ is a re-incarnation of Dharma.
14 *biswâ* is the twentieth part of anything; therefore, *bîs biswe* means "twenty twentieths," or the whole. Hindû arithmetic is throughout quarternary, and constantly presents multiples of four.
15 That is to say, Justice and Religion have but little currency in the Kali-yug.
16 This Passive construction combined with the Ablative expresses impossibility.

having become kings will inflict upon me excessive wrongs,[1] their burden I shall be unable to endure; from this fear I also am fleeing." Upon hearing this the King angrily said to the Kali-yug, "I [will] kill thee on the instant."[2] He agitatedly having fallen at the King's feet, entreatingly said, "Lord of the earth![3] now, indeed, I am come [under] your protection;[4] please indicate some place for me to remain in; because the Three Times and the Four Ages which Brahmâ created can in no way be obliterated."[5] Upon hearing this much, King Parîkshit said to the Kali-yug, "Dwell in these places [only],[6]—in gambling, lying, the alcohol market, harlots' houses, murder, theft, and gold." Having heard this, the Kali-[yug], for his part,[7] departed to his location, and the King fixed religion in his heart, [and] the Earth assumed[8] its proper form. The King then came [back] to the city, and began to rule religiously.

Some time [having] elapsed,[9] the King again once[10] went out to hunt, and [by] continuing the sport[11] became[12] thirsty. In the very [golden] crown on his head the Kali-yug was actually residing;[13] he, having found his opportunity, made the King ignorant. The King urged by[14] thirst, came where[15] the Rishi Lomas,[16] seated[17] [with his] eyes closed, engaged in the meditation

[1] *adharm* is plural, as is seen by the following *tin*.

[2] The Present tense used for the Future, to show the promptness of the act.

[3] For *Prithînâth* read *Prithwînâth*.

[4] *Lit.*, "into your asylum"; *saraṇ* should be *śaraṇ*, and the word is properly masculine.

[5] For *meṭe ne* read *meṭe na*; *lit.*, "in any way [one] may efface, they will not be effaced." This is highly idiomatic.

[6] The "only" is implied by *itnî*, "these many," which of course excludes other places.

[7] Here *to* indicates a contrast. The Kali-yug, for his part, does one act, and the King does another act.

[8] *mil ga,î*, "mingled with," "passed into."

[9] *bîte* is the Past Participle, with the Locative idea understood, as "on the lapse of a certain time."

[10] This text abounds in intrusive anuswâras. This *samaiñ* is for *samai*, the vulgar form of *samaya*. These blemishes are too numerous to be further specified.

[11] The repetition of *khelte* indicates the continued nature of the action.

[12] *bhayâ* is equivalent to *hu,â*. It is constantly found in poetry; and is colloquial in many places.

[13] Notice the emphatic particles here; *to*, "very," and *hî*, "actually."

[14] The Genitive to express "by" with a Past Participle is a useful idiom.

[15] For *kahâñ* read *wahâñ*.

[16] *Lomaśa* means "shaggy" or "hairy," and it is the name of a Muni or saint celebrated in the Mahâbhârata; but in the Âdi-parvan, § 40, &c., where the story of the Prem-Sâgar is told, the saint is named S'amîka, who was the brother of Vasudeva and the son of S'ûra, the grandfather of Krishṇa. S'ûra was of the Yadu or Lunar race. These relationships explain the antagonism between the Krishṇa party and that of the Kauravas mentioned later on.

[17] *âsan mâre* is a peculiar idiom; *âsan* is the seat or hams, and *âsan mârnâ* is to squat like a devotee.

of Hari, was performing austerity.[1] Having perceived him, Parîkshit began to say within himself, "This one, from conceit of his austerity, having seen me, is keeping his eyes shut." Having formed this evil opinion, he raised with [his] bow a dead snake [which] was lying there, [and] having thrown [it] on the neck of the Rishi, came [to] his own home. [On] taking off the crown, wisdom returned to the King; then [he], having reflected [on what had occurred], said, "Kali-yug's abode is in gold; this was on my head; hence I had so evil a thought that, having taken a dead snake [I] cast it on the Rishi's neck. Therefore, I now understand that Kali-yug has taken his revenge on me. How shall I escape from this grievous sin? Rather,[2] why did not all that I possess[3] depart to-day—wealth, caste-folk, wife, and kingdom? I know[4] not into what birth this wickedness will extend, that I have annoyed a Brâhmaṇ."

King Parîkshit, for his part, was in one place[5] sunk in this unfathomable ocean of cogitation; elsewhere several boys, playing about, came upon[6] [the spot] where the Rishi Lomas was. Having seen the dead snake on his neck they were astounded, and agitatedly said among themselves, "Brothers! let someone go [and] tell his son, who, in the grove on the banks of the river Kauśikî,[7] is sporting with the sons of the Rishis." One, upon hearing [this], ran [and] went [to] where Rishi S'ringî was playing with the children. [He] said, "Friend! are you playing here! Some wretch, having thrown a dead snake on your father's neck, has gone [off]." On hearing [this], the eyes of Rishi S'ringî became red, grinding his teeth together,[8] he quiveringly shook, and angrily said, "In the Kali-yug arrogant kings have arisen, by the intoxication of wealth having become blind, they

[1] *kar rahâ thâ* is the Progressive Imperfect. Every verb admits of this inflexion; and it implies that, at the time specified, the action spoken of was actually in progress. The next phrase gives the Progressive Present tense.

[2] *baran* is the Sanskrit *varam*, "better," "rather," "preferably." The mistake of considering this word to represent *varṇ*, "caste," has caused a general misapprehension of the meaning of this passage. The phrase occurs in the next page [p. 4] of the text without the word *baran*, because no preference is there intended.

[3] *merâ sab*, "my all," "all that I possess."

[4] *jânûñ*; this is really a Present Tense become aoristic by efflux of time. Colloquially, and in proverbs, the Aorist constantly preserves its original character.

[5] *yahâñ . . . jahâñ . . . tahâñ*, imply concurrence of action, i.e. while the King was doing one thing, in one place, elsewhere the boys were doing something else.

[6] *nikalnâ*, added to the base of another verb, imparts an idea of suddenness, or of the unanticipated, to it; thus *jâ nikalnâ*, "to meet with accidentally," *â nikalnâ*, "to come upon."

[7] The Kauśikî is the river Kosî, in Bihâr.

[8] The repetition of *pîs* and *thar* expresses the repetition of the act; *lagâ* belongs to *kâmpne* and *kahne*.

are become oppressors.[1] Now I will curse him;[2] he himself shall suffer that very death." Having spoken thus, Rishi S'ringî, having taken the water of the Kauśikî in the palm of the hand,[3] cursed King Parîkshit, thus, "This very snake, on the seventh day, shall bite thee."

Having in this way cursed the King, [and] come near his father, [he] removed the snake from the neck [and] said, "O father! be of good cheer![4] I have cursed him by whom the dead snake was placed on your neck." On hearing this statement the Rishi Lomas, having recovered consciousness [and] unclosed [his] eyes, after reflecting with his contemplative faculties, said, "O son! what [is] this [that] thou hast done? why didst [thou] curse the King? During his reign we have been[5] happy; no beast [or] bird even has been afflicted; so just has the government been that, during it, the lion [and] the cow were remaining together [and] saying nothing [amiss] to each other.[6] O son! what mattered it that [we] have been ridiculed by him in whose kingdom we have dwelt?[7] Why did [you] curse him [who] threw the dead snake? Thou hast committed a very great sin [by pronouncing] such a curse on a slight offence. [Thou] didst not reflect at all in [thy] heart; [thou] hast abandoned good, [and] chosen evil alone. A virtuous person ought to maintain an amiable disposition; to say nothing himself, to hearken [to the words] of others; to accept the good of all, [and] avoid the evil."

Having said this much, the Rishi Lomas, calling a pupil, said, "Do you go to King Parîkshit [and] inform him that the Rishi S'ringî[8] has cursed [him]. Good people,[9] indeed, will surely blame [S'ringî]; but let [the King] hear, and be heedful." Obeying this injunction of the preceptor, the pupil went onward to the place where the King [being] seated was meditating. On his arrival [he] said, "Mahârâj! the Rishi S'ringî has imposed this curse on you, that, on the seventh day, Takshak[10] shall bite

[1] Notice the rhyming transpositions here.

[2] For *dûhûn̄* read *dûn̄ hûn̄*. This is the Aorist fortified with the substantive verb, and it is a common colloquialism.

[3] Libations are offered by taking water in the two hands placed side by side and slightly hollowed. Such libations of water accompanied all solemn asseverations, and ceremonial observances.

[4] *Lit.*, "sustain thy body."

[5] The word *the* occasionally bears the sense of "have been"; but here the word is used, and the words are transposed, to produce a word-jingle between *sukhî* and *dukhî*.

[6] Implying that they were not at variance.

[7] *kyâ huâ*, "what has occurred?" or "what matters it?" *hañse* is plural, and the phrase is literally, "ridiculed of him." This use of the Genitive is of wide application.

[8] For *Srigo* read *S'ringî*.

[9] For *bhalâ* read *bhale*; it is a Gujarâtî inflexion, inadvertently employed by Lallû Lâl. Notice that *dehînge* is the emphatic Future, "will surely give."

[10] Takshaka is one of the principal Nâgas or snakes of Pâtâla, or the nether

[you]; now do you [so] order your actions that you may escape from the noose of Karma."[1] Upon hearing this, the King joyfully arose [and], with joined hands,[2] said, "The Rishi has conferred a great favour on me, in that[3] [he] has cursed [me]; because I had fallen into the boundless thought-ocean of delusion, [and he] has released me from that."[4] When the Saint's pupil departed, the King himself, for his part, took the Vairâgî vow, and having summoned Janamejaya,[5] [and] having given [him] the sovereignty, said, "O son! protect cows and Brâhmaṇs, and give contentment to the people." Having said this, he came [to] the female apartments, [and] beheld the women all dejected. The queens upon perceiving the King, having fallen at [his] feet, began bewailingly to say, "Mahârâj! we weak ones will be unable to endure separation from you;[6] than this, [it is] better [that] we should give up life with you." The King said, "Listen; it is fitting [that] a wife should do that by which her husband's piety may endure, and no obstacle be placed in [the path of] exalted duty."

Having said this, [and] having abandoned the illusion of wealth, caste-folk, family, and sovereignty, [and] having become free from [worldly] fascination,[7] went [and] sat on the banks of the Ganges, to accomplish his Yoga.[8] Whoever heard [of] this [circumstance] was deeply grieved and regretful,[9] [and] refrained not from tears. And when the sages heard the intelligence that King Parîkshit, in consequence of Rishi S'ringî's curse, had come

regions. These Nâgas are associated, in a friendly way, with the Krishṇa cult, Buddhism, and the Lunar dynasty.

[1] *Karma* is a sacro-philosophical term. It comprises acts committed in this life, all of which inevitably produce results in the future; it also means the aggregate result of those actions, which carries the unsanctified soul onwards to fresh states of existence conformable to the resultant of their forces; it furthermore implies, as in the text above, the result of actions performed in a previous existence, the consequences of which are now being endured. Parîkshit is invited to do something meritorious in order to neutralize the tendencies to ill-fortune which the Karma he brought into the world with him is manifesting. It is this which impels him to the voluntary surrender of state and dignity, and the pious exercises of his las few days.

[2] The attitude of respect.

[3] *jo* for "in that" is very idiomatic.

[4] *Lit.*, "that, having extracted, he has put out."

[5] *Janamejaya* means "causing men to tremble." He was the son of Parikshit, the son of Abhimanya, the son of Arjuna, one of the Pândava brothers engaged in the Mahâbhârata war. In revenge for his father's death, he performed a great sacrifice for the extermination of Nâgas; and Vyâsa related for his edification the whole of the Mahâbhârata poem.

[6] Notice the Genitive to express "from."

[7] For *niramohî* read *nirmohî*.

[8] *Yoga*, or "junction," is the re-union of the individual soul with the universal soul, and is, therefore, the attaining emancipation from continued transmigration. This extinction of individuality is to be attained by profound meditation.

[9] *pachhtâe pachhtâe*, "having repeatedly regretted," *hâe hâe kar*, "with sighs and sighs."

and sat down to die on the banks of the Ganges, then Vyâsa,[1] Vasishṭha,[2] Bhâradvâya,[3] Kâtyâyana,[4] Parâśara,[5] Nârada,[6] Viśwâmitra,[7] Vâsudeva,[8] Jamadagni,[9] &c., [in all] 88,000 Rishis came, and having spread [their] seats, sat down in rows, [and] each having reflected deeply [on his] own doctrine, began to rehearse

[1] *Vyâsa* means "the arranger"; it is the name or title conferred on the reputed arranger of the hymns of the Rig-veda, the Purâṇas, the compiler of the Mahâbhârata, and a number of other works, and the founder of the Vedânta philosophy. He was the son of Parâśara, and by command of his mother, became the father of Dhṛitarâshtra and Pâṇḍu (whose children fought out the Mahâbhârata contest), and Vidura, and S'uka, the narrator of the Bhâgavata-Purâṇa, the Tenth Section of which book is the Prem-Sâgar. Vyâsa is commonly known as Krishṇa-Dwaipâyana, because he was of dark complexion (*krishṇa*), and born on an island (*dwîpa*).

[2] *Vasishṭha* means "most wealthy." He was a famous saint of Vedic times, who specially cherished a miraculous cow, called Nandinî, who conferred all desired objects on him. He was the great champion of Brahmanic exclusiveness, and violently opposed Viśvâmitra, the saint of the military caste, who assumed priestly functions. Vasishṭha is stated to have descended from Mitra and Varuṇa, solar deities, and to have been the family priest of Sudâs, Ikshwâku, and Râmachandra, royal personages of the solar race. He is the Rishi, or author, of the seventh Maṇḍala of the Rig-veda.

[3] *Bhâradvâja* means "one of Bharadvâja's race"; a name applied to a great many people famous in Brahmanic lore, but here it means Droṇa, the preceptor of the Kauravas and Pâṇḍavas. This Droṇa played an important part throughout the Mahâbhârata contest, and afterwards became king of a part of Pânchâla.

[4] *Kâtyâyana* is the author of several famous works on grammar and ritual. He added the supplementary rules, or Vârtikas, to Pâṇini's Grammar; and he was the author of a grammatical treatise explanatory of the Yajur-veda, and of a celebrated liturgical work for the use of Advaryu priests, who performed all the manual functions at the sacrifices, such as preparing the ground, adjusting the vessels, procuring the animals, lighting the fire, killing the creature offered, &c. Kâtyâyana is considered to be the same as Vararuchi, the author of the Prâkrita-prakâśa, or grammar of the local dialects of ancient India.

[5] *Parâśara* was the son of Vasishtha and father of Vyâsa; but his genealogy is unsettled. He is the author of some hymns of the Rig-veda, and was also the compiler of a law-book. His name and association with Vasishṭha suggest a connection with Paraśu or Paraśu-Râma, the destroyer of the Kshatriya race.

[6] *Nârada* was one of the divine Rishis or saints, and author of several hymns in the Rig-veda. Mythologically he acts as messenger to the gods, and is spoken of as a son of Brahmâ. In the later literature he appears as the friend of Krishṇa, and as a kind of patron saint of music.

[7] *Viśvâmitra*, "the friend of all"; a famous Kshatriya, descended from Purûravas of the Lunar race. He is also said to have been the brother of Satyavatî, the mother of Jamadagni and grandmother of Paraśu-Râma; and the whole of the hymns of the Third Maṇḍala of the Rig-veda are ascribed to him, and members of his family. He is chiefly famous for his attempt at first to induce Vasishṭha to confer spiritual power upon him; and afterwards for his success in forcing himself into the priesthood in despite of the violent antagonism of his opponent. He is accounted the father of S'akuntalâ.

[8] *Vâsudeva*, "son of Vasudeva," is an epithet of Krishṇa. Vasudeva was the son of S'ûra, a descendant of Yadu of the Lunar line; and he was the brother of Kuntî, mother of the Pâṇḍava princes, who were thus cousins of Krishṇa.

[9] *Jamadagni*, "blazing fire," was descended from Bhṛigu, progenitor of the great Bhârgava family. He was only sixth in descent from the god Brahmâ, and was the father of Paraśu-Râma, the destroyer of the Kshatriyas. He is related to have joined Viśvâmitra in antagonism to Vasishṭha.

to the King various kinds of Dharma. Hereupon,[1] having perceived the King's faith, S'rî S'ukadev Jî[2] also arrived in a nude state[3] [with] a book under his arm.[4] On seeing him all the sages there rose up, [and] stood erect;[5] and King Parîkshit, also, standing [with] hands closed, supplicatingly said, "O abode of mercy! [you] have shown me much compassion in that, [at] this time, you have remembered me." [When the King had] said this much, the sage S'ukadev also seated [himself]; then the King said to the Rishis, "Mahârâjâs! S'ukadev Jî [is] indeed the son of Vyâs Jî and the grandson of Parâśar Jî; having seen him, you, although[6] very exalted sages, arose; that, indeed, was not fitting; tell [me] the cause of this, that the doubt of my heart may depart." Then the sage Parâśar said, "O King! how great [soever] we Rishis are, in knowledge we are quite inferior to S'uka; therefore all [of us] paid reverence to S'uka; some [too] in the hope that he is[7] the saviour of the saved; because from his very birth,[8] having become an Udâsî,[9] he has dwelt in the forest; and, O King! some great uprising of virtue[10] has taken place for thee also, in that S'ukadev Jî has come. He will declare[11] the most excellent creed of all creeds, from which thou, having escaped from birth and death, wilt cross[12] the ocean of existence." Having heard this speech King Parîkshit, having prostrated [himself], asked[13] S'rî S'ukadev Jî, "Mahârâj! explain religion to me; how shall I escape from the noose of Karma? what shall I perform in seven days? [My] impiety is boundless; how shall I cross the ocean of existence?"

S'rî S'ukadev Jî said, "O King! think not thou the time short; salvation there is in the meditation of only one hour; [just] as

[1] This use of *ki* to mark a change of subject is highly idiomatic; it is untranslatable; for it is *itne meñ*, which means "hereupon."

[2] S'ukadeva is the same as S'uka, son of Vyâsa, the narrator of the whole Bhâgavata-Purâṇa. Jî is a respectful adjunct to a name.

[3] *digambar*, "clothed with the atmosphere," therefore, naked.

[4] *Lit.*, "a book in the arm-pit."

[5] For *kharhe* read *khaṛe*.

[6] This use of *hoke* for "although" is very idiomatic.

[7] For *hai* read *haiñ*, to agree with *ye*. The implication is that S'ukadev, because of his piety, is to be the cause of others crossing the ocean of existence as well as himself.

[8] *Lit.*, "Since he took birth, from that very time," &c.

[9] Udâsîs are religious mendicants who have become indifferent to all mundane wants and emotions. They are distributed all over India, and form a prominent sect of the Sikh community.

[10] *puṇya-udaya*, as the word should be spelled, is a compound meaning "virtue's rise"; *huā* is often thus used for "has occurred" or "taken place." The King's virtuous merit has been enhanced by the mere presence of the sage.

[11] All the plural forms here are only respectful to S'ukadev.

[12] *pâr hogâ*, "wilt be on the other side."

[13] This use of *ko*, instead of *se*, with *pûchhna* is rare. It means "inquire about," "ask concerning." Colloquially, with the Imperative, a little irritation is often implied by it; as, *us ko pûchho*, "ask him (and don't bother me)."

the Saint Nârad imparted knowledge to King Shashṭângul,[1] and he in only two hours obtained salvation; to you, then, seven days are abundant. If with undivided attention[2] [you] should meditate, with your own knowledge you will understand all; such as,[3] 'What is the body? of what is it the abode? who manifests [himself] in it?'" Having heard this, the King delightedly[4] asked, "Mahârâj! what sort of religious duty is the best of duties? Kindly tell [me]." Then S'ukadev said, "O King! as among all religions the Vaishṇava religion is the best, so among Purâṇas the Bhâgavata [is best]. Wherever the worshippers of Hari[5] relate this story, all places of pilgrimage and [all] religion will come [together];[6] however many Purâṇas there are, there is not one [of them] equal to the Bhâgavata; [for] this reason I will relate[7] to you the twelve sections [of][8] the great Purâṇa, which the sage Vyâs imparted to me. Do thou, with faith and with delight, give attention [and] hear." Then, indeed, King Parîkshit, with pleasure, began to listen, and S'ukadev, as agreed,[9] [began] to recite.

When the saint had recited nine sections [of] the story, the King said, "Compassionate to the humble! now, mercifully, be good enough to relate the story of the incarnation of S'rî Krishṇa; because *he* is our helper and family deity." S'ukadev Jî said, "O King! you have given me much happiness in that [you] have asked [about] this topic. Listen, I [will] tell [you] with pleasure.[10] In the Yadu family there was, at first, a king named Bhajamân, whose son [was] Pṛithiku, Pṛithiku's [son was] Vidûrath, whose [son was] Sûrasen, who, having conquered the nine divisions of the earth, obtained renown. His wife's name was Marishyâ, who had[11] ten sons and five daughters; the eldest son among them [was] Vasudev, in the eighth pregnancy of whose wife S'rî Krishṇa-Chandra took birth. When Vasudev had arisen, the gods in Surapur played the instruments[12] of

[1] Shashṭângula means "the sixtieth finger"; but I have no knowledge of this early subject of death-bed repentance.

[2] A synonymous expression is *ekâgrachitt hokar*, "having the intellect fixed on one object."

[3] Here, again, is another most idiomatic use of *ki*.

[4] *harashke* is the Conjunctive Participle of *harashnâ*.

[5] Here also *sunâweṅ haiṅ* and *âweṅ haiṅ* give instances of the colloquial use of the substantive verb with the Aorist. *Hari* is a name of Krishṇa.

[6] Meaning that the merit will be as great as that of observing every duty and visiting every place of pilgrimage.

[7] Present Tense for the Future.

[8] It is quite idiomatic to omit the sign of the Genitive in such constructions; thus, "ten bighas of land" is *das bîghe jamîn*.

[9] *nem se*, or *niyam se*, may also mean "according to rule" or "in the prescribed way"; or "with self-restraint" or "devoutly."

[10] *Lit.*, "having become pleased."

[11] An ellipsis of *hâṅ*, "place," or *pâs*, "near," is indicated by the Genitive *ke*; and this is why the inflected masculine form is used irrespective of the gender of the thing possessed.

[12] The *n* at the end of *bâjan* is a sign of the plural.

rejoicing. And among the five daughters of Sûrasen, Kuntî was the eldest, who married Pâṇḍu, whose story is celebrated in the Mahâbhârata. But Vasudev Jî at first married King Rohan's daughter Rohinî,[1] afterwards seventeen [other wives]. When eighteen [royal] weddings had taken place, he married, in Mathurâ, Devakî, the sister of Kañs; upon which [2] a heavenly voice occurred, to this effect,[3] 'In the eighth pregnancy of this girl the destroyer [4] of Kañs will be produced.' Having heard this, Kañs shut up the sister [and] the sister's husband in a house, and S'rî Krishṇa took birth just there." On hearing this much of the story, King Parîkshit said, "Mahârâj! how did Kañs take birth? who conferred [this] great boon upon him? and in what manner [5] did Krishṇa arise? [and] further, by what method did he arrive [at] Gokul? This do you instructively relate to me."

S'rî S'ukadev Jî said:—[There was] a king of the city of Mathurâ named Âhuk; he had two sons; the name of one [was] Devak, [of] the other, Ugrasen. After a certain time, Ugrasen alone became king of that place; who had only one wife, named Pavanarekhâ. She was exceedingly beautiful and faithful, [and] at all times remained in sole obedience to her husband [6] One day she was menstruating; then, having received permission from her husband, accompanied by [her] friends and companions, having mounted a car, she went to play in a wood. There, amidst the densest trees, flowers of various kinds were blooming; a fragrance-laden most gentle and cool air was floating onwards; the cuckoo, the dove, the parrot, the peacock, were uttering their most sweet [and] heart-pleasing sounds; and in one direction the Jumna was rippling on quite apart. Hereupon the Queen, beholding this scene, descended from the car [and] walked on. Then suddenly [being] alone she turned aside mistakenly.[7] There a demon, named Drumalik, also, by chance, arrived. He, having perceived her youth and the beauty of her form, remained in astonishment, and began to say within himself, "With her I ought to have enjoyment." Having resolved on this, immediately assuming the appearance of King Ugrasen, [and] going before the Queen, said, "Embrace me." The Queen said, "Mahârâj! by day to sport amorously is not fitting; because, in this [conduct], virtue and religion depart. Are you not aware [of this], that you have contemplated so evil a thought?"

[1] Rohinî is the name of the ninth Nakshatra or Lunar asterism; she is, therefore, appropriately connected with the Lunar race.

[2] *tahâñ*, "there"; logically, "in that predicament."

[3] *ki* may occasionally be thus rendered.

[4] *Kâla*, "time," is also used for "destiny," and is often personified and invested with the attributes of Yama, the regent of the dead.

[5] *kaun rîti se*, for *kis rîti se*, is common enough colloquially.

[6] *âṭhoñ pahar*, "the eight watches," comprising both day and night; *âjñâ meñ*, "within the commands"; *rahe* is aoristic, "she remains."

[7] *Lit.*, "in one direction, [being] alone, having forgotten [the path], she issued forth," i.e. she lost her way, by mistake, while alone.

When Pavanarekhâ had spoken in this way, then, forsooth, Drumalik, having seized the Queen by the hand, drew [her towards himself], and what [he] desired [he] accomplished. By this trick having enjoyed [her, he] became again just as [he] was [before]. Then, indeed, the Queen, having become sorely pained [and] remorseful, said, "O impious, wicked Chaṇḍâl![1] what violence is this thou hast done, in that [thou] hast done away with my virtue! it is a curse to thy mother, [thy] father, and [thy] preceptor, who gave thee such understanding![2] Why was not thy mother barren, [rather] than bearing a son like thee! O wretch! he who having assumed man's form destroys the virtue of anyone, birth [after] birth falls into hell." Drumalik said, "O Queen! do not thou curse me; I have given to thee the fruit of my virtue. Perceiving thy womb [to be] barren, great anxiety was in my heart; that [is now] gone; from to-day hope of [your] pregnancy has begun; in the tenth month a son will be [born], and, from the excellence of my body, thy son will conquer the nine divisions of the earth,[3] and will war with Krishṇa. My name, at first, was Kâlanem; then [I] fought with Vishṇu; now, having taken birth, [I] am come [again]; therefore [I] am called [by] the name Drumalik. To thee I have given[4] a son; let no anxiety enter thy heart on any account." When Kâlanem departed, having said this much, then the Queen, having reflected somewhat, was encouraged—

"Intellect arises according to the destiny which is to be,
Destiny abides in the heart,—all remembrance is obliterated.[5]

In the meantime all the friends and attendants came up. Having perceived the Queen's ornaments disarranged, one of the attendants exclaimed, "Where have you loitered so long? and what has happened to you?"[6] Pavanarekhâ said, "Listen, damsel! you left me in this wood alone; a monkey came, he annoyed me much; from fear of that I am still trembling [and] shaking." Having heard this statement, one and all were alarmed, and quickly placing the Queen on the car, brought [her] home.

1 Chaṇḍâlas were the very lowest out-castes of ancient India, having a S'ûdra father and a Brâhmaṇ mother; this being esteemed the most odious union possible.

2 For *baddhi* read *buddhi*.

3 All previous editions of the text read *jît râj karegâ*, "having conquered will reign [supreme]." Capt. Hollings translates it thus, and so does Prof. Eastwick; but it is plain that the latter did not here look at his own edition.

4 The compound *de chalnâ* is of rare occurrence. It is formed on the model of *de jânâ*, the verbs *jânâ* and *chalnâ* being here regarded as synonymous.

5 This verse is given in extenuation of the pure-minded Pavanarekhâ's ready-witted deception which follows. The sense is that destiny itself produces the intellectual conditions which cause the acts predestined; destiny, therefore, has its seat in the heart; the teachings of experience vanish for the time being.

6 *ber lagnâ* is rare; it is on the model of *der lagnâ* and *der lagânâ*, which also mean "to loiter or delay"; *gati* means "state" or "condition."

When ten months were elapsed,[1] in full time a son was born, Then a violent storm arose, through [the effect] of which the earth began to shake; the darkness became such that day was turned into night,[2] and the stars, having broken into fragments,[3] began to fall, the clouds to thunder, and the lightning to crackle.

In this way, [in the month] Mâgh, on the 13th of the light-half, on Thursday, Kañs took birth. Then King Ugrasen, being pleased, having summoned all the musicians of the city, caused rejoicings to be made, and also sent to invite most respectfully all the Brâhmaṇs, scholars, and astronomers. They came; [and] the King, with great courtesy, offering each a place, caused [them] to be seated. Then the astrologers, having settled the [astronomical] conjunction [and] reflected on the moment [of birth], said, "Lord of the earth! this boy, named Kañs, who has arisen in your family, having become exceedingly powerful, [and] having taken demons [to his aid], will rule; and, having afflicted the gods and the worshippers of Hari, [and] having taken your kingdom, will at last die [by] the hand of Hari."

Having related this much of the story, the sage S'ukadev said to King Parîkshit:—O King! now I am relating the story of Devak, the brother of Ugrasen; that he had [4] four sons, and six daughters, which all six he gave in marriage to Vasudev. The seventh was Devakî, by whose birth the gods were delighted; and Ugrasen had, also, ten sons; but Kañs was the eldest of all. From [his] birth he began to commit this act of violence, to wit, going into the city, and repeatedly seizing little boys, he brought [them], and, shutting them up in a mountain-cave, slew them; [5] those who were older, he got on their chests and strangled.[6] From this affliction no one is anyhow allowed to escape; everyone conceals his own boy; the people say,[7] "This Kañs [is] a wretch; he is not of Ugrasen's family; some great sinner has been born by whom the whole city is plagued." Having heard this, Ugrasen summoned him and admonished [him] much; but what he said made not the least impression on the other's mind.[8] Then, becoming afflicted and regretful, he said, "[Rather] than the existence of such a son, why was I not sonless?"

It is said [9] [that] when a worthless son comes into a house, fame and virtue leave it. When Kañs was eight years old, he attacked the country of Magadh. Jarâsindhu, the king of that

[1] *bîjnâ*, as an intransitive, means "to elapse."

[2] Notice this useful idiom; "of day night became." It is applicable to every idea involving the conversion of one thing into another.

[3] The breaking into fragments is indicated by the repetition of the verb.

[4] See note [11], p. 11.

[5] All these repeated words indicate repetitions of the offence.

[6] *Lit.*, "he extracted the life [by] strangling"; *galâ ghoñṭnâ*, "to strangle."

[7] *pâwe*, *chhipâwe*, and *kahe* are Aorists with the sense of the Present Tense, to indicate the customary character of the acts.

[8] This is the Hindî equivalent of the Urdû *aṣar karnâ*.

[9] The third person plural can always be thus used impersonally.

place, was a great warrior. Having met him (i.e. Kañs) he wrestled; then he perceived the power of Kañs. Then, being defeated, he gave his two daughters in marriage [to Kañs]. He, having accepted [them], came into Mathurâ, [and] increased [his] enmity with Ugrasen. One day, angrily he said to his father, "Do you drop saying the name Râm, and [devoutly] repeat[1] [that] of Mahâdev." His [father] said, "He (i.e. Râm), verily, is indeed my creator, [and] the remover of grief; if I shall not worship him alone, then, having become impious, how shall I cross the ocean of existence?" Having heard this, Kañs, becoming angry, seized [his] father, and took possession of the entire kingdom; and proclaimed thus in the city, that no one should be allowed to perform sacrifice, [give] alms, [obey] the injunctions, do penance, [or call upon] the name of Râm. Iniquity increased so far that cows, Brâhmaṇs, and the worshippers of Hari, began to suffer affliction, and the Earth [from] excessive burdens to perish. When Kañs had completed the appropriation of the sovereignty of all kings, he, one day, taking his army, made an attack on King Indra.[2] There [his] minister said [to him], "Mahârâj! Indra's throne cannot be attained without the performance of austerity;[3] and Your Majesty should not be proud[4] of [your] strength; consider how pride swept away Râvan and Kumbhakaram,[5] so that not one of their family is left."

Having related the story so far, S'ukadev Jî said to King Parîkshit:—O King! when exceeding iniquity began to exist on earth, then [the Earth], pained [and] agitated, having assumed the form of a cow, went complaining into the celestial region, and entering Indra's Court [and] bowing the head, she related all her trouble, thus, "Mahârâj! in the world demons have begun to work exceeding wickedness: through fear of them Religion has departed, and, [if] you desire me,[6] I [will] abandon the abodes of men [and] go to the nether-region." Indra, having heard [this], taking all the gods with [him], went to Brahmâ. Brahmâ,

[1] *jap karnâ* is to mutter internally, or to repeat in the mind.

[2] Indra is the old Vedic god of the intermediate region, whose weapon is the thunderbolt, and who is the beneficent meteoric deity. In the later mythology he became the chief of the deities subordinate to the great triad, Brahmâ, Vishṇu, and S'iva. He passed over to Buddhism under the name Sakko, "the powerful," and became the recording angel of that creed; and the thunderbolt, his emblem, became an object of adoration among Buddhists. The fact that Kañs, the enemy of Krishṇa, makes war upon Indra is another instance of the connection between Krishṇa, Buddhism, and the Lunar cultus.

[3] *bin tap kiye*, "without austerity [being] performed," is a useful idiom, which can be availed of for the expression of an unlimited number of ideas, as extensions of the predicate.

[4] This is the respectful form of the aoristic *kare*.

[5] Râvana and Kumbhakaram are two of the leading personages in the Râmâyaṇa epic.

[6] *âjnâ ho*, "if the order should be," "if desired." This is a phrase in constant requisition colloquially.

having heard, conducted [them] all to Mahâdev. Mahâdev, also, having heard, taking [them] all with [him], went where, in the ocean of milk, Nârâyaṇ was sleeping on.[1] Perceiving him sleeping, Brahmâ, Rudra,[2] Indra, accompanied by all the gods, standing erect, [with] joined hands, supplicatingly began to praise the god;[3] "King of Kings! who can utter your greatness? having become fish-form, the sinking Vedas were extricated [by you]; assuming the tortoise-form, on [thy] back the mountain was supported; becoming a boar, the earth on [thy] tusk was placed [by you];[4] having become a dwarf, [you] tricked King Bali; taking the Paraśurâm incarnation [and] destroying the Kshatriyas, [you] gave the earth to the saint Kaśyapa;[5] [by you] the Râma-incarnation was adopted, then the most wicked Râvana was slain;[6] and whenever the Daityas[7] are afflicting your worshippers, you condescendingly protect [them]. Lord! now, through the oppression of Kañs, the Earth, greatly perturbed, is calling aloud; quickly bear her [in] remembrance; destroy the Asuras,[8] [and] give pleasure to the virtuous."

Thus celebrating [his] virtues, the gods spoke. Then there was a celestial voice, which Brahmâ expounded to the gods [thus], "This voice which has occurred, has directed you,—that all gods and goddesses, going to the district of Braj, should take birth in the city of Mathurâ; afterwards Hari, bearing four forms, will also become incarnate, in the house of Vasudev, in the

[1] See note [1], p. 6.

[2] Rudra is a Vedic deity; the god of the roaring storms. He has been held, by some, to be the prototype of the modern S'iva.

[3] All the older editions of the text here read *Vedastuti*, "praise of the Veda," and Prof. Eastwick follows Capt. Hollings in ascribing that sense to the passage; but it is plain that the Professor did not here look at his own text, which gives *Devastuti*, "praise of the god."

[4] Carefully observe this use of the intensive: *denâ* is used when the result of the action passes away from the actor; but *lenâ* when the result reverts to the actor. These two verbal adjuncts constitute the modern method of expressing the Sanskrit *parasmaipada*, "word for another," and *âtmanepada*, "word for oneself."

[5] Kaśyapa is, perhaps, the most important name in Brahmanism. He is described as the first human teacher of spiritual truths, which he received direct from the gods, and passed on, through the long line of succeeding teachers, to the present time. It was he who is said to have conquered the Soma, for the benefit of humanity; and his family are certainly the Rishis, or authors, of nearly all the hymns in praise of the Soma, found in the Rig-veda. He was, therefore, intimately connected with the Soma, or Lunar cultus, which played so important a part in the most ancient form of Brahmanism. In later mythological legends he is represented as having sprung from Marîchi, and to have been the husband of Aditi, and the father of Vishṇu.

[6] These various statements recount the well-known Avatârs, or incarnations, of Vishṇu.

[7] Daityas are enemies of the gods, and take their name from Diti, the daughter of Dakshâ, a wife of the divine Kaśyapa.

[8] Asuras are the same as Daityas, or the children of Diti, just mentioned; but in the Vishṇu-Purâṇa, they are said to have arisen from Brahmâ's thigh when he was in a condition of darkness. They preceded the gods in the order of creation.

womb of Devakî, and, by[1] childish sports, will give pleasure to Nand and Jasodâ." When Brahmâ [had] in this way instructed [them], then the Suras,[2] Munis,[3] Kinnaras,[4] and Gandharvas,[5] each with their own wives, severally took birth, and coming into the district of Braj, were called[6] Yadubañsîs[7] and cowherds. And those who were the texts of the four Vedas[8] said to Brahmâ, "Let us, also, becoming cowherdesses and taking incarnate form in Braj, serve the descendant of Vasudev." Having said this, they also came into Braj, and were called cowherdesses. When the gods had done coming into the city of Mathurâ, then, on the ocean of milk, Hari began to ponder thus, First of all let Lakshmaṇa become Balarâm; afterwards Vâsudev [shall] be my name; let Bharata become incarnate as Pradyumna, Satrughna as Aniruddha, and Sîtâ as Rukminî.[9]

---

## CHAPTER II.

The marriage of Devakî, Kañs's sister, to Vasudev—The death of Kañs announced from heaven—His sister's eighth son is to be his destroyer—He attempts to slay his sister—Kills her first six sons—The birth of Balarâm.

HAVING related this much [of] the story, S'rî S'ukadev Jî said to King Parikshit:—Mahârâj! Kañs, then, with this impolicy[10]

[1] The Conjunctive Participle *kar* or *karke* has become a mere case-ending, with the sense of "by," "through," "in consequence of," &c.

[2] Suras are the gods of the Vedic pantheon taken collectively.

[3] Munis were holy men, or inspired saints, who are generally spoken of as ascetic and solitary in their habits.

[4] Kinnaras are mythical beings with human forms and horses' heads. Their abode is beyond the Himâlaya Mountains, and they are indefinitely connected with wealth and music.

[5] The Gandharvas here alluded to are heavenly musicians, denizens of Indra's heaven. They are held to be particularly interested in female affairs, and are hence invoked at marriages. Their proper abode is the sky; they guard the sacred Soma juice, and are governed by Varuṇa, that is, the celestial vault personified. In the Rig-veda only one Gandharva is spoken of, who is the guardian of the Soma, which is forcibly taken from him by Indra for the benefit of humanity. This primal Gandharva is the parent of the first human couple, Yama and Yamî; and he is regarded as the source of medical science.

[6] This Passive sense of *kahânâ* or *kahlânâ* is very useful colloquially.

[7] Yadubañsî is a member of the family of Yadu, a great hero of the Lunar dynasty.

[8] The Richâs are female personifications of the texts of the Rig-veda.

[9] Sitâ was the wife of Râma; Lakshmaṇa, Bharata, and Satrughna were all concerned in the transactions of the Râma-incarnation. They are now to reappear, under the names indicated, to take part in the forthcoming manifestation.

[10] The Ablative is here adverbial, the phrase meaning "impoliticly." *Nîti* is the science of public policy, regulating the duties of sovereign and people.

began to rule in Mathurâ, and Ugrasen to be filled [with] grief.[1] Devak, who was Kañs's paternal uncle, when his girl Devakî was fit for marriage,[2] he went [and] said to Kañs, "To whom shall we give this girl?" He said, "Give her to Sûrasen's son Vasudev." On hearing this remark, Devak called a Brâhman, fixed a fortunate [astrological] conjunction, [and] sent nuptial gifts to Sûrasen's house. Then Sûrasen also, with great pomp, having prepared the marriage-procession, accompanied by the kings of all the various countries, came to marry Vasudev in Mathurâ.[3]

Hearing [that] the procession [was] come near the city, Ugrasen, Devak, and Kañs, taking with [them] their army, advanced [and] conducted [the procession] into the city. With exceeding courtesy having received [them, they] allotted [a proper] reception-hall [to them]. Having entertained [them with] food and drink, [and] having conducted the nuptial procession under the pavilion, [they] caused [them] to be seated,[4] and, with Vedic rites, Kañs gave the girl to Vasudev. In her dowry [he] gave fifteen thousand horses, four thousand elephants, eighteen hundred cars, numerous male and female slaves, [and] bestowed innumerable golden salvers, each filled with robes [and] ornaments studded with jewels; and having robed all the processionists also in vestments with ornaments, he escorted them all forth. There a celestial voice was [heard], "O Kañs! she whom thou hast escorted, her eighth son will arise thy destroyer; by his hand thy death is [to be]."

On hearing this, Kañs, with fear, trembled, and angrily seized Devakî [by] the back hair [and] dragged [her] down from the car. Taking sword in hand, and grinding [his] teeth together, [he] began to say, "The tree which should be torn up by the very roots, on that for what [purpose] will flowers and fruit be?[5] Now I will kill this one, [and] then reign without fear." Seeing and hearing this, Vasudev said within himself, "This fool has caused affliction, he knows[6] not virtue and vice. If I am now

[1] No case-sign is needed; for the verb *bharnâ* implies "to be full of" or "filled with"; thus *dukh bharnâ* = "grief-full."

[2] *byâhan* is the old Pûrbi Infinitive, constantly found in the old poetry, with which Lallû Lâl was very familiar. The standard Hindi form is *byâhne yogya*.

[3] Here, again, *byâhan* is an Infinitive, compounded with *âye* = "came to the marrying."

[4] *Janwâsâ* is a *vâs*, "dwelling," provided for the *janya*, "friends of the bridegroom." It is a part of the bride's house allotted to the family of the bridegroom during the marriage ceremony, who come in great numbers, and stay three or four days. In this hall the girl's friends make presents to the boy's friends on the third day of the festivities, and there the *âmantraṇ* verses are recited preparatory to the departure of the bride from her father's house. The *maṛhâ* is in the nature of an open marquee, formed by a wooden post fixed in the ground, on the top of which is a vessel containing sweetmeats, and from this wreaths of flowers are stretched on all sides. Under this the young couple sit, while the nine planets are worshipped, the ancestors are gratified, and the *ârtâ*, or four-wicked lamp, emblematical of Brahmâ, is waved round their heads.

[5] Meaning that if she has no offspring they can do no hurt.

[6] The *hai* is here redundant, and is considered unidiomatic with the negative.

angry, then the affair will be spoilt; therefore, on the present occasion, it is fitting to be patient. It is said—

> If an enemy draw a sword, a good man conciliates him;
> A fool after reflection regrets, as water puts out fire."

Having reflected thus, Vasudev, going before Kañs [with] joined hands, humbly said, "Listen, Lord of the Earth! no one in the world [is] as strong as you,[1] and all are dwelling under your shadow; being such a hero, [that] you should raise [your] weapon against a woman is exceedingly improper, and by the killing of a sister great sin is incurred; furthermore, a man may commit injustice if he knows that he will never die. Of this world, indeed, *this* is the custom—on the one hand, [we are] born; on the other, [we are] dead;[2] with a myriad efforts, by evil [and] virtue, anyone may cherish this body, but it will never become his own; and even wealth, youth, and kingdom will be of no avail;[3] therefore, please attend [to] my statement, and release your weak dependent sister." Having heard this much, [and] deeming her his destroyer, [he was] alarmed [and] still more enraged. Then Vasudev began to reflect, "This sinner, with[4] the intellect of an Asur, is fixed in his obstinacy;[5] that means should be employed by which[6] this one may escape from his hand." Thus reflecting he said within himself, "*Now*, from this [fellow] let me save Devakî [by] saying thus, Whatever son I may have[7] I will give to you. Who has seen [what is to be][8] hereafter? There may not even be a son;[9] or this wicked one may die. Let this occasion pass, then [what is to be] will be comprehended."[10] Having resolved thus in [his] mind, Vasudev said to Kañs, "Mahârâj! your death will not be by means of this one's son; because I have decided on one thing, that, as many sons as Devakî shall have, I will bring [and] give to you. This promise I have [now] given you." When Vasudev had made this statement, then having reflected [thereupon], Kañs assented, and released Devakî, saying, "O Vasudev! you have reflected well, in that [you] have saved me from so great a sin." Saying this, [he] bade them adieu; [and] they went to their home.

[1] *tum sâ balî*, "you-like strong"; a compound adjective.
[2] Meaning, "we are here to-day, and gone to-morrow."
[3] *kâj ânâ* or *kâm ânâ*, "to come [into] use," "to be useful." The *meñ* is not always elided.
[4] See note [8], p. 3.
[5] *Lit.*, "on the prop of his obstinacy."
[6] Notice *jis meñ* for "by which."
[7] See note [11], p. 11.
[8] The words *honewâlî bât*, "the affair that is to be," are understood; and that is why the verb is feminine.
[9] For *laṛkâî* read *laṛkâ hî*.
[10] Here the same ellipsis occurs. (Note [8] above.) The sense is, that if this crisis passes away, time will be given to obviate the future.

After remaining some time in Mathurâ, when Devakî had [her] first son, Vasudev, taking [it], went to Kañs, and crying placed the boy before [him]. Upon seeing [him], Kañs said, "Vasudev! you are very truthful; I have perceived that to-day; for you have not acted deceitfully towards me. Having become free from affection,[1] [you] have brought [and] given your son. From this one I have no fear; this child I have given to thee." Hearing this much, taking the child [and] prostrating [himself], Vasudev Jî went to his home. And, at that very time, the saint Nârad went [and] said to Kañs, "Râjâ! what have you done, that you have given the child back again! Are you not aware that, for the purpose of[2] attending on the descendant of Vasudev, all the gods have come into Braj [and] taken birth? and [that] in Devakî's eighth pregnancy S'rî Krishṇa, having taken birth [and] having destroyed all the Râkshasas,[3] will remove the earth's burden?" Having said this much, the saint Nârad drew eight lines, and caused [Kañs] to count [them]. When nothing but eight came out of the counting,[4] then, in alarm, Kañs sent to fetch Vasudev with the boy. The saint Nârad, having thus admonished [Kañs], departed; and Kañs, taking the child from Vasudev, killed [it]. Thus, when there [happened to] be a son, Vasudev brought [it] and Kañs killed [it]. In this way, six children were killed; then, in the seventh pregnancy, he who [is] the S'esh-formed revered Deity[5] came, [and] took up [his] abode.

Having heard this tale, King Parîkshit asked the saint S'ukadev, [thus], "Mahârâj! the great sin which the saint Nârad caused to be committed, explain its circumstances to me, so that the doubt of my mind may depart." S'rî S'ukadev Jî said, "O King! Nârad Jî well reflected that he [Kañs] would commit exceedingly great sin,[6] [and] then S'rî Bhagwân would be immediately manifested."

[1] For *niramohî* read *nirmohî*.

[2] "for the purpose of" is the equivalent of *ko*.

[3] *Râkshasas* are evil spirits of doubtful origin, sometimes being referred to Brahmâ's foot, sometimes being accounted descendants of Pulastya, and sometimes being called the children of Surasâ. They are of three kinds; the first being semi-divine, and acting as subordinate attendants in the realms of bliss; the second being demoniacal monsters who make war upon the gods; the third are ugly and distorted fiends and goblins who haunt the world by night, and annoy and prey upon devout and innocent human beings. These last are those alluded to in the Prem-Sâgar. Their headquarters is Lankâ or Ceylon, where their ruler, Râvaṇa, resides with his principal lieutenants; and a description of which is given in the Râmayaṇa.

[4] *Lit.*, "when, in counting, there came eight only eight," that is, each in turn became the eighth.

[5] This describes Balarâm, the brother of Krishṇa, who is esteemed the third deity bearing the name Râma, and to be an incarnation of the famous S'eshanâg, or seven-headed cobra.

[6] The repetition of *adhik* intensifies the meaning; and so does *hî* after *turant*.

## CHAPTER III.

Kañs persecutes the Yadu family—Balarâm, before birth, transferred from Devaki to Rohinî. by the miraculous interposition of Vishṇu—Devaki conceives Krishṇa—Kañs strictly guards her, to ensure the slaughter of this child.

THEN S'ukadev Jî began to say to Parîkshit:—O King! how Hari came into the womb, and Brahmâ and the others[1] praised[2] the fœtus, and in what manner Devî[3] conveyed Baladev to Gokul, in that way I am [about to] relate the tale. One day King Kañs came [and] sat in his Council, and as many Daityas as he had, he called for [and] said, "All the gods, having taken birth on earth, are come; among them Krishṇa, also, will assume incarnate form; this secret the saint Nârad has, admonishingly, imparted to me; therefore, now this is fitting, that you, going, all the Yadubansîs should so destroy that not even one should escape living."

Having received this order, one and all[4] prostrating [themselves] departed. Having come into the city [they] began hunting about, seizing, [and] binding; anyone who was found eating, drinking, erect, seated,[5] sleeping, waking, walking, moving about, was not spared. Surrounding [them, they] brought [them to] one place, and [by] burning, drowning, dashing to pieces, [and] tormenting, destroyed them all. In this way small [and] great [Daityas], assuming a variety of frightful disguises, began to hunt about [and] to kill [in] city [after] city, village [after] village, street [after] street, [and] house [after] house; and the Yadubansîs severally receiving affliction, abandoning the country, fled with bare life.[6]

At that time whatever wives of Vasudev there were, they also, together with Rohinî, came from Mathurâ into Gokul, where Vasudev Jî's best friend, Nand Jî, was staying. He most friendlily reassuring [them], kept [them in his care]; [and] they stayed

[1] The *âdi* means "beginning," the *ka* is a nominal affix; the compound implying "those beginning with Brahmâ," that is, "Brahmâ, &c."

[2] The use of *karâ* and *karî* for the Past tense of *karnâ*, instead of *kiyâ* and *kî*, is common throughout this book. It is sometimes, as here, used to force a rhyme; but it is a form in colloquial use, especially around Farrakhâbâd.

[3] *Devî* indicates Devî Durgâ, wife of S'iva, who was much interested in the incarnation of Krishṇa.

[4] The Genitive here intensifies the meaning. It is "the all of all," "one and all."

[5] Notice the participial change here; the Present Participle expresses continuing actions: the Past Participle expresses an action which was completed, though the result of it may continue. It accords with the idiom *mûsal hâth liye*. (See note [8], p. 3.)

[6] *Jî le le* means "taking [severally] life [only]." Notice the distributive sense of the repeated words in this paragraph, and the niceness with which this idiom discriminates between object, action, and actor; as, *nagar nagar*, "city after city," *khoj khoj*, "searching about," and *dukh pâe pâe*, "they severally receiving affliction."

[there] happily. When Kañs thus began to afflict the gods. and to act most sinfully, then Vishṇu produced from his own eyes an illusion,[1] [and] that. [with] joined hands, came before [him]. [He] said to it, "Do thou go at once into the world, assume incarnate form, in the city of Mathurâ, where the wicked Kañs is afflicting my worshippers; and Kaśyap and Aditi, who, as[2] Vasudev [and] Devakî, are gone into Braj, them [he] has incarcerated. Six children of theirs Kañs has slain; now Lakshmaṇ Jî is in the seventh pregnancy. Having removed him from Devakî's womb, [and] conveyed [him] into Gokul, so place [him] in Rohinî's belly that no wicked one may know [of it], and all the people of that place may celebrate thy glory."

Thus having instructed the Illusion, S'rî Nârâyaṇ[3] said, "Do thou at first go, execute this task, [and] take birth in the house of Nand; afterwards take incarnate form [in] Vasudev's place. I, also, am coming [in] Nand's house." On hearing this much, the Illusion came hastily into Mathurâ, [and] assuming the form of Mohanî,[4] entered in the house of Vasudev.

> The fœtus which was secretly abstracted [she] went [and] gave to Rohinî.
> All think [it] a first conception. Bhagwân became Rohinî's.

In this way, on Wednesday, the fourteenth [day of] the bright half [of] Sâwan,[5] Baladev took birth in Gokul; and the Illusion, going to Vasudev [and] Devakî, gave [them] a dream, thus, "I, having taken your son from the womb, have given [it] to Rohinî; therefore, do not have any anxiety [on its account]." On hearing this, Vasudev [and] Devakî woke up, and began to say to each other, "This, indeed, Bhagwân has done well, but at once [we] should inform Kañs, otherwise who knows[6] afterwards what affliction [he] may give [us]." Having thus pondered, [they] explained [the matter] to the guards. They having gone to Kañs, repeated [it], thus, "Mahârâj! Devakî's fœtus miscarried; the child was not at all completed."[7] On hearing this,

[1] *Mâyâ*, "Illusion," is constantly personified and identified with Durgâ; here the numeral *ek* shows that "an illusion" is intended.

[2] *ho* = "having become," which is here equivalent to "as," "in the character of"

[3] *Nârâyaṇa* is a name of Vishṇu, as being sprung from Nara, or the original male, the personified Purusha, or first human being. Ancient Hindûs say that the word is derived from *nâra* + *ayana*, "coming from the water."

[4] *Mohanî* is the name of a demoness, the daughter of Garbha-hantrî, and therefore a suitable disguise for the secret accomplishment of the purpose.

[5] That is, just on full moon of the month July-August.

[6] *kyâ jâniye*, "what is known?" The form *jâniye* is on the model of *châhiye*, "is wished," "is desirable." They are Passive Aorists, formed by the insertion of *î*; a method of forming the Passive largely availed of in Panjâbi.

[7] *kuchhî* is equivalent to *kuchh bhî*.

Kañs agitatedly said, "You this time[1] will be careful;[2] because to me there is fear of only the eighth fœtus; which the heavenly voice proclaimed."[3]

Having related the story thus far, S'rî S'ukadev Jî said:—O King! Baldev Jî, then, was thus manifested; and when S'rî Krishna came into the womb of Devakî, just then the Illusion went [and] took up [its] abode in the belly of Jasodâ, the wife of Nand. Both were with child.[4] During a certain festival,[5] Devakî went [to] the Jumnâ [to] bathe; there, by chance Jasodâ also came [and] was met [by her]; then, between themselves, conversation was started about [their] trouble. At last Jasodâ, giving this promise to Devakî, said, "Thy child I will keep; my own to thee I will give." Having thus promised, this one came [to] her home, and that one [to] hers.[6] Afterwards, when Kañs knew that there was an eighth pregnancy of Devakî, then, going [there], he surrounded Vasudev's house. All around, he placed a guard of Daityas, and, calling for Vasudev, said, "Now act not treacherously with me; bring your son, [and] give [him up]. Then[7] I regarded your mere statement."

Saying thus, [he] caused Vasudev [and] Devakî to wear gyves and manacles, shutting [them] in an apartment, placing lock upon lock, coming into [his] own palace, and, fasting through fear, [he] slept. Then, as soon as it was dawn, he went where[8] Vasudev [and] Devakî were. Perceiving the indication of pregnancy, he said,[9] "In this very cave of Yama[10] is my destiny. I could, indeed, slay [her]; but I fear the ignominy, because,

[1] *Lit.*, "the time of now"; it is the exact equivalent of the English "this time," when more or less of contrast is implied with some other time.

[2] *kariyo* is aoristic; but the respectful forms in *-o* convey a sense of futurity; as "You'll please be careful this time."

[3] *kah jânâ* is a little emphatic; and, therefore, implies more than "to say." Notice that the regimen follows the last member of the compound.

[4] The *ki* indicates a change of subject connected with the matter in hand. (See note [1], p. 10.)

[5] *Parb* means "knuckle" or "joint"; and the word indicates the "turning-points" in the calendar which are of felicitous augury; such as the full and change of the moon, the equinoctial and solstitial periods, an anniversary, &c., &c.

[6] The elision here is strictly idiomatic; it would be unidiomatic to insert the missing words.

[7] "Then" means "on that former occasion": hence, also, the use of the Past Perfect tense.

[8] For *wahoñ* read *wahâñ*.

[9] The Inceptive *lagnâ*, attached to another verb, need not necessarily be rendered by "to begin to ——"; for it expresses that which is resumed after an interval, and other similar ideas; *kahne lagâ* may thus mean, "he addressed himself to speaking," or, simply, "he said." In this passage, for *jagâ* read *lagâ*.

[10] *Yama*, "the restrainer," is the god who rules the spirits of the dead, and he has his abode in the southern quarter, whither all souls repair after death to receive from him the rewards or punishments due to their course of life on earth. He has many, and conflicting, attributes, according to various points of view from which different writers regarded his functions.

being exceedingly powerful, the killing [of] a woman [is] not[1] fitting. Better [that] I shall slay only her son." Saying thus, [and] coming out, he places there a guard [of] elephants, lions, dogs, and his greatest warriors; and himself, also, comes constantly on guard;[2] but, even for a moment, obtains no ease. Wherever [he] looks [during] the eight watches [or] sixty-four *gharîs*,[3] nothing but Destiny [in] the form of Krishṇa comes [in] sight. From fear of this, becoming apprehensive, night and day he spends in anxiety.[4]

On the one hand, of Kañs, then, there was this condition, on the other,[5] Vasudev and Devakî, [on] the days [of pregnancy being] complete, in great distress were invoking S'rî Krishṇa alone; when,[6] in the midst of this, Bhagwân, coming, gave them a dream, and saying this much removed the grief of their minds,[7] "We, very quickly having taken birth, are [about to] remove your anxiety; do not you now regret." Hearing this, Vasudev [and] Devakî awoke; thereupon Brahmâ, Rudra, Indra, &c., all the gods, leaving their chariots in mid-air [and] assuming invisible forms, came into the house of Vasudev, and severally joining [their] hands, [and] chaunting the Veda, began to praise the fœtus. Then they were not seen by anyone, but the sound of the Veda all heard. Perceiving this marvel, all the guards were astonished; and Vasudev [and] Devakî were satisfied thus, "Bhagwân speedily will remove our pain."

---

## CHAPTER IV.

Krishṇa is born—Supernatural manifestations of joy thereat—Vasudev, by divine aid, conveys the child to Gokul, and leaves it with Jasodâ, receiving in exchange a girl, miraculously born the same night.

S'RÎ S'UKADEV JÎ said:—O King! when S'rî Krishṇa-Chand began to take birth, in the mind of everyone such pleasures arose that even the name [of] affliction remained not; with

[1] For *nahoñ* read *nahîñ*.

[2] The Conjunctive Participle is here adverbial, meaning "guardingly," or "attentively."

[3] The eight *pahars* and sixty-four *gharîs* are alternative expressions; each indicates the entire period of day and night. A *gharî* is $22\frac{8}{16}$ minutes.

[4] All these Aorists with the sense of the Present tense should be in the Singular, as Lallû Lâl himself printed them.

[5] The words *idhar* . . . *udhar* are frequently thus used in stating concurrent events. It is quite colloquial.

[6] See notes [1], p. 10, and [4], p. 23.

[7] Here *itnâ* and *jo* are correlatives, the latter being necessitated by the former.

delight, woods [and] groves, severally becoming green, began to blossom and fruit; rivers, streams, [and] lakes to fill; on them various kinds of birds [began] to gambol; and [in] every city, village, [and] house festivities to be [celebrated]. Brâhmans [began] to perform sacrifice; the guardians of the ten regions[1] to rejoice; the clouds to revolve over the district of Braj;[2] the gods, seated in their respective chariots, to rain down flowers from space; Vidyâdhars,[3] Gandharvas,[4] Chāraṇas,[5] playing big-drums, kettle-drums, and pipes, [began] to sing the virtues [of the new-born]; and, in one direction, all the Apsarases,[6] beginning [with] Urvaśî,[7] were dancing on, when, in such a time, [on] Wednesday, the eighth [of] the dark half [of the month] Bhâdoñ, in the Lunar asterism [of] Rohinî, [at] mid-night, S'rî Krishṇa took birth; and being cloud-coloured, moon-faced, lotus-eyed, yellow-silk girdled, crown-wearing, wearing the five-element necklace,[8] and jewel-studded adornments, four-arm shaped,[9] holding the shell, the discus, the club, [and] the lotus, [he] revealed [himself] to Vasudev [and] Devakî. On seeing [him], being astonished, they both presciently reflected, then [they] knew [him] as Âdi-Purusha;[10] then, joining the hands, supplicatingly [they] said, "Ours [is] great fortune,[11] that your Honour has revealed [yourself], and brought to an end [our] births and deaths."[12]

Having said this much, [they] related the whole foregoing story; the various ways in which Kañs had afflicted them. There[upon] S'rî Krishṇa-Chand said, "Now do you have no more anxiety in [your] hearts on any matter; because I have become incarnate for the express purpose of removing your

[1] The regions of space are supposed to be presided over by a double set of guardians, one of which is astronomical, the other mythological. The sun, moon, and planets have separate quarters assigned to them; and along with them, also in separate quarters, Brahmâ, Indra, Yama, &c., hold sway. The word in the text should have been printed *dikpâl*.

[2] In a hot country rain-clouds produce happiness.

[3] *Vidyâdharas*, "magicians," were attendants on the gods, in possession of magical knowledge. Their functions were both good and evil, like genii or fairies.

[4] See note [5], p. 17.

[5] *Châraṇas* were celestial officials whose duty it was to panegyrize the gods.

[6] *Apsaras*, "moving in the aqueous." These are celestial nymphs, wives of the Gandharvas, whose residence is the aqueous medium in which clouds float. They sport about, dance, change their shape at will, and are fond of bathing.

[7] *Urvaśî*, the name of a nymph of Indra's heaven, who became the wife of Purûravas, and formed the heroine of Kâlidâsa's famous drama called "Vikramorvaśî."

[8] *Baijañti*, or, as it should have been printed, *Vaijayanti*, is a necklace of Vishṇu representing the five elements of nature—sapphire for the earth, pearl for water, ruby for fire, topaz for air, and diamond for ether.

[9] The form *kiye* may be used thus with substantives, like the English termination *-ed*, to give a participial sense.

[10] *Âdi-Purusha* is primeval spirit or the first male; it is a term often applied to Vishṇu.

[11] *bhâg* or *bhâgya*, "fortune," is generally treated as plural.

[12] That is, "released us from further transmigrations."

affliction; but, for the present, convey me [to] Gokul; and at this very time Jasodâ has had[1] a daughter; bring that [and] give [it] to Kañs. I [will] state the reason for my going; hear it:

Nand [and] Jasodâ performed austerity, having brought
  [their] hearts to me alone;
[They] wish to see the joy of offspring, I [will] go [and]
  stay some time [with them].

Afterwards, having killed Kañs, I will return [to you];[2] do you fix fortitude in your hearts." Having thus instructed Vasudev [and] Devakî, S'rî Krishṇa, as a child,[3] began to cry, and spread his illusion around; then the [spiritual] knowledge of Vasudev [and] Devakî departed, and they thought thus, "We have a son." Thinking this, [and] vowing in [their] hearts [an offering of] ten thousand cows, raising the boy on [their] lap, [they] embraced [him]. Looking again and again [at] his face, both of them repeatedly heaving deep sighs, [they] began to say to each other, "If, by any way, we could send away this boy, then [he] would escape from the hand of the sinner Kañs." Vasudev said:—

Without Destiny no one preserves [anything]; the fate
  [that is] written, that same becomes fruitful.[4]
Then, joining [her] hands, Devakî says, "[Our] friend
  Nand dwells in Gokul;
Jasodâ will remove our pain; your wife Rohinî [is] there.

Convey this child there." Thus having heard, Vasudev perplexedly said, "How shall I be released from this firm binding, [and] convey [him] away?" As this statement was uttered, all the gyves and manacles[5] fell open, the encircling gateways went open,[6] the watchmen were subdued [by] profound sleep.[7] Then Vasudev Jî having placed S'rî Krishṇa in a winnowing-basket, put [him] on [his] head, and hastily departed for Gokul.

Above the god rains; behind a lion who roars;
Vasudev is reflecting, having seen the Jumnâ [in] excessive
  flood.

Standing on the river's bank, Vasudev began to reflect, thus, "Behind a lion is roaring, and in front the unfordable Jumnâ is

[1] See note [11], p. 11.
[2] *ân milnâ*, "to come and meet with," is a compound implying "to return to anyone."
[3] The Conjunctive Participle *ban*, "having been made," or "becoming," is often used as the equivalent of the English "as."
[4] The Hindûs believe that a person's fate is written on his forehead.
[5] For *dathkaṛî* read *hathkaṛî*.
[6] For *ḍaghaṛ* read *ughaṛ*.
[7] There is an ellipsis here; more fully the sentence is *achet nīñd ke bas meñ baye*, "they were in the power of unconscious sleep."

flowing, now what shall I do?" Having spoken thus, [and] fixed [his] thought on Bhagwân, he entered the Jumnâ. As he proceeded forwards, the river was rising; when the water came up to [his] nose, then he was exceedingly agitated. Knowing him to be perplexed, S'rî Krishṇa, having stretched forth his foot, gave the *hûñkâr*.[1] On [his] foot touching [it] the Jumnâ became fordable. Vasudev having crossed, arrived at Nand's gate; there he found the door open, [and] having gone within, [he] looks; then all are lying asleep. Devî has thrown [over them] such a fascination that there was no remembrance to Jasodâ even of the existence of a girl. Vasudev Jî put Krishṇa then to sleep beside Jasodâ, and having taken the girl, quickly took his way [home]. Having crossed the river, [he] returned to where Devakî was seated reflecting, [and] giving the girl, [he] told the happy [circumstances] of that place [i.e. Gokul].[2] On hearing [that], Devakî, being pleased, said, "O husband! now let Kañs slay [me], still [there is] no anxiety [on that account], because from the hand of this wicked one the son has escaped."

Having related this much [of the] tale, S'rî S'ukadev Jî said to King Parîkshit:—When Vasudev had brought the girl, the doors closed up just as they were before, and both of them wore [their] manacles [and] gyves. The girl cried out; [and] having heard the noise of the weeping the guards awoke; then each seizing his weapon, [and] becoming alert, began to discharge their firelocks. Hearing the noise of these, the elephants began to trumpet, the lions to roar, and the dogs to bark. At the same moment, in the midst of the dark night, in the rain, a watchman came [and] said to Kañs, [with] joined hands, "Mahârâj! your enemy has arisen." Hearing this, Kañs fainted [and] fell.

---

## CHAPTER V.

Kañs attempts to destroy the substituted girl—She escapes into space—And derides Kañs—He learns that his future destroyer has escaped him—He persecutes the worshippers of Vishṇu.

ON hearing [of] the birth of the child, Kañs arose, fearing [and] trembling, [and stood] erect; and having taken sword in hand, falteringly, [with] dishevelled hair, bathed in sweat, in an agitated condition, he drew near to [his] sister. When he snatched the

[1] That is, "uttering the syllable *hûm*." This is a mystical incantation as old as Vedic times.

[2] There is an elision of *bât* here, as is shown by the gender of the verb.

girl from her hand, she [with] joined hands, said, "O, brother! this girl is thy niece; do not kill her; she is my last child.[1] The boys are killed; pain on their account exceedingly troubles me; needlessly killing the girl, why aggravate the sin?" Kañs said, "I will not give the girl to thee living. He who marries this one will kill me." Having said this, [and] having come out, just as he wished that, by swinging [her] round he [will] dash [her] on a stone, at that instant, escaping from [his] hand, the girl went to the sky, and, crying out, proclaimed this, "O Kañs! what has [resulted] from dashing me down? Thy enemy has somewhere taken birth;[2] now thou wilt not be preserved alive."

Hearing this, Kañs having repented,[3] came to where[4] Vasudev [and] Devakî were. On arriving [he] cut the manacles [and] gyves from their hands [and] feet, and supplicatingly said, "I have committed great sin in that [I] have killed your sons; how will this stain be remitted? in what birth will my salvation take place? Your deities were false who said that in Devaki's eighth pregnancy there will be a boy; that not having taken place, a girl has been [born instead]; that, also, having escaped from [my] hand, is gone to heaven. Now, compassionately, keep not my fault in [your] soul; because [what is] written by Fate,[5] no one is able to obliterate; from being come[6] into this world, the living, dying, association, [and] dissociation, of humanity is not [to be] escaped. They who are wise, esteem dying [and] living [as] just the same; but the conceited regard [them] as friends [and] enemies. You, indeed, are very virtuous [and] truthful, in that, for our sake, [you] have brought your sons [to me]."

Having said this, when Kañs began repeatedly to entreat,[7] Vasudev Jî said, "Mahârâj! you say true; in this there is no fault of yours; Fate wrote this in our destiny." Hearing thus, Kañs, becoming pleased, most friendlily conducted Vasudev [and] Devakî [to] his own house, caused [them] to be fed, [and] dressed [in] robes, very courteously re-conducted them both [to] the same place [in which they previously were]. And calling for his Minister, said, "Devî has declared[8] [thus], 'Thy enemy is born into the world;' hence, now, wherever you may find the gods, kill [them]; for *they* uttered to me the false[9] statement, that 'In the

[1] *poñchhnâ*, "to wipe," *pet poñchhan*, "womb-wiping," hence "the last child."

[2] Notice the use of *le chukâ*. It is the first time the form has occurred in the book. It expresses that "the thing has been done," notwithstanding the counter efforts of Kañs.

[3] Many of these jingling repetitions (*achhtâ pachhtâ*) have occurred, and will occur; they are quite colloquial, and not to be despised.

[4] For *jâhâñ* read *jahâñ*.

[5] See note [14], p. 5.

[6] Notice the Passive Participle here; the sense is, "once entered in this world."

[7] "To clasp the hands" here means "to entreat."

[8] See note [3], p. 23.

[9] For *jhuṭhî* read *jhûṭhî*.

eighth pregnancy thy enemy will be [born].'" The Minister said, "Mahârâj! what great affair is their destruction? they, forsooth, are beggars by birth; whenever your Honour may be angry they will flee away.[1] What power have they, that they should confront you? Brahmâ, for his part, remains all day in thought [and] meditation; Mahâdev[2] consumes [the intoxicants] *bhang* and thorn-apple; nothing of Indra's prevails against you;[3] there remains Nârâyaṇ that understands not war, he remains with Lakshmî, mindful of happiness."

Kañs said, "Where shall we find Nârâyaṇ, and [in] what way conquer [him]? tell [me] that." The Minister said, "Mahârâj! if you wish to conquer Nârâyaṇ, then destroy now the house of those [with] whom [he] ever remains—Brâhmaṇs, Vaishṇavas, Jogîs,[4] Jatîs,[5] Tapasîs,[6] Sannyâsîs,[7] Vairâgîs,[8] &c., as many as are Hari's worshippers, among them, from the boy up to the old man, not even one should remain living." Hearing this, Kañs said to his chief adviser, "Do you go and slay all." Having received [this] order, the Minister, accompanied by many Râkshasas, taking leave, went into the city and began, by fraud [and] force, to search out [and] slay cows, Brâhmaṇs, children, and worshippers of Hari.

---

## CHAPTER VI.

**Rejoicings in the house of Nand over the birth of Krishṇa—The cowherds seek to propitiate Kañs—Vasudev warns them of their danger.**

HAVING said this much [of] the tale, S'ri S'ukadev Jî said:—O King! on one occasion Nand [and] Jasodâ performed great

[1] Notice the idiomatic use of the Genitive in *janm ke bhikhârî*, "beggars of, or from, birth." It is used in a great variety of similar expressions. The form *koĩ yegâ* is respectful, with a sense of futurity, "when you may please to be angry."

[2] *Mahâdev* is a name of S'iva or Rudra.

[3] This is a peculiar sentence. *Indra kâ kuchh*, "anything of Indra," *tum par*, "upon, or against, you," *na*, "not," *basâe*, "prevails," the Aorist of *bashnâ*, from *vaś*, "power," a verb not found in the dictionaries, in the sense of "to prevail," "have power over." This verb occurs further on, and in Chapter LVIII.

[4] *Jogîs*, or, more properly, *Yogins*, are devotees who practise the Yoga philosophy, which leads to the belief that by effective meditation the powers of nature can be abrogated, and the limitations of time and space removed.

[5] *Jatîs*, or, rather, *Yatins*, are devotees who hold their passions under restraint.

[6] *Tapasîs* are those who practise *tapas*, or bodily torments, by way of devotion.

[7] *Sannyâsins*, which should be thus spelled, from *sam + ni + as*, "to lay aside," are ascetics who have set aside, or renounced, the world, in order to give their lives to religious exercises.

[8] *Vairâgins* are ascetics who are free from worldly desire, or passion; they have attained indifferentism.

austerity for a son; there[1] S'rî Nârâyaṇ himself granted the boon, thus, "We shall take birth in your house." When S'rî Krishṇa came, at the time of midnight, on Wednesday, the eighth [day] of the dark half of [the month] Bhâdoñ, then Jasodâ, as soon as she awoke, perceiving the face of a son, spoke to Nand. [She] felt excessive joy, and thought [that] her life [was] fruitful. As soon as it was dawn, having arisen, Nand Jî sent for the Paṇḍits and astrologers; they came, bringing each of them his book and calendar. Giving each of them a seat, [he] courteously caused them to sit down. They, by the rules of the S'âstras, having settled the year, month, lunar station, the day, the lunar mansion, the conjunction [of planets], [and] Karaṇa,[2] having reflected on the zodiacal sign, and settled the moment, [they] said, "Mahârâj! in considering our S'âstras it thus appears, that this boy having become a second Vidhâtâ,[3] [and] having slain all the Asuras, [and] removed the burden of Braj, will be called the Lord of Cowherdesses. All the world will sing the glory of this one."

Hearing this, Nand Jî vowed [an offering of] two hundred thousand cows dressed in silk, with golden horns, silver hoofs, [and] copper backs; and making many presents, giving fees to Brâhmaṇs, [and] receiving blessings, [he] dismissed [the Paṇḍits, &c.]. Then he called for all the musicians of the town; they severally came [and] each began to manifest his special attainment; musicians played, dancers danced, singers sang, [and] male and female panegyrists [began] to celebrate the glory [of the inviter]; and as many cowherds as belonged to Gokul, causing their wives to bring vessels of curds on their heads, [and] making up various kinds of disguises, dancing [and] singing, came to offer congratulations to Nand. On their coming they played so [heartily] at *dadhikâdo*[4] that in Gokul [the ground] was made nothing but curds.[5] When the game of *dadhikâdo* was ended, then Nand Jî, giving food [and] drink to all, and dressing [them] in robes, making the *tilak*,[6] [and] giving betel-leaf, dismissed [them].

In this way, for several days, congratulation continued; during this [time] whoever came [and] asked anything obtained from Nand Jî what [they] severally wanted. Having become free from the congratulations, Nand Jî called all the cowherds and said, "Brothers! we have heard that Kañs is sending to seize children; there is no knowing, some wicked one may say something [about

[1] See note [2], p. 12.
[2] *Karaṇas* are lunar periods of time, two of which are equal to a lunar day, or the time during which the moon travels 6° of space. There are eleven Karaṇas, having separate names.
[3] A name of Brahmâ.
[4] A game of pelting each other with curds and clay, on Krishṇa's festival.
[5] *Lit.*, "curds [and] curds was made."
[6] That is, making marks on the forehead, between the eyebrows, for ornamental or religious purposes. Coloured earths are generally employed.

us]; hence it is proper that, taking presents, we should go all together, and pay [our] yearly tribute."[1] Accepting this direction, all severally brought from their houses milk, curds, butter, and money, loading [them] on carts, accompanied by Nand, going from Gokul [they] came [to] Mathurâ. Having met with Kañs [they] made their presents,[2] [and] having paid every *kauṛî*,[3] being dismissed, [and] having saluted,[4] [they] took their way [homewards].

As soon as [they] were come to the bank of the Jumnâ, hearing the news, Vasudev Jî arrived [there also, and] having met with Nand Jî [and] asked [about his] welfare, said, "There is no kinsman and friend of ours like you in the world; because, when there was a load of misfortune upon us, then [we] sent the pregnant Rohinî [to] your place. She had a boy, that you have nurtured, and brought up. How far can we extol your virtue?"[5] Having said this much [he] again inquired, "Tell [me], are Râm-Krishṇa and [your] wife Jasodâ well?" Nand Jî said, "By your honour's favour all are well; and the source of our life, your Baldev Jî, is also prosperous, [during] the existence of whom, by your virtue and power, we have had a son; but one of your afflictions afflicts us." Vasudev said, "Friend! nothing prevails against Vidhâtâ; the line of destiny is obliterated by no one; hence having come into the world, [and] experienced the pain [of] affliction; who regrets?" Thus having imparted wisdom [he] said,—

"Do you go speedily [to] your home; Kañs has committed heavy oppression;
The mean [wretch] is sending to search for children; the death of virtuous subjects has occurred.

You, forsooth, have come along here, and Râkshasas are going about searching; none knows, some wicked one, having gone, may be exciting mischief in Gokul!" On hearing this, Nand Jî, agitatedly, taking all with [him], reflecting, went from Mathurâ to Gokul.

---

## CHAPTER VII.

Kañs sends Pûtanâ, a demoness, to destroy Krishṇa—But the latter sucks out her life—She falls dead—The cowherds cut up her body.

S'RÎ S'UKADEV Jî said:—O King! the Minister of Kañs, then, taking many Râkshasas with [him], was solely [engaged in] going

[1] Notice the addition of *ânâ*; idiom requires one to say "give and come back," or "go and come back," or "do and come," &c.

[2] There is here a play on the words *bheṭnâ*, "to visit," and *bheṭ* "a present."

[3] *chukânâ*, "to finish," "to settle"; here it means "to satisfy every *kauṛî*," i.e. the shells used for small change.

[4] The *juhâr* is a kind of prostration before a superior.

[5] Meaning that they cannot sufficiently thank him. The interrogative is often thus employed to indicate a negation.

about slaughtering; when [1] Kañs called a Râkshasî named Pûtanâ [and] said, "Go thou; as many children as thou findest of the Yadubansîs, kill." Hearing this, she, being pleased, prostrated [herself, and] departed; then [she] began to say within herself,—

"Nand has had a son; deserted [is] Gokul village;
By stratagem immediately I will bring [it]; becoming a
cowherdess, I will go."

Saying this, with the sixteen ornaments [and] twelve decorations, putting poison in her breast, assuming a fascinating form, deceitfully, holding a lotus-flower in [her] hand, decked out, [she] went as [if] the adorned Lakshmî may be going to her husband. Having arrived in Gokul, smiling [she] went into Nand's mansion. Having seen her, one and all, becoming fascinated, remained as though forgetting [themselves]. This one, going, seated [herself] near Jasodâ, and asking [her] welfare, gave a blessing, thus, "Thy hero Kâhn,[2] may [he] live a myriad years." Thus putting forward friendship, having taken the boy from the hand of Jasodâ [and] placed [it] on [her] lap, as [she] began to give [him] milk, S'rî Krishṇa, with both hands seizing the nipple [and] applying [his] mouth, began to drink the milk with the life. Then, indeed, becoming exceedingly alarmed, Pûtanâ cried out, "What sort [of being is] thy son, Jasodâ; [he is] not human; this is the messenger of Yama. Thinking [it] a cord, I have grasped a snake; if from this one's hand I shall escape living, then I will never again come into Gokul." Thus having said, [and] having fled, [she] came out of the village; but Krishṇa did not release [her]. At last her life was taken. She, writhing [in agony], fell as falls [3] the thunderbolt from the sky. Hearing the tremendous sound, Rohinî and Jasodâ came, weeping [and] wailing, where Pûtanâ was lying dead, covering two *kos* [of ground]; [4] and after them all the village [folk,] arising, ran. They see, then, Krishṇa on its breast mounted, sucking away [at] the milk. Quickly raising [him], kissing [his] face, [and] embracing [him, they] conveyed [him] home; [then] inviting the skilful, they began exorcising; and the cowherdesses [and] cowherds standing near Pûtanâ were saying among themselves, that, "Brother! hearing the crash of this one's falling we feared so that our breast is still throbbing; none knows what the condition of the child must have been." [5]

In the meantime Nand Jî arrived from Mathurâ; then what does he see?—a Râkshasî lying dead, and the crowd of inhabitants of Braj standing around. [He] asked, "What [is] this mischief

[1] See note [3], p. 4.
[2] A form of the name Krishṇa, found in the name of the city Kâhn-pur or Cawnpore.
[3] For *girâ* read *girî*. [4] About four miles.
[5] Notice this use of the Presumptive Perfect, *huî hogî*, "must have been." These forms are colloquially in constant requisition.

[which] has occurred?" They said, "Mahârâj! at first, this one, being exceedingly beautiful, went giving blessings [in] your house; having seen her, all the women of Braj remained forgetful. This one, taking Krishṇa, began to give him milk; afterwards we know not what circumstance happened." Hearing this much, Nand Jî said, "It was great good fortune that the child was saved, and [that] this one fell not on Gokul; otherwise not even one had remained living, all had been crushed to death beneath her."[1] Having spoken thus, Nand Jî came home [and] began to [give] alms and perform meritorious acts; and the cowherds, with axes, mattocks, spades, [and] hatchets, cutting up Pûtanâ's hands [and] feet, were digging [and] digging holes [and] burying [them]; and collecting together the flesh [and] skin, burnt [them]. By the burning of that such an odour was diffused that the world was filled with the fragrance.

Having heard this much [of] the tale, King Parîkshit asked S'ukadev Jî, "Mahârâj! that Râkshasî [was] most foul [and] a consumer of alcohol [and] flesh; how [comes it that] fragrance issued from her body? kindly tell me [that]." The saint said, "O King! S'rî Krishṇa-Chand, having drunk [her] milk, gave [her] salvation; [for] this reason a sweet smell issued."

---

## CHAPTER VIII.

Festivities when Krishṇa is twenty-seven days old—The demon S'akatâsur attempts to destroy him, but is killed by Krishṇa—The demon Triṇâwart killed by Krishṇa when five months old.

S'RÎ S'UKADEV, the saint, said,—

> The asterism [in] which Mohan was [born] came round;[2]
> Mother Jasodâ prepared everything [according to] rule, all four congratulatory festivities.

When Hari was of twenty-seven days,[3] Nand Jî sent an invitation to all Brâhmans and inhabitants of Braj. They came; [and he] caused them, courteously, to be seated; afterwards,[4] bestowing

[1] Notice the use of the Present Imperfect in these sentences, with its sense of "had remained" and "had died."

[2] For *paiyauṅ* read *paryau*; *paryau âî*, "happened to come," "it fell to come." Mohan is a name of Krishṇa.

[3] The ordinary expression for "twenty-seven days old." The same idiom is used for any other period of time.

[4] *âge* means "afterwards" as well as "before," because it expresses events which occur by going "forward" in a course of action.

much liberality on the Brâhmaṇs, [he] dismissed them, and dressing the brotherhood [in] robes, caused them to enjoy the six flavours.[1] At that time the lady Jasodâ was playing the hostess; Rohinî was engaged in household duties; the inhabitants of Braj were laughing away [and] feasting; the cowherdesses were singing on; all were in this way absorbed in joy, that there was no thought of Krishṇa to anyone. And Krishṇa under a heavy cart, in a cradle, was sleeping unconsciously; when, in this [state of affairs], becoming hungry, [he] awoke. Having placed [his] big toe in [his] mouth, he began to cry, [and] fidgeting about looked around. Just at that conjuncture a Râkshas, flying by, came upon [the scene, and] perceiving Krishṇa alone, said within himself, "This, forsooth, is some very strong one born; but to-day I will take revenge for Pûtanâ on him." Having thus resolved [he] came [and] sat on the cart; [and] from this very [circumstance] his name has become *Sakaṭâsur* (i.e. cart-demon). When the cart creakingly moved, S'rî Krishṇa [while] sobbing struck such a kick that that [demon] died, and the cart, breaking to pieces, fell down; then as many dishes of milk [and] curds as were [there], were all broken to pieces, and, like a river of milk, flowed forth. Having heard the sound of the breaking of the cart and the splitting of the vessels, the cowherds and cowherdesses came running [there]; on arriving, Jasodâ raising up Krishṇa, kissed [his] face, [and] embraced [him]. Perceiving this wonder, all said among themselves, "To-day Fate has effected great happiness, in that the child has remained safe, and the cart alone is broken up."

Having related the tale so far, S'rî S'ukadev said:—O King! when Hari was of five months [age], Kaṅs sent Triṇâwart; he, becoming a whirlwind, went into Gokul. Nand's wife, holding Krishṇa in [her] lap, was seated in the middle of the courtyard, when, all at once, Kâhn became so heavy that Jasodâ, through the weight, set [him] down from [her] lap. Hereupon such a storm came that day became night,[2] and trees [one after another] began to be torn up [and] fall, [and] roofs to fly [by the wind]. Then becoming alarmed, Jasodâ Jî essayed to lift up Krishṇa, but he was not raised. As soon as her hand was removed from his body, Triṇâwart, taking [him] to the sky, flew away; and said to himself, thus, "To-day I will not remain [with] this one unkilled."

He, for his part, holding Krishṇa was there this meditating; here Jasodâ Jî, when [she] found [Krishṇa] not before [her], weeping bitterly began to cry out "Krishṇa! Krishṇa!" Hearing her noise, all the cowherdesses [and] cowherds came, [and] accompanying [her], ran to search. In the darkness they went feeling about by guess; furthermore, stumbling, [and] falling about.

[1] The six recognized flavours are, sweet, sour, salt, bitter, acrid, and astringent; and they are held to comprise every alimentary delicacy.

[2] See note [2], p. 14.

The cowherdesses roam searching the woods of Braj; on this side Rohinî [and] Jasodâ are talking [of the affair];
Nand [with] the noise of a thunder-cloud is shouting; the cowherdesses [and] cowherds are crying out excessively.

When S'rî Krishṇa saw all the inhabitants of Braj, along with Nand [and] Jasodâ, exceedingly pained, swinging Triṇâwart round [and] bringing [him] into the courtyard, [he] dashed [him] upon a stone, so that his life vanished from [his] body. The storm was hushed; it became light [again]; all [who had] mistakenly strayed came home. They saw, then, the Râkshas lying dead in the courtyard; S'rî Krishṇa was playing on the chest. On arriving, Jasodâ, taking [him] up, pressed [him to her] neck, and bestowed many gifts on Brâhmaṇs.

---

## CHAPTER IX.

Vasudev sends his family priest to name Balarâm and Krishna—Krishṇa steals the butter-milk—And when caught contrives to escape—He eats dirt—And his mother beholds, instead, the three worlds in his mouth.

S'RÎ S'UKADEV Jî said:—O King! one day Vasudev Jî, sending for the saint Garg, who was a great astrologer and family priest of the Yadubansîs, said, "Do you go to Gokul, fix the name of the boy, [and] return.

Rohinî has been with child; a son is [born] to her;
How long [is to be his] life, what [his] strength, [and] what is [to be his] name.

And Nand Jî has had a son; he also having invited [you] departed." On hearing [this] the saint Garg, being pleased, went, and arrived near Gokul. Then someone, having approached Nand Jî, said, "The family priest of the Yadubansîs, the saint Garg Jî, is coming." Having heard this, Nand Jî, delightedly, collecting together the cowherd-children, taking presents, rose up, [and] hastened; and spreading carpets of silk-cloth, conducted [him] with musical instruments. Having reverenced [him and] seated him on a seat, [and] having received the nectar of his feet,[1] women [and] men, [with] joined hands, began to say, "Mahârâj! we [have] great fortune that your Honour compassionately having permitted a view [of you] has purified the house. By

[1] It is considered meritorious to drink the water in which the feet of a Brahman have been washed. This is called *charaṇâmrita*, "foot's nectar."

your majesty two sons have been [born]; one Rohinî's [and] one ours; kindly fix a name for them." The saint Garg said, "Such name-fixing as this is improper;[1] because, should this affair be spread about, that the saint Garg had gone into Gokul to fix the name of the boys, and Kañs should get [to] hear [of it], then he will know this that someone has conveyed Devakî's son [to] the house of Vasudev's friend; on this account the family priest Garg has gone; having understood this, he will send to seize me, and none knows what mischief [it] may bring upon you also; hence do not you spread [it] about at all; secretly have the name fixed in the house."[2]

Nand said, "Garg Jî! you have spoken true." Saying this much [he] conducted him within the house, [and] seated [him]. Then the saint Garg, having inquired from Nand Jî the time and lunar day of the birth of both, having examined the zodiacal conjunction, [and] fixed the name, said, "Listen,[3] Nand Jî! of the son of Rohinî, the wife of Vasudev, there shall be these-many names:—Sankarshan, Revatîraman, Baladâû, Balarâm, Kâlindî-bhedan, Haladhar, and Balabîr. And the Krishṇa-formed one, who is your boy, his names are unnumbered; but [at] some time [he] was born in the house of Vasudev, therefore [his] name has become Vâsudev; and, it occurs to me, that both these boys of yours, during the four ages, when they are born, are born only together."[4]

Nand Jî said, "Tell [me] their qualities." The saint Garg replied, "These are second Vidhâtâs; their condition is inconceivable;[5] but I know this, that having killed Kañs they will remove the burden of the earth." Having spoken thus, the saint Garg silently departed, and going to Vasudev, related[6] all the news [to him].

Afterwards both the boys day by day began to grow in Gokul, and to delight Nand and Jasodâ by childish sport. Dressed in blue [and] yellow frocks, [pretty] little curls scattered over their foreheads, amulets [and] charms fastened [on], necklets placed on their necks, holding toys in their hands, they were playing; in the courtyard crawling along, they tumble about, and prattle lispingly. Rohinî and Jasodâ follow close behind [them], lest the boys, [from] fear of anything, should stumble [and] fall.[7] When,

[1] For *nahoñ* read *nahiñ*.

[2] Notice the use of the double causal *dharwânâ* to express "to have it fixed."

[3] For *munoñ* read *suno*.

[4] *janmeñ haiñ* are Aorists with the substantive verb as auxiliary. The sense is, "when they are born" or "may be born." It is quite common colloquially. They are not Past tenses.

[5] Here the Ablative is understood (see note [16], p. 4), the construction being, "his condition is not understood anyhow [by anyone]."

[6] The plural *kahe* is needed; because *samâchâr*, "news," is generally treated as a plural noun.

[7] The idiom is peculiar here; the sentence is really Imperative, meaning literally, "On this account, to wit, Let not, anyhow, the boys, fearing anything, stumble and fall!"

having caught hold of the very little calves' and heifers' tails, [they] rise up, and tumble down, then Jasodâ and Rohinî most affectionately, having raised, embraced them, [and] given [them] milk, fondle them with various kinds of endearments.

When S'rî Krishṇa was grown up, one day, accompanied by cowherd-children, he went into Braj to steal curd [and] butter.

> Going [they] search in empty house; what [they] find, that [they] cause [others] to steal.[1]

Those whom [they] find sleeping in a house, [they] take [and] bring away their curd-vessels [which are] placed [there] covered up. Where he sees [anything] placed [high] on a netting, there on a stool a plank, on the plank a wooden mortar setting, making a companion stand [on that, and] mounting upon him, [they] take [it] down, eat some, steal [some], and spill [some]. Thus [they] constantly steal [from] the various houses of the cowherdesses.[2]

One day, they all took counsel and allowed Mohan to enter a house. As, having entered inside the house, [he] wishes that [he] may steal butter [and] curd, going [and] catching [him, they] said, "Day by day [you] are coming, night [and] morning; now where will you go, butter-thief?" Thus having said, when all the cowherdesses together, taking Kanhaiyâ, went to give a complaint to Jasodâ, then S'rî Krishṇa acted so trickily that he caused that [cowherdess] to hold the hand of her own son, and himself running away [re]joined his cowherd-children. They went on [and] having approached Nand's wife, falling [at her] feet, said, "If you should not be displeased, we will tell [you] what a mischievous [thing] Krishṇa has resolved on.

> "Milk, curds, butter, butter-milk, nothing escapes in Braj.
> Such thefts he perpetrates, returning morning and evening.

Wherever they find [a vessel] placed, covered up, they fearlessly take [it] up, and bring it thence. Some they eat, [some] they cause [others] to steal. Should anyone point out the curds attached to his mouth, he retorts to her saying, 'Thou thy very self put [it there].' In this way they are continually coming thieving. To-day we have caught [him], therefore we have brought [him] to show [him] to you." Jasodâ said, "Sister! whose son have you seized [and] brought? Since yesterday, my prince Kanhâ,i has not gone even outside[3] the house. Such truth [as] this are you speaking!" Hearing this [and] seeing only her own child in [her] hand, they, laughing, were abashed. There[upon] Jasodâ having called Krishṇa, said, "Son! don't go

[1] The plurals are respectful to Krishṇa.
[2] Notice all these Aorists about here. They indicate the customary character of the different actions.
[3] For *bâhir* read *bâhar*.

in anyone's place; what you may wish, take [and] eat in the house."

> Having heard [this] Kâhn says lispingly, "Mother! don't believe them;
> These false cowherdesses tell lies; they roam about close behind me.

In places they get me to hold the milk-pails [and] calves; sometimes they get me to do house-work; having set me to watch at the door they go about their work; then deceptively, having returned, they tell tales to you." Hearing thus, the cowherdesses, severally looking [at] the face [of] Hari, smiled [and] went away.

One day later on Krishṇa [and] Balarâm were playing in the courtyard with [their] companions, when Kâhn ate [some] dirt; thereupon one companion went [and] informed Jasodâ.[1] She angrily, taking a switch in [her] hand, got up [and] ran [towards him]. [He] having perceived [his] mother coming filled with passion, wiped [his] mouth [and] stood [there] frightened. As soon as [she] got [to him] she said, "How now![2] why hast thou eaten dirt?" Krishṇa, fearing [and] trembling, said, "Mother! who has told thee?"[3] She said, "Thy friend." Then Mohan angrily asked the friend, "How now! when did I eat dirt?"[4] He, fearing, said, "Brother! I know nothing [of] what thou sayest; what shall I say?" As soon as Kâhn began to expostulate with the companion, Jasodâ went [and] seized him. Thereupon Krishṇa began to say, "Mother! be not thou angry; do human beings ever eat dirt?" She said, "I will not listen to thy prevarication;[5] if thou art true, show thy mouth." When S'rî Krishṇa opened [his] mouth, the three worlds were seen within it.[6] Then knowledge came to Jasodâ, therefore she began to say within herself, "I am a great fool, in that I am esteeming as my son the Lord of the Three Worlds."

Having related the tale thus far, S'rî S'ukadev said to King Parîkshit:—O King! when Nand's wife thought thus, Hari dispersed his illusion; hereupon Jasodâ, having fondled Mohan [and] pressed [him to her] bosom, conducted [him] home.

[1] The word *bât* is understood.

[2] *Lit.*, "Why? fellow!"

[3] For *tuj se* read *tujh se*; but Lallû Lâl himself wrote *tuj*.

[4] Notice that Krishṇa is made to use the more correct form *maṭṭî* or *miṭṭî*, while his mother uses the rustic *mâṭî*.

[5] Present tense for Future: *aṭpaṭî bât* = "incoherent statement," "shuffling," or "prevarication."

[6] The idiom *drishṭi ânâ* is useful; *meñ* is understood; and it, therefore, means "to come into sight." The Hindû notion is that rays of sight pass from the person to the object, not *vice versâ*. A knowledge of this fact will explain this and other related idioms. The Singular is used because *tîn lok*, "the three worlds," implies "entire creation [was seen]."

## CHAPTER X.

Churning as busily practised in Nand's house—Krishṇa breaks the churning-sticks—Upsets the butter-milk—His mother ties him to a wooden mortar to stop his pranks.

ONE day, thinking [it] time for churning curds, Nand's wife arose quite early, and, having awakened all the cowherdesses, called [them to her]; they, having come, swept the house, [and] cleaned [it, and] smeared [and] plastered [it with cow-dung], each taking her own churning staff, began to churn curds. Thereupon Nand's wife, also, having taken a largish vessel [and] placed [it] on a porter's knot, spreading a seat [for herself, and] sending for cord and churning-stick, and carefully selecting fresh curd-vessels, sat down to churn for Râm Krishṇa. At that time, in the house of Nand, such a noise of curd-churning was going on, as though a cloud were thundering. Hereupon Krishṇa woke up, [and] set-to crying [and] calling out[1] "Mother! mother!" When nobody heard his shouting, he himself came to Jasodâ, and [his] eyes filled with tears, ill-humouredly sobbing on [and] lisping, he said, "Mother! [I] called thee several times, but [thou] didst not come to give me breakfast; is not thy work done yet?" Having said this much he became cross, [and] pulling the churning-stick from the vessel, [and] thrusting in both [his] hands, he began to take out [and] fling about the butter, to besmear [his] body, to stamp about [with his] feet, [and] to drag at the skirt's end and cry. Then Nand's wife, alarmed, angrily said, "Son! what conduct [is] this [which you] have developed?

"Come, get up, I will give thee breakfast." Krishṇa said,
"Now I will not take [it];
At first why was [it] not given, Mother? [if it] were taken
now, [it would be] my misfortune."

At length Jasodâ, having flattered [him, and] affectionately kissed [his] face, took [him] up on [her] lap, and gave [him] curds, butter, [and] bread, to eat. Hari laughing away was eating; Nand's wife was feeding him [under] a screen formed by the bottom of [her] dress, so that no one should see.[2]

In the meantime a cowherdess came [and] said, "You, forsooth, are seated here; there all the milk has boiled over[3] on the hearth. On hearing[4] this, hastily putting Krishṇa down from [her] lap, [she] rose [and] ran; and having gone, saved the milk.

[1] *pukâran lâge* is the Braj form of *pukârne lage*.
[2] Here *us par* is understood; meaning that "the sight of anyone should not be *on him*."
[3] For *ûphan* read *uphan*.
[4] For *sante* read *sunte*.

Here Kâhn, having broken the vessels of curds and butter-milk, snapped the churning-stick, [and] having taken a pot full of butter, ran among the cowherd lads. He found a mortar placed upside down, on which he got [and] sat, and causing [his] companions to sit around, began to laugh away, [and] to share among them the butter [and] to eat.

In [the midst of] this Jasodâ, having taken off the milk, came [and] saw, that, in the courtyard and hall, there was a mess of curds and butter-milk. Then, indeed, having reflected, [she] took a switch in [her] hand, [and] went forth; and, searching about, [she] came where S'rî Krishṇa, having made a circle [of his companions], was eating [and] causing [others] to eat the butter. As soon as [she] on going [to him] caught [his] hand from behind, Hari, then seeing his mother, crying and beseeching said, "Mother! who upset the butter-milk? I don't know. Let me go." Having heard such humble speeches, Jasodâ, having laughed [and] thrown the switch from [her] hand, and, being immersed in joy, [under] the guise of anger,[1] pressed [him to her] breast, [and] taking [him] home, began to tie him to a mortar. Then S'rî Krishṇa so acted that with whatever string [he] was bound it should become [too] short. Jasodâ[2] sent for all the strings of the house, still [he] was not bound. At last, perceiving [that his] mother was pained, he himself allowed the binding [to be effected]. Nand's wife, having bound [him, and] administered an oath of [not] unfastening [him] to the cowherdesses, recommenced [her] domestic occupation.

---

## CHAPTER XI.

Krishṇa goes to release Nal and Kûvar from a curse pronounced in a former birth—He drags the wooden mortar along with him—He tears up the trees in which the victims are confined—Their gratitude therefor.

S'RÎ S'UKADEV JÎ said:—O King! to S'rî Krishṇa while bound came the remembrance of a former birth, that Kuver's[3] sons had been cursed by Nârad [and that] their deliverance should be effected. Having heard this, King Parîkshit asked S'ukadev Jî:—Mahârâj! how did Nârad, the saint, curse the sons of Kuver?

[1] For *riske* read *ris ke*.
[2] For *Jaaodâ* read *Jasodâ*.
[3] Kuvera is the god of riches generally; and his resi'ence is placed in one of the loftiest peaks of the Himâlaya mountains. He is accounted regent of the northern region.

explain that [to me]. S'ukadev, the saint, said :—Kuver's two sons, named Nal [and] Kûvar,[1] were in Kailâs ;[2] they, by assiduously serving S'iva, became exceedingly wealthy. One day, taking [their] wives with [them], they went [to] the woods for diversion. Having gone there [and] drunk wine, [they] became intoxicated. Then, along with [their] wives, having become naked, [they] began to bathe in the Ganges; and, throwing [their] arms round [each other's] necks, began to indulge in a variety of sports; hereupon Nârad, the saint, [unexpectedly] came there. On seeing him, the women, for their part, came forth and dressed [themselves]; [but] those drunken [men] remained standing where [they were]. Perceiving their condition, Nârad Jî said within himself, "These have become proud of their wealth, [and] therefore having become intoxicated [they] esteem pleasure [and] anger as happiness. The poor man has no conceit, [but] to the wealthy, where is the thought of virtue [and] vice? Fools, by affection for a false body, forget [themselves]; having regarded [their] wealth [and] family [they] are elated. The virtuous do not bring the pride of wealth into [their] hearts; they esteem fortune [and] misfortune as equal." Having said this much, Nârad, the saint, cursed them, thus, "For this sin, go you into Gokul, [and] become trees; when S'rî Krishṇa shall take incarnate form he will give you deliverance." Nârad, the saint, cursed them thus; in consequence of that they came into Gokul [and] became trees; their name then became Yamalârjun.

Having related the story thus far, S'ukadev Jî said :—Mahârâj! having remembered this affair, S'rî Krishṇa dragged along the wooden mortar to the place where the Yamalârjun trees were. On going there, having cast the mortar cross-wise between both those trees, [he] gave such a jerk that both the trees were uptorn from the root; and two handsome men, having issued from them, [with] joined hands, praising [him] began to say, "O Lord! who but you would take thought of such great sinners as us?" S'rî Krishṇa said, "Listen. Nârad, the saint, had great compassion on you in that [he] gave [you] deliverance in Gokul. By his favour you have found me; now ask the boon which may be in your hearts."

Yamalârjun said, "Lord of the humble! this is the favour of Nârad Jî alone that [we] have touched your Honour's feet and seen [you]; now we have no wish for anything; but please grant only this much that your service may ever remain in our hearts." Hearing this [and] granting the boon, [and] smiling, S'rî Krishṇa-Chand dismissed them.

[1] For *Kâvar* read *Kûvar*. This misreading was made by both Hollings and Eastwick.

[2] Kailâsa was the paradise of S'iva, as well as being the residence of Kuvera; and was situated beyond the Mânasa lake, among the Himâlaya mountains.

## CHAPTER XII.

The cowherds find Krishṇa by the uprooted trees—Nand and his followers escape from Gokul to Brindâban—Krishṇa, at five years old, slays the demon Bachchhâsur, and the demon Bakâsur.

S'RÎ[1] S'UKADEV, the saint, said:—O King! when both those trees fell, having heard their sound, Nand's wife agitatedly ran. She came where Krishṇa had been bound to the mortar;[2] and all the cowherdesses and cowherds also came after her. When [she] did not find Krishṇa there, having become alarmed, Jasodâ, calling out "Mohan! Mohan!" went along saying, "Where has gone [he who] was bound? O mother! has anyone seen anywhere my boy Kanhâ,î?" Hereupon a Brajwoman[3] came forward [and] said, "Two trees have fallen, Murârî[4] has escaped there."

Hearing this, all went forward [and] saw[5] that [in] very truth the trees are lying uprooted, and Krishṇa between them, bound to the mortar, seated [in a] contracted [attitude]. On going [to him] Nand's wife released Kâhn from the mortar, [and] crying, embraced [him]; and all the cowherdesses, thinking [him] frightened, began to snap [their fingers, and] to clap away [with their hands] to amuse [him]. Thereupon Nand [and] Upanand began saying to each other, "These trees [which] have been growing from age to age, how did [they] come rooted up? this comes to [our] minds [as] a marvel; their secret is not at all to be understood [by us]." Hearing this much, a boy related the circumstance of the falling trees just as it occurred; but no one understood it. One said, "How can this child understand this secret?" Another said, "Perhaps it may be so; who can understand Hari's actions?" In this way, making various kinds of remarks, taking S'rî Krishṇa, all joyfully came into Gokul. Then Nand Jî [gave] much alms [and] performed virtuous [acts].

After some time had elapsed, Krishṇa's birthday came round; then Jasodâ Rânî sent an invitation to all the family, and, preparing a festivity, tied the birthday-knot. When all having met had sat down to the treat, Nand-Râ,e said, "Listen, brethren! now in this Gokul how is [it possible] to remain? Day by day dreadful oppressions are occurring; come, let us go to some such place where we may obtain the comfort of grass and water." Upanand said, "Should [you] go [and] dwell [in] Brindâban,

[1] For *S'î* read *S'rî*.
[2] Lallû Lâl here wrote *ulûkhal*, not *ukhal*.
[3] The punctuation of the text is here quite misleading.
[4] Murârî (properly *Mura + ari*), "the enemy of Mura," a name of Krishṇa.
[5] *dekhen̄* is the Aorist, with the sense of the Present, and means "they are looking."

then [you] will remain [there] with delight." Having heard this statement, Nand Jî caused all to eat [and] drink, [and] having distributed betel-leaf [and] made [them] sit down, and forthwith having summoned an astrologer, asked the [propitious] moment for the journey. That one, having reflected,[1] said, "For a journey in this direction to-morrow is exceedingly good ; on the left-hand [is] Yoginî,[2] Diśâśûla[3] [is] behind, and the Moon is [in] front. Undoubtedly your Honour can set out quite early [to-morrow]."

Having heard this, all the cowherdesses and cowherds, at that time, went each to his own home ; but early in the morning each loaded his own goods and chattels on carts [and] came [and] collected together. Nand Jî accompanied [them] with [his] family, and proceeding on and on, [and] crossing the river, [in] the evening they arrived [at their destination]. Having propitiated the goddess Brindâ,[4] and occupied Brindâban, they all began to reside there with happiness [and] ease.

When S'rî Krishṇa was five years old, he said to [his] mother, "I will go to graze calves ; do thou tell Baladâ,û not to leave me alone in the wood." She said, "Son! there are plenty of calf-grazers your servants ; do not you be [for] an instant concealed from before my eyes, darling!" Kâhn said, "If I shall go into the wood to sport, I shall eat food ; otherwise not." Having heard this, Jasodâ, calling the cow-boys, [and] consigning Krishṇa to [the care of] Balarâm, said, "You will not go[5] far to graze calves ; and before dusk[6] come home with both [of them]. You will not leave these alone in the wood ; remain in their very company ; you are their guardians." Having spoken thus, [and] having given [them] food, [she] dispatched Râm Krishṇa along with them.

They, having gone, began to graze calves [on] the bank of the Jumnâ, and to sport among the cow-boys ; when, hereupon, Bachchhâsur, sent by[7] Kañs, having assumed a deceitful form, arrived. Upon seeing him, all the calves, frightened, fled hither and thither. Then S'rî Krishṇa indicated by a sign to Baladev Jî, thus, "Brother! this [is] some Râkshas come." When he, grazing on forwards, approached near to effect [his] ambuscade,[8]

[1] For *bichâr ke* read *bichârke*.

[2] A Yoginî is a female demon possessed of magical power ; eight of them attend upon Durgâ, to perform ill-omened offices.

[3] For *diśâśul* read *diśâśûla*, as Lallû Lâl wrote it. It means *diśâ* + *sûla*, "the quarter of death" ; and is the ninth astronomical Yoga, in which direction it is unpropitious to travel.

[4] *Brindâ* is a name of the *tulsî*, or sweet basil, plant. It is fabled that Krishṇa loved a nymph and turned her into the *tulsî*-plant, which Hindûs now adore.

[5] The respectful Imperative in *-iyo* conveys a sense of futurity as well as request.

[6] *sâñjh na hote*, "twilight not being," that is, "before dusk."

[7] See note [14], p. 5.

[8] That is, to accomplish his treacherous purpose.

S'rî Krishṇa, having seized the hind leg [and] whirled [him] round, so dashed [him] down that his life issued from [his] body.

Having heard [of] the death of Bachchhâsur, Kañs sent Bakâsur. He, having come into Brindâban [and] arranged his ambuscade, [on] the bank of the Jumnâ went [and] sat, like a mountain. Having seen him, struck with fear the cow-boys began to say to Krishṇa, "Brother! this, forsooth, [is] some Râkshas, come as a crane; how shall we escape from his hand?"

These, then, on the one hand, were thus speaking to Krishṇa; and, on the other hand, that [Râkshas] also was thus reflecting in [his] mind, "To-day I will not go without killing him." Hereupon, when S'rî Krishṇa went near him, he, having lifted him (Krishṇa) in [his] beak, closed [his] mouth. The cow-boys, becoming alarmed, looked about on all sides, [and] crying [and] calling again and again,[1] began to say, "Alas! alas! Haladhar, too, is not here; what shall we go [and] say to Jasodâ?" Perceiving them to be exceedingly pained, S'rî Krishṇa became so hot that he could not hold [him] in [his] mouth. When he disgorged him, then he (Krishṇa) seized him [by] the beak, [and] having pressed the beak under [his] foot, he rent [him] up; and having collected the calves, accompanied with [his] companions, he went home laughing [and] playing.

---

## CHAPTER XIII.

**The serpent-demon Aghâsur swallows Krishṇa and all his companions—Krishṇa swells out monstrously, and bursts the serpent.**

S'RÎ S'UKADEV said:—Listen, Mahârâj! At dawn one day S'rî Krishṇa proceeded to the wood to graze calves; along with him all the cow-boys, also, each taking food from his home, accompanied [him]; and having entered the pasturage, set down the food, [and] set free the calves to graze, they began to smear about their bodies with chalk [and] red ochre, and making [and] putting on ornaments of wild fruits [and] flowers, [they began] to play, and imitating the sounds of beasts [and] birds, [and] with various kinds of pastime, [began] to dance [and] to sing.

Hereupon the Râkshas named Aghâsur, sent by Kañs, came. He, having become an exceedingly large dragon, sat [with] open

[1] "Again and again" is indicated by the repetition of the Conjunctive Participles.

mouth; and, with all the companions, S'rî Krishṇa, also, sporting about, [happened to] go just where he, having arranged [his] ambuscade, was seated open-mouthed. Having perceived him from afar, the cow-boys began to say among themselves, "Brother! this, forsooth, is some great mountain, the cavern of which is so large." Saying thus, and grazing the calves, they approached near him; then one boy, perceiving his mouth open, said, "Brother! this, indeed, is some exceedingly frightful cavern; we will not go within it; we are afraid as soon as [we] look [at it]." Then a companion named Tokh said, "Come on, let us go in; what should frighten us, as long as Krishṇa [is] with [us]; if it should be some Asur, then it will be killed in the manner of Bakâsur."

All the companions, standing, were thus merely conversing, when he drew so deep a breath that all the cow-boys, along with the calves, flying, went [and] fell into his mouth. As soon as the poisonous hot vapour was felt, then the calves, becoming alarmed, began to bellow, and the companions to cry out, "O beloved Krishṇa! quickly take thought [of us]; otherwise, we all [shall be] burnt to death." As soon as [he] heard their cry, becoming distressed, S'rî Krishṇa, also, advanced [1] into his mouth. He (the dragon), becoming pleased, closed [his] mouth; thereupon S'rî Krishṇa increased his own body so much that his (the dragon's) stomach burst open. All the calves and the cow-boys fell out. Then delightedly the gods, having rained down flowers and nectar, removed the anguish of all [sufferers]. Then the cow-boys began to say to S'rî Krishṇa, "Brother! having killed this Asur, to-day thou hast well preserved [2] [us]; otherwise all had perished."

---

## CHAPTER XIV.

Brahmâ steals away Krishṇa's companions and the cows and confines them in a cave—Krishṇa creates illusive imitations of them—He frightens Brahmâ by causing his illusions to appear more god-like than the divinities.

SRÎ S'UKADEV said:—O King! having thus killed Aghâsur, S'rî Krishṇa Chand collected the calves [and], taking the companions with [him], set forth. Having gone some distance, standing in the shade of a *kadam*-tree [and] playing the flute, [he] called to all the cowherd lads [and] said, "Brothers! this is a nice place; leaving this, where should we go further on? Sit down just here

[1] For *baṛ gaye* read *baṛh gaye*. [2] For *bachâyo* read *bachâye*.

[and] let us eat the food." Upon hearing this, they drove away the calves to graze, and having brought the leaves of swallow-wort, bastard-teak, fig, kadam, and lotus, [and] having made plates [and] cups, [and] brushed [and] cleaned, [they] sat down around S'rî Krishṇa [in] rows on rows; and each opening his own [packet of] food, began to share it among themselves.

When they had done sharing, S'rî Krishṇa Chand, standing in the midst of all, having himself first raised a mouthful, gave the order to eat. They began to eat. Among them, wearing a peacock-crown, a floral wreath on the neck, holding a club, assuming the triply-bent form,[1] wearing yellow silk, covered with yellow cloth, [and] laughing away, S'rî Krishṇa, also, was feeding all [of them] from his [packet of] food; and taking up [a little] from the plate of each [and] tasting [and] tasting, he was going on declaring the flavours—the bitter, sweet, hot, [and] pungent; and in that assembly he appeared as beautiful as the moon among the stars. Then Brahmâ [and] all the other gods, seated in their chariots, were looking on, from the sky, [at] the happiness of the cowherd assembly, when Brahmâ, coming from among them, stole away all the calves. And hereupon the cowherd lads, [while eating], becoming anxious, said to S'rî Krishṇa, "Brother! we, forsooth, are sitting [and] eating away carelessly; no one knows where the calves might have strayed away to."

Then Kanhâ,î says to the cowherds, "Do you all remain at the feast, brothers!
Let no one arise [or] be anxious; I will collect [and] bring everyone's calf."

Having spoken thus, [and] having gone some distance in the wood, when [he] perceived that "Brahmâ has taken away the calves from here," then S'rî Krishṇa made [and] brought others just like [them]. Having come here [again, he] sees that the cowherd boys also have been picked up [and] carried away [by Brahmâ]. Then he made [others] also just as they were; and, perceiving it had become evening, taking all with [him, he] came [to] Brindâban. The cowherd boys went each to his home; but no one knew this secret, that, these [are] not our children [and] calves; rather, day by day the delusion went on increasing still more.

Having rehearsed this much [of] the story, S'rî S'ukadev said:—Mahârâj! on that side, Brahmâ having taken the cowherd boys [and] calves, [and] having filled [them] into the cave of a mountain, [and] put a block of stone on its mouth, forgot [the affair]; and, on this side, S'rî Krishṇa Chand was continually indulging in various fresh sports. In this [way] a year passed

[1] Many images of Krishṇa have the legs, loins, and neck bent. It is a characteristic mark.

away, then the remembrance occurred to Brahmâ; therefore he began to say within himself, "Of me, indeed, there has not been even one moment, but [it] has become a year of men; hence now, come, it should be seen what has taken place in Braj without cowherd boys and calves."

Having reflected thus, [he] arose [and] came where they had all been shut up in the cavern. Having raised the stone, [he] sees that the boys and calves are lying sleeping in a profound sleep. Going from there [and] coming into Brindâban, having seen the children and calves all just as they [formerly] were, being astonished, [he] began to say, "How came the cowherd boys and calves here? or has Krishṇa created them afresh?" Having said this much, [he] again went to look at the cavern. In the interval in which he could look from there [and] back, within that, on this side, S'rî Krishṇa Chand produced such an illusion that, as many cowherd-boys and calves as there were, all became four-armed, and before each [of them] Brahmâ, Rudra, [and] Indra, are standing [with] joined hands.

> Seeing [this], Biranch[1] became like a picture; [he] forgot [everything]; knowledge, thought, all went.
> As a stone four-faced Devî [is] afflicted [when] become deprived of worship [and] adoration.

And, having become afraid, [he] closed [his] eyes, [and] began to tremble [and] shiver. When the soul-regulating S'rî Krishṇa Chand perceived that Brahmâ is exceedingly disquieted, [he] appropriated the share of all,[2] and himself remained quite alone, just as separated cloud may become one.

---

## CHAPTER XV.

Brahmâ asks pardon of Krishṇa—He releases the real kine and cowherds, after a twelvemonth's incarceration.

S'RÎ S'UKADEV JÎ said:—O King! when S'rî Krishṇa had dissipated his illusion, then Brahmâ acquired knowledge of his own person; therefore, having reflected [and] approached Bhagwân, with extreme humility falling [at his] feet, supplicatingly standing with joined hands, he began to say, "O Lord! you have

[1] *Birañch* is an epithet of Brahmâ; it should be *Virach* or *Virachi*, "the creator." The expression "to become like a picture" means "to be struck motionless with astonishment."

[2] *anś harnâ* means "to appropriate a share [in some common property]," *anś-hârâ* is "a co sharer," "the taker of a share [with another]." The sense here is

acted very kindly in that [you] have removed my pride ; through this I was remaining blind. Of whom is there such intelligence that, without your compassion, he may understand your actions. By your illusion everything is fascinated; who is he that may fascinate you? You are the creator of all ; in each hair of your [body] many Brahmâs such as me are lying. Of what account am I?[1] Compassionate to the humble ! now mercifully forgive [my] transgression ; take no heed [of] my fault."

Having heard this much, S'rî Krishṇa Chand smiled. Then Brahmâ brought all the cowherd boys and calves fast asleep [and] gave [them to him] ; and having become abashed, [and] having offered praise, [he] went to his own place. Just such an assembly as formerly was, was produced ; a year had elapsed, that no one knew. As the cowherd-boys' sleep passed away[2] Krishṇa collected the calves [and] brought [them] ; then boys among them[3] said, "Brother ! thou, indeed, hast brought the calves quickly ; we have not found [time] even to eat."

> Hearing [this] statement, laughing, Bihârî says, "I was anxious [on] your account ;
> [They] were found near in one place grazing ; now go home ; [you] came at dawn."[4]

Thus talking among themselves, taking the calves, all, laughing [and] playing, came [to] their homes.

---

## CHAPTER XVI.

**Balarâm slays the demon Dhenuk, who had assumed the form of an ass.**

S'RÎ S'UKADEV said:—Mahârâj ! when S'rî Krishṇa was eight years old, one day he said to Jasodâ, "Mother ! I will go to graze cows ; do thou persuade father,[5] that he may send me with the cow-

that the illusive cow-boys were co-sharers in the attributes of Krishṇa ; and that the latter re-absorbed into himself all the portions of his essence appearing in the illusions, and thus became again one. The word *ansu*, means "filament," and if this were the word intended the sense would be just the same ; for it would imply the filaments of his essence reaching out into the illusions.

[1] "In what reckoning" literally ; because Hindûs, in enumerating a list of virtuous persons, estimate their worth by watching the falling of chalk in water, as a kind of divination. See *Hitopadesa*, Introduction, verse 15.

[2] For *to* read *toṅ*.

[3] In the four previous editions, three by Lallû Lâl himself, and one by Pandit Yogadhyân Misra, this phrase is *tin se larke*.

[4] See note [14], p. 5. The Genitive here gives the meaning "[You who] are come [here] from dawn, go home."

[5] For *tu* read *tû*, and for *kaho* read *kah*. Lallû Lâl was not guilty of this ungrammatical jumble.

herds." On hearing this Jasodâ spoke with Nand Jî. He having settled a propitious moment, and called the cowherd-boys, on the eighth of the bright half of Kârtik, having caused Krishṇa to worship a cow-shed, humbly said to the cowherds, "Brothers! do you continue from to-day to take Râm Krishṇa also with you to graze cows; but keep close to him; do not leave him alone in the wood." Having spoken thus [and] given food, marking Krishṇa [and] Balarâm [on the forehead] with curds, he dismissed [them] with all [the others]. They, being delighted, along with the cowherd-boys taking cows, arrived in the wood. There, seeing the beauty of the wood, S'rî Krishṇa began to say to Baladev, "Dâ,û![1] this is an exceedingly agreeable [and] pleasant place; see, how the trees are bending [and] bending; and various kinds of beasts [and] birds are sporting." Saying thus, [they] went [and] ascended a lofty hillock, and began to wave about [their] scarves, [and] to shout out, saying, "Black, white,[2] grey, purple, brown, blue" (the colours of the cows). On hearing [this] all the cows, lowing [and] snorting, ran up. At that time there was such beauty as if, from all sides, variously coloured clouds might have been collected.

Then S'rî Krishṇa Chand, having driven the cows to graze, [and] eaten [his] food with [his] brother, under the shade of a *kadam*-tree, resting his head on the thigh of a companion, slept. After a time, when he awoke [he] said to Balarâm Jî, "Dâ,û! listen; let us play this game;—having arranged separate armies, let us fight." Having said this much, sharing the cows and cowherd boys, [they] took half each. Then, gathering wild fruits [and] flowers, and filling wallets [with them, they] began to play, with [their] mouths only, trumpets, pipes, horns, tambourines, drums, [and] kettle-drums, [and] to fight, and to shout, "Kill! kill!" They fought thus for some time; then each taking his own company apart, [they] began to pasture the cows.

In the midst of this, a companion said to Baladev Jî, "Mahârâj! at a shortish distance from here there is a palm-grove, in which there are fruits like nectar; there, [in] the form of an ass, a Râkshas keeps guard." On hearing this statement, Balarâm, along with the cowherd boys, entered that wood; and began, hitting away [with] bricks, stones, clods, and sticks, to knock down fruit. Hearing the noise, the ass named Dhenuk came braying; and he, on coming, turned round [and] kicked with both heels, on the chest of Baladev Jî; then he, raising him (the ass) up, dashed [him down]. Then he, having rolled about, got up, pawed the ground, pressed back [his] ears, [and] backing, began to strike out with both heels. He kept on fighting thus

[1] *Dâ,û* is a familiar abbreviation of the name *Baladev*; it is often applied to fathers and elder brothers.

[2] Eastwick follows Hollings in inserting "yellow," although it is not in his text; Lallû Lâl, and former editions, did, however, insert *pîrî* here.

for a long time ; at last Balarâm Jî, having seized both his hind legs [and] swung [him] round, flung him on to a high tree. He, on falling down, died, and along with him that tree also was broken down. By the falling of both [of them] there was an exceeding noise, and all the trees of the forest shook violently.

Having seen [this] from afar, Murârî says, "The trees have shaken ; there has been a loud noise."
Just then a friend of Haladhar came, "Come along, Krishṇa ! you are called hastily ;

an Asur is killed, that same is lying [dead]. On the hearing of this statement, S'rî Krishṇa also went [and] drew near to Balarâm. Then the companions of Dhenuk, as many as were Râkshasas, all advanced to the attack. Those S'rî Krishṇa Chand Jî quite easily killed [and] overthrew. Then, indeed, all the cowherd boys, being delighted, fearlessly gathered fruits, [and] to their own satisfaction filled wallets. And having brought the cows together, S'rî Krishṇa said to Baladev, "Mahârâj ! it is a long time since we came ; now please go home." On hearing this speech, both the brothers, taking the cows, along with the cow-boys, laughing [and] playing, in the evening returned home ; and the fruit which they had brought, [they] had distributed in all Brindâban. Having dismissed all, he himself slept. Again, on rising at early dawn, S'rî Krishṇa, having called the cowherd-boys, made breakfast, took the cows, [and] went to the wood ; and by keeping on grazing the cows, arrived at Kâlîdah.[1] There the cowherds caused the cows to drink water in the Jumnâ, and themselves also drank. As they rose up, [after] drinking the water, [they], together with the cows, through the poison, all rolled about. Then S'ri Krishṇa, having looked [at them] with a glance[2] of immortality, restored all to life.

---

## CHAPTER XVII.

Krishṇa conquers the poisonous snake Kâli—He compels him to remove his residence to Ramaṇaka Dwîpa.

SRÎ S'UKADEV Jî said :—Mahârâj ! having thus protected all, S'rî Krishṇa began to play at ball with the cow-boys. And where Kâlî was, for a distance of four *kos*, the water of the Jumnâ,

[1] *Kâlîdah* is a whirlpool on the Jumnâ, where the serpent Kâli is said to have resided. The serpent's name should be *Kâlîya* throughout.
[2] For *drishṭh* read *drishṭi*.

through his poison, was boiling. No beast [or] bird was able to go there. Whoever mistakenly went [there], scorched by the glow, fell into the whirlpool, consumed,[1] and on the bank no tree even was produced. One solitary eternal Kadam-tree was on the bank, and no more.[2] The King asked,—Mahârâj! how was that Kadam-tree saved? The Saint said,—At one time, holding nectar in [his] beak, Garuḍa came [and] sat on that tree; from his mouth one drop fell; on this account that tree was saved.

Having related this much [of] the story, S'rî S'ukadev Jî said to the King:—Mahârâj! S'rî Krishṇa Chand Jî resolved in his mind on the death of Kâlî. Playing on at ball [he] went [and] ascended the Kadam-tree. As from below a friend threw the ball, it fell[3] into the Jumnâ, [and] S'rî Krishṇa, also, jumped in along with it. Having heard, with [his] ear, the sound of his jumping, he began to vomit poison, and darting forth hisses like fire, to exclaim, "What sort of a one is this, who is still living in the whirlpool? Perhaps the undecaying tree, unable to endure my violeuce, has broken down; or some great beast [or] bird has come, in that still in the water there is a noise."

Having said thus, he was vomiting forth poison from all [his] one hundred and ten hoods, and S'rî Krishṇa was swimming around. Then the friends, weeping, and severally stretching forth [their] hands, were calling out; the cows, [with] mouths open, on all sides, were lowing, snorting, [and] running about. The cowherds quite apart were saying, "S'yâm! please come forth quickly; otherwise, having gone home without you, what answer shall we give?" These, then, here, being grieved, were thus speaking; [and] while this was going on, someone went to Brindâban [and] stated that "S'rî Krishṇa has jumped right into the whirlpool of Kâlî." Hearing this, Rohiṇî, Jasodâ, and Nand, along with the cowherdesses and cowherds, weeping [and] beating [their breasts] rose [and] ran; and one and all, falling and stumbling, came to the whirlpool of Kâlî. There not seeing S'rî Krishṇa, becoming alarmed, Nand's wife went straight forward to fall into the water. Then the cowherdesses, going just between, seized [her], and the cowherd boys, having stopped Nand Jî, were saying thus—

Having abandoned the great forest [and] come [into] this
wood, still Daityas greatly annoy [us].
Much good fortune has happened from Asuras; now how
will Hari issue from the whirlpool?

Hereupon, from behind, Baladev Jî also came there, and,

[1] For *partâ* read *pachtâ*, as in all previous editions.

[2] Notice this idiom; *lit.*, "one eternal Kadam was on the bank; that alone was."

[3] For *chalkyâ* read *chalâ,î*, and for *girâ* read *girî*. As *gẽnd* is feminine the verbs should agree with it, as Lallû Lál made them.

addressing all the inhabitants of Braj, said, "The imperishable Krishṇa will come [forth] presently; why are you dejected?

To-day I did not accompany him; Hari plunged into the whirlpool without me."

Having related thus much [of] the story, S'rî S'ukadev Jî said to King Parîkshit:—Mahârâj! on the one side Balarâm Jî was thus inspiring all with hope, and, on the other, as S'rî Krishṇa by swimming approached him, he (Kâlî) wrapped [himself] round his (Krishṇa's) whole body. Then S'rî Krishṇa became so bulky that, on releasing him, it was well.[1] Then as that one was repeatedly hissing and darting [his] hoods against him, this one kept on saving himself. At last, perceiving that the inhabitants of Braj were exceedingly grieved, S'rî Krishṇa suddenly sprang up [and] mounted on his (Kâlî's) head.

Assuming the weight of the three worlds, Murârî became ponderous;
He dances about on hood after hood, he beats time with his feet.

Then, indeed, through the weight, Kâlî began to die; and dashing [his] hoods again and again [on the ground],[2] he put forth his tongues; from them streams of blood flowed out. When the poison and the pride of strength was gone, then he perceived in his heart that "Âdi-Purush[3] has assumed incarnate form; otherwise, in whom is there so much power that he should escape from my poison?" Having realized this, he abandoned the hope of life, and remained benumbed.[4] Then the serpent's wife having come, joined [her] hands, [and] inclined [her] head, entreatingly said to S'rî Krishṇa Chand, "Mahârâj! your Honour has done well in that you have removed the pride of this tormentor and exceedingly conceited one; now his [good] fortune has awakened, in that [he] has obtained a sight of you. The very feet which Brahmâ, and all the other gods, meditate on, with prayer and self-mortification, are resplendent on the head of Kâlî."

Having said this much, she again spoke, "Mahârâj! have compassion on me, [and] please release this one; otherwise, slay me also, along with him; for death itself is excellent for a woman

[1] A confusion of persons has made this sentence puzzling It implies that Krishṇa became so bulky that, on (Kâlî's) releasing him, it turned out well (for Kâlî); in other words, it was well for Kâlî that he released him. The verb *ban ânâ* means "to succeed," "be fortunate," "turn out well."

[2] This describes a peculiarity in the attack of a snake. In striking at, and missing an object, the head knocks on the ground, and ejects a portion of the poison; on this being repeated several times a snake becomes temporarily less dangerous. Snake-catchers avail themselves of this peculiarity when encountering large poisonous snakes.

[3] *Âdi-Purush*, "the first male," or primary soul; a name generally applied to Vishṇu.

[4] For *sithal* read *śîtal*; but *sithal* is colloquial.

without a husband. And if you please to reflect, then of him even there is no fault; this is the nature of the species, that it should be fed on milk, [and] the poison should increase."

Having heard this statement from the serpent's wife, S'rî Krishṇa Chand descended from him (Kâlî); then Kâlî, reverentially, with joined hands, said, "Lord! please to forgive my fault; I ignorantly darted my hood upon your Honour; I am a low-caste snake; where [could] we [get] so much knowledge, that we should recognize you?" S'rî Krishṇa said, "Well! what was was; but now do not you remain here; go dwell with your family in Raunak Dîp." [1]

Hearing this, Kâlî, fearing [and] trembling, said, "Lord of Mercy! should I go there Garuḍa will eat me up; from fear of that very one I fled [and] came here." S'rî Krishṇa said, "Now do thou go there fearlessly; [2] from seeing the print of our feet on thy head, no one will say [anything] to you." Having spoken thus, S'rî Krishṇa Chand at once called for Garuḍa and expunged fear from the heart of Kâlî. Then Kâlî, having performed worship, according to precept, with incense, lamps, and consecrated food, [and] having placed before S'rî Krishṇa many presents, [with] joined hands, supplicating, bidding adieu, said,—

> "[For] four *gharîs* you danced [on] my forehead; this friendship bear in mind, O Lord!"

Having spoken thus [and] saluted, Kâlî, with [his] family, went to Raunak Dîp; and S'rî Krishṇa Chand came out of the water.

---

## CHAPTER XVIII.

Krishṇa frightens his companions by producing a conflagration around them—He tranquillizes them by drinking it up.

HAVING heard the tale so far, King Parîkshit asked S'rî S'ukadev:—"Mahârâj! Raunak Dîp was a nice place; why did Kâlî come from there? and for what purpose did he stay in the Jumnâ? Explain this to me, that the doubt may leave my mind." Srî S'ukadev said:—O King! in Raunak Dîp, Garuḍa, the vehicle of Hari, remains. He is exceedingly powerful; in consequence, the greatest serpents of that place acknowledging [themselves] de-

[1] *Raunak Dîp* is a corruption of *Ramaṇaka Dwîpa*, "the charming island," which is the name given in the Bhâgavata-Purâṇa, and also in the Sukha-Sâgara, or Hindî rendering of Bâbû Makkhan Lâl. It is the imaginary spot where Garuḍa, the enemy of the serpent race, is reposing from his labours. The word has nothing to do with the Arabic *raunaq*, as suggested by Prof. Eastwick.

[2] For *nirabhaya* read *nirbhaya*.

feated, were accustomed to give him constantly a snake. They come [and] place [it] on a tree; he comes and eats [it] up. One day Kâlî, the son of Kadrû, the Nâginî, conceited of his venom, went to eat up the food of Garuḍa. Hereupon Garuḍa came there, and there was a great fight between the two. At last, recognizing [his] defeat, Kâlî began to say within himself, "Now how shall I escape from this one's hand? and where shall I go?" Having said this much [he] reflected, thus, "I will go [and] stay in Brindâban, then I shall be saved; for this one is unable to go there." Having thus thought, Kâlî went just there. Then King Parîkshit asked S'rî S'ukadev, thus,—"Mahâraj! why was he unable to go there; tell that secret?" S'ukadev said,—O King! [at] a certain time, the Rishi Saubhari was seated [on] the banks of the Jumnâ [engaged] in self-mortification. Garuḍa having gone there, killed a fish [and] ate [it]. Then the Rishi angrily cursed him thus, "If thou shalt come again [to] this place, thou shalt not remain living." [For] this cause he is not able to go there; and since Kâlî went there, the name of that place has been the Whirlpool of Kâlî.

Having related this much of the tale, S'rî S'ukadev Jî said:—O King! when S'rî Krishṇa Chand came forth [from the water], Nand [and] Jasodâ, through delight, [gave] much alms [and] performed virtuous [acts]. Having seen the face of [their] son, happiness was given to [their] eyes; and life came into the souls of all the dwellers in Braj also.

While this was taking place, it became evening; then they began to say among themselves, "Now, all day being tired out, fatigued, hungry, [and] thirsty, where[1] shall we go home? let us pass the whole night just here. [When it is] become morning we will go to Brindâban." Saying this, all stayed [and] slept.

> When half the night had passed, a heavy gloomy storm
> occurred;
> A fire burst out all around; very furiously burnt trees, forests,
> [and] cattle.

As soon as the fire occurred all woke up, and agitatedly looking round, [and] stretching out [their] hands, they began to exclaim, "O Krishṇa! O Krishṇa! save [us] speedily from this fire, otherwise it, in a moment, will burn all up, [and] reduce [us] to ashes."[2] When the inhabitants of Braj along with Nand [and] Jasodâ had cried out thus, S'rî Krishṇa Chand Jî, on rising up, having, in a twinkling, drank up that fire, removed the anxiety from the hearts of all. As soon as it was morning all came to Brindâban, [and] in every house there were rejoicings [and] congratulatory songs.

[1] The interrogative here implies that going home is out of the question.
[2] Present tense for the Future, to mark the imminence of the act.

## CHAPTER XIX.

**Balarâm destroys the demon Pralamb, by blows of his fist.**

HAVING told the story thus far, S'rî S'ukadev Jî said :—Mahârâj ! Now I am about to explain the seasons ; the different sports which S'rî Krishṇa Chand played in them, attentively listen to. First, the warm season came. That, on coming, took happiness from all the world, and having heated the earth [and] atmosphere, made [them] like fire ; but, by the power of S'rî Krishṇa, in Brindâban there was only perpetual spring. Where on the trees of dense arbours climbing-plants flourish, various coloured blossoms were blooming, swarms on swarms of bees were humming on ; on the branches of the mango trees the kokilas were warbling ; peacocks were strutting in the coolest of shades ; the sweetest of perfume-laden airs were blowing ; and, on one side of the wood, the Jumnâ was displaying its beauty quite apart ; there Krishṇa [and] Balarâm, together with [their] companions, leaving the cows, were sporting on, in various surprising games, among themselves. Hereupon the Râkshas named Pralamba, wearing the form of a cowherd, sent by Kañs, came [among them]. On seeing him, S'rî Krishṇa Chand, with a sign, said to Baladev Jî,—

"[This is] not a friend of ours, Balabîr ! this [is] an Asura in a disguised body ;
Take means to slay him ; he should not be killed [in] the cowherd form ;
When he bears his own form, then do you that instant kill him."

Having pointed out this much [of] the matter to Baladev, S'rî Krishṇa Jî laughingly called Pralamb near [him, and] taking [his] hand said,—

"Your appearance [is] most excellent ; without guile [you are] an excellent friend of ours."

Having said thus, taking him with [him, and] dividing the cowherd-lads, took half [himself], and gave half to Balarâm Jî. Causing two boys to be seated, he began to ask and tell the names of fruits and flowers. In this [game], indicating [name after name], S'rî Krishṇa was defeated ; Baladev won ; then those on the side of S'rî Krishṇa [1] mounted the companions of Baladev on [their] shoulders [and] carried [them] off. Thereupon Pralamb took Balarâm Jî [and] hurried on beyond all [the others], and entering the wood, increased [the size of] his body. [At] that time, on that jet-black mountain-like [demon], Baladev Jî was as resplen-

[1] Notice the use of *-wâlâ* here. Although an affix usually, it is here employed as an independent word, otherwise the gender of *kî* would have changed.

dent as the moon on a dark cloud ; and the glitter of his earrings was flashing like lightning ; the perspiration was falling like rain. Having related this much of the story, S'rî S'ukadev Jî said to King Parîkshit :—Mahârâj ! as soon as he got [him] alone [and] was about to slay Balarâm Jî, at once the latter, by blows of the fist, slew [and] overthrew him.

---

## CHAPTER XX.

**Krishṇa provokes and extinguishes a second conflagration.**

S'RÎ S'UKADEV Jî said :—O King ! when Balarâm, having slain Pralamb, came forward, the dark blue cloud (Krishṇa) came, with the companions, [and] met him ; and the cowherd lads who were grazing cows in the wood, they also, hearing that an Asura had been slain, left the cows [and] went thither to see. During that time, on this side, the cows, grazing on, passing from the *ḍâbh* [and] *kâñs* [grasses], entered the *munj* wood. Having returned thence, both the brothers [when] looking here, then there is not even one cow [to be seen].

Scattered [are] the cows, scattered the cowherds ; forgetting [the path] they are wandering about the *munj* [and] palm forest ;
Mounted on trees, they are mutually shouting ; again and again [calling] names, they are waving waist-cloths.

In this [state of things] a friend came, [and with] joined hands, said to S'rî Krishṇa, "Mahârâj ! the cows have all entered the *munj* forest ; after them the cowherd lads dispersedly are searching, [and] wandering about." Upon hearing this statement, S'rî Krishṇa, having mounted on a Kadam-tree, played [his] flute at a high pitch ; the cowherd lads and cows, having thus heard, rending the *munj* forest, came [and] joined him, as the rivers of the Sâwan [and] Bhâdoñ [months], cleaving the high waves, go [and] mingle with the ocean. Meanwhile, what do they behold ? From all sides a raging conflagration is closing in [upon them]. Perceiving this, the cowherd lads and companions, exceedingly agitated, being afraid, cried out, "O Krishṇa ! O Krishṇa ! save [us] speedily from this fire ; or immediately, in a single instant, all [will] be burnt to death." Krishṇa said, "Do you all shut your eyes." When they had shut [their] eyes, S'rî Krishṇa Jî, in a twinkling, put out the fire, and performed another illusion, to wit, having taken all the cowherd lads with the cows into a fig-tree forest, he said, "Now open [your] eyes."

The cowherds, opening [their] eyes [and] looking about, say,
"Where is that fire gone, Murâri?
When did the fig-tree forest come back? This is a marvel,
Balabîr!"

Having spoken thus, taking the cows, collectively, with Krishṇa [and] Balarâm, [they] came [to] Brindâban; and all, going to their own houses, said, "To-day, in the forest, Balarâm Jî killed the Râkshas named Pralamb; and in the *munj* forest there was a conflagration, that also, by the power of Hari, was extinguished."

Having related this much [of] the story, S'rî S'ukadev Jî said:—O King! hearing this statement from the mouths of the cowherd lads, all the dwellers in Braj went indeed to see; but they obtained no clue to the proceedings of Krishṇa.

---

## CHAPTER XXI.

### Description of the Rainy Season.

S'RÎ S'UKADEV, the saint, said:—Mahârâj! having perceived the exceeding hardship of the hot season, King Rain, reflecting compassionately on the beasts, birds, and living creatures of the parched earth, having collected together an army [of] clouds from all sides, advanced to the contest. Then the clouds which were thundering were very drums sounding; and the variously coloured clouds which were gathered round, were heroes, warriors, and champions.[1] In the very midst of them the flash of the lightning was like the glitter of weapons; rows of cranes, [in] different places, were like white banners[2] being fluttered; frogs [and] peacocks, [in] the manner of bards, were celebrating praises; and a very great shower of drops was pouring, like a shower of arrows. Perceiving Rain coming with this pomp [and] pride, the Hot Season, abandoning the field, escaped with his life. Then the cloud-lover, raining, gave happiness to the earth. She who, after eight months of separation from a husband, was conjoined [with him], took full enjoyment from him. The breasts fell [and] became cool, and the fœtus remained; from that eighteen bearings of sons arose, they also, each taking presents of fruit [and] flowers, began to do homage to [their] father. Then the land of Brindâban became as beautiful as a lovely woman decorated with ornaments; and in all directions rivers, streams [and] lakes were full, [and] on them

[1] For *râwate* read *râwat*.
[2] For *ddhajâ* read *dhwajâ*; and in the next line, for *bûndoṅ kîṅ* read *bûndoṅ kî*.

swans [and] cranes [1] were giving surpassing beauty [to the scene]. The branches of very lofty trees were waving, on them cuckoos, rain-drop cuckoos, pigeons, parrots, were seated and continued [their] noisy chatter; and [in] various places, wearing crimson [and] safflower [dyed] dresses, the cowherdesses [and] cowherds, swinging about on swings, in very high strains were singing rain-songs. Again and again going near them, S'rî Krishṇa [and] Balarâm also, playing away at childish sports, were exhibiting additional happiness. In this delight the rainy season passed. Then S'rî Krishṇa began to say to the cowherd lads, "Brothers! now the pleasure-giving autumn season is come.

> Now I know [that] the happiness of all [is] great; I recognize the flavour, the odour,[2] [and] the beauty;
> The constellations at night [are] brilliant [in] the sky; lucid as[3] Brahma void of qualities.
> Those who [for] four months have tarried at home; [when] it became autumn, they abandoned dalliance;
> Each hastened to his occupation; the king advanced against the foreign country."

---

## CHAPTER XXII.

The virtues of Krishṇa's flute extolled.

S'RÎ S'UKADEV JÎ said:—O Mahârâj! having said this much, S'rî Krishṇa Chand again, taking the cowherd lads with [him], began to sport; and while Krishṇa is grazing cows in the wood, all the cowherdesses, seated within doors, are singing Hari's praises. One day S'rî Krishṇa played his flute in the wood; then, hearing the sound of the flute, all the young women of Braj arose precipitately [and] ran; and having met [in] one place, sat down on the road. Thereupon they began to say among themselves, "Our eyes will then be fully gratified when they obtain a sight of Krishṇa; just now, indeed, Kành, with the cows, in the wood, is singing [and] dancing about; at evening time he will come hither, then we shall get a look [at him]." Hearing this a cowherdess said,—

> "Listen, friend! he has played on the flute; behold the greatness of the bamboo tube!" [4]

[1] After *sâras* insert *saras*, "surpassing," as in all previous editions. It is difficult to guess what Prof. Eastwick was translating about here.

[2] For *sugangh* read *sugandh*.

[3] *mânahu* = *mânoṅ*, "let it be esteemed," "deemed," or "considered," and hence commonly used to express "as though," "as if it were."

[4] The bamboo is honoured by the condescension of the great player. Notice that *bajâ,î* is here governed by the Nominative, not the Agent.

"How is there in it so much virtue, that all day it continues applied [to] the mouth of S'rî Krishṇa, and, drinking the nectar of [his] lip, [and] raining delight, resounds like a cloud? What! [is] this more loved even than us, that, night [and] day, Bihârî continues holding [it]?

> This [thing] made in my presence, has become a rival [wife], mounted on [his] body.

When S'rî Krishṇa, having wiped it with [his] yellow robe, plays [on it], then gods, saints, Kinnaras, [and] Gandharvas, each bringing his wife along [with him], seated severally on cars, eagerly come to listen; and having heard, having become fascinated, remain motionless[1] as pictures. What corresponding mortification has this one inflicted [on itself], that all [things] are subservient to it?"

Hearing this statement a cowherdess replied, "First, then, this, having been produced in the tube of a bamboo, [constantly] remembered Hari; afterwards, [it] took upon [itself] heat, cold, [and] water; lastly, having become fragments [and] having burnt [itself, it] inhaled the smoke.

> What sort of mortification are they performing[2] like this? It (the flute) became perfect, [and] obtained such a reward as this."

Hearing this, a woman of Braj said, "Why did not the Lord of Braj make us flutes, that, night [and] day, we had remained with Hari?" Having related this much [of] the story, S'rî S'ukadev Jî began to say to King Parîkshit:—Mahârâj! until S'rî Krishṇa, having grazed the cows, came from the wood, the cowherdesses were constantly[3] celebrating the virtues of Hari.

---

## CHAPTER XXIII.

**Krishṇa steals the cowherdesses' clothes while they are bathing—He expounds the spiritual meaning of his action.**

S'RÎ S'UKADEV, the saint, said:—On the passing away of the autumn season, the winter season came, and excessive cold [and] frost began to occur. [At] that time the Braj girls began to say

[1] *jahâñ ke tahâñ* means "just in the same place," that is, without change of position, or motionless.

[2] *karte haiñ* is here impersonal; the third person plural, without an expressed nominative, is often thus used. The sense is, "What greater penance than this does anyone perform?"

[3] For *nitt* read *nit* or *nitya*.

amongst themselves,[1] "Listen, companion! by bathing in the [month of] Ag̓han, the sins of birth after birth are departing; and the desire of the heart is accomplished; thus we have heard from the mouth of ancient people." Hearing this statement, it occurred to all of them, thus, "We should bathe [in] Ag̓han; undoubtedly we would obtain S'rî Krishṇa [as] a boon."

Having thus reflected, as soon as [it was] dawn, getting up, donning dresses [and] ornaments, all the Braj girls together came to bathe [in] the Jumnâ. Having bathed [and] offered an oblation to the Sun, [and] come out of the water, [and] made an earthen [image of] Gaur,[2] [and] offered sandal-wood, unbroken rice, flowers, [and] fruit, [and] having placed before [it] incense, a lamp, [and] consecrated food, [and] having worshipped, [with] joined hands, inclined head, [and] having gratified Gaur, [they] said, "O Goddess! we have repeatedly asked from you this boon, that S'rî Krishṇa should become our lord." According to this rule, the cowherdesses are continually bathing, fasting all day, eating curds and boiled rice in the evening, [and] sleeping [at night] on the earth, so that they might speedily obtain the reward of their vow.

One day all the Braj girls, collectively, went to an unfrequented *ghâṭ* to bathe, and having gone there [and] taken off their clothes [and] placed [them] on the bank, becoming naked, [and] entered the water, they began to sing repeatedly the virtues of Hari, and to sport [in] the water. At that very time S'rî Krishṇa also, seated in the shade of a fig-tree, was grazing cows. [By] chance having heard the sound of their singing, he also silently approached, and began to look on, concealedly. At last, as he gazed, when something entered his mind, [he] stole all the clothes [and] went [and] ascended a Kadam-tree; and tying [them in] a bundle, placed [them] before [himself]. Hereupon, when the cowherdesses looked, [and saw] there were no clothes on the bank, then, in alarm, rising up on all sides, they began to look about, and to say among themselves, "Just now not even a bird came here; who has taken away the clothes, Mother?" In the meantime a cowherdess saw that, with a crown on [his] head, a staff in [his] hand, with a yellow sectarial mark, a necklace of wild flowers, wearing yellow robes, with a tied-up bundle of clothes, preserving silence, S'rî Krishṇa mounted on the Kadam-tree, is seated, concealed. On seeing him [she] cried, "Friend! behold him, the stealer of our hearts, the stealer of clothes, on the Kadam-tree, holding the bundle,

[1] For *maiñ* read *meñ*.

[2] *Gaur* or *Gaurî* is a name of Pârvatî, daughter of the Himâlayas, and bride of S'iva. Early legends state that Umâ was the name of the daughter of the Himâlayas, and that she performed *sati*, burning herself for devotion; in consequence of S'iva's frantic grief thereat, she was given back to him in the form of Pârvatî. In this form he complained of her dark hue, and she, by pious exercises, attained a golden tint, and was then called Gaurî. She is, under other forms, known as Durgâ and Kâlî.

[seated] resplendent." Hearing this speech, and all the young women having seen Krishṇa, ashamed, entered the water, joined [their] hands, bowed [their] heads, supplicated, [and] coaxingly said,—

"Compassionate to the humble! beloved remover of grief!
O Mohan! please give our clothes."
Hearing thus, Kanhâ,î says, "I will not give thus, appealing [to] Nand, [I swear];[1]
Come out one by one, then you'll receive your clothes."

The Braj girls angrily said, "This is a nice lesson you have learnt, in that you are saying to us 'Come out naked.' We will go at once [and] tell our fathers [and] friends, then they will come [and] seize you as a thief; and we will go [and] relate [this] to Nand [and] Jasodâ, then they also will properly impart to you instruction. We are ashamed of something; you have blotted out all recognition [on our part]."

On hearing this statement, angrily, S'rî Krishṇa Jî said, "Now you shall obtain the clothes when you fetch them [yourselves], not otherwise." Hearing this [and] fearing, the cowherdesses said, "Compassionate to the humble! you yourself hold us in remembrance, you are the protector of our husbands;[2] whom shall we bring? For you alone, having made vows, we are bathing in the month Mangśir." S'rî Krishṇa said, "If you, with sincerity, on my account are bathing [in] Ag,han, then abandon shame [and] evasion, [and] come [and] take your clothes." When S'rî Krishṇa Chand had said this, the cowherdesses, having reflected among themselves, began to say, "Come, friends! what Mohan says, that alone we should respect; because he knows all [the state][3] of our body [and] mind; what shame [is there] in this?" Having thus settled among themselves, obeying the direction of S'rî Krishṇa, concealing with the hands the breast [and] privities, all the young women issued from the water, with heads bowed down, [and] when they went [and] stood before [him] on the shore, S'rî Krishṇa laughingly said, "Now, with joined hands, come forward, then I will give the clothes." The cowherdesses said,—

"Why are you deceiving [us], Darling of Nand! we are plain simple Braj girls.
A trick has been played; consciousness [and] sense are gone; you have played this prank, O Hari!
Fortifying [our] hearts we have committed shame; now do you do something, O Ruler of Braj!"

Having said this, when the cowherdesses joined [their] hands,

[1] The equivalent of "I swear by Nand."
[2] Meaning "you take thought for our general welfare, you preserve the reputation of our husbands by making us good women."
[3] *bât* or *gati* is understood here.

S'rî Krishṇa Chand Jî, having given the clothes, came to them [and] said, "In your hearts, do not be anywise displeased at this affair; I have given you this lesson, because in the water is the abode of the god Varuṇa,[1] hence if anyone becomes naked [and] bathes in the water, all his virtue passes away. Perceiving the affection of your hearts, [and] being delighted, I have imparted this secret to you. Now go home; then, in the month of Kâtik, come [again, and] sport with me."

S'rî S'ukadev, the saint, said:—Mahârâj! Hearing this speech, [and] being pleased [and] contented, the cowherdesses then went to their own homes; and S'rî Krishṇa, having come to the fig-tree, taking with [him] cowherds, cows, cowherd lads, [and] companions, moved forward. Then looking again and again on the dense forest all around, he began to recount the greatness of trees, saying, "Behold! these having come into the world, how much they are taking on themselves [and] giving happiness to [other] people! It is fortunate that such-like charitable [people] come into the world." Speaking thus, [and] advancing onwards, they reached [a spot] near the bank of the Jumnâ.[2]

---

## CHAPTER XXIV.

Krishṇa sends to beg food from the Brâhmaṇs of Mathurâ—They refuse to give when asked—Their wives, on the contrary, run with food—Spiritual reward of the women—The husbands repent.

S'RÎ S'UKADEV Jî said:—When S'rî Krishṇa, having arrived near the Jumnâ, was standing, resting [on] a staff, under a tree, all the cowherd lads and companions came, with joined hands, [and] said, "Mahârâj! we are now very hungry; whatever food we brought has been eaten, still hunger has not departed." Krishṇa said, "Observe that smoke which is appearing; the Mathurâ folk, from fear of Kañs, secretly are performing sacrifice. Go to them, having mentioned my name, [and] saluted, with joined hands, stand still; from a distance ask food with such humility as a beggar, being dependent, asks."

Hearing this direction, the cowherds moved on, [and] went where the Mathurâ folk were seated performing sacrifice. On going there, they, having bowed down, with great humility

[1] *Varuṇa*, "the all-enveloper," that is, the welkin or celestial dome. He is the oldest and grandest of the Vedic deities; but becoming associated with ideas of water, through the rain-clouds, &c., his status gradually changed, until at length he became a kind of Neptune, whose abode was the ocean itself.

[2] Prof. Eastwick has omitted the whole of this sentence, for some reason.

having joined [their] hands, said, "Mahârâjas! S'rî Krishṇa Chand has sent to tell you respectfully through us, thus, 'I am very hungry, kindly send something to eat.'" Hearing this statement from the mouths of the cowherds, the Mathurâ folk angrily said, "You, forsooth, are great fools, that you are telling us this just now. Until the sacrifice is finished we shall give nothing to anyone. Listen; when we shall sacrifice and anything shall be left, we will share [it]." Again the cowherds, supplicatingly much besought, saying, "Mahârâjas! by causing to be fed the hungry who are come to a house, much virtue arises." But they paid no attention to their words; on the contrary, turning [their] faces from them, they began to say among themselves,—

"Great fools [are these] low cattle-feeders; they ask for rice in the midst of a sacrifice."

Then these [cowherds], becoming hopeless, came from thence regretfully to S'rî Krishṇa [and] said, "Mahârâj! [we] have asked alms [and] lost honour [and] dignity; still we have met with nothing to eat. Now what shall we do?" S'rî Krishṇa Jî said, "Now do you go to their wives and ask; they are very compassionate [and] virtuous souls. Mark their devotion! they, as soon as they see you, will courteously give food." Hearing this, these again went where those [women] were seated cooking. On going [they] said to them, "In the wood S'rî Krishṇa [while] grazing cows is become hungry, therefore he has sent us to you; should there be any food, then give [some]." On hearing that speech from the mouth of the cowherds, they all, being pleased, taking [and] filling severally golden dishes with food of six flavours,[1] rose up [and] hastened, and were hindered by no obstruction.[2]

The husband of one Mathurâ woman did not allow [her] to go; then she meditating [on Krishṇa] abandoned the body, and before all [the others] went [and] united [with him], as water goes [and] unites with water; and afterwards all, proceeding on, came where S'rî Krishṇa Chand, with the cowherd lads, under the shade of a tree, with [his] hand on the shoulder of a companion, in triple-bent beauty,[3] was standing with the flower of a lotus [in his] hand. On coming, having placed the dishes before [him], prostrating, [and] looking again and again [on] the face [of] Hari, they began to say among themselves, "Friend! this indeed is the son of Nand, whose name [we], having many times heard, were fixing our thoughts on; now, looking on the moon-face, render the eyes fruitful, and take the reward of life." Having conversed thus, with joined hands, they began to say, entreatingly, to S'rî Krishṇa, "Lord of compassion! without

[1] See note [1], p. 34.
[2] *Lit.*, "obstructed by anyone, they were not hindered." See note [5], p. 35, for a similar idiom.
[3] See note [1], p. 46.

your favour when does anyone have a sight of you? To-day our fortune [is] felicitous, that [we] have obtained the sight, and have lost the sin of birth upon birth.

> The foolish Brâhmaṇ, avaricious and conceited, [with] mind soiled [by] prosperity, pride, [and] covetousness;
> [He] esteems God as man; blinded by delusion, how should he recognize [anything]?
> For whose sake prayer, mortification, [and] sacrifice is performed, to him why not give food?

Mahârâj! that very wealth, relation, [and] modesty is felicitous which is useful to you; and that alone is mortification, prayer, [and] knowledge, in which your name enters." Hearing this statement, S'rî Krishṇa Chand, asking after their welfare, said,—

> "Do not pay reverence to me; I am Nand the chieftain's dark one.

Do they who cause themselves to be worshipped by Brâhmaṇs' wives gain any greatness in the world? You, thinking me hungry, compassionately, coming into the wood, bore [me in] remembrance. Now what hospitality can I show you here?

> Brindâban, our home, [is] far; in what way can we show respect for you?

Had we been there, we had brought [and] laid before [you] some flowers [and] fruit.[1] You, for our sake, accepting trouble, have come into the jungle; and here, from us, nothing has rewarded your service; there is nothing but regret for this." Thus courteously again he spoke, "[Since] you came, some time has elapsed; now please set out home; because your Brâhmaṇ [husbands] must be looking out for you; for without a wife a sacrifice is not fruitful." Hearing this speech from S'rî Krishṇa, they, with joined hands, said, "Mahârâj! we feeling affection for your lotus-feet, have entirely abandoned the illusion of family; for how can we go to the house of those whose words having disregarded, [we] arose [and] hastened [here]? If they should not allow us to enter the house, then where should we dwell? hence it were well that we should remain under your protection. And, O Lord! a woman, having formed the desire of seeing you, was coming with us; her husband stopped her; then that woman, distractedly, gave up her life." Upon hearing this statement, laughing, S'rî Krishṇa Chand showed her who, having abandoned [her] body, had come. [He] said, "Listen! he who acts kindly towards Hari is never destroyed. This one came [and] joined me before you."

Having related this much [of] the story, S'rî S'ukadev Jî said:—

[1] Notice this rendering of the Indefinite Imperfect tense.

Mahârâj! on seeing her, for a time, all remained astounded; afterwards sense returned; then they began to celebrate the praise [of] Hari. In the meantime S'rî Krishṇa Chand, having eaten, said to them, "Now depart to [your] place; your husbands will say nothing." When S'rî Krishṇa had thus counselled them, they took leave, prostrated [themselves, and] departed [to] their own homes. And their husbands, having reflected, remorsefully were saying, "We have heard a story in the Purâṇa, that, at some time, Nand [and] Jasodâ had performed great austerity for a son; thereupon Bhagwân, having come, granted this boon, 'I, in the family of Yadu, having become incarnate, will go to your house.' That very one, having taken birth, is come; who sent to ask food by means of the cowherd lads. What have we done, in that the First Male asked, and [we] gave not food?

For whose sake sacrifice and religion were established,
before him to-day we have not been.
The First Male we esteemed a man; we did not regard the
speech of the cowherds.
We [are] fools, sinners, conceited; we had no compassion,
[nor] understood the ways of Hari.

Curse to our minds! and to this sacrifice! that [we] did not recognize Bhagwân [and] do [him] service. Women even are better than we; who, without prayer, austerity, [or] sacrifice, bravely went [and] beheld S'rî Krishṇa, and [with] their own hands gave him food." Having repented in this strain, the Mathurâ folk, [standing] before their wives, with joined hands, said, "Felicitous [is] your fortune! in that you have seen Hari [and] returned; [it is] only your life [that] is fruitful."

---

## CHAPTER XXV.

**Krishṇa seduces the cowherds from the worship of Indra—He induces them to worship the mountain Gobardhan—He personates that mountain-god for deceptive purposes.**

S'RÎ S'UKADEV JÎ said:—Mahârâj! as S'rî Krishṇa Chand raised the mountain Gobardhan, and humbled the pride of Indra, now I am [about to] relate that very story; do you listen attentively. All the dwellers in Braj, at the anniversary on the fourteenth of the dark half of Kâtik, having bathed [and] washed, [and] filled a square place with saffron and sandal, [and] having placed various kinds of sweetmeats and confections, with incense [and] lamps, were performing the worship of Indra.[1] This custom, in their place, had come down traditionally. Once that very day arrived; then Nand Jî caused much preparation for a feast to be made; and in each house of the dwellers in Braj festal preparations were in progress. Thereupon S'rî Krishṇa coming asked [his] mother, thus, "Mother, dear! the confections and sweets which are preparing in each house, what [does it all mean]? Explain to me the secret of this, that the doubt of my mind may depart." Jasodâ said, "O son! now there is no leisure for me to tell you this, go [and] ask your father, he will explain [the matter]." Hearing this, having come to Nand [and] Upanand, S'rî Krishṇa said, "O father! to-day, for the worship of what god is there this ostentatious display; for whom confections [and] sweets are preparing? What sort of a bestower of faith, salvation, [and] boons is he? Tell me his name and qualities, that the doubt of my mind may depart."

Nand, the chieftain, said, "Hast thou not as yet understood this secret? that this is the worship of the master of the clouds, who is lord of the gods, by whose favour increase [and] prosperity is met with in the world, and grass, water, [and] food are produced; woods [and] groves blossom[2] [and] fruit; through him all living creatures,[3] beasts [and] birds, remain in happiness. This custom of Indra-worship has come down, [in] our family, from [our] early ancestors; no new [matter] has been invented just to-day." Hearing this from Nand Jî, S'rî Krishṇa Chand said, "O father! though our ancestors, wittingly [or] unwittingly, worshipped Indra or not,[4] still now why are you, knowingly, abandoning the path of religion [and] pursuing an impassable way? Nothing comes from heeding Indra, for he is not the bestower of faith [and] salvation; and who obtained increase [and] prosperity from him? You just say this, to whom did he grant a boon?

"Yes! one thing is this, that through performing austerity and sacrifice, the gods having made [him] their king, seated [him] on the Indra-throne; from this anyhow he cannot be a supreme deity. Listen! when by the Asuras he is frequently defeated, [he] flees, goes somewhere, [and] passes his time in concealment. Why should you respect such a coward? For what reason do you not recognize your religion? From what Indra has done, nothing can arise; what is written in destiny, that alone takes place; happiness, prosperity, wife, brethren, friends—these, even, all are met with, according to virtue and fate; and the sun which, for eight months, dries up the water, that same [sun], in four months, causes rain to fall; from this alone there is, on the earth, grass, water, [and] food. And Brahmâ, who created the four castes—Brâhmans, Kshattriyas, Vaiśyas, [and] S'ûdras,—attached to each of them his particular destiny; thus, the Brâhman should study

[1] In this sentence for *dhup* read *dhûp*, and for *pujâ* read *pûjâ*.
[2] For *phulte* read *phûlte*. [3] For *jîv, jannu*, read *jîvajantu*.
[4] Notice the construction here: *Indra kî pûjâ kî to kî*.

Vedic science; the Kshattriya should protect all; the Vaiśya [should practise] agriculture [and] trade; and the S'ûdra should keep in the service of these three.

"O father! we are Vaiśyas; the cows increased; from that Gokul arose; from that alone the name cowherd came about. This only is our destiny, that we should practise agriculture [and] trade, and keep in the service of cows [and] Brâhmans. It is a command of the Veda, that one should not abandon the custom of his family. Those people who abandon their own duty, and devote themselves to the duty[1] of another, they are as a wife of good family would be who should love a strange man. Therefore, now, please give up the worship of Indra, and worship woods [and] mountains; for we are dwellers in woods; our king is he in whose kingdom we remain happily; to abandon him [and] to worship another is not proper for us; therefore, now, take all the confections, sweets, [and] food, [and] go, and worship Gobardhan."

Upon hearing this statement, Nand [and] Upanand, arising, went where the greatest cowherds were seated at the [usual] meeting-place. They, upon going, related to them all the statements made by S'rî Krishṇa. They, as soon as [they] heard, said, "Krishṇa says the truth; do not you, deeming him a child, set aside his words. Well! do you, indeed, reflect; who is Indra? and why should we respect him? He who nourishes, his worship alone is proper.

What business have we with the lord of the gods; let us
worship the woods, streams, [and] mountain king."

Having said thus, then all the cowherds said,—

"Kânhar has given good counsel; let us abandon all the
gods;
The Gobardhan mountain [is] great; let us perform his
service."

On hearing this speech, Nand Jî, being pleased, caused an announcement [by beat of drum] to be made in the village, that "To-morrow all we dwellers in Braj will go [and] perform worship to Gobardhan; whatever confections and sweets are prepared at home for the worship of Indra, take each of you the whole [of it, and] as soon as it is dawn, go on to the Gobardhan [mountain]." Having heard this much, all the dwellers in Braj rose, at early dawn next day, [and] having bathed [and] meditated, having filled all the large baskets, trays, dishes, baskets, [and] cauldrons, [and] causing [them] to be placed on carts and buggîs, proceeded to Gobardhan. Then Nand [and] Upanand also, with [their] family, taking all [their] material, accompanied all [the others], and proceeded on, with the sound of musical instruments, [and] arrived all together [at] Gobardhan.

Having arrived there, having swept, cleaned, [and] sprinkled

[1] For *gharm* read *dharm*.

water all round the mountain, they arranged [and] placed [in order] confections [such as] Ghewar, Bâbar, Jalebî, Laḍḍû, Khurmâ, Imratî, Phenî, Perâ, Barfî, Khâjâ, Gûñjhâ, Maṭharî, Sîrâ, Pûrî, Kachaurî, Seb, Pâpaṛ, Pakauṛî, &c.,[1] and various kinds of food, [and] sauces, insomuch that the mountain was hidden [with them], and having decorated [it] above with garlands of flowers,[2] stretched out various coloured silk awnings.

The splendour of that time is indescribable.[3] The mountain was as beautiful as [if] someone may have clothed [it with] jewels [and] dresses, [and] adorned it from top to toe.[4] And Nand, having summoned the family-priest, accompanied by all the cowherd lads, offered *tilak*-mixture, unbroken rice, [and] flowers, [and] having performed [what is usual with] incense, lamps, [and] consecrated food, [and] having given betel, areca, [and] sacrificial presents, performed worship according to the precepts of the Veda. Then S'rî Krishṇa said, "Now do you meditate on the mountain-king with a pure mind, then he, having come, [and] revealed [himself], will eat [the offered food]."

On hearing this from S'rî Krishṇa, all the cowherdesses [and] cowherds, along with Nand [and] Jasodâ, joining the hands, closing the eyes, [and] fixing the thought, stood [still]. [At] that time, Nand's darling, on the one side, taking a second body, exceedingly gross [and] ponderous, with vast hands [and] feet, becoming lotus-eyed [and] moon-faced, wearing a crown, [and] a necklace of wild flowers, dressed in yellow robes, and jewel-studded ornaments, with gaping mouth, silently issued from the lower part of the mountain; and, on the other side, he himself, looking at his second form, shouting out, said to all, "Look! the mountain-king has manifested [and] revealed [himself], whose worship you, with fixed mind, performed." Having uttered this speech, S'rî Krishṇa Chand Jî prostrated himself to the mountain-king. Seen by them, all the cowherdesses [and] cowherds, bowing down, began to say among themselves, "When did Indra manifest himself in this way? We have uselessly kept on worshipping him; and who knows why our ancestors, neglecting so manifest a deity, paid attention to Indra? This is incomprehensible."

They were all talking thus when S'rî Krishṇa said, "Now what are you looking at? The food which you have brought, feed [him] with." On hearing this direction, the cowherdesses [and] cowherds, filling the six-flavoured food on to dishes [and] trays, raising [them] up, began to give; and Gobardhan the lord, stretching forward [his] hand, [and] taking again and again,

[1] Attempts to find equivalents for these confections are futile; besides, the student must ever recognize and speak of them by their native names.

[2] For *phuloñ* read *phûloñ*.

[3] This is a passive construction, from *baranâ*, "to relate"; *kisî se* is understood. Similarly also *samajhî nahîñ jâtî*, at end of next para.

[4] *tak* or *talak* is understood after *nakh*; *singârâ ho,e*, is the Contingent Perfect tense governed by the Agent *kisî ne*.

began to eat. At last as much preparation as the dwellers in Braj, together with Nand, had brought, was eaten up; then that form subsided into the mountain. In this way, performing wonderful sports, S'rî Krishṇa Chand, taking all with [him], and circumambulating the mountain, next day moving from Gobardhan, laughing [and] playing came [to] Brindâban. Then, in every house, rejoicings, festivities, [and] congratulations occurred; and the cowherd lads, [having painted] all the cows [and] calves various colours, [and] fastened on their necks amulets, little bells, [and] tinkling ornaments, separately continued their sports.

---

## CHAPTER XXVI.

Indra's anger—He attempts to destroy the cowherds—Krishṇa protects them by holding the mountain Gobardhan over them, on the tip of his finger.

HAVING related thus much of the story, S'rî S'ukadev, the saint, said :—

The worship of the Ruler of the Gods was abandoned, and the service of the mountain [was] performed;
Then, indeed, Indra, incensed in mind, summoned all the gods.

When all the gods had approached Indra, he began to ask them thus, "Do you inform me; yesterday, in Braj whose worship was [celebrated]." Meanwhile Nârad Jî arrived, and began to say to Indra, "Listen, Mahârâj! everybody reverences you; but one inhabitant of Braj does not; for Nand has had a son, and everyone does what he says.[1] He, having abolished the worship of you, yesterday caused the mountain to be worshipped by all." Upon hearing this statement, Indra angrily said, "The wealth of the inhabitants of Braj has increased, therefore they have become exceedingly proud :—

They have abandoned prayer, penance, sacrifice, [and] vows, to me; [and] have invited famine and poverty.
The human Krishṇa they revere as a god; his statements they think [to be] true.
That child [is] foolish [and] ignorant, a great talker, [and] has conceit;
Now I will remove his pride; I will do away with the cattle, [and] deprive him of prosperity."

Thus chattering irritatedly, the Ruler of the Gods sent for the

[1] *tisî kâ kahâ*, "said of that one," or "said by him." The Participle in such constructions has the force of a substantive.

Ruler of the Clouds. He, upon hearing, fearing [and] trembling, with joined hands, came [and] stood before [him]. Upon seeing him, Indra, with vehemence, said, "Do you at once go, taking with [you] all your host, and flood with rain the district of Braj, together with the Gobardhan mountain, so that nowhere may a trace of the mountain or the name of the Brajbâsîs remain."

Having received this order, the Ruler of the Clouds prostrated [himself, and] took leave of Indra, and, returning to his place, called for the greatest clouds [and] said, "Listen, the King's command is that you [are] at once to go [and] flood with rain the district of Braj." Hearing this direction, all the clouds, each taking his cloud-armies with him, accompanied [1] the Ruler of the Clouds. He, on arriving, surrounded the district of Braj, and thundering violently, with great drops began to rain down torrents of water,[2] and to indicate the mountain with his finger.

Having stated the story so far, S'rî S'ukadev Jî said to King Parîkshit :—Mahârâj ! when, in this way, on all sides loud-sounding clouds began to pour down an unbroken [sheet of] water, then all the cowherdesses and cowherds, together with Nand [and] Jasodâ, being afraid, drenched, [and] trembling violently, went to S'rî Krishṇa and cried out, "O Krishṇa ! how shall we escape from the water of this great cataclysm ?[3] Then, indeed, you abolished the worship of Indra, and caused the mountain to be adored ; now be good enough to summon him speedily, that [he] may come [and] protect [us]; otherwise, in a moment [we] shall be drowned, along with the town."[4] Hearing this statement, and seeing they were all afraid, S'rî Krishṇa Chand said, "Have no anxiety in your minds about anything ; the king of the mountain coming immediately will protect you." Having spoken thus, by [his] energy [he] heated Gobardhan [and] made [it] like fire; and raised [and] supported it on the little finger of the left hand. Then all the inhabitants of Braj came with their cattle [and] stood beneath it ; and looking severally at S'rî Krishṇa Chand, began to say among themselves in amazement,—

[1] [*ke*] *sâth ko lenâ* = "to accompany."

[2] *mûs'â*, "a club, pestle," *dhâr*, "a stream" ; *mûslâ-dhâr barasânâ*, "to rain down a stream of clubs."

[3] *Pralaya* means "dissolution," and it is of four kinds; the first is incidental; the second is elemental; the third is absolute ; and the fourth is constant. The last two are special and do not concern us here ; the incidental *pralaya* is a general dissolution of the world which takes place at the end of every day of Brahmâ. All moisture is then absorbed, and whirlpools of eddying flame consume created matter ; afterwards clouds appear and pour down torrents of rain, extinguishing the vast conflagration, and ultimately form a universal ocean on which the mighty Brahmâ reposes during his stupendous night. On his reawakening the work of creation recommences, until the completion of the period of Brahmâ's lifetime, when the *Mahâpralaya*, or elemental dissolution, takes place ; and the entire universe is resolved into ether, which is taken up by intellect, and merged into supreme spirit. The *Pralava* spoken of in the text is the cataclysmal torrent which extinguishes a blazing universe.

[4] Present tense used for the Future, to indicate the imminence of the act.

This is some incarnation of the Primeval Male ; Murârî is the god of even gods ;
How can Mohan [be] mortal, O brother ! he has raised a mountain on his little finger ! [1]

Having related the story so far, S'rî S'ukadev, the saint, began to say to King Parîkshit :—On the one hand, the Ruler of the Clouds, with his legions, was angrily pouring down torrents of water ; and, on the other, [the rain] falling on the mountain, hissing, became [like] a drop on a baking-plate. Hearing this intelligence, Indra also angrily himself advanced to the attack, and continuously, in that way, for seven days rained ; but in Braj, by the power of Hari, not even one drop fell. When all the water was expended, the clouds came [and], with hands joined, said, "O Lord ! as much water as [that] of a Mahâpralaya has all been [expended] ; now what shall we do ? " Hearing thus, Indra with his knowledge [and] thought reflected thus, " The Primeval Male has become incarnate ; otherwise, in whom had there been [2] so much power that, having supported a mountain, he could have protected Braj." Having thus reflected, Indra regretfully returned with the clouds to his own place, and the clouds having cleared off, there was light. Then all the inhabitants of Braj, becoming pleased, said to S'rî Krishṇa, " Mahârâj ! now please place down the mountain ; the cloud has departed." On hearing this remark, S'rî Krishṇa Chand set down the mountain just as it was before.

---

## CHAPTER XXVII.

**The astonishment of the cowherds at this last miracle.**

S'RÎ S'UKADEV said :—When Hari placed down the mountain from [his] hand, then all the greatest cowherds, perceiving this surprising incident, were saying thus, " He by whose power the district of Braj has been this day saved from this Mahâpralaya, how shall we call him the son of Nand ? Verily, at some time, Nand [and] Jasodâ performed [some] great austerity, [and] for this [reason] Bhagwân has come [and] taken birth in their house." And the cowherd lads, coming severally [and] successively embracing S'rî Krishṇa, began to ask, " Brother ! how did you support the weight of this heavy mountain on this soft lotus-like hand ? " And Nand [and] Jasodâ tenderly embraced [their] son, [and] rubbing [his]

[1] *kyoñ* here merely indicates an exclamation.
[2] *thî* here is Indefinite Imperfect, instead of the more usual *hotî*, "had there [be]en."

hand, [and] making [his] fingers crack, began to say, "Seven days the mountain rested on the hand; the hand must be giving pain." And the cowherdesses coming to Jasodâ, celebrating all the recent recreation of Krishṇa, began to say,—

This boy who is your son, may he live long, the guardian of Braj!
[He] has destroyed Dânavas, Daityas,[1] [and] Asuras; wherever has he not delivered the people of Braj?
As Garg, the prince of Rishis, said, each particular thing is coming to pass.

---

## CHAPTER XXVIII.

**Indra acknowledges Krishṇa's superiority.**

S'RÎ S'UKADEV, the saint, said:—Mahârâj! as soon as it was dawn, all the cows, and cowherd lads together, each taking his food, [and] Krishṇa [and] Balarâm playing the flute and singing the sweetest songs, as they proceeded to the forest to graze the cows, Râjâ Indra, accompanied by all the gods, placing in front Kâmadhenu,[2] mounted on the elephant Airâwat,[3] proceeding onwards from Suralok,[4] having arrived in Brindâban, stood stopping the road to the forest. When S'rî Krishṇa Chand appeared to him at a distance, [he] descended from the elephant, [and] came barefoot, with cloth thrown around [his] neck, trembling violently, [and] fell at the feet of S'rî Krishṇa; and with deep remorse [and] many tears, began to say, "O Lord of Braj! have compassion on me![5]—

I[6] have been exceedingly conceited and proud; and gave [my] mind to Passion and Darkness;[7]

[1] For *Daiyata* read *Daitya*, as in the edition of Pandit Yogadhyân Misra, and as required by the metre.

[2] *Kâmadhenu* is the cow of plenty, belonging to the Rishi Vasishṭha. It granted every desire of its possessor.

[3] *Airâwat* is the elephant which bears Indra; it was produced at the churning of the ocean, in mythological story; and is regarded as the prototype of the elephant race.

[4] *Suralok* is the name of the special heaven of Indra.

[5] For *muj* read *mujh*.

[6] The sign of the Agent is generally omitted in poetry; it is found in only six of the verses of this book.

[7] There are three Guṇas, or qualities, termed *sattwa*, *rajas*, and *tamas*, varying proportions of which enter into every constitution and differentiate all objects in creation. They are usually rendered by the words Goodness, Passion, and Darkness; and in proportion as one or other of these qualities disturbs the equipoise, that quality acquires conspicuousness in the disposition. This idea is chiefly favoured by the Sânkhya philosophy.

Intoxicated with wealth, [I] have deemed riches [to be] enjoyment ; [I] knew nothing of your secret ;
You [are] the Supreme Ruler, the lord of all ; who other [than you is] lord of the universe ?
Brahmâ, Rudra, and other givers of boons, have obtained prosperity given by you.
You [are] Father of the world ! dwelling in the Nigama ;[1]
Kamalâ[2] continually serving [you] has become [your] servant ;
[For] the good of creatures, taking incarnate form, then and then[3] [you] are removing the burden of the earth.
Put afar all my error ; I am very presumptuous [and] foolish."

When, having become thus submissive, Indra had praised [him], S'rî Krishṇa Chand, becoming compassionate, said, "Now, indeed, thou hast come with Kâmadhenu ; therefore thy fault is pardoned; but please be not proud again, because from being proud knowledge departs, and evil ideas increase, [and] from this disgrace results."

Upon hearing this statement from the mouth of S'rî Krishṇa, Indra arose [and] worshipped [him] according to Vedic rites ; and calling[4] him Govind, [and] accepting the *charaṇâmrit*,[5] [he] performed perambulation.[6] Then Gandharvas, playing away [on] various kinds of instruments, began to sing the glories of S'rî Krishṇa ; and gods seated in their cars [began] to rain down flowers from the sky. Then the time[7] was such as though[8] again S'rî Krishṇa had taken birth. When Indra had completed the worship, he stood before [Krishṇa] with hands joined ; then S'rî Krishṇa gave [this] order, "Now do you go, along with Kâmadhenu, to your own city." On receiving the order, Kâmadhenu and Indra, taking leave, prostrated [themselves, and] departed to Indra's abode ; and S'rî Krishṇa, having grazed the cows, [when] it became evening, taking all the cowherd lads, came to Brindâban. They each departing to his own home said, "To-day we, by the power of Hari, have seen Indra in the forest."

Having related this much [of] the story, S'rî S'ukadev Jî said

[1] *Nigama* implies a text or precept, especially a text of the Vedas ; also the Vedas themselves.

[2] *Kamalâ*, "desirous" ; a name of the goddess Lakshmî.

[3] This is the correlative of *jab jab*, omitted by poetic license. The sense is "*whenever* you take incarnate form you remove the burden of the earth."

[4] *nâm dharnâ* is to give a name to anyone, to dub, to style.

[5] The *charaṇâmrit* is the water in which the feet of a holy person have been washed. It is deemed highly meritorious to drink this water.

[6] *parikramâ* is an act of adoration, by passing three times round the sacred object keeping the right side turned towards it.

[7] *samâ* for *samaya*, means not only "time" but the general condition and circumstances of things at any particular moment.

[8] *mâno* or *mânoṅ*, from *mânnâ*, "to deem," "esteem," means "be it deemed," or "as one should suppose," and is the equivalent of "as though."

to King Parîkshit:—Râjâ! this story of Govind which I have related, from hearing it, all the four objects—merit, wealth, desire, emancipation—are attained.[1]

---

## CHAPTER XXIX.

Nand is seized by the servants of Varuṇa while bathing in the Jumnâ; but is released by Krishṇa—Varuṇa acknowledges his superiority Krishṇa creates a heaven similar to that of Vishṇu, to gratify the curiosity of the people of Braj.

S'RÎ S'UKADEV Jî said:—Mahârâj! once Nand Jî, abstaining, performed the vow of the eleventh day;[2] the day was passed in bathing, meditation, adoration, prayer, [and] worship; and the night was spent in wakefulness. When six *gnaṛis*[3] of the night remained, and the twelfth day had begun, then rising [and] purifying the body, perceiving [that] it was dawn, [he] took [his] loin-cloth, bathing-towel [and] ewer, [and] went [to] the Jumnâ to bathe. Several cowherds also followed after him. Having gone to the bank, saluted, [and] taken off [his] clothes, as Nand Jî entered the water, the servants of Varuṇa,[4] who were guarding the water, that no one should bathe at night, they, going to Varuṇa said, "Mahârâj! someone is now bathing in the Jumnâ; what is [your] order to us [with respect to this]?" Varuṇa said, "Seize [and] bring him at once." On receiving the order, the servants again came where Nand Jî, having bathed, was standing in the water praying. On arriving, [the servants] throwing a noose unawares, conveyed Nand Jî to Varuṇa. Then the cowherds who had gone with Nand Jî, came and said to S'rî Krishṇa, "Mahârâj! the attendants of Varuṇa, having seized Nand Râe Jî from the bank of the Jumnâ, have conveyed him to Varuṇa's place." On hearing this statement, S'rî Govind arose hastily with anger, and in a moment reached the vicinity of Varuṇa. On seeing him, he (Varuṇa) stood up, and with joined hands meekly said,—

"My birth is to-day propitious; [I] have obtained, O Lord
of the Yadus, a sight of you;

[1] The four objects of existence are held to be the acquisition of religious and virtuous merit; the gain of fame, wealth, and such-like objects; the gratification of desires generally; and the obtaining of final emancipation from transmigrations into continued existences. It is probably impossible to find four English words conveying all that is implied by these technical terms.

[2] The eleventh day of the half-month is especially sacred to Vishṇu; fasting on that day is held to be very efficacious.

[3] About 3 o'clock in the morning.

[4] Varuṇa is the deity specially connected with water.

Remove afar all my sins; [your] father Nand was for this reason entrapped;
You are celebrated as the Father of All; we know not your father.

Seeing [him] bathing at night, [my] attendants unwittingly seized [and] brought [him]; well! [by] this stratagem I have obtained a sight of you. Now have mercy, bring not my fault into mind." Thus, with extreme humility, having brought many presents, [and] placed them before Nand and S'rî Krishṇa, when Varuṇa, with joined hands [and] bowed head, stood before [him], S'rî Krishṇa, accepting the presents, going thence along with [his] father, came [to] Brindâban. On seeing him, all the inhabitants of Braj came [and] met [him]. Then the chiefs of the cowherds asked Nand Râ,e, "Where did the servants of Varuṇa convey you?" Nand Jî said, "Listen! just as they, having seized [me], bore me hence to Varuṇa, immediately after S'rî Krishṇa arrived. On seeing him, he, rising from the throne, [and] falling at his feet, began beseechingly to say, 'Lord! please forgive my fault; this fault was [committed] by me[1] unwittingly; bring it not in mind.'" On hearing this statement from the mouth of Nand Jî, the cowherds began to say among themselves, "Brother! we, of a truth, knew this, when S'rî Krishṇa Chand by supporting Gobardhan protected Braj, that, in the house of Nand, the chieftain, the Primeval Male had come [and] taken incarnate form."

Having conversed thus among themselves, all the cowherds then, with joined hands, said to S'rî Krishṇa, "Mahârâj! you have misled[2] us for a long time, but now all your secret is discovered. You are the Creator of the world, the Remover of pain. O Lord of the three worlds![3] having mercy, kindly now show us Vaikuṇṭh."[4] Having heard this remark, S'rî Krishṇa Jî in a moment created a Vaikuṇṭh [and] showed [it] to them in Braj itself. On seeing it the inhabitants of Braj attained knowledge. Then, joining hands [and] inclining heads, [they] said, "O Lord! your greatness is infinite; we can say nothing; but by your favour we this day know that you are Nârâyaṇ, and have taken birth [and] come into the world to remove the burden of the earth."

S'rî S'ukadev Jî said:—Mahârâj! when the inhabitants of Braj had said thus much, S'rî Krishṇa Chand fascinated all [of them, and] removing the Vaikuṇṭh which he had created, [he] diffused his illusion [over them]; then all the cowherds regarded [it] as a dream, and Nand Jî also, being subject to the illusion, esteemed S'rî Krishṇa as merely his own son.

[1] For *muj* read *mujh*. [2] For *bharamâyâ* read *bhramâyâ*.

[3] Heaven, Earth, and Hell.

[4] *Vaikuṇṭha* is the paradise or heaven of Vishṇu. It is described as situated in the northern ocean, and also on the eastern peak of Mount Meru. Originally there were seven Lokas or spheres of delight; Vaikuṇṭha or Go-loka is an eighth, and probably sectarial addition. It is the paradise appointed as the special reward of those who have their daughters married at nine years old.

## CHAPTER XXX.

Krishṇa dances with the cowherdesses—He takes them to the lake Manasarowar.

HAVING related so much of the tale, S'rî S'ukadev Jî said :—

As Hari danced [and] sported with the cowherdesses,
That same I will relate [in] five chapters ; as [my] understanding enlightens [me].

When S'rî Krishṇa Jî had taken away the clothes, he promised the cowherdesses thus, "In the month of Kârttik we will dance with you." From that time the cowherdesses, longing for the dance, were dejected in mind ; and constantly on rising were propitiating the month Kârttik alone. It happened, [while] they were [thus] propitiating, the pleasure-giving autumn season arrived.

From the time when the month of Kârttik began, [there was] an end of heat, cold, [and] rain ;
Lakes were full of pure water, lotus blossoms were flourishing ;
The white lotus [and] partridge, the lover [and] mistress, looking [at] the moon [at] night are delighted ;
The ruddy-goose and the blue lotus droop, who ever regard the sun as a friend.

Saying thus, S'rî S'ukadev, the saint, again said:—Lord of the Earth ! one day S'rî Krishṇa Chand, on the night of the full moon in Kârttika, starting from home, went out. [He] saw, then, in the clear sky, the stars sprinkled, and the moonlight diffused over the ten quarters [of space] ; a cool scented, gently moving air was blowing, and [on] one side the beauty of the dense forest gave enhanced beauty [to the scene]. On perceiving such circumstances it came into his mind that he had promised the cowherdesses that, in the autumn season, he would dance with them, therefore it was desirable to fulfil [that promise]. Thinking this, going into the forest, S'rî Krishṇa played the flute. Having heard the sound of the flute, all the Braj girls, being pained by desire through separation [from Krishṇa], were greatly agitated ; at last, abandoning the illusion of the family, breaking through modest reserve, abandoning household duties, in confusion, adorning themselves at random, they rose [and] hurried [forth]. One cowherdess who as she rose to go from near her husband, he went in the way [and] stopped her, and brought her [to] the house again. [He] did not allow [her] to go. Then, indeed, she, meditating on Hari, abandoned the body, [and] before all [the others] went [and] met [him]. Perceiving the affection of her heart, S'rî Krishṇa Chand immediately gave [her] final emancipation.

Having heard the tale so far, King Parîkshit asked S'rî S'ukadev Jî thus :—Lord of Compassion ! the cowherdess did not esteem S'rî Krishṇa Jî knowing [him to be] God ; but regarded him as a sensual object of desire ; how was she emancipated ? Explain that to me, that the doubt of my mind may depart. S'rî S'ukadev, the saint, said:—Incarnation of Justice ! they who celebrate the virtues of the greatness of S'rî Krishṇa Chand even unwittingly, they too undoubtedly obtain the emancipation of faith. Just as [if] anyone should drink *amrit* unknowingly, he also becoming deathless will live ; and should he drink knowingly, to him also the excellence will be [imparted]. All know this that the quality and fruit of anything cannot remain unmanifested ;[1] just so is the force of the worship of Hari. Should anyone with any purpose worship, he will be emancipated. It is said,—

> Prayer, the rosary, body-marks, forehead-marks, all [are] entirely without use ;[2]
> [With] an imperfect mind [anyone] antics purposelessly ; [with] a true [mind he] gratifies Râm.

And hearken ! I am now declaring with what, [and] what many, [and with] what different dispositions S'rî Krishṇa [was] revered, [and] salvation obtained ; thus, Nand, Jasodâ, and others, knew [him] as a son ; the cowherdesses understood [him] as a friend ;[3] Kañs worshipped [him] by fear; the cowherd lads called on [him] as a friend ; the Pâṇḍavas knew [him] as a benefactor ; Sisupâl honoured [him] as an enemy ; the Yadubañsîs made [him] as themselves ; and Yogîs, Yatîs, [and] Munis meditate on [him] as God ; but, at last, everyone of them obtained emancipation. If one cowherdess, by meditating on the Lord, crossed [the ocean of existence], what wonder is it ?

Hearing this, King Parîkshit said to the saint S'rî S'ukadev :—Lord of Compassion ! the doubt of my mind is gone ; now kindly tell [me] the rest of the story. S'rî S'ukadev Jî said :—Mahârâj ! when all the cowherdesses, each in her own party hurrying met S'rî Krishṇa Chand, the light of the world, the ocean of beauty, which was[4] as rivers of the four [rainy] months violently go meet the

[1] This idiom requires consideration : *hu,e* means "been," and hence "occurred," or "taken place" ; *bin hu,e* therefore means "without having taken place" or "without manifesting itself." The import of the phrase being that a quality and its result cannot exist without its purpose being effected. For *padârath* read *padârth*.

[2] For *na,e kau* read *na ekau*, as Lallû Lâl printed in his last edition, and as Paṇdit Yogadhyán Miśra has it. The "marks" are lines and figures made on the body and forehead to indicate particular forms of devotion.

[3] The word *yâr* has, in India, a disreputable sense, when applied to a woman.

[4] "which was" is here the equivalent of *ki*.

ocean, the beauty of the decoration of Bihârî Lâl [1] at that time is indescribable. Decked [in] all ornaments, wearing the guise [of] a juggler, so fascinating, beautiful, [and] charming he was that the Braj maidens, on seeing Hari's beauty, were amazed. Then Mohan, having asked their health and prosperity, said roughly, "Tell [me]; [at] night time—the time of ghosts [and] goblins—having passed the fear-inspiring road, wearing clothes and ornaments [thrown on] at random, exceedingly agitated; having abandoned the illusion of the family, how did you come in this vast forest? It is not proper for women to act so boldly; a woman is told that, 'However a husband may be a coward, vicious, stupid, deceitful, ugly, leprous, blind of one eye, stone-blind, maimed,[2] lame, [or] poor, still it is proper for her to serve him. In this is her prosperity, and reputation in the world.' It is the duty of a well-born and faithful [woman] not to quit her husband for an instant, and the woman who leaving her own husband goes to another man, [in] birth [after] birth obtains a dwelling in hell."[3] Having spoken thus, [he] again said, "Listen! you having come have seen the dense forest, the pure moonlight, [and] the beauty of the banks of the Jumnâ; now go home [and] attentively serve [your] husbands. In this for you there is every kind [of] good." On hearing this declaration from the mouth of S'rî Krishṇa, all the cowherdesses at once became senseless [and] fell in a boundless ocean of thought. Afterwards,—

> [They] looked down [and] heaved sighs;[4] [they] were scratching the ground with the nails of their feet;
> Thus from the eyes escaped a stream of tears, as though [they were] a broken necklace of pearls.

At length, exceedingly agitated by grief, [and] crying violently, [they] began to say, "O Krishṇa! you are a great deceiver; at first, playing the flute, [you] stole away, unawares, our knowledge, thought, mind, [and] wealth; now, having become compassionless, deceptively uttering harsh speeches, you will to take [our] lives." Having spoken thus, again [they] said,—

> "Folk, family, house, [and] husband are abandoned, abandoned is [care for] the reproaches of society.
> We are protectorless; [there is] no one [to help us]; assign [us] an asylum, O King of Braj!

And people who remain at your feet do not desire corporal form, wealth, modesty, [or] greatness; of them, indeed, you alone are, [in] birth [after] birth, the husband, O Deity in the form of life!

[1] Bihârî Lâl is a name of Krishṇa. Prof. Eastwick did not notice the Genitive sign after *Lâl*, which makes his translation impossible. Capt. Hollings is right here.

[2] For *lulâ* read *lûlâ*. [3] For *nark* read *narak*. [4] For *la,t* read *la,īñ*.

Where are we to go [and] make a home? [our] souls are
enwrapped [in] love of you!"

On hearing this much, S'rî Krishṇa Chand having smiled, called all the cowherdesses near [and] said, "If you are imbued [with] this affection, then dance a dance with me." Hearing this speech [and] abandoning grief, the cowherdesses, with delight, gathered around, and Hari's face regarding attentively, began to render [their] eyes fruitful.

As the dark-blue one[1] stood [in] the midst [of] the assembly,
the beauty [of] the sporting women [was] such,
As though golden creepers had grown from beneath a blue
mountain.

Afterwards S'rî Krishṇa Jî commanded his Illusion thus, "We will dance; do thou construct a good place for that, and remain here; whoever desires any thing, that same bring [and] give." Mahârâj! he, on hearing [this], went [to] the bank of the Jumnâ, [and] formed a golden circular-shaped large terrace, [and] having studded [it with] pearls [and] diamonds, [and] having planted all around it stems of sprouting plantain, [and] having fastened on them wreaths and garlands of various flowers, [came and] told S'rî Krishṇa Chand. He, upon hearing [that], being pleased, taking all the young women of Braj with him, went to the bank of the Jumnâ. [They] go there [and] look; then the splendour of the dancing circle was yielding four times more brilliance than the moon's orb; all around it the sand was spread out like moonlight; the sweetest of cool scented airs was blowing; and [on] one side, the verdure of the dense forest was deriving increased beauty from the brilliant night.

On viewing this scene, all the cowherdesses becoming delighted, [and] going to the bank of a lake called Mânasarowar, [which] was near that place,[2] [and] putting on pleasing [and] elegant dresses [and] ornaments, adorning [themselves] from head [to] foot, they came with excellent instruments—lutes, timbrels, and so forth—[and] composing melodies; and, becoming intoxicated [with] love [and] passion, abandoning reflection [and] modesty, [they] joined with S'rî Krishṇa, [and] began to play, to sing, [and] to dance. Then S'rî Govind, in the centre of the circle of cowherdesses, appeared as beautiful as the moon in the starry firmament.

Having related the tale so far, S'rî S'ukadev Jî said:— Listen, Mahârâj! when the cowherdesses, having abandoned knowledge and discrimination, in the dance, mentally regarded Hari as their natural husband, and thought him subject to them,[3] then S'rî Krishṇa Chand reflected in [his] mind thus,—

[1] For *jušyâm* read *ju šyâm*.

[2] Notice the construction of this sentence. It is a method of introducing a parenthetical phrase in Hindî.

[3] That is, under their influence.

"Now, having become fascinated, they think [me in] their power; [I] come into [their] mind as a natural husband;
Modesty having quitted [their] persons they are become ignorant; [they] cling to [and] embrace [me with] lover-like affection;
Knowledge [and] meditation [they] have altogether forgotten; I shall leave them [and] go; they have increased their pride.

Let me see what they [will] do without me, afterwards in the forest, and how they will be." Having reflected thus, S'rî Krishṇa Chand, taking S'rî Râdhikâ with [him], became invisible.[1]

---

## CHAPTER XXXI.

**Krishṇa roams through the forest alone with Râdhikâ—He suddenly deserts her.**

S'RÎ S'UKADEV, the saint, said:—Mahârâj! On suddenly not perceiving S'rî Krishṇa Chand, it became dark before the eyes of the cowherdesses; and, becoming exceedingly pained, [they] were as agitated as a snake, having lost [his] jewel, is alarmed.[2] Hereupon a cowherdess began to say,—

"Tell [me], friend! where has Mohan, having deserted us, gone?
[His] arm was placed [on] my neck, he was fondling [me].

Just now he was dancing [and] sporting in close union with us. In only this much [of time] where has [he] gone? Did not even anyone among you see him going?" Hearing this, all the cowherdesses becoming exceedingly dejected through the separation, heaving sighs, said,—

"Where shall [we] go? how shall [we] act? on whom shall [we] call?
Where is he? does nobody know anything? how is Murârî to be met with?"

Having said this, [and] becoming intoxicated [with] love [of] Hari, all the cowherdesses began to search about all around, repeatedly singing [his] praises, [and] crying bitterly, began to exclaim,—

[1] For *antaradhyân* read *antardhyân*.

[2] It is believed in India that certain snakes bear a jewel in their heads, the loss of which is a great grief to them.

"Why have you left us, O lord of Braj! we have given up everything to you?"

When [they] found [him] not there, they went forward, [and] said among themselves, "Friend! here, forsooth, we see no one; from whom shall we ask, 'Whither has Hari gone?'" Hearing thus, a cowherdess said, "Listen, darling! it has occurred to me that as many animals, birds, and trees as are [here] in this forest, are all sages [and] saints; these have assumed incarnate form [and] come to see the sports of Krishṇa. Do you ask from these; they are standing looking on; they will point out whither Hari may have gone."[1] On hearing this direction, all the cowherdesses, disconsolate by [reason of] separation [from Krishṇa], began to ask from one [by] one, whether inanimate or animate,—

"O *baṛ*, *pîpal*, *pâkaṛ*, *bîr*![2] your lofty form was obtained by meritorious acts;
You, indeed, have been beneficent to others, [and] have assumed on earth the shape of trees;
[You] have endured the pains of heat, cold, [and] rain; [you] have remained standing for the advantage of others;
O bark, blossoms, root, fruit, branches! with these [you] are doing good to others;
The darling of Nand having taken the heart [and] possessions of all, has [he] gone hitherwards? kindly tell [us].
O *kadamb*, *amb*, [and] *kachnâri*![3] have you seen Murâri going anywhere?
O *aśoka*, *champâ*, *karbîr*![3] have you seen Balabîr passing by?
O *tulsî*[4] greatly beloved of Hari! from [his] body [he] nowhere keeps [you] separate;
O blossoming one! has Hari come [and] met you to-day? Who [will] point out to *us* [where he is]?
O dear *jâtî*, *juhî*, *mâlatî*![5] has the youthful Kanhâ,î gone forth this way?"
The women of Braj, crying out, said to the deer, "Have you seen the Banwârî[6] going in this direction?"

Having related this much, S'rî S'ukadev Jî said:—Mahârâj! in this way the cowherdesses, continually inquiring of beasts, birds, trees, and climbing plants, becoming replete with Krishṇa, began to represent the slaughter of Pûtanâ, and all the other childish sports [which] S'rî Krishṇa himself had performed, and to search about. At length while searching on, [and] having gone some distance, they see, then, the mark of S'rî Krishṇa Chand's feet,

[1] For *gay* read *gaye*.
[2] Names of various kinds of fig-trees.
[3] Names of trees.
[4] The *tulsî* is deemed sacred, and employed in religious ceremonies.
[5] Different kinds of jasmine.
[6] *Banwârî*, equivalent to *Banmâlî*, "the garland-wearer," an epithet of Krishṇa.

with lotus, barley-mark, standard, and elephant-goad,[1] glittering on the sand. On seeing [this], the Braj women, having prostrated [themselves] before the dust which gods, men, and saints are searching for, placing [it] on the head,[2] [and] with a fixed hope of meeting with Hari, [they] advanced thence. Then [they] saw that quite close to the marks of those feet were imprinted the feet of a woman also. Seeing them, with astonishment, [they] advanced further, [and] beheld, [in] one place, on a bed of soft leaves, a beautiful jewel-studded mirror lying down. They began to ask that. When, filled [with the pain of] separation, that also spoke not, then they began to ask among themselves, [thus], "Say, friend! why was this taken?" Then one who knew [the affairs][3] of the hearts of lover and beloved, gave answer, thus, "Friend! when the lover was seated to plait [his] sweetheart's hair, and the beautiful form had disappeared from sight; then the beloved one, taking the mirror in hand, showed [it] to the lover;[4] then the reflection of S'rî's face came before [her]." Hearing this statement, the cowherdesses were not at all angry; on the contrary, they began to say, "She worshipped[5] S'iva and Pârvatî excellently, and performed great austerity, who sports fearlessly in private with the Lord of Life."[6] Mahârâj! all the cowherdesses, then, on the one side, intoxicated with the passion of separation, were idly chattering on [and] merely hunting about; on the other, S'rî Râdhikâ Jî, feeling excessive delight with Hari, [and] thinking [her] lover in her power, fancying herself greater than all, conceit coming into [her] mind, said, "O beloved one! now I can go no further,[7] place [me on your] shoulder, [and] convey [me in that way]." On hearing this expression, the annihilator of pride, the knower of secrets, S'rî Krishṇa Chand, having smiled [and] seated [himself], said, "Please come [and] get on my shoulder." When she, having stretched forth [her] hand, was about to ascend, S'rî Krishṇa vanished. As her hands were outstretched, so with extended hands she remained standing; just as, by pride, lightning may have been separated from the cloud, or the moonlight, angry with the moon, may have remained behind; and the brilliance from her fair form, escaping [and] spreading on the earth, gave forth such beauty as though she were standing on a ground of beautiful gold. A stream of tears was flowing from her eyes; and she could not drive away even those bees near her face who, attracted by the sweet savour, were coming again and again and settling

[1] These are marks of divine beauty on the feet of Krishṇa.

[2] To place on the head is to show reverence to anything by placing it above oneself.

[3] After *man kî* the word *bât* is understood.

[4] "showed it" here means presented it so that the reflection of the lover could be seen in it.

[5] For *pujâ* read *pûjâ*.

[6] *Prâṇapati* implies both the Supreme Being, and also a husband.

[7] See note [3], p. 68; *Hindî Manual*, p. 169. For *muj* read *mujh*.

[on it]; and heaving deep sighs, through separation [from the loved one], was so standing alone in the forest that, hearing the sound of her crying, all beasts, birds, trees, [and] climbing plants were crying [also]. And she was thus saying,—

"Alas, Lord! chief of benefactors! where, O capricious Bihârî! are you gone?
I [am] the slave of the asylum of thy feet; O ocean of compassion! hold me in remembrance."

Hereupon[1] all the cowherdesses also, [in] searching on, came up to her; and embracing her again and again, all respectively meeting [with her] felt the same pleasure as anyone would feel [who], having lost great treasure, should find, in the way, half the wealth. At length, all the cowherdesses also, perceiving her [to be] greatly distressed, taking her with them, entered the great forest; and, as far as moonlight was seen the cowherdesses searched for S'rî Krishṇa Chand in the forest. When in the darkness of the dense forest no path was found, then they all returned thence, [and] taking courage, with the hope of meeting [the lost one], they came and sat on the bank of the Jumnâ where S'rî Krishṇa Chand had given [them] exceeding pleasure.

---

## CHAPTER XXXII.

Krishṇa abandons all the cowherdesses, in order to test the strength of their affection.

S'RÎ S'UKADEV JÎ said:—Mahârâj! all the cowherdesses having seated themselves on the banks of the Jumnâ, being intoxicated with the passion of love, began to celebrate the actions and virtues of Hari, thus, "O beloved one! since you came into Braj the fresh and fresh pleasures have here come [and] diffused [themselves]. Lakshmî, reposing confidence[2] in your feet, has come [and] made a fixed abode [here]. We cowherdesses are your slaves; in compassion speedily take us in remembrance; since we saw your beautiful, dark-complexioned, handsome form,[3] we have become your slaves without purchase; your eye-arrows have struck our hearts; beloved one! why is not that [in] your

[1] Here the untranslatable *ki* most idiomatically marks a sudden transition of thought or circumstances.
[2] The text should read *Lakshmî ne kar tumhâre charaṇ kî âs,* as in the previous editions. The *kar* of *âs kar* was thrown out of position by Lallû Lâl merely to secure the rhyme of *âs* and *bâs*. Lakshmî is the goddess of prosperity.
[3] For *murati* read *mûrtti*.

account?[1] Our souls are passing away; now have compassion; abandon harshness, [and] speedily show [thyself]. If your sole [wish] was to destroy, why were we saved from the poison-bearing [serpent], from fire, and from the inundation? then why were [we] not allowed to die? You are not alone Jasodâ's son; you, indeed, Brahmâ, Rudra, Indra, and all the other gods, humbly have brought for the protection of the world.

"O Lord of Life! it is a great surprise to us, that if you will kill your very own, then whom will you protect? Beloved one! you being the searcher of hearts, why not remove our grief [and] fulfil the hope of [our] hearts? Art thou heroic only against weak women! O loved one! when your gentle smiling love-full glances, and the bend of [your] eyebrows, the coquetry of [your] eyes, the undulation of [your] neck, and the brilliance of [your] discourse, come into our minds, then what manifold pain do we not experience! and when you were going into the forest to graze the cattle, then, thinking of your soft feet, the stones and thorns of the forest were paining our hearts. [You,] gone at dawn, were returning at evening,[2] yet to us the four watches were appearing like four ages. When, having seated [ourselves] opposite we were looking [at your] beautiful body, then we were thinking in our minds that Brahmâ is a great fool in that [he] made an eyelid to place an obstacle in our fixed gazing."

Having related the tale thus far, S'rî S'ukadev Jî said:—Mahârâj! in this way all the cowherdesses, through [the pain] of separation, celebrating again and again, in various ways, the actions and virtues of S'rî Krishṇa Chand, were tired out; still Bihârî did not come. Then, indeed, having become greatly dejected, [still] with the hope of meeting [him], having abandoned the hope of life, becoming senseless from exceeding faint-heartedness, falling down, [they] so cried [and] exclaimed that, by hearing [them], animate [and] inanimate creatures also were heavily afflicted.

---

## CHAPTER XXXIII.

Krishṇa returns to the cowherdesses, and tells them why he left them.

S'RÎ S'UKADEV JÎ said:—Mahârâj! when S'rî Krishṇa Chand, the searcher of hearts, knew that "Now the cowherdesses[3] will no [longer] be saved alive without me,"—

[1] Notice that the verb is singular, *nahīñ hai*, and is so in all editions. Neither Hollings nor Eastwick have remarked this, and have both mistranslated in consequence. Prof. Eastwick has had to invent a verb, *lekhnâ*, "to be accounted," in order to give some sense to the passage.

[2] For *sâñj* read *sâñjh*.

[3] For *gopiyoñ muj* read *gopiyâñ muih*.

Then, in their very midst, the son of Nand appeared,
As a juggler disappears, by closing the sight, and appears again.
When Hari was seen come, all arose conscious,
As [when] the vital airs alight on a corpse the senseless members revive.
[While he] was unseen the minds of all were agitated,
As though a heart-agitating[1] snake, having bitten all, had departed.
The lover, knowing [their] pain to be sincere, came [and] arrived;
Having revived all, [he] sprinkled the creepers [with] nectar.
As lotuses are dejected at night, just so [were] the Braj women;
Having seen the beauty of the sun's orb, [their] large eyes expanded.

Having related the tale so far, S'rî S'ukadev said:—Mahârâj! on seeing S'ri Krishṇa Chand, the root of joy, all the cowherdesses at once issuing from the ocean of loneliness, [and] going near him, were as pleased as anyone, having been immersed in a bottomless ocean, having found the bottom, becomes delighted; and [they] stood around [him] on all sides. Then S'rî Krishṇa, taking them with [him], came where formerly [they] had danced [and] sported. On going there, one cowherdess removed her upper garment [and] spread it for Krishṇa to sit upon. As he sat upon it, several cowherdesses angrily said, "Mahârâj! you are a great deceiver! you know [how] to steal away the hearts [and] wealth [of] others, but do not recognize any obligation to anyone." Having spoken thus, they began to say among themselves,—

"[He] forsakes goodness; [he] accepts badness; deceit is pleasing [to him];
See, friend! having reflected [on this], how [shall we] stay with him?"

Having heard this, one among them said, "Friend! do you remain aside; [from] our speeches [we] derive no benefit; see, I [will] cause Krishṇa himself to tell [us]." Having said thus, she, smiling, asked S'rî Krishṇa, "Mahârâj! one, without good being done, acknowledges good; a second, makes return for a good action; a third, in return for good, does evil; a fourth, does not bear in mind even the good which anyone has done. Among these four, who is good, and who bad? Explain this [matter] to us." S'rî Krishṇa Chand said, "Do you all listen attentively; the good and the bad I [will] explain [and] tell [you]. The

[1] *manmatha* means amorous passion or desire, or heart-disturbing affection; it is also a name of Kâmadeva, the Indian Cupid, and therefore we have here a play on words.

best, indeed, is he who does [good] without having [good] done; as a father loves a son. And from doing [good] on [good] being done there is no virtue; that is as a cow gives milk on account of the milking fodder. He who esteems good to be evil [you] should regard [as] an enemy. The worst of all [is] the ungrateful who obliterates what has been done."

On hearing this statement, when the cowherdesses looking among themselves at each other's countenances, began to laugh, S'rî Krishṇa Chand was alarmed [and] said, "Listen; I am not in the reckoning of these four, as you think [and] laugh about; on the contrary, my method is this, that whoever desires anything from me, the desire of his heart I satisfy. Perhaps you may say, 'If this is your course, then why did you go [and] leave us in this way?' The reason is this, I tested[1] your love. Do not think this wrong; believe what I say to be quite true." Having spoken thus [he] afterwards said,—

"Now I have tried you; you remembered [and] meditated on me;
You have increased [your] affection for me alone, like a poor person [who] has acquired wealth;
Thus you came [for] my service, [you] abandoned regard for the world [and] the Vedas;
As a Vairâgî abandons [his] home, and giving his heart, entertains love for Hari.
How shall I confer greatness on you? I cannot recompense you;[2]
Should I live a hundred of Brahmâ's years, still I should not be free from the debt [I owe] you."

---

## CHAPTER XXXIV.

**Krishṇa dances, with the cowherdesses, his special dance—The reason for the dance explained.**

SRÎ S'UKADEV, the saint, said:—O King! when S'rî Krishṇa Chand in this way had uttered this agreeable speech all the cowherdesses, giving up anger, being pleased, arose, [and] joining with Hari, experiencing a variety of pleasures, being immersed [in] joy, began to sport. Then,—

[1] For *parikshâ* read *parîkshâ*.
[2] In this idiom *ham pai* is the equivalent of *ham se*. In standard Hindî the phrase would be *ham sẹ palṭâ dij â nạ jâ ẹ*. See note [7], p. 82.

Krishṇa used the Yoga-illusion, [and his] body became many parts;
To all the pleasure [they] were wishing [he] gave, sport [and] the highest affection.

As many cowherdesses as were [there,] just so many bodies S'rî Krishṇa Chand assumed; [and] taking all [of them] on the terrace of that dancing ring, again began to dance [and] sport.

Two [and] two the cowherdesses joined hands, between each two [was] Hari the companion;
Each thinks that he is at her side, and does not recognize another [of the illusions];
Finger is placed in [his] fingers; they whirl round delighted, taking Hari with [them],
Cowherdess [and] Nand's son, alternately, [like] a dense cloud [and] lightning all round;
The dark Krishṇa, the fair Braj women; like a gold and sapphire necklace.

Mahârâj! in this way standing, the cowherdesses and Krishṇa began to tune various kinds of musical instruments, to run over the airs of many very difficult melodies, to play [instruments, and] to sing; and selecting tunes [and] extemporizing in shrill, sharp, solemn [tones, those] raised a half-tone, a tone, [and] a third; [and] dancing so as to represent speech. And in the joy they became so absorbed, that no recollection remained to them of even body or mind. Here the breasts of some were uncovered; there the diadems of others had slipped; on the one side, the pearl necklaces being severally broken were falling; on the other side, the wild-flower wreaths. The drops of perspiration on [their] foreheads were glittering like strings of pearls; and the ringlets on the most fair faces of the cowherdesses were dishevelled as if young snakes, from lust of nectar, having flown up, had attached [themselves] to the moon. At times a cowherdess joining with S'rî Krishṇa's flute, was singing in treble pitch; sometimes one was tuning her notes quite alone. And when anyone, having stopped the flute, was bringing forth from [her] throat its note entire, exactly as it was, then Hari remained as forgetful [of all else] as a child seeing his face in a mirror is forgetful.

In this way, singing [and] dancing on, practising various kinds of coquetry [and] ogling, they were giving [and] receiving enjoyment, and mutually pleased, laughing merrily, embracing repeatedly, [they] were making offerings of clothes [and] ornaments. Then Brahmâ, Rudra, Indra, and all the other gods, and Gandharvas, each with his wife, seated in cars, looking on at the pleasure of the dancing-circle, with delight were raining down flowers. And the wives gazing on that pleasure, enviously were saying in their hearts, that "Had we been born in Braj, then we also had danced [and] sported with Hari." And there was such harmony of the Râgs and Râginîs,[1] that, by hearing it, wind [and] water also no longer flowed; and the moon, together with the starry firmament, being astonished, rained down nectar with its rays. Meanwhile night advanced; then six months had passed away, and no one was aware of it. From that time the name of that night has been The Night of Brahmâ.

Having related the tale so far, S'rî S'ukadev Jî said :—Lord of the Earth! while engaged in the sport of dancing, a fancy entered the mind of S'rî Krishṇa Chand; then taking the cowherdesses [he] went to the bank of the Jumnâ, entered the water [and] sported in the stream, [and] having relieved fatigue, [and] come out, [and] satisfied the desire of all, [he] said, "Now four *gharîs* of the night remain, do you all go home." Hearing this direction [and] becoming dejected, the cowherdesses said, "Lord! how can we leave your lotus-feet [and] go home? Our greedy mind, indeed, does not at all agree [to what you have] said." S'rî Krishṇa said, "Listen; as Jogîs[2] meditate on me you also should meditate; wherever you may be I will be near you." On hearing this remark, having become satisfied, all took leave [and] each went to her own home; and no one among their families knew this secret, that they had not been there.

Having heard thus much of the story, King Parîkshit asked S'rî S'ukadev Jî, the saint, thus, "Compassionate to the humble! explain to me this, If S'rî Krishṇa Chand, indeed, took incarnate form [and] came [into the world] in order to slay Asuras [and] remove the burden of the earth, and to give happiness to good [and] pious [people, and] to promote the course of virtue, why did he dance [and] sport with the wives of others? This, indeed, is the act of a libertine, who[3] enjoys the wife of another." S'ukadev Jî said,—

> Listen, King! you do not understand this mystery, [and] regard God as human;
> By the remembrance of whom sin departs, effulgent cleansing fires are [his] body;
> As anything falling into a fire, that same, having become fire, burns.

[1] *Râgs* and *Râginîs* are different modes of constructing melodies according to the Indian principles of music. There are six Râgs, or principal modes, and each of these has five dependent methods, or Râginîs. Sometimes the total number is reckoned as thirty-two. These different forms of melody have nothing in common with European principles of composition; but depend upon the arrangement of sounds in a way best calculated to awaken special sentiments; thus the melodies of the various Râgs are allotted to different periods of the day.

[2] Notice *jan* as the sign of the plural; and remark that the form *kîjiyo* is used because a sense of futurity is intended. The meditation is to take place in the subsequent course of the women's lives.

[3] For *joṅ* read *jo*.

What are not the powerful doing? They, indeed, by acting, interfere with destiny; as S'iva Jî took poison, and having swallowed [it] adorned his throat, and made a necklace of a black snake.[1] Who knows their course of action? They, indeed, do nothing for themselves; [but] they who hold their worship in remembrance [and] ask any boon, they give to them just such [a boon as they ask].

Of them, then, this is the method, that they appear united to all; but, having reflected, you will perceive [that] they show [themselves] as separate from all, as the leaf of the lotus in water [is from the water]. I have already informed you of the birth of the cowherdesses, that the goddesses and the texts of the Veda, to see [and] touch Hari, came [and] took birth in Braj. And in this way S'rî Râdhikâ also, having obtained the boon from Brahmâ, for the purpose of serving S'rî Krishṇa Chand, came [and] took birth, and remained in the service of the Lord.

Having said this much, S'rî S'ukadev Jî said:—Mahârâj! it is said thus, "Revere the actions of Hari, but do not give [your] mind to the doing of them." If anyone celebrates the fame of the Lord of Cowherdesses, [he] attains, fearless [and] unmoved, the highest dignity; and the fruit which results from bathing at sixty-eight places of pilgrimage, just such result is met with by singing the praises of S'rî Krishṇa.

---

## CHAPTER XXXV.

**Krishṇa gives salvation to Sudarśan—He slays S'ankhachûṛ, and gives his jewel to Balarâm.**

S'RÎ S'UKADEV, the saint, resumed:—O King! I am [about to] relate the episode how S'rî Krishṇa Jî caused Vidyâdhar to cross [the ocean of existence] and slew S'ankhachûṛ;[2] do you listen attentively. One day, Nand Jî, having called for all the cowherds, said to them, "Brothers! when the birth of Krishṇa took place, I made this promise to the family goddess Ambikâ,[3] that when Krishṇa should be twelve years old, on that day I would go out, with the city [folk], and with the sound of musical instru-

[1] These statements refer to the legend that, at the mythical churning of the ocean for the production of the water of life, S'iva swallowed the poison previously generated, which turned his throat blue. The blueness of S'iva's neck is held to enhance his beauty. The snake, also, which S'iva wears as a terrifying symbol, becomes an adornment by reposing on his person.

[2] *Vidyâdhar*, means "the bearer of spells," and is reckoned one of a class of genii. *S'ankhachûṛ* means "one whose top-knot is in the form of a shell."

[3] *Ambikâ* is a name of Pârvatî, the wife of S'iva; it is also the name of one of the female domestic deities of the Jaina sect.

ments perform [her] worship. That day, by her favour, we have seen to-day; now we should go forth, and perform worship."

On hearing this speech from the mouth of Nand Jî, all the cowherds rose [and] ran, and each of them hastily fetched from his house the materials for worship. Then, indeed, Nand Râ,e also caused the apparatus for worship, and milk, curds, [and] butter to be placed on carts and *bahangîs*,[1] accompanied by [his] family, and went on [until] he arrived at the place [sacred to] Ambikâ. Having gone there [and] bathed in the waters of the Saraswatî, Nand Jî called the Purohit, [and] taking all with [him, he] entered the temple of the goddess, [and] worshipped according to the Scriptures. And the things which had been brought to be offered were placed before [her, and] having perambulated [ceremoniously, and] joined hands, [he] said with humility, "Mother! by thy favour Kânh has become twelve years old."

Having spoken thus, [and] prostrated [himself, he] came out of the temple, [and] fed a thousand Brâhmans. Hereupon, as it had become late, Nand Jî, with all the inhabitants of Braj, having performed their vows of pilgrimage, remained on the spot. At night they were sleeping, when a dragon came [and] seized the foot of Nand Râ,e, and began to swallow [it]. Then on seeing that, with fear [and] agitation, he began to exclaim, "O Krishṇa! speedily remember me, otherwise this [creature] will devour me."[2] On hearing his voice all the Braj-dwellers, both men and women,[3] started from sleep, [and] having gone near Nand Jî, [and] procured light, they saw a dragon was lying there, holding his foot. Meanwhile S'rî Krishṇa Chand Jî having arrived, as soon as he, before them all, had placed his foot on the back [of the dragon], it at once changed its form, [and] becoming a handsome man, making obeisance, stood before [Krishṇa] with joined hands. Then S'rî Krishṇa asked him, "Who art thou? and for what sin didst thou become a dragon? tell [me] that." He, hanging his head, meekly said, "Searcher of Hearts! you know all my origin, that I am the magician named Sudarśan. I was dwelling in Surapur, and, through pride, esteemed nobody anything in comparison with my beauty and excellence.

"One day, seated in a car, I went out for a turn; then, where the Rishi Angiras[4] was seated performing penance, I went back-

[1] Bamboo poles laid over the shoulder, with goods attached to each end, for easy carriage.

[2] Here the Present tense stands for the Future, to show the imminence of the act. Notice, also. the form *nigle* (not *nigal*). This participial form increases the emphasis and rapidity of the idea. See *Hindî Manual*, p. 190. In all previous editions *he Krishṇa!* is repeated; and as Eastwick himself translates.

[3] It would have been more in conformity with practice to have written *kyâ strî kyâ purush*; but in all previous editions it is as in text.

[4] *Angiras* is a famous Rishi, or saint, and the author of many hymns of the Rig-veda. He is one of the seven great Rishis, and had a miraculous origin from Brahmâ's mouth. He is reputed the father of several gods, the sacred hymns, and even of mankind.

wards and forwards over him a hundred times. Once, as he saw the shadow of the car, he looked up [and] angrily cursed me, thus, 'O conceited one! become a dragon-snake!'

"This much issued from his mouth, when I, becoming a dragon, fell down. Then the Rishi said, 'Thy deliverance will be through S'rî Krishṇa Chand'; on this account I came and seized the foot of Nand Râe Jî, that you, by coming, might deliver me; therefore, Lord of Compassion! you, having come, have kindly delivered me." Having said which, Vidyâdhar performed perambulation, [and] receiving the command from Hari, [he] prostrated himself, took leave, mounted [his] car [and] went to Surlok. And, having witnessed this incident, all the Braj-dwellers were amazed. At length, as soon as it dawned, having presented themselves before the goddess, they went all together to Brindâban.

Having related the story so far, S'rî S'ukadev, the saint, said:—Lord of the Earth! once Haladhar and Gobind, with the cowherdesses, were singing away delightedly, one moonlit night, in the wood, when, in the midst of it, a Yaksha named S'ankhachûṛ, an attendant on Kuver,[1] on whose head [was] a jewel, and [who was] exceedingly strong, [suddenly] came [upon them]. [He] saw, then, on one side, all the cowherdesses engaged in sport, and,[2] on the other side, Krishṇa and Baladev, enraptured, singing away as if intoxicated. When some [idea] occurred to him, [he] surrounded the Braj girls, [and driving them] before [him] was carrying them off. Then the Braj women, being frightened, cried out, "Save [us], Krishṇa! Balarâm!"

On hearing this issuing from the mouth of the cowherdesses, both the brothers, tearing up a tree [and] bearing it in their hands, ran forward, as a raging elephant rushes on a lion; and, having come there, said to the cowherdesses, "Fear no one, we are arrived." On perceiving them like Death, the Yaksha was terrified, abandoned the cowherdesses, [and] fled for his life. Then Nandalâl left Baladev Jî with the cowherdesses; and went himself, seized [the Yaksha] by the back-hair [and] threw [him] down; finally, striking transversely, [he] cut off his head, took the jewel, came [back and] gave it to Balarâm Jî.

---

## CHAPTER XXXVI.

The cowherdesses sing the praises of Krishṇa.

S'RÎ S'UKADEV, the saint, said:—O King! while Hari is grazing cows in the forest, the Braj girls come to Nand's wife, sit down, [and] sing the glory of the Lord. The sports which S'rî

[1] The god of riches.

[2] For *sau* read *aur*.

Krishṇa played in the woods, the cowherdesses related, seated at home.

" Listen, Friend! [when] he is playing the flute, animals and birds find gratification.
Devî, with her lord, reclined [in] the car; [their] ears, hearing the sound, were fascinated.
Bracelet [and] ring fall from the hand, [the sound] has stolen away recollection from the perturbed mind and body.[1]
Just then," says a woman of Braj, " the clouds, quite overcome, left off thundering;
Hari is singing with unwavering delight; eyebrows, hand, and cheek, [he] sways [to the metre];
The doe, with her loved one, hearing the flute, is brought to a standstill; the Jumnâ is deflected, the cows are there collected together.
The fascinated clouds form a shade, like an umbrella held over Krishṇa;
Now Hari hastens to the thick arbour, [and] again all come [with him] to the fig-tree;[2]
The roaming cows are following; [when] collected he took them to water.
It is become evening; now Hari returns; the cow lows, the flute sounded."

Having related the story thus far, S'rî S'ukadev Jî said to King Parîkshit:—Mahârâj! in this way, the cowherdesses all day are continually celebrating the virtues of Hari, and at eventide, going forth [and] meeting with S'rî Krishṇa Chand, the source of joy, they joyfully conduct [him home]; and then the lady Jasodâ also, having affectionately wiped the dust-covered face of [her] son, embraces [him, and] feels delight.

---

## CHAPTER XXXVII.

**Krishṇa slays an Asura in the form of a bull, and himself bathes at all the places of pilgrimage, miraculously brought together, to expiate the crime—Kañs endeavours to entrap him at an entertainment—The mission of Akrûr for that purpose.**

S'RÎ S'UKADEV JÎ said:—Mahârâj! one day S'rî Krishṇa [and] Balarâm, having grazed the cows, were returning home at night from the wood; hereupon an Asura came, as a very large bull, and mingled with the cows.

[1] *parahiñ* is 3rd pers. plural Aorist of *paran* (for *parnâ*), "to fall"; *hari* is the Past tense of *harnâ*, and agrees with its object *sudhi*, as usual. Both Eastwick and Hollings failed to catch the meaning of this passage.

[2] *ab . . . puni*, "now . . . and again," mean that at one time he does one thing, and at another time something else.

His body reached to the sky ; [he] made [his] back as hard as a stone ;
Two great horns, sharp [and] erect, [were his] ; [his] red eyes were filled with excessive rage ;
With tail up-lifted, he careers about roaring ; stopping [and] stopping, wandering about, [he] drops dung ;
[His] shoulder writhes, [he] moves [his] ears ; all the gods, abandoning [their] cars, took flight ;
With [his] hoof [he] digs up the river-banks ; and upsets a mountain with [his] back ;
Then everyone became affrighted ; the guardians of the world [and] those of the [ten] quarters [of space] trembled ;
The earth shook ; S'esha quivered ; woman and cow miscarry.

On seeing this all the cows scattered to the right and left, and the Braj-dwellers running came where, behind all, Krishṇa [and] Balarâm were coming along. Making obeisance [they] said, "Mahârâj ! in front an exceedingly great bull is standing ; save us from him." Upon hearing this statement, the Searcher of Hearts, S'ri Krishṇa Chand, said, "Do not fear him at all ; that low creature, assuming the form of a bull, has come ; he wishes his death from us." Having said this much, [he] went forward, [and] looking at him the Forester said, "Come to us, thou who hast assumed a deceitful body, why art thou terrifying others ? why art thou not coming near me ? That which is called the enemy of the lion does not rush upon the deer. See ! I myself am Gobind in the form of Death. I have slain [and] extirpated many such as you."

Having spoken thus, then, striking his arms [defiantly], he challenged [thus], "Come : fight with me." On hearing this speech, the Asura rushed on as angrily as though the thunderbolt of Indra were come. As often as Hari forced him back, so often he, regaining strength, was coming on. Once as he (Hari) dashed him down, he irritatedly arose and squeezed Hari between both [his] horns. Then S'rî Krishṇa Jî, also, dexterously slipping out, quickly put [his] foot on [the Asura's] foot, and, seizing his horns, wrung [them] round as anyone wrings round a wet cloth. At length he sank [and] fell, and his life departed [from him]. Then all the gods, seated each in his car, joyfully began to rain down flowers, and the cowherdesses and cowherds began to celebrate the glory of Krishṇa. Hereupon S'rî Râdhikâ Jî came and said to Hari, "Mahârâj ! in that you have killed a bull-formed [object], sin has resulted, therefore do you now come [and] bathe at a place of pilgrimage, then touch anyone."[1] On hearing this expression,

[1] The sense is, as sin has been incurred by slaying an object which was merely in the form of a cow, therefore purification should be performed before touching anyone. Notice *is kâ*, meaning "from this."

the Lord said, "I [will] summon all places of pilgrimage into Braj itself." Saying this, he went to Gobardhan [and] caused two deep pits to be dug. There all the places of pilgrimage came in bodily form, and each pronouncing his own name threw water in those [pits], and departed. Then S'rî Krishṇa Chand having bathed in them, came out, gave many cows in alms, fed numerous Brâhmaṇs, [and] became purified. And from that very day those [tanks] have been renowned as[1] the Tank of Krishṇa [and] the Tank of Râdhâ.

Having related this episode, S'rî S'ukadev, the saint, said:—Mahârâj! one day Nârad Muni Jî came to Kañs, and when, in order to increase his anger, he expounded to him the existence of Balarâm and S'yâm,[2] the coming of Mâyâ, and the secret of the departure of Krishṇa, Kañs angrily said, "Nârad Jî! you speak the truth.

> At first he came [and] gave a son, increasing the confidence [of my] mind;
> As a cheat, having shown something, takes all one's wealth, [and] runs off."

Having said this, he summoned Vasudev, seized [and] bound [him], and placing [his] hand on [his] shoulder, said with emotion,—

> "I have discovered [that] thou wast a deceiver; I thought thee a good person;
> Thou didst send away Krishṇa [and] gave [him] to Nand; Devî came [and] revealed to us [the affair];
> In [thy] mind was one thing, the mouth said something different; to-day surely I will kill [thee], just here;
> The friend, kinsman, servant, [or] helper, [who] practises deceit [is] a great sinner;
> [Thy] mouth was sweet, [thy] mind filled [with] poison, through deceit;
> He who [is] self-interested [and] inimical to others, than him a fiend is better."[3]

Having chattered thus, Kañs began to address Nârad Jî thus, "Mahârâj! I have not discovered anything of the secret of this [fellow's] mind; there was a boy, and a girl was brought and shown; he whom [they] said had been miscarried, went into Gokul [and] became Baladev." Having said this much, [he] angrily bit [his] lip [and] raised [his] sword, when just as he was about to slay Vasudev,[4] Nârad, the saint, seizing [his] hand said,

[1] Notice this use of *karke* for "as."

[2] *S'yâm*, "the dark blue"; a name of Krishṇa.

[3] *ju*, in the second hemistich, is the relative, *us se* is the correlative; *âpakâj* or *âpakâjî* is "one who labours for self," and *para-drohiyâ*, is "one who injures another."

[4] *Lit.*, "as he wished thus, 'Let me slay Vasudev.'"

"O King! keep Vasudev to-day, and act so that Krishṇa and Baladev may come here."[1] When Nârad, the saint, had thus counselled [and] departed, Kañs shut up Vasudev [and] Devakî in a chamber, but himself becoming disturbed by dread, he called for the Râkshas named Kesî [and] said,—

> "O mighty one! thou [art] my retainer; I have great hope from thee;
> Do thou go at once into Braj, [and] having slain Râm [and] Krishṇa, show [their bodies] to me."

Upon hearing this direction, Kesî,[2] having received the order, took leave, prostrated [himself, and] departed to Brindâban; and Kañs sent for Sâl, Tusâl, Chânûr, Arishṭ, Byomâsur, and others his ministers. They came, [and he] began to instruct them, thus, "My enemy has come near to dwell; do you, having reflected in your minds, extract the thorn which rankles in my heart." The ministers said, "Lord of the Earth! you yourself are powerful, whom do you fear? What great thing is it to slay Râma [and] Krishṇa? Do not be anxious; we will point out [to you] the device by which they may come here, by stratagem or force.

"In the first place, let us have constructed here, in a good fashion, such a beautiful arena, that, upon hearing of its splendour, the folk of the various cities and villages shall arise and hurry to see [it]; afterwards, do you cause a sacrifice to be offered to Mahâdev, and have goats [and] buffaloes sent for, as offerings. Having heard this news, all the Braj-dwellers will bring offerings, and with them Râma [and] Krishṇa will also come. Then some wrestler will overthrow them, or some other strong [fellow] will slay them at the gate." On hearing this statement,—

> Kañs, giving heed, said, "Good advice the ministers have given."
> He summoned wrestlers, treated [them] respectfully, [and] gave [them] betel.[3]

He then convened a meeting [and] said to his greatest Râkshasas, "When our nephews Râma [and] Krishṇa come here, let someone among you slay them, that the worry of my mind may depart." Having instructed them thus, he next called his Mahout, and said [to him], "A violent elephant is in thy power; do thou take [him] to the gate [and] stay there.[4] When those two

[1] *jis meñ*, "in that which" may induce Krishṇa and Baladev to come, do thou act.
[2] For *tî* read *to*.
[3] The throwing down of betel was a challenge to a difficult exploit; those who took up the betel pledged themselves to attempt the task.
[4] Notice the Respectful Imperative in *-iyo*, because implying an idea of futurity.

shall come, and place foot on the door, do thou cause them to be torn in pieces by the elephant. Let them not escape by any means. If thou shalt slay those two, thou shalt receive whatever you may ask."[1]

Thus having addressed [and] admonished all, [and] having fixed the fourteenth of the dark half of Kârttik for the sacrifice to S'iva, Kañs, at eventide, summoned Akrûr, received [him] most courteously, conducted [him] within the house, placed [him] near him on a throne, took [his] hand, [and] with exceeding affection said, "You are the greatest in the family of Yadu, intelligent, religious, [and] brave; therefore, all know [and] honour you. There is no one who, having seen you, is not pleased; hence, as Bâwan[2] went [and] effected the object of Indra, and by stratagem deprived Bali of the whole of his kingdom, and sent Râjâ Bali to Pâtâla; so do you perform my work. Then at once go to Brindâban, and, as best you can,[3] by force or fraud, bring hither the two sons of Devakî. It is said, 'They who are great, themselves bearing the pain, effect the object of others.' Herein to you, indeed, is [committed] the entirety of my reputation. What more shall we say? As best you can, bring them here; then here they will be quite easily killed; either, on seeing [them] Chânur will overthrow [them], or the elephant Kubaliyâ will seize [and] tear [them] to pieces. Otherwise, I alone will arise [and] slay [them], and will effect my purpose with my own hand; and, having slain those two, afterwards I will kill Ugrasen, because he is very deceitful, [and] wishes my death. Afterwards Devakî's father Devak, having burnt with fire, I will submerge in water, [and] along with him, having slain Vasudev, I will eradicate the worshippers of Hari. Then reigning free from annoyance, I will go [and] unite with Jurâsindhu, the fierce, who is my friend, from fear of whom the nine divisions [of the universe] tremble, and whose attendants are Narakâsur, Bânâsur, and other most large [and] mighty Râkshasas;—provided you bring [here] Râma [and] Krishṇa."

Having said these words, Kañs began to instruct Akrûr, thus, "Do you, having gone into Brindâban, say in the house of Nand, 'There is a sacrifice to S'iva; a bow is set up, and there will be various other sports there.' Hearing this, Nand, Upanand, with the cowherds, will bring goats [and] buffaloes as presents; along with them Krishṇa [and] Baladev will also come to see. This device for bringing them I have pointed out to you; for the rest, you are intelligent; if any other story will succeed, then make it up [and] say [it]. What more should I say to you? It is said,—

[1] *muñh-mâñgâ-dhan*, "mouth-asked-wealth," anything the mouth may ask. This idiom is often brought into requisition.

[2] *Bâwan*, "the dwarf," the fifth incarnation of Vishṇu.

[3] *jyoñ bane*, "as it may be"; an idiom often employed to express, "to the best of one's ability," "anyhow one can."

Should the ambassador be of surprising [capacity]; whose intelligence [is] his strength;
Bold in the affairs of others; place confidence in him."[1]

On hearing this statement, at first Akrûr reflected in his mind thus, "If I now say anything honestly to him, then this [person] will not regard [it]; it is, therefore, better that now I should say what is pleasing [and] agreeable to his mind. So it is said in another place, 'Say that which pleases one.'" Having reflected thus, Akrûr, joining [his] hands [and] inclining [his] head, said, "Mahârâj! you have given good advice; we also have accepted this direction most respectfully.[2] Nothing has power over fate.[3] A man forms many designs [and] hurries [to their realisation], but obtains the mere [previously] written result of fate. They project one thing; another happens. [The design] imagined in one's mind does not occur.[4] Binding the future, you have excogitated this affair. It is not known what will happen. I have accepted your direction; to-morrow at dawn I will go, and Râma [and] Krishṇa I will bring." Saying thus, [and] taking leave from Kaṅs, Akrûr came home.

---

## CHAPTER XXXVIII.

**Krishṇa destroys the Asuras Kesî and Byomâsur.**

S'RÎ S'UKADEV Jî said:—Mahârâj! I am [about to] relate all the particulars, how S'rî Krishṇa Chand killed Kesî, and Nârad went [and] praised [him, and] afterwards [how] Hari killed Byomâsur; do you listen attentively. As soon as it was dawn, Kesî came into Brindâban as an exceedingly high terrific horse; and, with very red eyes, distended nostrils, ears [and] tail erect, [he] began to paw about [and] tear up the ground, and to neigh [and] writhe [his] shoulders repeatedly, and to kick.

On seeing him, the cow-boys, feeling dread, ran off, [and] went [and] told S'rî Krishṇa. He, having heard, came where he was, and, having seen him, tightening [his] girdle for the fray, striking [his] arms, [and] roaring like a lion, said, "O thou who art greatly beloved of Kaṅs, and hast come as a horse! why art thou following others about? Come, fight with me, that I may see thy might. How long wilt thou flutter round the lamp like a

[1] *tâtanau* should be one word; it is a Braj form for "of him."
[2] *sir chaṛhâ,e*, "having raised it to the head," as a sign of submission.
[3] *Lit.*, "no power moves over fate."
[4] After *chîtâ*, a Participle used adjectivally, some such word as *abhiprâya* is understood.

moth? Thy death has drawn near." Hearing this speech, Kesî angrily began to say within himself, "To-day I will see this one's might, and having seized [and] chewed [him] up like sugar-cane, I will accomplish Kañs's object."

Having said this much, opening [his] mouth, [he] ran as though he would swallow up the whole world. On coming up at first, as he stretched forth [his] mouth at S'rî Krishṇa, the latter at once with a push forced [him] backwards. When the second time, having recovered [himself, he] stretched forth [his] head [and] ran, S'rî Krishṇa putting his hand in his mouth, making [it] like an iron staff, so extended [it] that he stopped his ten orifices with it. Then Kesî agitatedly said within himself, "Now [my] body is splitting. How is this? [I] myself have taken my own death into [my] mouth. As a fish, swallowing the hook, gives up life, so I also have lost my life."

Saying this, he made many attempts to get the hand out, but not one were of avail. At last, breath being stopped, the stomach burst, and staggering [he] fell. Then from his body the blood flowed forth like a river. At that time, the cow-boys severally coming began to look on; and Krishṇa, going forward into the wood, stood under the shadow of a Kadam-tree.

Meanwhile, Nârad Muni Jî arrived [there] with a lute in [his] hand. Making obeisance, standing up, [and] sounding the lute, recounting all the sports and actions of S'rî Krishṇa Chand's past [and] future, said, "Lord of Compassion! your sports are infinite! In whom is there so much capacity that he can recount your exploits? But I know your compassion so far that you, to give happiness to worshippers, and for the preservation of the good, and for the purpose of destroying wicked Asuras, again [and] again taking incarnate form, becoming manifest in the world, are removing the burden of the earth."

On hearing this speech, the Lord dismissed Nârad, the saint. He prostrating [himself] set forth; and [Krishṇa] himself, accompanied by all the cow-boys [and] friends, having seated [himself] under a fig-tree, first having made one a minister, another a councillor, another a general, himself becoming King, they began to play the game of royalty, and afterwards blind man's buff. Having told the story so far, S'rî S'ukadev Jî said:—Lord of the Earth!—

"He killed Kesî early in the morning," Kañs heard this remark;
He says to Byomâsur, [with] shuddering, trembling frame,
"Foe-destroying Byomâsur, the powerful! thy frame is excellent in the world,
As the Son of the Wind[1] [was the assistant] of Râma, just so [art] thou my messenger of death;

[1] "Son of the Wind" (in Sanskrit *pavanâtmaja*) is an epithet of Hanuman, the monkey, who was the friend of Râma.

Slay [and] bring [here] the son of Vasudev ; to-day perform
my object [and] return."

Having heard this, joining [his] hands, Byomâsur said, "Mahârâj ! whatever shall be possible I will do to-day ; my body is at your service. They who are greedy of life, feel abashed [at] giving life for their master. The glory [and] virtue of [both] servant and wife is in this, that he [or she] gives up life for the master's sake." Having said thus [and] taking up the betel on [account of] Krishṇa [and] Baladev,[1] [and] making obeisance to Kañs, Byomâsur went to Brindâban. Going along the road, having assumed the disguise of a cowherd, he proceeded on, [and] arrived where Hari was playing blind man's buff with the cow-boys [and] friends. On going [there], when from afar he joined [his] hands [and] said to S'rî Krishṇa Chand, "Mahârâj ! cause me also to play with you," then Hari calling him near said, "Do not keep the desire of anything within thyself ; play with us whatever sport thou desirest." Having heard this, becoming pleased, [he] said, "The game of wolf and rams is a good one." S'rî Krishṇa Chand smilingly said, "Very well ; do thou become the wolf, and the cow-boys be the rams." They began to play together.

Then that Asura, taking them one by one, and placing [them] in a cave of the mountain, placing a stone across its mouth [and] confining [them], came back. When he had so placed them all [and] returned, and S'rî Krishṇa remained alone, [he] challenged [him, and] said, "To-day I will accomplish the object of Kañs, and will slay all the Yadubañsîs." Having spoken thus, abandoning the disguise of a cowherd, [and] becoming in truth a wolf, as he sprang upon Hari the latter seized [him], gripped [his] throat, [and] with blows of the fist beat [him] to death, as they slaughter a goat for sacrifice.

---

## CHAPTER XXXIX.

**Akrûr arrives at Brindâban, and delivers his message.**

S'RÎ S'UKADEV, the saint, said :—Mahârâj ! Kesî and Byomâsur were killed on the 12th of the dark half of Kârttik ; and, quite early in the morning of the 13th, Akrûr came to Kañs, took leave, mounted [his] chariot, [and] reflecting within himself as follows, set out towards Brindâban : "What devotion, penance, sacrifice, alms, pilgrimage, [or] vow, have I performed, of such [a nature] that, by its merit, I should obtain this result ? As far as I know, all this life [I] have never invoked the name of Hari.

[1] See note [3], p. 95.

[I] have always remained in the society of Kañs; where should I get the secret of worship? Yes! [in some] previous birth, [I] may have performed some virtuous act, and this, probably,[1] is the result of the force of its merit, that Kañs has sent me to bring S'rî Krishṇa Chand, the source of joy. Now, [by] going [and] getting a sight of him [I] shall render my birth profitable.

"Having joined [my] hands, I shall fall at [his] feet; then, the dust of the feet on [my] head I will place.[2]
Those feet which the removers of sin, S'rî Brahmâ and the rest, are worshipping;
Those feet which alighted [on] the head of Kâlî; those feet filled with the breast [and] sandal;[3]
They danced well the circular dance; the feet which roamed after the cows;
[By] the dust of which feet Ahilyâ crossed [the ocean of existence]; from which feet the Ganges issued;
Having tricked Bali, [those feet] accomplished the object of Indra; those feet I shall see to-day.
Omens are to me propitious; herds of deer are passing to the right."

Mahârâj! having reflected thus, Akrûr then began to say within himself, "Let them by no means suppose me the messenger of Kañs!" Again he reflected, "He whose name is 'The Searcher of Hearts' regards the affection of the heart, and recognizes every friend [and] foe. He will never think thus; on the contrary, upon seeing me, he will embrace [me, and] place his soft lotus-like hand on my head; then I shall give pleasure to my Chakor-like eyes,[4] [by] regarding fixedly that moon-body of which Brahmâ, Rudra, Indra, and all the other gods are continually thinking."

Having related the story thus far, S'rî S'ukadev Jî said to King Parîkshit:—Mahârâj! in this way reflecting, [and] driving [his] chariot, Akrûr Jî went from this direction; and from the wood, [in] the other direction, S'rî Krishṇa [and] Baladev, with the cow-lads, having grazed the cattle, were also come. Then there

[1] *ho to ho* = "may probably be."

[2] *parihauñ* and *dharihauñ* should have been printed as here, and not divided into two, as in text.

[3] Eastwick considers *kucha chandana* to stand for *kuchandana*, "red sanders"; but the latter word is formed by the prefix *ku*, "bad," "inferior," and the poet is not likely to have selected the inferior sandal-wood as the stuffing for the sacred feet. Hollings expands the word *kuch*, "the breast," into "the milk of the breast," and he probably took counsel from Indians on the point. The allusion is most likely to the softness and smoothness of the sandal-scented feet. The phrase does not occur in the Sukha-Sâgar, nor in the Bhâgavata-Purâṇa. [But a later edition reads: *je pad kuchh chandan soñ bhare*.]

[4] The Chakor, or red partridge, is supposed to derive much delight from gazing fixedly at the moon.

was a mutual meeting of them both[1] just outside Brindâban. On perceiving Hari's beauty from afar, Akrûr descended from the chariot, [and] running with extreme agitation, went [and] fell at his feet; and was so enraptured that speech came not from [his] mouth. With excessive delight, water began to rain from [his] eyes. Then S'rî Krishṇa Jî raised him up, [and] embracing [him] with exceeding tenderness, took [his] hand, [and] conducted [him] home. There Nand Râ,e, on seeing Akrûr Jî, was pleased, arose, [and] embraced [him], and did [him] much honour. Having caused [his] feet to be washed, [he] seated [him].

> The bath-attendants came bearing oil; having applied sweet-smelling unguents, [they] caused [him] to be bathed;
> Jasodâ gave [him] a cooking-place [and] a board [on which to sit and eat, and] fed [him] with the six-flavoured delicacy.

When, having rinsed his mouth, [he] sat down to eat betel, then Nand Jî, having asked after [his] welfare, said, "You, indeed, are a very worthy person among the Yadubañsîs, and have always preserved your dignity; tell [me] now, how are you faring with the wicked Kañs, and what is the condition of the people there? tell the whole secret." Akrûr Jî said,—

> "Since Kañs has been [in] Madhupurî,[2] [he] has given pain to everyone.
> [You] have asked, what [is] the city's prosperity; the condition of the subjects is miserable.
> As long as Kañs is in Mathurâ, how will the Yadu family escape?
> As the hunter is the enemy of animal, rams [and] she-goats,
> So is Kañs [the enemy] of the subjects; everyone suffers distress."

Having said this, again [he] spoke, "You, indeed, know the proceedings of Kañs; what more shall we say?"

---

## CHAPTER XL.

**Krishṇa accepts the invitation, and goes to Mathurâ with Nand and all the cowherds—Akrûr, on the road, sees Krishṇa in his celestial form.**

S'RÎ S'UKADEV Jî said:—Lord of the Earth! when Nand Jî had done conversing, Krishṇa [and] Balarâm, calling Akrûr by a sign, led [him] apart.

[1] *in se un se;* the juxtaposition of inflexions in this way implies mutuality.
[2] *Madhupurî*, "the city of honey"; a name of Mathurâ.

Respectfully [they] asked [his] welfare ; "Tell [us], paternal uncle, the affairs of Mathurâ;
Are Vasudev [and] Devakî well ? Has the king fallen out their foe ?
Exceedingly wicked is our maternal uncle Kañs, who has done away with the whole Yadu race.

Some violent disease of the Yadu family has taken birth [and] come; that has plagued all the Yadubañsîs ; and, if you ask the truth, Vasudev [and] Devakî are getting all this misery for our sake ; had they not concealed us, they would not have got [into] all this trouble." Having spoken thus, Krishṇa again said,—

"What did they say to you [when you were] going, they whose debtors we shall ever remain ?
They must be thinking of us, in [their] difficulty, suffering deep distress."

Hearing this, Akrûr Jî said, "Lord of Compassion ! you know all. How shall I relate the injustice of Kañs, who has friendship with no one. Vasudev and Ugrasen are constantly meditating on death ; but, up to the present time, they have escaped by their destiny ; but since Nârad, the saint, came [and] stated circumstantially all the particulars of your existence, gyves and manacles have been placed on Vasudev, [and he] is kept in great misery. And to-morrow, at his (Kañs's) place, there is [to be] a sacrifice to Mahâdev, and a bow has been set up, everybody will come to see ; therefore [he] has sent me to call you, telling [me] this, 'You go [and] cause to be brought [here] Nand Râ,e with offerings for the sacrifice, along with Râma [and] Krishṇa' ; therefore I am come to take you." Having heard this statement from Akrûr Jî, Râma [and] Krishṇa came [and] said to Nand Râ,e,—

"Kañs has called for [us], listen, Father ; Uncle Akrûr has told [us] this affair.
Take milk, rams, [and] she-goats ; it is the sacrifice of the bow ; give these [as offerings].
Let all go together along with you ; the king has spoken ; there should be no tarrying."

When S'rî Krishṇa Chand Jî had thus counselled [and] spoken to Nand Jî, Nand Râ,e Jî immediately summoned criers, and sent round a proclamation through all the city, saying this, "To-morrow, as soon as dawn [breaks], everyone assembling will go to Mathurâ ; the king has summoned [us]." From hearing this statement, as soon as it was dawn, each taking a present, all the Braj-dwellers arrived ; and Nand Jî also, taking milk, curds, butter, rams, goats, [and] buffaloes, causing carts to be yoked, accompanied them ; and Krishṇa [and] Baladev also, taking with them their cow-lads [and] friends, mounted a chariot.

In front were Nand [and] Upanand; after all [were] Haladhar [and] Govinda.

S'rî S'ukadev Jî said:—Lord of the Earth! all at once hearing of S'rî Krishṇa Chand's departure, all the Braj cowherdesses, having become exceedingly agitated [and] distressed, abandoning home, rising in confusion, ran; and lamenting, raving, stumbling [and] falling, came where S'rî Krishṇa Chand's chariot was. As soon as they came, having stationed [themselves] around the chariot [with] joined hands, beseechingly they began to say, "Why are you leaving us, Lord of Braj? Everything is given [into] your possession; the affection of the good never diminishes; it ever remains, like the lines on the hand; but the affection of a fool remains not, like a wall of sand. What fault has been committed against you such that you are going [with your] back towards us?" Having thus addressed S'rî Krishṇa Chand, next the cowherdesses, looking towards Akrûr, said,—

"This Akrûr is very cruel;[1] [he] knows nothing of our pain;
Without whom for an instant, everyone [of us] is widowed, that one [he] is taking away with him;
Deceitful Krûr has become hard-hearted; who gave the name Akrûr in vain?
O Akrûr! perverse, void of understanding! why [are you] afflicting the weak [and] helpless?"

Uttering such very bitter expressions, abandoning reflection [and] modesty, seizing the chariot of Hari, [they] began to say among themselves, "The women of Mathurâ are exceedingly wanton, cunning, beautiful, [and] accomplished; Bihârî forming friendship with them, becoming subject to their accomplishments and graces will remain there; then why should he think of us? They are very fortunate who will remain with the beloved one. What fault has happened in our devotion [and] penance, for which S'rî Krishṇa Chand is deserting us?" Having said thus among themselves, again they began to say to Hari, "Your name is the Lord of Cowherdesses, why are you not taking us along with you?

"Without you how will each moment pass? [when] for an instant concealed, the bosom bursts [with grief].
Having shown affection, why are you causing separation? relentless, pitiless, you bear no affection."
The beautiful ones are thus praying there; fallen into the ocean of misery, [they] are thinking.
They remained gazing steadfastly towards Hari; like a charmed doe [or] the Chakor [gazing at] the moon;
Tears are bursting forth from [their] eyes; [their] locks having become loosened, are scattered over [their] faces.

[1] *Akrûr*, "kind," *krûr*, "cruel." A play on words.

S'rî S'ukadev, the saint, said :—O King ! at that time the cowherdesses were in the condition which I have stated ; and Jasodâ Rânî, with motherly affection, embracing [her] son, weeping greatly, with exceeding affection was saying, "Son ! take provision for the number of days [that may elapse till] you return thence ; having gone there, make friendship with no one ; speedily come [back, and] show yourself to your mother." Hearing this speech, S'rî Krishṇa descended from the chariot, [and] having instructed [and] counselled all, [and] taken leave of [his] mother, prostrating [himself, and] receiving [her] blessing, [he] again mounted the chariot [and] departed. Then, from the one direction, Jasodâ Jî, with the cowherdesses, exceedingly agitated, crying greatly, were calling out "Krishṇa !" and from the other direction, S'rî Krishṇa, standing on the chariot, was keeping on calling out [and] saying, "Do you go home ; don't worry about anything ; in only four or five days we shall be back again."

Thus calling out and gazing on, when the chariot had disappeared [in] the distance, and the dust had spread to the heavens, insomuch that even the pennon of the chariot was no longer visible, then, becoming disconsolate, all at once, the whole of them, convulsed like fishes without water, swooned [and] fell. After a time, regaining consciousness, [they] arose ; and fixing the hope of the engagement [to return] in mind, [and] consoling [herself], in the one direction, Jasodâ Jî, taking all the cowherdesses, went to Brindâban ; and, in the other direction, S'rî Krishṇa Chand, with all [his party], proceeding on, arrived at the bank of the Jumnâ. There the cow-lads drank water, and Hari also stopped the chariot in the shade of a fig-tree. When Akrûr, thinking to bathe, descended from the chariot, S'rî Krishṇa Chand said to Nand Râ,e, "Do you, please, take all the cow-lads [and] proceed onwards ; let Uncle Akrûr bathe, afterwards, we also [will] come [and] join [you]."

Hearing this, taking all [the party], Nand Jî advanced ; and Akrûr Jî, having undressed, washed [his] hands [and] feet, rinsed [his] mouth, [and,] having gone to the bank, entered the water, taken a dive, worshipped, [offered] a libation, prayed, [and] meditated, again dived, [and] opening [his] eyes, looked in the water, then S'rî Krishṇa appeared there with his chariot.

> Again, having raised [his] head, he beheld [that] the Yadu Chief is seated [in] the very same place;
> He is astonished, reflecting [in his] heart, "Murâri [is] on the chariot afar ;
> Both [the brothers] are seated [under] the shade of the fig-tree ; [yet] I see those very [two] in the water;
> I don't apprehend the mystery[1] [of their being] out [and] in [the water] ; which shall I call [their] true forms ?"

[1] For *med* read *bhed*.

Mahârâj! Akrûr Jî continuing to observe one and the same form out [and] in [the water], was simply reflecting, when, in the midst of it, at first, S'rî Krishṇa Chand Jî, becoming four-armed [and] bearing the shell, discus, club, [and] lotus, appeared in the water with all [his] worshippers, Suras, Munis, Kinnaras, Gandharvas, and others; and, afterwards, having become S'eshaśâ,î,[1] [he appeared again]. Then Akrûr, having seen [that], was still more perplexed.

---

## CHAPTER XLI.

Akrûr celebrates the glory of Krishṇa.

S'RÎ S'UKADEV Jî said:—Mahârâj! [while] continuing to stand in the water, knowledge [came] to Akrûr, by meditating on the Lord, during a long time; then, joining [his] hands [and] making obeisance, [he] began to say, "O Bhagwân! you alone are Creator [and] Destroyer! for the sake of worshippers, having come into the world, you assume endless shapes; and gods, men, [and] saints are [but] parts of you; having become manifest from you alone, they are so contained in you alone, as water [which,] having issued from the ocean, is received [back] into the ocean! Your greatness is incomparable! who can utter it? you ever remain Virâṭ-swarûpa![2] [Your] head [is] heaven, the earth [is your] foot, the sea [your] belly, the sky [your] navel, the clouds [your] hair, trees [are] the down [of your body], fire [your] mouth, the ten quarters [your] ears, [your] eyes [are] the moon and sun, Indra [is your] arm, [your] intellect [is] Brahmâ, [your] self-consciousness [is] Rudra, thunder [is your] speech, air [is your] breath, water [is your] semen, the closing of [your] eyes [is] night [and] day. In this form you are ever resplendent! Who can recognize you?" In this way having offered praises, Akrûr, meditating on the feet of the Lord, said, "Lord of Compassion! keep me in your protection!"

[1] *S'eshaśâ,î*, "the sleeper on S'esha." This alludes to the mythological sleep of Vishṇu on the back of the snake S'esha, before the creation of the present world. While so reposing Brahmâ arose from out of his form, and proceeded with the work of creation.

[2] *Virâṭ-swarûpa*, "consisting of Virâj." The first progeny of Brahmâ, or the primary male power, produced from the female portion of Brahmâ's own substance, was named Virâj, or "the resplendent." From Virâj all animated creation arose, and thus the term Virâṭ-swarûpa intimates that Krishṇa is Creation embodied.

## CHAPTER XLII.

**Krishṇa and his companions enter Mathurâ—Description of the city—Krishṇa robs the King's washerman, and then kills him.**

S'RÎ S'UKADEV Jî said :—Mahârâj ! when S'rî Krishṇa Chand had exhibited [himself] in a variety of forms in the water, like the delusions of a juggler, [and] had withdrawn [the illusion], Akrûr Jî, having issued from the water [and] come to the bank, performed obeisance to Hari. Then the beloved of Nand asked Akrûr, thus, "Uncle ! in the cold season, why stay so long a time in the water ? We were anxious about you, [asking] Why has uncle forgotten to think of going on the journey ? Having gone [into the water], did you see anything strange ? [1] Explain this [matter], that the doubt of our minds may depart."

Having heard [this], Akrûr, closing [his] hands, said, "You know all, Lord of Braj !
[You] revealed [yourself] admirably in the water ; no action of Krishṇa [need occasion] surprise ;
I have become confident of you ; quickly, O Lord ! set foot [towards] Mathurâ.

Please delay not here ; speedily go [and] accomplish the work." On hearing this statement, Hari hastily seated [himself] on the chariot, [and] taking Akrûr with [him], departed, [and] stopped [at the halting-place]. And Nand, all the cowherds, and the rest, who had gone on ahead, had pitched [their] tents outside Mathurâ ;—and watching for Krishṇa [and] Baladev, with exceeding anxiety, began to say among themselves, "Why so much delay [in] bathing ? and why has Hari not yet come ?"—where, hereupon, coming along, the Source of Joy, S'rî Krishṇa Chand, also went [and] met [them]. Then, [with] hands joined [and] head bent down, beseechingly, Akrûr Jî said, "King of Braj ! now come [and] make my house holy ; and revealing [yourself] to your worshippers, give [them] happiness." On hearing this request, Hari said to Akrûr,—

"First discharge [your] duty towards Kaṅs, then point out your dwelling ;
Present the submission of all who had [previously] gone away." [2] Having heard [this], Akrûr went [with] downcast head.

[1] Eastwick omits this phrase from his translation. Hollings does not.

[2] The expression *ju jâ,e* has been evaded by both Hollings and Eastwick. It means "they who having gone"; but its grammatical connection with the rest of the line is not evident. Krishṇa directs Akrûr to present the humble respects of all those who had previously left Mathurâ, but who were now returned to attend the great sacrifice. The expression does not occur in the Sukha-Sâgar nor in the Bhâgavata-Purâṇa.

Proceeding onwards, for a certain time, [he] descended from [his] chariot [and] arrived where Kañs was seated [in] an assembled council. On seeing him, [the King] arose from the throne, came down, [and] with exceeding friendliness met [him], and very courteously taking [his] hand, [and] conducting [him], caused [him] to sit near him on the throne, [and] asking his welfare, said, "Tell me news of where you went."

Having heard [this], Akrûr, instructing, said, "The greatness of Braj is unutterable.
How shall I express the greatness of Nand? I placed your direction on [my] head;[1]
Râma and Krishṇa are both come; all the Braj-dwellers have brought offerings;
[Their] tents are pitched on the river-bank; carts [and] a great crowd have alighted."

Hearing this, Kañs joyfully said, "Akrûr Jî! to-day you have done a great thing for me, in that [you] have brought Râma [and] Krishṇa; now go home and repose."

Having related the story so far, S'rî S'ukadev Jî said to King Parîkshit:—Mahârâj! having received the command of Kañs, Akrûr Jî went to his house. He began to reflect; and [outside the city,] where Nand [and] Upanand were seated, Haladhar and Gobind [went and] asked them, thus, "Should we receive your permission, we will inspect the city." Having heard this, at first Nand Râ,e Jî brought out some sweetmeats to eat, [which] both the brothers ate together; afterwards [he] said, "Well, go, see, [and] return; but stay not long."

As soon as this direction had issued from the mouth of Nand, the chieftain, gladly both the brothers, accompanied by their cow-boys [and] friends, proceeded to see the city. Advancing forwards, [they] saw then [that] there are, outside the city, all around, woods, groves, flowers, [and] fruits; on them birds are seated warbling a great variety of pleasing notes; and very great lakes filled with pure water, in them blossoming lotuses, on which swarms on swarms of bees are humming; and on the banks swans, cranes, and other [water-]birds are disporting [themselves]; a cool, perfumed, gentle breeze is blowing; and at the enclosures of the very large gardens betel-grounds were planted; in the very midst, beds of various kinds of flowers extending for miles are blooming; in various places, at the stone wells [and] water-pits, wheels [and] buckets were in motion; [and] gardeners, singing away sweet songs, were irrigating.

Having gazed upon this beauty of the woods [and] groves, being delighted, the Lord, with all [his companions], entered the town

[1] See note [2], p. 97; but for *chaṛâ,î* read *chaṛhâ,î*.

of Mathurâ. What is that city like? around which [are] copper forts, and a strongly built wide ditch with water; four crystal gates, whose panels were of eight metals, inlaid with gold; and in the city, palaces of various colours—red, yellow, green, [and] white—of five storeys [and] seven storeys, so high that they were holding converse with the clouds, the brilliance of whose spires [and] pinnacles shone like lightning; banners [and] streamers were fluttering; from lattices, windows, [and] apertures, came the sweet savour of incense; at each door were placed pillars of plantain-tree and golden vessels filled with [growing] sprouts; garlands [and] wreaths were formed; in every house instruments were playing; and, on one side, a variety of jewelled golden palaces, belonging to the King, were glittering, the beauty of which cannot be described. Such [was] the beautiful, delightful city of Mathurâ, which S'rî Krishṇa [and] Baladev, taking the cow-lads with [them], went to see.

There was great bustle [in] the city of Mathurâ, [on] the coming [of] Nand's son;
[On] hearing [it], all the people of the city ran, forgetting house [and] work;
And the beautiful women of Mathurâ, hearing [the news with their] ears [were] really much agitated,
They called out this speech to each other, "Balabhadra [and] Murâri are coming,
Akrûr is bringing them; come, Friend, now our eyes will see;"
Some left [their] food [and] bathing; some rose [and] left dressing [their] hair.
They forgot the amorous dalliance of [their] husbands; ornaments [and] clothes were put on anyhow;
Just as they were [they] rose [and] ran; [they] came to look [upon] Krishṇa;
Laying aside shame, modesty, [and] fear, some [at] the windows, some at the balconies; some stood [at] the doors, some ran wandering about the lanes;
Wherever the women stood, stretching out [their] arms, [they] pointed to the Lord;
"In blue dress [was] the fair Balarâm; [with] yellow silk Ghanaśyâm [1] was covered;
These are the two nephews of Kañs; from them no Asura escapes;
Of whose accomplished manhood [2] we are hearing, their form let us see with full eyes;
In a former birth someone did [some] meritorious act; therefore Providence has given this manifestation [as a] reward."

[1] *Ghanaśyâm*, "dark-blue cloud," a name of Krishṇa, referring to his dark colour.
[2] *purushârth* means "man's object," and comprises all the lofty purposes for which man exists. The implication in the text is that Krishṇa was the embodiment of all that man should be and desire.

Having related the tale thus far, S'rî S'ukadev, the saint, said:—Mahârâj! in this way, all the citizens, whether women or men, were keeping on conversing in a variety of ways, [and] looking on [the brothers], were in ecstasy; and in whatever market, road, [or] square, Krishṇa [and] Balarâm, with all [their entourage] were happening to be,[1] there, each standing at his own house, sprinkling respectively perfume [and] sandal-scent, joyfully they (the people) were raining down flowers; and these regarding steadfastly the splendour of the city, kept on saying thus to the cow-lads, "Brothers! let no one mistake [the way]; and if anyone should mistake, let him go to the last encampment." Meanwhile, having gone some distance, what do they see?—the washermen of Kañs, laden [with] bundles of washed clothes, bearing large packages, intoxicated, besmeared with colour, singing the praises of Kañs, were coming along from outside the city. Seeing them, S'rî Krishṇa Chand said to Baladev Jî, "Brother! snatch from them all the clothes; dress yourself, and cause the cow-lads to be dressed [in them]; what remains allow to be plundered." Having instructed the brother thus, Hari, having gone near the washermen with all [his companions], said,—

"Give us clean clothes; after we have met the King [and] returned, take [them] back;
The dresses [of honour] we shall get from the King, some from among them we shall give to you."

On hearing this statement, the chief washerman among them laughingly began to say,—

"Having folded, we shall deposit [them]; do you come up to the King's door;
Then, having approached the gate, take [them]; give [us] what you please.
[You] are roaming from wood to wood grazing cows; cowherds [by] caste, wearers of blankets;
Having assumed the guise of jugglers [you] are come; the wearing of royal garments suits [your] inclination;
Joining together [and] proceeding to the King [in] the hope of obtaining dresses [of honour],
What good hope of life [you have], that same [you] are again now about to lose."

Having heard this remark of the washerman, Hari again smiling said, "We, for our part, are asking in a straightforward manner, why do you understand us in a reversed sense? No harm will happen to you through giving us the clothes; on the other hand, there will be acquisition of fame." Hearing this statement, the washerman angrily said, "Just look at the face [of

[1] *ho nikalnâ*, though separated, should be construed together; the compound verb means "to pass," "pass by," "happen to be," or "to turn up."

the fellow who wants] to wear the King's cloth ; go from before me, otherwise I [will] slay [you] at once." On hearing this speech, angrily S'rî Krishṇa Chand struck [him] obliquely [a blow with] one hand, that his head flew off like an ear of Indian corn. Then all the companions and servants who were with him, one and all, abandoning the bundles [and] packages, fled for their lives, and going to Kañs cried out. On the other side, S'rî Krishṇa Jî took all the clothes, and having dressed himself, [and] caused [his] brother to be dressed, [and] shared [some] among the cow-lads, the rest he gave to plunder. Then the cow-lads, each being exceedingly pleased, began to put on the clothes in random fashion.

> Having tightened the waist, they put the coat [on their] feet, and thrust the drawers on their arms ;
> They knew not the secret of dressing ; Krishṇa was laughing in his heart.

As they were advancing onwards from there, a tailor having come, prostrated [himself], stood up, joined [his] hands [and] said, "Mahârâj ! I, so to speak, am called Kañs's servant, but in [my] heart I am ever celebrating your virtues alone. Kindly bid [me], then I will fit the clothes, by which [means] I shall be called your servant."

As soon as this speech issued from his mouth, the Searcher of Hearts, S'rî Krishṇa Chand, knowing him to be his servant, called him near [and] said, "Thou art come at a good time ; good, fit [the clothes]." Then he quickly unseaming, opening, cutting, trimming, sewing, accurately adjusting, [and] arranging, dressed all [of them], together with Râma [and] Krishṇa, in the clothes. Then the beloved of Nand, giving him emancipation, [and] taking [him] with him, proceeded onwards.

> There came the gardener Sudâmâ, [and] respectfully took [the party] to [his] house ;
> He dressed them all in garlands ; [in] the gardener's house were rejoicings.

---

## CHAPTER XLIII.

**Kubjâ offers service to Krishṇa, and is promised a reward—Krishṇa breaks the bow of Mahâdev, and slaughters the guard.**

S'RÎ S'UKADEV JÎ said :—Lord of the Earth ! perceiving the attachment of the gardener, [and] being gratified [thereby], S'rî Krishṇa Chand, having conferred beatitude upon him, moving forward thence, [he] sees before [him] in a lane a hump-backed woman, with cups filled with saffron and sandal, placed in the middle of a tray, [which she] held in [her] hand, awaiting [him]. Hari asked her, "Who art thou? and where art thou taking this?" She said, "Compassionate to the Lowly! I am the servant of Kañs; my name is Kubjâ; I constantly rub [and] apply sandal to [the body of] Kañs; but with [my] heart I am celebrating your virtues; by the power of this [mental service] to-day, having obtained a sight of you, [I] have made [my] birth advantageous, and have received profit from [my] eyes. Now the desire of [this] servant is this, that I may receive the Lord's command, then [with] my own hands I may apply sandal [to your body]."

Perceiving her deep devotion, Hari said, "If there is [any] satisfaction to thee in this, then apply [it]." Upon hearing this declaration, when Kubjâ, with great affection [and] earnestness had rubbed sandal on Râma [and] Krishṇa, then S'rî Krishṇa Chand, perceiving the affection of her heart, kindly placing foot on foot, [and] applying two fingers under [her] chin, drew [her] up, [and] made her straight. On the application of the hand of Hari she became very beautiful, and with exceeding meekness began to say to the Lord, "Lord of Compassion! as you have kindly made this servant's body straight, compassionately now come [and] make [her] home holy, and, taking rest, give happiness to [this] servant." Having heard this, Hari, taking her hand, smiling, began to say,—

"Thou hast removed our fatigue, having met [us, thou] hast applied cool sandal;
[Thy] beauty, disposition, [and] qualities, O fair one! [are] excellent; my affection for thee will be endless;
Having slain Kañs I will come [and] meet you." Saying thus, Murâri moved onwards.

And Kubjâ, having returned home, [and] having filled a *chauk*[1] with saffron [and] sandal, [and] fixing in [her] mind the hope of meeting Hari, began to indulge in rejoicings.

The women of Mathurâ come there, [and] having seen [her] are astonished [and] say,
"Great indeed is thy fortune, O Kubjâ! to whom the Creator has shown affection.
What difficult penance have [you] performed, such [that] the Lord of Cowherdesses has met [and] embraced you?
We, well [formed], have not seen Hari; thee [he] has met, [and] been exceedingly loving to."
All the women are talking thus there; Murâri is roaming about, looking [at] Mathurâ.

[1] A *chauk* is a square place which, at marriages and other festive occasions, is filled with sweetmeats, etc., which are consecrated and distributed among visitors.

In the midst of looking about [in] the city, the Lord, with all [his companions], arrived at the gate of the bow. On perceiving them hilariously coming, with their [bodies] stained with colour, the gate-keepers angrily said, "Whither are you coming along, in this direction, boors! Stand off; this is the royal portal." Pretending not to hear what the door-keepers said, Hari, with the others, went straight on, and proceeded to the place where the bow of Mahâdev, [which was] as long as three palm-trees, massive, [and] heavy, had been placed. On reaching [it, he] quickly took [it] up, [and] having drawn [it] with the greatest ease, broke [it] as an elephant breaks a sugar-cane.

Hereupon all the guards placed there by Kañs, who were watching the bow, attacked [Hari]. The Lord slew [and] overthrew them also. Then the citizens, having seen this act, by reflection having become assured [in their minds], began to say among themselves, "Behold! the King, seated in his house,[1] has invited his own death; he will not escape alive from the hands of these two." And Kañs, having heard the tremendous sound of the breaking bow, being terrified, began to ask his people, "What was this the great sound of?" Hereupon several of the King's people, who, standing afar, were seeing [what had occurred], uncovering [their] heads, went [to the King, and] exclaimed, "We swear by the King![2] Râma [and] Krishṇa, having come, have excited a great bustle in the city; having broken the bow of S'iva, [they] have slain all the guards."

On hearing this statement, Kañs, calling many soldiers, said, "Do you go with these, and by fraud [or] force slay Krishṇa [and] Baladev immediately, [and] return." As soon as this direction issued from the mouth of Kañs, each taking his arms [and] weapons went where both the brothers were standing. As soon as these challenged them, they came and slew all these also. When Hari saw that, "No servant of Kañs now remains here;" he said to Balarâm, "Brother! it is very long since we came; we should go to the tents; because Father Nand, keeping on watching for us, must be anxious [on our account]." Having spoken thus, taking all the cow-lads with [him], the Lord, proceeding with Balarâm, came where the tents had been pitched. On coming [there] he said to Nand, the chieftain, "Father! we, having gone into the city, have witnessed good sport, [and] returned"; and he showed his clothes to the cowherds.

Then, having looked, Nand, counselling, said, "Kânh! your
habit is not departing [from you];
This is not our village [in] the Braj forest; it is the place of
Kañs Râ,e;
Here do not violence; bear in mind my instruction, O son!"

[1] *ghar baiṭhe*, "seated at home," means that the danger was needless. A king in the discharge of his duties may expect to meet death, but here Kañs, "in a perfectly uncalled-for way," invited his own destruction.

[2] *Lit.*, "the oath of the King!"

When Nand Râ,e Jî had ended this counsel, the beloved of Nand very affectionately said, "Father! [we] are hungry; please give what our mother has sent [for us] to eat." On hearing this, he brought out [and] gave the comestible matter which had come with [them]. Krishṇa [and] Baladev, having accepted [it], in conjunction with the cow-lads, ate [it] up. Having related the story so far, S'rî S'ukadev, the saint, said:—Mahârâj! on the one hand, these, having come, [and] with great gratification having supped, slept; and, on the other, hearing again and again[1] of the doings of S'rî Krishṇa, in the mind of Kañs exceeding anxiety arose; then he had no peace either sitting or standing. He was fretting [in his] heart of hearts, [but] his pain [he] was not telling to anyone. It is said,—

> As the weevil eats into wood, [and] no one knows the pain [the wood suffers],
> So anxiety being in the mind, intelligence, strength [and] the body, diminish.

At last [he] became greatly agitated; then having gone into the palace, he went to sleep on the bed; but through fear sleep did not come to him.

> Three watches [of] the night passed [he] remaining awake; [he] closed [his] eyelids, there was sleep for a moment.
> Then he saw a dream in [his] mind,—the phantom of [his] body is going about without a head;
> Sometimes naked [he] bathes in sand; having taken poison, mounted [on] an ass, he hurries along;
> Accompanied by demons he dwells [in] a cemetery; [on his] breast a garland of blood-red flowers.
> [He] saw flaming trees all around, [and] young children seated on them.

Mahârâj! when Kañs saw such a dream, then he, becoming exceedingly agitated, woke up, and reflecting seriously, having got up, [he] came out. Having summoned his advisers [he] said, "You go at once, [and] have the arena swept, sprinkled [and] prepared; and having summoned all the Braj-dwellers, along with Nand [and] Upanand, and Vasudev and the rest of the Yadubañsîs, into the arena, have [them] seated; and all the various countries' kings who are come [here, invite] them also; in the interim, I also [will] come."

Having received the command of Kañs, the ministers came into the arena. Having had it swept [and] sprinkled, [and] having spread there silken screens, [and] having had affixed [there] flags, banners, wreaths [and] garlands, [and] having caused various kinds of instruments to be played, [they] sent to summon everyone. They came, and each severally going seated

[1] Lallû Lâl, and previous editions, have the repetition *sun sun* here.

[himself] on his own platform. Hereupon Râjâ Kañs also, filled with excessive pride, came [and] seated [himself] on his daïs. Then the gods, seated in their cars, began to look on from the sky.

---

## CHAPTER XLIV.

### Krishṇa slays the elephant Kubaliyâ.

S'RÎ S'UKADEV Jî said:—Mahârâj! at dawn, when Nand, Upanand, and all the remaining very great cowherds, went into the assembly of the arena, then S'rî Krishṇa Chand Jî said to Baladev Jî, "Brother! all the cowherds have gone before; now make no delay, quickly proceed, with the cow-lads [and] friends, to see the arena."

On hearing this speech, Balarâm Jî arose [and] stood up, and said to all the cowherd companions, "Brothers! come on; let us see the preparation of the arena." On hearing this direction, immediately all accompanied [him]; at last S'rî Krishṇa [and] Balarâm, disguised [as] jugglers, taking with [them] cow-lads [and] companions, moving on, having come to the gate of the arena, stopped where the furious elephant Kubaliyâ, strong as ten thousand elephants, was standing swaying [backwards and forwards].

Having seen the furious elephant [at] the door, Balarâm called out to the elephant-keeper,
"Listen, Mahaut! to our advice; do you take the elephant [to] a distance from the door.
Allow us to go near the King, otherwise the destruction of the elephant will occur.
I tell [you; it is] no fault of ours; do not think[1] Hari a child.

This is the Lord of the Three Worlds; having destroyed the wicked, he is come to remove the burden of the earth." Having heard this, the driver angrily said, "I know; having grazed cows, he is become Lord of the Three Worlds; therefore, having come here, like a great hero, he is standing hesitating. Do not fancy [this] bow-breaking; my elephant has the strength of ten thousand elephants; until you fight with this you shall not go inside. You, indeed, have slain many strong ones; but to-day, should you escape from the power of this one, I shall think you are very mighty."

[1] *jâno* must be *jâne*, as in previous editions.

Then, becoming angry, Haladhar said, "Listen, O low-caste fool!
I will dash [you] down with [your] elephant; say [your] observations with restrained mouth.
Delay is not good, as the elephant will die [1] immediately.
I tell thee loudly; at once obey what I say."

On hearing these words, angrily the driver urged on the elephant. As he charged upon Baladev Jî, the latter, swinging round [his] hand, struck such a blow that he, shrinking up [his] trunk [and] screaming, retreated back. Seeing this exploit, the greatest warriors of Kañs, who were standing looking on, despairing of their lives, [in their] inmost hearts began to say, "Who will be able to conquer these very powerful ones?" And the driver also, perceiving the elephant in retreat, feeling much fear, began to reflect in [his] mind, thus, "If these boys should not be killed, then Kañs will not leave me living." Having reflected thus, he again, goading on, inflamed the elephant, and urged [him] upon the two brothers. On coming up, having seized Hari with [his] trunk, [and] thrown [him] down, as he angrily squeezed [him] with [his] tusks, the Lord, making his body minute, escaped between the tusks.

Immediately all arose with fear,—gods, saints, citizens [and] women.
Having passed between the two tusks, [he] escapes; the Lord, the Treasury of Strength, gives the challenge;
He rises together with the elephant; then [in] sport [he] drives [him] along.
Immediately [the people] had a master,[2] having seen all the exploits of S'yâm.
Hearing the driving [noise, his] great anger was increased; twitching [his] trunk, again the elephant rushed [forward];
Murâri remained ensconced under [his] belly; thinking [him] gone, the elephant kept looking for [him];
Appearing behind, Hari again shouted out; Baladev went round in front;
They both began to make the elephant gambol; everybody was frightened [at] seeing [this].

Mahârâj! sometimes Balarâm, seizing the trunk, was pulling him; sometimes S'yâm [by] seizing the tail; and when he was coming to catch them, they slipped away. For some time they kept on sporting with it thus, as they used to sport with calves, in [their] infancy. At last Hari, seizing the tail [and] swinging [it] round, dashed it down, and killed it with blows. [He] drew

[1] *marihai* = *maregâ*.
[2] *sanâth* means "with a lord," or possessed of a lord or ruler; the implication being that, previously, the people were without a competent ruler.

out the tusks, then, from its mouth, blood, like a river, flowed forth. On the death of the elephant, the driver came defiantly; the Lord quickly slew him also, [and] threw [him] under the feet of the elephant; and laughing away, both the brothers, disguised as jugglers, each with a tusk of the elephant in [his] hand, went [and] stood within the arena. Then each of those who saw the beloved of Nand perceived him according to his own individual nature; the wrestlers esteemed [him] a wrestler, the kings thought [him] a king, the gods understood [him as] their Lord, the cow-lads [as] a friend, Nand [and] Upanand supposed [him] a boy, and the young women of the city [thought him] the treasury of beauty; and Kañs and the rest of the Râkshasas looked [upon him] as Death. Mahârâj! on looking at them, Kañs, being greatly afraid, cried out, "O wrestlers, seize [and] kill them, or drive [them] from before me."

As these words issued from the mouth of Kañs all the wrestlers, taking with [them] teachers, sons, [and] pupils, disguised in various ways, striking their arms [defiantly], for the purpose of joining [in battle], came round S'rî Krishṇa [and] Balarâm, on all sides. As they came on, these [brothers] also, gathering strength, stood [to receive them]. Then from among them Chânur, looking towards them, impertinently said, "Listen! to-day our king is somewhat dejected, therefore, to divert [his] spirits, [he] wishes to see your fighting; for you, having rusticated in a forest, have acquired all knowledge; but do not be anxious in [your] mind about anything; wrestle with us [and] give pleasure to your king."

S'rî Krishṇa said, "The King's Majesty, with great kindness, has invited us to-day; what shall we do to effect his purpose? You are exceedingly strong [and] accomplished; we [are] ignorant boys; how shall we join hands [in wrestling] with you? It is said [that] marriage, enmity, and friendship, should be made with equals. But we have no power over the King's Majesty; therefore we agree to what you say. Spare us; do not exert strength [and] fling us down. It is fitting to both of us [that] that should be done in which duty resides, and unitedly [we] should give pleasure to our King."

Hearing [this], Chânur, being fearful, says, "Your conduct is incomprehensible;
You two [are] not mortal children; [you] are some dissembling strong ones.
Playing [with] the bow [you] broke [it] in two pieces; Kubaliyâ was instantly killed [and] crossed [the ocean of existence];
[Who] fights with you, experiences no loss;[1] everyone knows these things."

[1] Meaning that, if killed, he obtains salvation by Krishṇa, as the elephant mentioned in the preceding line.

## CHAPTER XLV.

Krishṇa and Balarâm engage in a wrestling match, and kill their antagonists—Krishṇa then slays Kañs.

S'RÎ S'UKADEV, the saint, said :—Lord of the Earth ! with such-like statements as these, Chânur, striking [his] arms, confronted S'rî Krishṇa, and Mushtak came [and] joined battle with Balarâm Jî. Mutual wrestling began between them.

[They] joined head to head, arm to arm, eye to eye ;
Gripping each other's feet, leaping, clinging [together], snatching at, [and] shaking [each other].

Then all the people, looking on at both parties, began to say among themselves, "Brothers ! there is great injustice in this meeting ; behold ! what are these children, treasuries of beauty, [compared with] these powerful wrestlers, like thunder-bolts ! If [we] prohibit [the contest], Kañs will be angry ; if [we] do not prohibit [it], our virtue is gone ; therefore it is now not proper to remain here, because we have no power [in the matter]."

Mahârâj ! on the one hand all the people were speaking thus ; on the other, S'rî Krishṇa [and] Balarâm were wrestling with the wrestlers. At last these two brothers threw down [and] killed those two wrestlers. On their death, all the [other] wrestlers rushed upon [them] ; the Lord, in an instant, killed [and] overthrew them also. Then the worshippers of Hari, being delighted, severally played musical instruments [and] began to cry, "Victory ! victory !" and the gods, seated in their cars, [began] respectively to celebrate Krishṇa's praises from the sky, [and] to rain down flowers ; and Kañs, getting extremely pained, being agitated, [and] angry, began to say to his folk, "Fellows ! why are you playing instruments ? Is the victory of Krishṇa agreeable to you ?"

Thus having spoken, [he next] said, "These two boys are very wanton ; seize [and] bind them [and] take them out of the assembly, and seize the treacherous Vasudev, [and] Ugrasen along with Devakî, [and] bring [them along]. First slay them ; afterwards kill these two also." As soon as this direction had issued from the mouth of Kañs, Murâri, the friend of worshippers, in an instant slaying all the Asuras, [and] leaping up, mounted [the place] where, on an exceedingly lofty daïs, wearing a coat of mail, helmeted, with shield [and] sword, in great pride Kañs was seated. He, on perceiving this one near, like Death, in terror stood up, and began to tremble violently.

He wished from [his] heart to fly ; but through shame he could not fly. Raising up shield [and] sword, he began to aim blows. Then the beloved of Nand, watching his opportunity, was escaping from his blows ; and gods, men, saints, [and] Gandharvas, respectively seeing this great fight, being alarmed, were crying out, "O Lord! O Lord! speedily slay this wicked one." For some time the fight lasted on the daïs; at length the Lord, knowing them all to be pained, seizing his hair, flung him down from the daïs, and himself also leaped from above, so that his (Kañs's) life passed out from the body. Then all the people of the assembly cried out, "S'rî Krishṇa Chand has slain the fellow Kañs." Having heard this cry, gods, men, [and] saints were all exceedingly delighted.

The gods, delighted, again and again uttered praises [and] rained heaps of flowers;
Being pleased, [they] caused drums to beat, [and] said, "Victory! victory! Nand! Nand!"
The men [and] women of the town of Mathurâ [had] all their hearts expanded [with joy],
Having seen the moon-face of Hari, just as the beautiful lotus [in] the wood is expanded [by seeing the moon].

Having related the tale so far, S'rî S'ukadev Jî said to King Parîkshit:—Incarnation of Virtue! on the death of Kañs, his eight exceedingly strong brothers advanced to fight. The Lord killed [and] overthrew them also. When Hari saw that no Râkshas remained there, he dragged along the corpse of Kañs [and] brought [it] to the bank of the Jumnâ; and both the brothers sat down [and] took rest. From that day, the name of that place has been Viśrânta Ghâṭ.

Subsequently, having heard of the death of Kañs, the wives of Kañs, together with the wives of his younger brothers, being greatly agitated, grieving bitterly, came where, on the bank of the Jumnâ, the two heroes, with the corpse, were seated; and each severally looking on the face of her husband, [and] calling to mind the happiness [he had conferred on them, and] celebrating [his] virtues, in agitation falling about, were on the point of death.[1] Hereupon the Treasury of Compassion, Kânh, kindly going near them said,—

"Mother! listen; grieve not; give water[2] to uncle dear.
No one lives for ever; he [is] false who calls [anything] his own.
No one [is] mother, father, son, [or] relation; there is nothing but a succession of birth [and] death;
As long as a relation[3] remains with one, so long, by associating [with him] should one derive happiness."

1 *Lit.*, "began to die."

2 "To give water," means to pour out a libation of water mixed with sesamum seeds, to propitiate the manes. It is an essential part of the funeral obsequies; and is also called *tilânjalî denâ*, from *til*, "sesamum seed," and *anjalî*, the two hands held together like a cup to hold water.

3 *sanmand* is a corruption of *sambandh*, "a connection," or "relation." This word is not found in dictionaries, nor in Eastwick's Vocabulary.

Mahârâj! when S'rî Krishṇa Chand had counselled the queens thus, they rose up thence comforted, came to the bank of the Jumnâ, [and] poured out the libation to [their] husband. And the Lord himself, with [his] own hand, applying the light [to the pyre] of Kañs, performed his funeral rites.[1]

## CHAPTER XLVI.

Krishṇa releases Vasudev and Devakî from prison, places Ugrasen on the throne, and dismisses the cowherds to Brindâban—Krishṇa and Balarâm are invested with the Brahmanical thread, and pursue Vedic studies—He slays the Asura S'ankhâsur, and takes his shell as his own weapon.

S'RÎ S'UKADEV, the saint, said:—O King! the queens, together with the brothers' wives, having bathed, washed, [and] lamented, went thence to the royal palace. And S'rî Krishṇa [and] Balarâm, having come to Vasudev [and] Devakî, [and] having struck the manacles [and] gyves from their hands [and] feet, prostrating [themselves], stood before [them, with] joined hands. Then, perceiving the form of the Lord, knowledge came to Vasudev [and] Devakî. Then they, satisfied in their own minds, knew that these are both Creators; having taken incarnate form [and] slain the Asuras, they are come into the world to remove the burden of the earth.

When Vasudev [and] Devakî knew this in their minds, then Hari, the Searcher of Hearts, diffused his illusive power, [and] that removed the impression from their minds. Then again they esteemed him as a son; in the meantime S'rî Krishṇa Chand, with exceeding humility, said,—

"You, for a long time, have suffered heavy affliction; [and] are bearing us much in remembrance.

In this [there is] no fault of ours; because since you placed us in Gokul, [in] the house of Nand, we have been subject to others; we have had no power. But this was ever coming into [our] minds, '[We] have never given any happiness to her in whose womb, after remaining ten months, [we] took birth; nor have we[2] seen the happiness of [our] parents; [we] have wasted life to no purpose [in] the house of strangers. They have endured great affliction for us; from us nothing originated [for]

[1] It is the duty of the nearest relative, or successor, to apply the torch to the funeral pyre of a dead per·on.

[2] *ne* should come after *ham hîñ*, as Pandit Yogadhyân Miśra prints the passage.

their service. In the world they alone are capable who serve their parents. We remained their debtors, [and] were unable to serve [them].' "

Lord of the Earth! when S'rî Krishṇa Jî had thus stated the grief of his heart, then, with the greatest joy, those two [parents] affectionately embraced these two [sons], and feeling happy lost all [their] recent affliction. Having thus given happiness to [their] parents, both the brothers, proceeding on from thence, came to Ugrasen, and joining [their] hands, said,—

"Grandfather dear! please now to reign; to-day is a lucky day,—the stars are propitious."

As soon as this issued from the mouth of Hari, Râjâ Ugrasen got up, drew near, [and] falling at the feet of S'rî Krishṇa Chand, began to say, "Lord of Compassion! hear my humble petition. As you, having slain the very wicked Kañs with all the Asuras, have given happiness to worshippers, be pleased to sit on the throne; rule now over Madhupurî, [and] cherish the subjects." The Lord said, "Mahârâj! the Yadubañsîs have no regal rights; everyone knows this. When King Jajâti[1] was become old, he summoned his son Yadu and said, 'Give me your youth, and accept [in exchange] my old age.' Hearing this he reflected within himself thus, 'If I shall give youth to father, [he] having become this youth will indulge [sexually], in this sin will accrue to me; therefore, the not doing of this is better.' Having reflected thus, he said, 'Father! this cannot be [done] by me.' On hearing this, King Jajâti angrily cursed Yadu thus, 'Go; in thy family a king shall never be.'

"In the midst of this, his younger son named Puru, coming before [him] with hands joined, said, 'Father! give me your aged condition, and do you accept my youthfulness; this body is of no use [to me]; if it is useful to you, what can be better?' When Puru had thus spoken, King Jajâti, being pleased, gave his old state, [and] accepting the youthful condition of that [son], said, 'The succession to the throne shall remain in thy family.' Therefore, grandfather dear! we are Yadubañsîs; it is not proper for us to reign.

"Do you sit [on the throne, and] reign; set aside all doubt;
We will execute every order which you may give us;
He who will not execute your commands, him we will severely punish;
Have no other care [or] anxiety; [but] with justice give happiness to the subjects;
Those of the Yadu race who [from] fear of Kañs, having left the city have gone abroad,

[1] *Jajâti*, properly Yayâti, was a famous monarch of the Lunar race. The particulars of his life are related in the Sambhava-parvaṇ of the Âdi-parvaṇ of the Mahâbhârata.

Now search for, [and] recall them ; give [them] happiness, [and] cause them to dwell in Mathurâ ;
Worship Brâhmaṇs, cows, [and] gods ; give [your] mind to the preservation of these."

Having related the tale so far, S'rî S'ukadev, the saint, said :— Incarnation of Justice ! the king of kings, benefactor of worshippers, S'rî Krishṇa Chand, knowing Ugrasen to be his worshipper, having instructed [him] thus, [and] seated [him] on the throne, gave [him] the mark of royalty [on the forehead], and having displayed the umbrella [of authority], both the brothers, [with] their own hands, acted as fanners.

Then all the inhabitants of the town, being immersed in exceeding delight, began to utter thanks, and the gods [began] to rain down flowers. Mahârâj ! having thus placed Ugrasen on the throne, both the brothers took many dresses and ornaments with them. Proceeding thence, they came to Nand Râ,e Jî, and standing in his presence [with] joined hands, most submissively said, "How can we make [enough of] your greatness? if there were a thousand tongues, we should not be able to express your goodness. You, loving us greatly, cherished us as your own sons, [and] showed [us] tender kindness ; and [our] mother Jasodâ, also, loves [us] greatly, [and] fixes her affection upon us alone, deeming us always her own sons, never even mentally esteeming us as strangers."

Having spoken thus, again S'rî Krishṇa Chand said, "O Father ! having heard this declaration do not you think ill of it. We utter the thought of our hearts, [when we say] that you alone shall we call parents. But now, for some time, we shall stay in Mathurâ, [and] having seen our caste-folk, we shall hear the condition of the Yadu family, and, having rejoined our parents, we shall give [them] happiness ; for they have endured much misery for our sakes. Had they not conveyed us to your [place] there, they would not have received [this] affliction." Saying this much, [and] placing the dresses [and] ornaments before Nand, the chieftain, the Lord, having become free [from the trammels of] affection, said,—

"Express [our] respects to mother ; [and] do you continue to love us."

As soon as this statement issued from the mouth of S'rî Krishṇa, Nand Râ,e, being greatly dejected, began to sigh deeply ; and the cow-lads reflecting [began] to say in their inmost hearts, "They are saying a strange thing ; from this it appears to us that they treacherously wish to leave [us]; otherwise [they] would not have uttered such a harsh speech." Mahârâj ! at length, from among them, a companion named Sudâmâ said, "Brother Kanhaiyâ ! what work hast thou now in Mathurâ, that harshly abandoning [thy] father, [thou] remainest here ? [It] was well done [that you] killed Kaṅs ; all the work is accomplished ; now please accompany Nand, and having gone into Brindâban, rule [there]; having seen the royalty of this place, do not covet [it] in your heart; you will not get such happiness [here] as there.

"Listen! having seen royalty, fools forget [themselves]; having seen elephants [and] horses [they] are puffed out [with pride]. Do not leave Brindâban to reside anywhere else. There it is always spring-time. The beauty of the dense woods, and of the Jumnâ, is never forgotten by the mind. Brother! if you give up that happiness, [and] do not attend to what we say, [and] having abandoned the illusion of parental affection, should stay here, what greatness will be yours in [doing] this? You will serve Ugrasen, and night [and] day will be in anxiety. You will be subject to him to whom you have given the government. How will you endure this discredit? This is better than that, that you should not give pain to Nand Râ,e, [but] accompany him [back].

Reflect on the woods, streams, [and] sports of Braj; do not let the remembrance of the cows pass from [your] mind,
We will not abandon [you], O Lord of Braj! all will go along with you."

Having related the story thus far, S'rî S'ukadev, the saint, said to King Parîkshit:—Mahârâj! [when they had] said several such things, about ten or twenty remained with S'rî Krishṇa [and] Balarâm Jî, and they advised Nand Râ,e saying, "Do you, taking all [with you], go on before without hesitation; afterwards we, also, bringing these with [us, will] come along." On hearing these words, [then] became—

Disturbed [in mind] all the herdsmen; like [people] stung by a snake;
Irresolutely looking [at] the face [of] Hari; fixed, as a painted picture.

Then Baladev Jî, seeing Nand Râ,e greatly pained, began to counsel [him] thus, "Father! why are you feeling such grief? In a few days, having finished [our] work here, we also [will] come. We dismiss you in advance for this [reason], that our mother, being alone, must be disquieted; by your being gone [hence] she will be somewhat comforted." Nand Jî said, "Son! do you come with us at once, then, having met [your mother], return [here]."

Having spoken thus, becoming much agitated Nand remains embracing the feet [of Krishṇa];
[His] radiance was wasted away, [his] understanding dimmed, [he] could not retain the water of [his] eyes.

Mahârâj! when S'rî Krishṇa Chand Jî, free from illusive power, saw that Nand, the chieftain, together with the cowherd-lads, were greatly agitated, he reflected within himself thus, "[If] these shall be separated from me, then [they] will not remain living."

At once he released his illusive force by which all the world is kept in delusion. On [its] coming, it made Nand Jî, with all [the others], unwise. Then the Lord said, "Father! why do you regret so much? first consider this, that between Mathurâ and Brindâban the mere interval is what?[1] We are not going to any distance from you, that you [should] experience so much affliction. The people of Brindâban must be troubled, therefore we send you on in advance."

When the Lord had thus explained [the matter] to Nand, the chieftain, the latter feeling comforted, [with] joined hands, said, "O Lord! if it appears thus to *your* mind, what power have I [to gainsay it]? I am going; [I] cannot set aside your direction." As soon as this declaration issued from the mouth of Nand Jî, Hari dismissed Nand Râ,e, with all the cowherds [and] cow-lads, to Brindâban; and the two brothers themselves, with some of the companions, remained in Mathurâ. Then the cowherds, along with Nand—

> Went along all the way thinking deeply, like a gambler [who] has lost everything;
> Some [with] consciousness, some without consciousness; [with] staggering feet, falling in the way;
> Going [to] Brindâban, [but] looking [to] Madhuban;[2] [with] agitated frames, the pain of separation increased.

In this way, somehow or other, they arrived at Brindâban. On hearing of their coming Queen Jasodâ, much agitated, came running; and not seeing Râma [and] Krishṇa, becoming greatly distressed, began to say to Nand Jî,—

> "O husband! where have you lost the sons? you are coming bringing dresses [and] ornaments;
> [You] have thrown away gold [and] preserved glass; abandoning nectar, [you] have foolishly tasted poison;
> As a blind person, having obtained the philosopher's stone, [and] thrown it away, then, on hearing [its] virtues, strikes [his] forehead.

So you also have lost the sons, and have brought in return dresses [and] ornaments. Now, without them, what will you do with your wealth, O foolish husband? For whom, [on] the eyelids being closed, the breast is rent, say, without them, how will the time pass?[3] When they spoke to you of separation, how was your heart?"

Hearing these words, Nand Jî was much grieved, and, holding down [his] head, made this remark, "True it is that S'rî Krishṇa

[1] Implying that the interval is very short.

[2] *Madhuban* is a name of Mathurâ. (See note [2], p. 101.)

[3] Meaning that, losing sight of them during even the twinkling of the eye was the cause of anguish, what, then, must be the result of any protracted separation!

gave these clothes [and] ornaments, but I have no recollection as to who brought [them here]. And how shall I say what Krishṇa said? Having heard [then] thou, also, wilt become pained.

> Having slain Kañs, [he] then came to me, [he] uttered love-removing speeches;
> They became the sons of Vasudev; having fascinated our [affection, they] are gone;
> I, then, O wife! was astounded; [they] spoke of our nourishing [them].[1]
> Now, [do] not, O wife! say 'son' in speaking to Hari; know [him as] God, and continue worshipping [him].

Him, I, at the very first, knew to be Nârâyaṇ; but, [under] the force of illusion, [I] esteemed [him] as a son." Mahârâj! when Nand Râ,e Jî had related [these] perfectly true statements made by S'rî Krishṇa, then, becoming subject to the illusion, Queen Jasodâ, sometimes thinking the Lord her son, grieving in [her] inmost heart, repeatedly agitated, was crying; and sometimes, with wisdom, knowing [him as] God, meditating on him, celebrating [his] praises, [she] was losing the grief of [her] heart. And, in this fashion, all Brindâban-dwellers, whether women or men, saturated with the love of Hari, were saying various kinds of things; these I have not the power to describe; therefore, now, I am relating the sports of Mathurâ; do you listen attentively.

Thus,—When Haladhar and Govind, having dismissed Nand Râ,e, went to Vasudev [and] Devakî, then they, [by] seeing him, forgetting misery, experienced such happiness as an ascetic, having performed asceticism, feels when he gains the fruit of his penance. Afterwards Vasudev Jî said to Devakî, thus, "Krishṇa [and] Baladev have remained with strangers; they have eaten [and] drunk with them; and do not know even the customs of their caste; therefore, it is now fitting that [we] should send for [and] question the Purohit. What he may say, that we will do." Devakî said, "Very well."

Then Vasudev Jî sent for his family priest Garga Muni Jî. He came. This one, having told him all about the doubt of his heart, asked thus, "Mahârâj! now kindly tell us what is fitting for us to do." Garga, the saint, said, "First summon [by] invitation all the caste-brethren; afterwards, having performed the caste ceremonies, invest Râma [and] Krishṇa with the sacrificial cord."[2]

[1] *poshaṇ-bharaṇ*, is a compound substantive, meaning "nourishment," "maintenance." The separation of the compound has led to mistranslation here.

[2] *karma* implies the ceremonial observances practised by the members of the different castes; the *jane,u*, is the thread with which all members of the Brahmanical community are invested when admitted to participation in sacrificial acts.

As soon as this direction had issued from the mouth of the Purohit, Vasudev Jî sent an invitation into the city, [and] invited all the Brâhmaṇs and Yadubaṅsîs. They came, [and he] caused them to be seated with much courtesy.

Then, at first, Vasudev, according to prescription performing the caste-rites, had the horoscope written, [and] gave to the Brâhmaṇs ten thousand cows, with golden horns, copper backs, [and] silver hoofs, [and] draped in yellow silk, which [he] had vowed at the time of S'rî Krishṇa Jî's birth. Afterwards having a festival prepared, [and] having observed all customs [and] observances according to the prescriptions of the Veda, [he] invested Râma [and] Krishṇa with the sacrificial thread; and giving something to the two brothers, sent [them] forth to study learning.

They proceeding on, came to the place of a highly scholarly and very intelligent Rishi, named Sândîpan, of the town of Awantikâ, who was in the city of Kâśî. Prostrating [themselves, and] standing [with] joined hands before [him], with exceeding humility [they] said:—

> "Rishi Râ,e! have compassion on us; give heed, [and] bestow [upon us] the gift of knowledge."

Mahârâj! when S'rî Krishṇa [and] Balarâm had spoken thus humbly to the Rishi Sândîpan, then he very affectionately placed them in his house, and began to instruct [them] very kindly. After a time they, having studied the four Vedas, the Upavedas, the six S'âstras, the nine Grammars, the eighteen Purâṇas, the Mantras, Yantras, Tantras, Âgama, Jyotish, Vaidik, Kok, Sangît, [and] Pingala,[1] they became treasuries of the fourteen [branches of] knowledge. Then, one day, the two brothers, [with] joined hands, most meekly said to the preceptor, "Mahârâj! it is said that if one should take incarnate form [in] many births, [and] give bountifully [in each], still a [suitable] return for [the gift of] knowledge would not be given; but you, taking into view our ability, should order a preceptor's fee, then

[1] The four *Vedas* are the Rig-veda, Yajur-veda, Sâma-veda, and Atharva-veda; the *Upavedas*, according to the Bhâgavata-Purâṇa, whence the Prem-Sâgar originated, are four treatises on medicine, military science, music, and mechanics, respectively; but I suspect the term is here used as synonymous with Vedânga, or the six supplementary treatises to the Vedas, on phonetics, ceremonial, verbal inflection, etymology, metre, and the calendar; the six *S'âstras* are the six Darśanas, or schools of philosophy, named Mîmâṅsa, Vedânta, Nyâya, Vaiśeshika, Sânkhya, and Yoga; the nine Grammars, and the eighteen Purâṇas, or mythological cosmogonies, are self-explanatory; the *Mantras* are spells or incantations; *Yantras* are amulets or mystic formulæ; the *Tantras* are treatises professing to teach methods for the attainment of superhuman power, and other such mysteries; *Âgama* may mean "traditional doctrine," or a special treatise inculcating the worship of S'iva and his S'akti, but the latter is, probably, not the meaning here; *Jyotish* is astronomy; *Vaidik* or *Vaidya* means medical science; *Kok* a treatise on philoprogenitiveness, connected with ancestral worship; *Sangît* is the art of music; and *Pingala* is the name of the author of a famous treatise on prosody.

we, having given to the extent of [our] power, [and] receiving [your] blessing, will go [to] our home."

As soon as this statement had issued from the mouth of S'rî Krishṇa [and] Balarâm, the Rishi Sândîpan, having risen from there, went inside the house reflecting deeply, and he explained to his wife their secret, thus, "These [two], Râma [and] Krishṇa, who are both boys, are the imperishable Primordial Male; having taken incarnate form for the sake of worshippers, [they] have come into the world to remove the burden of the earth. I witnessed their sports [and] discovered this secret; for they who are studying uninterruptedly, again and again taking birth, even they cannot reach the bottom of the sea of knowledge; and, behold! with this state of childhood, in a very short time, these [two] have crossed such an impassable [and] limitless ocean. Whatever they wish done they can do in an instant." Having said this, then [he] added,—

"What should be asked from them, O wife?" Having heard [this], the beauty, having reflected, says,
"Do you go [and] ask [for our] dead son. If he be Hari, he will bring [and] give it."

The Rishi Sândîpan, with [his] wife, having come out from the house reflecting thus, facing S'rî Krishṇa [and] Balarâm Jî, [with] joined hands, humbly said, "Mahârâj! I had a son; taking him with [me], I with the family, on a certain festival went to bathe in the sea. Having arrived there [and] taken off [our] clothes, as [I] began to bathe, with all, on the bank, a great wave of the ocean came, [and] my son was washed away in it. He never came out again; some shark swallowed him; I have great grief for him; if you wish to give a preceptor's fee, then bring [back, and] give that son, and remove the affliction of our hearts."

Having heard this, S'rî Krishṇa [and] Balarâm, making obeisance to the preceptor and the preceptor's wife, ascended the chariot, proceeded towards the sea, for the purpose of bringing their son; and, proceeding on, after a certain time, [they] came to the shore [of the sea], when, perceiving them coming on angrily, the sea, having become terrified, assumed man's form, [and] bringing many presents, issuing from the water, came [and] stood before them, trembling [and] shaking, on the shore, and setting down the presents [and] prostrating [himself, with] joined hands, [and] head drooping, with great humility, said,—

"Great [is my] fortune! the Lord has revealed [himself]; what affair has occurred to bring you here?"

S'rî Krishṇa Chand said:—"Our preceptor divinity came here with [his] family to bathe; his son which you washed away with a wave [and] took, bring [back, and] return. For this purpose we are come here."

Hearing [this], the sea, with bowed head, said, "I did not wash away [and] take him ;
You are the preceptor of all, the Lord of the World ; [you] are the Lord [who] assumed the form of Râma.

I have greatly feared since then, and have kept within the limits [of my duty]." Hari said, "If thou didst not take [him], then who else took him away from here?" The sea said, "Lord of Compassion! I [will] explain this mystery. There is within me an Asura named S'ankhâsur, in the form of a shell. He gives trouble to all creatures moving in the water ; and if anyone comes to bathe on the bank, [he] seizes [and] takes them away. Probably he may have taken away your preceptor's son ; I do not know. Please come in yourself [and] see."

Hearing thus, Krishṇa eagerly entered, [and], going on, reached the centre of the sea ;
Upon seeing S'ankhâsur [he] killed [him]; rending open [his] stomach, [he] cast [him] out;
[He] did not find the preceptor's son in him; [he] said regretfully [to] Balabhadra,

"Brother! I have killed this one to no purpose." Balarâm Jî said, "Do not [be] anxious. Now do you bear this [as an emblem]." Hearing this, Hari made that shell his weapon. Afterwards, proceeding onwards thence, the two brothers came into the city of Yama,[1] the name of which is Sanyamanî (*i.e.* "restraining"), and Dharmarâj is the ruler there.

On seeing them, Dharmarâj rose from his throne, [and] coming forward, courteously conducted [them in]. Having seated [them] on the throne, washed [their] feet, [and] accepted [their] foot-water, [he] said, "Happy [is] this place! happy [is] this city! where the Lord having come, has manifested [himself], and has fulfilled the purpose of his worshippers! Now please give some command that [your] servant may execute it." The Lord said, "Bring my preceptor's son [and] give [him to me]."

As soon as this direction issued from the mouth of Hari, Dharmarâj went quickly [and] brought the lad, and [with] joined hands, humbly said, "Lord of Compassion! by your favour I knew from the very first that you would come to take the preceptor's son; therefore I preserved him carefully. Up to the present [I] have not given to this boy a [second] birth." Mahârâj! having said thus, Dharmarâj gave the boy to Hari. The Lord accepted [him], and immediately seating him on the chariot, proceeded thence, [and], in a certain time, bringing [him], stood before the preceptor. And the two brothers, having joined [their] hands, said, "Divine Preceptor! now what order is there?"

[1] Yama, the Regent of the Dead.

Hearing these words [and] seeing the son, the Rishi Sândîpan, being greatly pleased, gave many blessings to S'rî Krishṇa [and] Balarâm, [and] said,—

"Now what should I ask, O Murâri? [You] have given me a son [and] great happiness;
A disciple such as you [is] a great glory to me; [in] peace [and] happiness now set forth home."

When the preceptor had thus ordered, both the brothers, taking leave [and] prostrating [themselves], seated on the chariot, proceeded on from there [and] came near the city of Mathurâ. Having heard of their coming, the Râjâ Ugrasen, with Vasudev, [and] the citizens, both women and men, all rose up [and] hurried [to him], and having come out of the city, met [him], obtained great happiness, [and] spreading silken carpets, conducted the Lord, with sounding instruments, into the city. Then in every house festivities began to take place, and congratulatory songs to resound.

---

## CHAPTER XLVII.

**Krishṇa sends Ûdho to Brindâban to comfort the cowherds and cowherdesses.**

S'RÎ S'UKADEV JÎ said:—Lord of the Earth! I am [about to] relate the diversion how S'rî Krishṇa Chand remembered Brindâban, do you listen attentively. One day Hari said to Balarâm Jî, "Brother! all the residents at Brindâban, by remembering me, must be experiencing great grief, because the limit [of time] I had fixed with them has expired; therefore it is now fitting that someone should be sent there, that [he] may go, console them, [and] return."

Having thus advised [his] brother, Hari called for Ûdho [and] said, "O Ûdho! for one thing, you are a great friend of ours, for another, [you are] very clever, wise, and bold; therefore we wish to send you to Brindâban, that you may go [and] impart knowledge to Nand, Jasodâ, and the cowherdesses, [and] console them, [and] return; and bring Mother Rohinî [here]." Ûdho said, "Whatever order [is given shall be obeyed]."

Then S'rî Krishṇa Chand said, "First of all, do you cause knowledge to arise in Nand the chieftain, and in Jasodâ Jî, [and] clear away their mental fascination, [and] in this way counselling [them], say that they should think me near [and] abandon grief, and abandoning the idea [of] son, [they] should worship [me] as God. Afterwards say to those cowherdesses, who, for my service, have abandoned respect for the world [and] the Vedas, [and] day and night are celebrating the glory [of my] sports, and, [on] the hope of the limit [of my absence] being formed, have taken their lives in [their] hands,[1] thus, Do you abandon the idea [of] husband, [and] worship Hari as God, and give up grieving at separation."

Mahârâj! having directed Ûdho thus, both the brothers together wrote a letter, in which were written suitable courtesies, compliments, [and] blessings, to Nand, Jasodâ, the cowherds [and] the lads, and having advised all the young women of Braj [to practise] devotion, gave [it into] the charge of Ûdho, and said, "You alone will read out this letter; as far as you are able advise them all [and] return speedily."

Having uttered this message, the Lord, dressing Ûdho in his own clothes, ornaments, [and] crown, and seating [him] in his own chariot, dismissed [him] to Brindâban. He driving the chariot, proceeding on, for a certain time, from Mathurâ, drew near to Brindâban. Then what does he see there? that, on the trees of deeply embowered arbours, various kinds of birds are uttering fascinating melodies, and [that] hither and thither, white, yellow, brown, [and] black cows, like clouds, are roaming about; and [that], in various places, cowherdesses, cowherds, [and] cow-lads, are singing the glories of S'rî Krishṇa.

Rejoicing [on] seeing this beauty, [and] reverencing [it on] recognizing [it as] the place of the Lord's sport, as Ûdho Jî went near the village someone from afar, having recognized the chariot of Hari, came near, [and] having asked his name, went to Nand the chieftain [and] said, "Mahârâj! disguised as S'rî Krishṇa [and] with his chariot, someone named Ûdho is come from Mathurâ."

Upon hearing this statement, just as Nand Râ,e was seated at the village-green, in the midst of the assembled cowherds, rising up [he] hurried, and immediately went near to Ûdho Jî. Recognizing [him as] a companion of Râma [and] Krishṇa, [he] met [him] cordially, and asking [about his] prosperity very courteously conducted him to [his] house. First having his feet washed, [he] gave [him] a seat to sit upon; then causing six-flavoured food to be prepared, [he] hospitably entertained Ûdho Jî. When he (Ûdho) had fed with relish, then [Nand] had a nice white bed, [soft] as foam, prepared. After a time, when Ûdho had slept [and] arisen, Nand the chieftain went [and] sat near him, and began to say, "Tell me, Ûdho Jî! is the son of Sûrasen, our excellent friend Vasudev Jî, with his family, in happiness? and what affection has he for us?". Having spoken thus, [he] added,—

[1] That is, that they are ready to sacrifice if disappointed in their hope of meeting him again.

"Tell me the welfare of our son, with whom you ever remain;
Does he ever remember us? without him we experience great affliction.
Having said to all [that he was] coming, [he] departed; the interval has elapsed some time ago.

Continually arising, Jasodâ, having churned the curd [and] made the butter, puts [it aside] for Hari. Does Kânh ever remember her, and the young women of Braj, who are imbued with love for him; or not?"

Having related the story thus far, S'rî Sukadev Jî said to King Parîkshit:—Lord of the Earth! in this way keeping on asking news, and recounting over the former sports of S'rî Krishṇa Chand, Nand Râ,e Jî, saturated [with] the delight of love, having said thus much, meditating on the Lord, became silent.

He has slain the very powerful Kañs, and others; why should Krishṇa now forget us?

Meanwhile, greatly agitated, forgetful of personal considerations, mentally distressed [and] weeping, Jasodâ Rânî, having come near to Ûdho Jî, asked about the prosperity of Râma [and] Krishṇa, [and] said, "Tell [me], Ûdho Jî! how has Hari stayed there so long without us? and what message has [he] sent? and when will [he] come [and] show [himself]?" Upon hearing this, at first, Ûdho Jî read out S'rî Krishṇa [and] Balarâm's letter to Nand [and] Jasodâ; afterwards he began to counsel them, thus, "Who can declare the greatness of those in whose house Bhagwân took birth, and conferred happiness by [his] childish sports? You are very fortunate; for he who [is] the Âdi-Purush, the Creator of the eternal S'iva and Viranch,[1] who has neither mother, father, brother, nor relative, you are considering [and] treating him as your own son, and remain with your minds ever fixed in meditation on him. When can he remain far from you? It is said,—

Hari is ever near [those in] the power of love; who bears a body for the good of human-kind;
How can anyone be high [or] low, to one who has neither friend nor enemy?
Whoever bears in mind [his] adoration [and] worship, will unite with [and] become a follower of Hari.

As the bee takes away an insect, and moulds [it into] its own form; and as the female bee remains enclosed in the blossom of the lotus, and the male bee continues all night buzzing over her, [and] quits her not to go elsewhere, just so those who love Hari and meditate on him, he also conforms to himself, and ever remains close to them."

Having spoken thus, Ûdho Jî then added, "Now do you no

[1] *Virancha* and *Viranchi* are names of Brahmâ.

longer consider Hari as a son; esteem [him] as God; He, the Searcher of Hearts, the befriender of worshippers, the Lord, having come [and] revealed [himself], will fulfil your desire. Do not be anxious on any account."

Mahârâj! in this way, repeating and listening to various kinds of statements, when all night had been passed, and the four last *gharîs* remained, then Ûdho Jî said to Nand Râ,e, "Mahârâj! now it is time to churn curds; if I receive your directions, [I will] go and bathe in the Jumnâ." Nand the chieftain said, "Very well." Having said this, he remained seated there in deep meditation; and Ûdho Jî rising, hastily seated [himself] in the chariot, [and] came to the bank of the Jumnâ. [He] first removed [his] clothes [and] purified [his] body; afterwards, going near the water, [and] placing dust [on his] head, joining [his] hands, [and] singing the great praises of Kâlindî,[1] [and] rinsing the mouth, [he] entered the water; and having completed [his] bathing, washing, morning ceremonies, worship, [and] oblations, [he] began to pray. At that time all the young women of Braj also got up; and each brushing her house, swept, plastered, [and] smeared [with fresh cow-dung, and burnt] incense [and lighted] lamps, began to churn curds.

The churning of the curds thundered like clouds; they sang [and] the sound of their anklets was clanging.
Having churned the curd, [they] took the butter; [they] did the work of the house;
Then, all together, the fair ones, the women of Braj, went [for] water.

Mahârâj! those cowherdesses, distracted [at] the absence of S'rî Krishṇa, [and] singing his praises alone, in their respective companies, meditating [on] his love, began to sing the sports of the Lord, as they went along.

One says, "I have met Kanhâ,î"; another says, "He has gone off to hide;
Having caught[2] my arm from behind, Hari is standing [in] the shadow of [that] fig-tree."
One says, "[I] saw [him] milking cows"; another says, "[I] saw [him] at early dawn";
One says, "He is grazing cattle; listen, pay attention; [he] is playing the flute;
This road we will not go, Mother! the young Kanhâ,î will ask alms [of us].
He will loosen the knots [and] break [our] pitchers; having looked [at us] for a moment, he will steal [our] hearts.

[1] *Kâlindî*, an abbreviation of *Kalî Nadî*, "the black river." A name of the Jumnâ.

[2] *lukâ,î* and *pakrî* are Conjunctive Participles, for *lukâ,e* and *pakre*, under the influence of *Kanhâ,î*.

He is hidden somewhere ; he will come running [out upon us] ; then where shall we be able to go ? "
Speaking thus, the women of Braj proceeded on ; agitated [by reason of] separation [from] Krishṇa, [with] bodies heavy [from grief].

---

## CHAPTER XLVIII.

**Ûdho delivers his message—The cowherdesses are deeply distressed by it—They reproach Krishṇa for leaving them, but accept perforce the philosophy of Ûdho.**

S'RÎ S'UKADEV, the saint, said :—Lord of the Earth ! when Ûdho Jî had finished prayer, then having issued from the water, put on [his] clothes [and] ornaments, [and] seated [himself] in the chariot, as he proceeded from the banks of the Kâlindî towards [1] the house of Nand, then the cowherdesses who had come out to draw water, saw the chariot coming along the road from some distance. On seeing [it], they began to say among themselves, "Whose is this chariot coming along ? Look at it [first], then advance forwards." Hearing this, one cowherdess among them said, "Friends ! may it by no means be that that deceitful Akrûr has come [2] who took away S'rî Krishṇa Chand and caused [him] to dwell in Mathurâ, and to slay Kañs !" Hearing this much, another from among them said, "Why has this treacherous one come again ? Once he took away the source of our life, will [he] now take the life [itself] ?" Mahârâj ! saying various things of this kind among themselves—

The Braj women stopped there, having taken the pitchers from [their] heads [and] placed [them] down.

Hereupon, when the chariot drew near, the cowherdesses, having seen Ûdho Jî, at some little distance, began to say among themselves, "Friend ! this is some dark-coloured, lotus-eyed, crowned, garland-wearing, yellow silk clothed, yellow scarf dressed, S'rî Krishṇa Chand like [person], seated in a chariot, coming along looking towards us." Then one cowherdess from among them said, "Friend ! this one, indeed, came, since yesterday, to Nand's place ; his name is Ûdho ; and S'rî Krishṇa Chand has sent some message through him."

Upon hearing this statement, seeing [that it was] a lonely

[1] For *hî* read *kî*.
[2] *kahîñ . . . na*, "by no means." This very idiomatic phrase implies, "Let us hope that it is not that deceitful Akrûr come again !"

spot, the cowherdesses, laying aside all consideration [and] modesty, running [forward] went near to Ûdho Jî, and regarding [him as] the friend of Hari, prostrating [themselves], [and] asking about the welfare [of Krishṇa], with hands joined, [they] stood around the chariot on all sides. Perceiving their affection, Ûdho also descended from the chariot. Then all the cowherdesses, seating him in the shadow of a tree, seated themselves also all around [him], and affectionately began to say,—

"[You] have done well, Ûdho! [that] you are come; you have brought news of Mâdho;[1]
[You] remain ever near Krishṇa; tell [us] the message he delivered [to you];
[You] were sent for the sake of the mother and father; [he] takes thought of no one else.
[We] gave everything [into] his possession; [our] souls are entangled with [his] feet.
[He] is become quite selfish; now, giving pain to everyone, [he] is gone.

And as a bird abandons a tree destitute of fruit, just so has Hari left us. We gave all we possessed to him, still he has not become ours." Mahârâj! when, absorbed in love, the cowherdesses had uttered many expressions of this character, Ûdho, having perceived the firmness of their affection, as he was about to arise to make obeisance, a certain cowherdess, seeing a black bee sitting on a blossom, spoke to Ûdho [under] the pretence [of speaking to this].

"O honey-maker! thou hast drunk the sweets of Mâdhava's lotus-feet, for this [reason] thy name became Madhu-kar; and [thou] art the friend of the deceiver, on this account he has made thee his messenger [and] sent [thee]. Do not thou touch our feet; because we know [that] as many as are dark-coloured are all deceivers. Such as thou art, just such is S'yâm; therefore do not thou make obeissance to us. As thou roamest about taking sweets from flower after flower, and belong to none, so he also, having made love, belongs to nobody." The cowherdess was speaking thus when another black bee came. On seeing that, a cowherdess named Lalitâ said,—

"O bee! do you remain apart; go [and] tell this in Madhu-purî,—

Where the hump-backed queen and S'rî Krishṇa Chand are enjoying themselves,—Are we speaking [of this as the practice] of one birth? this is your practice in birth after birth. Bali Râjâ gave everything, [you] sent him to Pâtâla,[2] and a virtuous wife such as Sîtâ [you] turned out of doors [for] no fault. When you

[1] *Mâdho*, properly *Mâdhava*, "honey-like." A name of Krishṇa.
[2] *Pâtâla* is one of the principal hells.

made their condition [such as] this, what has happened to us?"[1] Speaking thus, again all the cowherdesses, together, [with] joined hands, began to say to Ûdho, "Ûdho Jî! we, without Krishṇa, are widowed; do you take us with you."

S'rî S'ukadev Jî said:—Mahârâj! as soon as this speech had issued from the mouth of the cowherdesses, Ûdho Jî said, "The message which S'rî Krishṇa Chand wrote [and] sent, I [will] expound [to you]; do you attentively listen. It is written, 'Do you give up the hope of enjoyment [and] practise devotion; I will never be absent from you.' And it is said, 'Night and day you are meditating on me; therefore no one is loved by me equal [to] you.'"

Having said this much, then Ûdho Jî added, "He who is the Âdi-Purush, the eternal Hari, with him you have made unending love; and him whom everyone describes as the invisible, imperceptible, [and] the inscrutable, you have regarded as your husband. Just as earth, air, water, fire, [and] ether are resident in the body, so the Lord is resplendent in you; but by virtue of illusion he appears distinct. Bear him in mind [and] meditate [on him]. He ever remains [in] the power of his worshippers.[2] And, from being near, knowledge [and] meditation are destroyed; therefore Hari, having gone, has made [his] residence at a distance. And S'rî Krishṇa Chand has also counselled me thus, 'Playing on the flute, [I] called you into the wood; and when [I] saw the manifestation of [your] love and abandonment, then I, joining with you, frolicked.'

When you forgot the God-hood, Yadu Râe vanished.

Then when you, by knowledge, meditated on Hari in [your] minds, knowing the devotion of your hearts, the Lord came [and] revealed [himself]." Mahârâj! as soon as this declaration had issued from the mouth of Ûdho Jî—

Then the cowherdesses angrily said, "[We] have heard [your] statement, now stand apart [from us];
You have told us of knowledge, devotion, [and] intelligence; [you say], 'Abandon meditation,' [and you] point out [to us] the sky.
Who calls him Nârâyaṇ whose mind is fixed on sport?[3]
He who gave pleasure from childhood, why has he become the invisible [and] imperceptible?
He who is endowed with every [good] quality [and is] beautiful in form, why has he become void of qualities and formless?
Since our souls [are] in [his] beloved body, who will listen to your words?"

[1] Implying that their little inconvenience is as nothing compared with the great injuries done to the others.

[2] That is, accessible to them, and willing to help them.

[3] Here Eastwick follows Hollings's mistranslation without noticing the word *ko* or the punctuation of his own text.

One friend, having arisen [and] reflected, said, "Let us conciliate Ûdho Jî;
Friend! say nothing to him; continue to look [on his] countenance [and] listen to [his] words."
One says, "[It is] not this one's fault; he is come, sent by Kubjâ;
Now he is singing the song which Kubjâ taught him.
S'yâm never speaks as this one has come into Braj [and] spoken.
Who can listen to such a thing, Mother! Having heard [it] a pain arises,—we cannot endure it.
[He] says, 'Abandon pleasure [and] practise devotion'; how will Mâdhava say such [a thing]?
Prayer, penance, self-restraint, vows, [and religious] observance,—all this [is] the practice of widows.
Live [from] age [to] age, young Kanhâ,î,—the bestower of happiness on our heads.
Who brings [into use] the ashes of cow-dung [while her] husband [is] living? Say; where is this practice current?
To us, vows, devotion, [and] fasts, in this world, [is] constant affection [for] the feet [of] the son of Nand.
Ûdho! who will blame you? Kubjâ causes all to dance this dance."

Having related the story thus far, S'rî S'ukadev, the saint, said:—Mahârâj! when he heard such expressions, imbued with affection, from the mouth of the cowherdesses, Ûdho, regretting in his inmost heart [his] having mentioned the subject of devotion, being ashamed, preserved silence, [and] remained with bent-down head. Then a cowherdess asked, "Say; is Balabhadra well? and does he also ever think of childhood's affection [and] call us to mind, or not?"

Hearing this, some other cowherdess among them gave answer thus, "Friend! you, indeed, are cowherdesses [and] rustics; and Mathurâ has beautiful women; being [in] their power, Hari disports [himself]; why should he now think of us? Since [he] has gone there [and] resided, O Friend! he has become the beloved of others. If at first we had known this, how would [we] have allowed [him] to go? Now, by regretting, nothing is gained; it is more fitting that, laying aside grief, we continue hoping [for the expiry] of the stipulated time; because, as [for] eight months, earth, woods, [and] mountains, with the hope of rain, endure heat, and that [rain] having come, cools them, so Hari, also, having come, will meet [us]."

One says, "Hari has accomplished [his] purpose; [he] has slain [his] enemy [and] taken the kingdom;
Why should [he] come to Brindâban? Why abandon royalty [and] graze cows?

Abandon, O Friend! [all] hope of the limited time; doubt should depart, [his return] has become hopeless."
One woman said, agitatedly, "Why should hope [of] Krishṇa be abandoned?

The woods, mountains, and banks of the Jumnâ, wherever S'rî Krishṇa [and] Balabîr sported, looking upon each place the recollection of Hari, our soul's lord, comes up." Having said thus, she added,

"This Braj has become an ocean of misery; [his] name [is] a boat [in] the midst [of] the stream;
[We] are sinking [in] the water of abandonment and separation; when will Krishṇa take [us] across?
[He] was 'Lord of Cowherdesses'; why is the remembrance [of that] departed? Is there not any shame at the name?"

Having heard these words, Ûdho Jî, reflecting in his inmost heart, began to say, "Praise to these cowherdesses, and to their fortitude, who have resigned everything [and] are absorbed in the meditation of S'rî Krishṇa Chand!" Mahârâj! Ûdho Jî, having seen their love, was in the act of praising [it] in his inmost heart, when, at that moment, all the cowherdesses arose, [and] stood up, and very courteously conducted Ûdho Jî to their abode. Perceiving their affection, he also went there [and] ate [with them], and having rested [and] related the story of S'rî Krishṇa, [he] gave them much happiness. Then all the cowherdesses, having shown [their] veneration for Ûdho Jî, [and] placed before [him] many presents, [with] joined hands, said with great humility, "Ûdho Jî! do you go to Hari [and] say, 'Lord! formerly you were showing great kindness; taking [us by] the hand, you used to lead [us] about; now, having attained nobility, [at] the suggestion of the city-woman Kubjâ, [you] have written [to us about] devotion. We weak, impure [creatures] are not yet become even the mouth of the preceptor;[1] what knowledge can we have?'

For him [we have] the affection of childhood; what do we know of the method of devotion?
Why is that Hari conferring union [and] departing?[2] this is not an affair for a message;
Ûdho! explain [to him, and] say, Our lives are going; come [and] preserve [them]."

[1] Meaning that they have never been instructed by a spiritual preceptor, and are therefore unable even to repeat what he may have said to them.

[2] Here is a complicated play on words. *Yog* means "conjunction," "union," and, therefore, spiritual union with the Divine, rendered in the translation by "devotion." Krishṇa counsels them to seek spiritual union; and they ask why he gives a lesson on *union* while *disuniting* himself from them. The name *Hari* is also used on account of its double etymology, from *hri*, "to take away," "remove," and *hri*, "to blush," "be ashamed." This is emphasized by the pronoun *we*.

Mahârâj! having said thus much, all the cowherdesses, meditating on Hari, were absorbed; and Ûdho, prostrating [himself before] them, rose from thence, seated [himself] on the chariot, [and] came into Gobardhan. There he stayed some time, then, when he departed thence, he went wherever S'rî Krishṇa Chand Jî had sported; and remained two or three days at each place.

At length, after a time, he returned to Brindâban, and going to Nand [and] Jasodâ, having joined [his] hands, [he] said, "Having seen your affection, I have stayed thus-long in Braj; now should I receive [your] command, [I] will go to Mathurâ."

On hearing these words, Jasodâ Rânî, going into the house, brought milk, curds, butter, and plenty of sweetmeats, and giving [them] to Ûdho Jî, said, "You will give[1] this to the beloved S'rî Krishṇa [and] Balarâm, and say to sister Devakî thus, 'Send my Krishṇa [and] Balarâm; do not delay.'" Having uttered this message, Nand's wife, being exceedingly agitated, began to weep. Then Nand Jî said, "Ûdho Jî, what more can we say to you? You yourself are clever, virtuous, and intelligent; on our part, go [and] speak so to the Lord that he, reflecting on the sorrow of the Braj-dwellers, may come [and] show [himself], and not to lose remembrance of us."

Having said this much, when Nand Râ,e shed tears, and as many of the Braj-dwellers, whether men or women, who were standing there, they also were all crying, then Ûdho Jî, counselling [and] instructing them, giving [them] hope, [and] fortifying [them], took leave, [and] taking Rohinî with [him], started for Mathurâ, and, proceeding on for a certain time, arrived at [the abode of] S'rî Krishṇa Chand.

On seeing him, S'rî Krishṇa [and] Baladev rose up [and] embraced [him], and very affectionately asking about his prosperity, began to inquire the news of Brindâban. "Tell [us], Ûdho Jî! are all the Braj-dwellers, as well as Nand [and] Jasodâ, in happiness? and are they ever thinking of us, or not?" Ûdho Jî said, "Mahârâj! the greatness of Braj, and the affection of the Braj-dwellers, is more than I can express. You are their life; night and day they are thinking of you alone. And I saw [that] the affection of the cowherdesses, is as the method of perfect worship. [As] told by you, [I] went [and] delivered the message concerning devotion; but I got from them the [real] secret of devotion."

Having delivered this news, Ûdho Jî said, "Compassionate to the humble! what more should I say? You, the Searcher of Hearts, know [the secrets] of every heart. In very few [words] please understand that in Braj, all [things], whether irrational or rational, without a sight of you, are very miserable; they are only hoping for the [expiry of the] limited period [of your absence]."

On hearing this statement, when both the brothers were

[1] *tum . . . dená*, a respectful form of the Imperative.

become dejected, Ûdho Jî, taking leave of S'rî Krishṇa Chand, having conveyed the message of Nand [and] Jasodâ to Vasudev [and] Devakî, went home; and Rohinî Jî, having met S'rî Krishṇa [and] Balarâm [once more], with great joy dwelt in her own palace.

---

## CHAPTER XLIX.

**Krishṇa redeems his promises to Kubjâ and Akrûr.**

S'RÎ S'UKADEV, the saint, said :—Mahârâj ! one day, S'rî Krishṇa, the sportive, the benefactor of worshippers, reflecting on the affection of Kubjâ, [in order] to redeem his promise, taking Ûdho with [him], went to her house.

> When Kubjâ knew [that] Hari was come, [she] had silk foot-cloths spread [for him].
> Rising, [she] showed great delight; the accumulation of former merit was all on the alert;[1]
> Causing Ûdho to take a seat, Murâri entered the interior of the palace.

Having gone there, he sees that, in a picture-gallery, a bright carpet is spread; on it a beautiful couch, adorned with flowers, is prepared. Hari went [and] reclined on that, and Kubjâ, going into another apartment, anointed [herself with] fragrant unguents, bathed, washed, combed her hair, put on clean clothes [and] ornaments, adorned herself from head to foot, ate betel, applied scent, [and] went towards S'rî Krishṇa Chand as amorously as Rati[2] may have approached her husband. And veiled from modesty, with fear at the first interview, she remained apart, standing silent. On seeing [her], S'rî Krishṇa Chand, the source of joy, taking [her] hand, seated her near himself, and fulfilled her wish.

> Then arising, [he] came towards Ûdho; smiling, [and] casting down [his] eyes, [he] was ashamed.

Mahârâj ! having thus given happiness to Kubjâ, taking Ûdho Jî with [him], S'rî Krishṇa Chand returned to his house, and began to say to Balarâm Jî, " Brother ! I said to Akrûr Jî that I would go see his house; therefore, first we should go there; afterwards, having sent him to Hastinâpur, let us inquire the news of that place."

Having said this much, both the brothers went to Akrûr's house. He, on perceiving the Lord, found much happiness, [and] bowing down [and] placing the dust [of Krishṇa's] feet

[1] The merit acquired in former births was about to be recompensed.
[2] Psyche, or the Goddess of Love, and wife of Kâma-deva.

on [his] head, [with] joined hands, humbly said, "Lord of Compassion! you have been very kind to come [and] show [yourself], and make my house pure." Hearing this, S'rî Krishṇa Chand said, "Uncle! why are [you] exalting [me] so much? We are your children." Having spoken thus, [he] added, "Uncle! by your merit the Asuras were destroyed; but there is only one anxiety in my mind, in that [we] hear that Pâṇḍu has departed [to] Vaikunṭh, and [that] by the hand of Duryodhan our five brothers are afflicted.

[My] aunt Kunti[1] is greatly troubled; who, except you, will go [and] console [her]?"

On hearing these words, Akrûr Jî said to Hari, "Do not be anxious on this point; I will go to Hastinâpur, and, having consoled her, will come [and] bring tidings of that place."

---

## CHAPTER L.

Akrûr is sent to Hastinâpur to inquire after the Pâṇḍavas—He finds them tyrannized over by the Kauravas—End of the first half of the story.

S'RÎ S'UKADEV, the saint, said:—Lord of the Earth! when S'rî Krishṇa Jî heard thus from the mouth of Akrûr, he dismissed him to get tidings of Pâṇḍu. He, having seated [himself] on the chariot, proceeded on, in the course of time reached Hastinâpur from Mathurâ; and, descending from the chariot, [and] going where Râjâ Duryodhan was seated on a throne in his court, saluting [him], stood [there]. On seeing him, Duryodhan, with the [whole] assembly, rose [and] embraced [him], and very courteously causing [him] to be seated beside him, [and] asking after his welfare, said,—

"[Are] Sûrasen [and] Vasudev well? Are Mohan [and] Balarâm well?

"Râjâ Ugrasen [is] beneficial to no one; he remembers no one;

"Having slain [his] son, he rules; he has no concern with anyone."[2]

[1] Kunti was the first wife of Pâṇḍu.

[2] This rendering is doubtful. For "well" we might substitute "good," and take the verse satirically; or it may be affirmative. In the second verse *kihuñ* is a misprint; Lallû Lâl wrote *kihi*; but to give the meaning I have ascribed to the passage it should be read *kehi hit*. *Kihi* is interrogative, and is the equivalent of *kis ko* (not *kisî ko*), and *het* is the poetic form of *heti*, "a sword" or "weapon"; this would translate literally, "To whom is not Râjâ Ugrasen a sword?" but this seems contradicted by the second half of the verse, "he thinks of no one." I favour Prof. Eastwick's version; Hollings is all at sea here.

When Duryodhan spoke thus, Akrûr listened [and] remained silent, and began to say in his inmost heart, "This is an assemblage of sinners. It is not fit that I should remain here; because if I shall stay, this [fellow] will utter many similar expressions. When shall such be heard by me? Therefore it is not good to stay here."

Having reflected thus, Akrûr Jî arose [and], taking Vidur with [him], went [to] the abode of Pâṇḍu. Having gone there, he sees that Kunti, from grief for her husband, with great agitation, is crying. Going near her [he] sat down; and began to console [her], thus, "Mother! no one has any power over Vidhanâ,[1] and no one, becoming immortal, continues living for ever. Creatures having bodies endure pain [and] pleasure; therefore it is not proper for man to be anxious; for by becoming anxious nothing is gained; there is only the giving of pain to the heart."

Mahârâj! when Akrûr Jî, thus advising [and] consoling, spoke to Kunti, she became thoughtful [and] silent, and, asking after his welfare, said, "Tell [me], Akrûr Jî! are my mother, father, and brother Vasudev Jî, with the family, well? And does S'rî Krishṇa [and] Balarâm ever remember their five brothers, Bhîma, Yudhishṭhira, Arjuna, Nakula, [and] Sahadeva?[2] These are here fallen into the ocean of grief; when will they come [and] save them? We cannot endure the affliction of this blind Dhṛitarâshṭra; because he follows the advice of Duryodhana. Day [and] night he continues plotting the destruction of the five [brothers]. Several times [he] has mixed poison; [once] my Bhîmasen drank that."

Having said this much, Kunti added, "Tell [me], Akrûr Jî! when all the Kauravas are thus inimical, to whose face are these my children to look,[3] and how shall [they] escape death [and] grow up? This is a great affliction; how shall I describe [it]? As a doe separated from the herd is terrified, so I also continue ever dejected. They who slew Kañs and the other Asuras, are my protectors.

"Go [and] tell [them] the affliction of the brothers Bhîma, Yudhishṭhira, [and] Arjuna."

When Kunti, thus humbly had uttered [these] words, Akrûr, having heard [her], wept; and exhorting [her] said, "Mother! be not at all anxious. These who are your five sons are very powerful [and] famous. They will utterly destroy enemies and wicked ones; S'rî Govind is [on] their side." Having spoken thus, Akrûr Jî added, "S'ri Krishṇa [and] Balarâm telling me this, sent me to you, 'Say to aunt, be not pained at anything; we are coming to you very quickly.'"

[1] Vidhanâ is a name of Brahmâ.

[2] These are the names of the five Pâṇḍava princes, the heroes of the Mahâbhârata war.

[3] *chahnâ* is one of the many words omitted from the Vocabulary. It means "to look towards," in the sense of expecting assistance.

Mahârâj! having thus stated what S'rî Krishṇa had said, Akrûr Jî, having counselled, consoled, [and] rendered Kunti hopeful, took leave, [and], accompanied by Vidur, went to Dhṛitarâshṭra, and said to him, "You are an old man, why are you acting so unjustly? in that, having become subject to [your] son, you have seized the government of your brother, [and] are afflicting [your] nephews? Where is this [deemed] right, that you are committing such wrong?

"The eyes being gone, it is not seen [in] the heart, [that]
the family is passing away, through wickedness.

Why did you, [when] prosperous without exertion [of your own], seize the kingdom of [your] brother, and afflict Bhîma [and] Yudhishṭhira?" On hearing these words, Dhṛitarâshṭra, taking the hand of Akrûr, said, "What can I do? No one listens to what I say. All these follow each his own opinion; I am become as a fool before them; therefore I say nothing in their affairs. Sitting apart, silently, I worship my Lord." When Dhṛitarâshṭra had thus spoken, Akrûr Jî, prostrating [himself], rose up thence, ascended the chariot, [and] proceeding on from Hastinâpur, came into the city of Mathurâ.

[He] told the words of Pâṇḍu to Ugrasen [and] Vasudev;
[That] the sons of Kunti [are] greatly afflicted, [and] their
bodies are become emaciated [with grief].

Having thus related to Ugrasen [and] Vasudev Jî all the news of Hastinâpur, Akrûr Jî then, going to S'rî Krishṇa [and] Balarâm Jî, [and] making obeisance, [with] joined hands, said, "Mahârâj! I went into Hastinâpur [and] saw [that] your aunt and five brothers are greatly afflicted at the hands of the Kauravas. What more shall [I] say? You are the Searcher of Hearts. Nothing is concealed from you of the condition and contrarieties of that place." Having spoken thus, Akrûr Jî, having delivered the message of Kunti, took leave, [and] went home. And having heard all the news, S'rî Krishṇa [and] Baladev, who are the gods of all gods, sat down, after the manner of men, and began to reflect anxiously on removing the burden of the earth.

S'rî Sukadev, the saint, having related the story to King Parîkshit thus far, said:—Lord of the Earth! what I have sung of the glory of the Braj-forest [and] Mathurâ is called the first half; now I shall sing the latter half, if I receive strength from the Lord of Dwârakâ.[1]

**END OF THE FIRST HALF.**

[1] *Dwârakâ* means "the gated," or possessed of many gates. It is the name of the capital of Krishṇa, on the western point of Gujarât, now submerged.

# CHAPTER LI.

## THE LATTER HALF OF THE STORY IS NOW BEING WRITTEN.

Jurâsindhu invades Mathurâ with a vast army, but is defeated—He attacks seventeen times with fresh armies, and is each time defeated—Nârad incites Kâlayaman to attack Krishṇa, and he advances with an army of barbarians —Krishṇa then abandons Mathurâ, and retires with his tribe to Dwârakâ on the sea.

S'RÎ S'UKADEV JÎ said :—Mahârâj ! I am about to relate the whole story how S'rî Krishṇa Chand, with his army, having conquered Jurâsindhu,[1] and destroyed Kâlayaman,[2] and effected the salvation [3] of Muchakund,[4] left Braj and went to reside in Dwârakâ ; be attentive, and listen heedfully. Râjâ Ugrasen, then, was ruling the city of Mathurâ with politic skill ; and S'rî Krishṇa and Balarâm, like servants, were obedient to his orders ; hence, the king and his subjects were happy, but, exceptionally,[5] the queens of Kañs alone, from grief for their husband, were very unhappy. They neither slept, nor felt hunger or thirst, but all day long were in a state of dejection.

One day the two sisters, with deep concern, said to one another, "As subjects without a king, and night without the moon, attain no splendour, so a woman also, without a husband, has no beauty. Now, having become husbandless, it is not good to remain here ; therefore it is better that we go to our father's house, and stay there." Mahârâj ! the two queens, having thus arranged between themselves, sent for a car, mounted upon it, and proceeding on from Mathurâ, came to their father's place in the district of Magadha ; and those two, with many tears, related to their father all the news as to how S'rî Krishṇa and Balarâm Jî had killed Kañs, along with all the Asuras.

On hearing this, Jurâsindhu angrily entered his council, and said, "What powerful ones are these who have arisen in the Yadu family, who have killed the very powerful Kañs, with all the Asuras, and have made my daughters widows ? I will at once hasten with my whole army to attack them ; and having burnt the city of Mathurâ, with all the Yadubañsîs, will bind Râma and

[1] This should be *Jarâsandha*, a king of Magadha and Cheḍi, father-in-law to Kañs. He was slain in single combat, by Bhîmasen, the second of the Pâṇḍava princes.

[2] This should be *Kâlayavan*, an Asura destroyed by a stratagem.

[3] *Lit.*, "caused to cross" [the ocean of repeated existences].

[4] This is *Muchukunda*, the son of Mandhâtṛi, who rendered assistance to the gods in the subjugation of certain demons.

[5] This use of *ek*, "one," is highly idiomatic. It means "special," "peculiar." "unique." Indians will sometimes say, *Angrezî log bhî ek bare hî dânâ haiñ*, "The English are singularly wise."

Krishṇa, and bring them alive; then is my name Jurâsindhu, not otherwise."

Having said this, he immediately wrote letters to the kings all around, telling them to come to him bringing their respective armies, as he intended to take revenge for Kañs, and to exterminate the Yadubañsîs. On receiving the letter of Jurâsindhu, the kings of all the various countries came on quickly, each accompanied by his army; and, on his side, Jurâsindhu also put the whole of his army into thorough order. At length, when Jurâsindhu, accompanied by the whole army of Asuras, marched from the district of Magadha towards the city of Mathurâ, there were with him twenty-three complete armies. This is the sum of a complete army:—twenty-one thousand eight hundred and seventy chariots, the same number of elephants, one hundred and nine thousand three hundred and fifty footmen, and sixty-thousand horsemen.

Twenty-three such complete armies were with him; and to what extent shall I describe how powerful each Râkshas among them was? Mahârâj! when Jurâsindhu, accompanied by the whole army of Asuras, noisily advanced, the guardians of the ten regions began to tremble violently, and all the gods to fly, through fear. The earth, from the mere weight,[1] began to sway like a roof. At length, in the course of time, he arrived, and surrounded the city of Mathurâ on all sides. Then the citizens, being exceedingly terrified, went to S'rî Krishṇa Chand, and exclaimed, "Mahârâj! Jurâsindhu has come and surrounded the city on all sides. Now, what shall we do, and where shall we go?"

On hearing this statement, Hari began to reflect a little. Meanwhile, Balarâm Jî came and said to the Lord, "Mahârâj! you have taken incarnate form for the purpose of removing the afflictions of worshippers. Now please assume a body of fire, burn up the forest formed of Asuras, and remove the burden of the earth." Hearing this, S'rî Krishṇa Chand went with him to Ugrasen, and said, "Mahârâj! Give *us* the order to fight, and do you, taking all the Yadubañsîs, protect the fort."

Having said this, as he approached his parents all the citizens surrounded him, and, with great agitation, began to say, "O Krishṇa! O Krishṇa! now how shall we escape from the hands of these Asuras?" Then Hari, perceiving that all, including his parents, were distracted by fear, admonished them thus, "Do not be in any way anxious; this army of Asuras which you see, in a single instant, in this very spot, will disappear, as bubbles of water vanish in a pool." Having spoken thus, and admonished and encouraged all, and taken leave from them, as the Lord advanced the gods sent two chariots for them filled with weapons.

[1] I have considered *bojh* to have been intended for a verbal noun, from *bojhnâ*, with which *nyârî* agrees. Both Hollings and Eastwick failed to give a good rendering of this passage.

They came and stopped before them; then these two brothers seated themselves on those two chariots.

The two Yadu-chiefs issued forth; they went and arrived amidst the army.

They came upon the place where Jurâsindhu was standing. On seeing him, Jurâsindhu, with much haughtiness, said to S'rî Krishṇa Chand, "O thou! fly from before me; how should I slay thee? thou art not my equal, that I should move a weapon against thee. Well! I will look at Balarâm." S'rî Krishṇa Chand said, "O conceited fool! what is this thou art chattering? They who are valiant do not utter great speeches to anyone; they show humility[1] to all. When occasion arises they show their strength. Are they at all worthy who sound their praises with their own mouths? It is said that what thunders does not rain.[2] Hence, what avails this useless chattering?"

On hearing these words, Jurâsindhu became enraged, and S'rî Krishṇa and Balarâm, retiring, stood ready. He also, with all his army, rushed after them, and shouting out, cried, "O wicked ones! where will you fly from before me? Having for a long time escaped alive, what have you imagined in your hearts? Now you will not be allowed to remain living. I will send you also, with all the Yadubañsîs, just where Kañs and all the Asuras are gone." Mahârâj! as soon as these wicked words had issued from the mouth of that Asura, having gone a certain distance, the two brothers again stood ready. S'rî Krishṇa Jî took all the weapons, and Balarâm Jî the plough and pestle. When the Asura army went near them, both the heroes, shouting, rushed at them as lions rush upon a herd of elephants, and began to smite with their weapons.

Then the drum which was sounding was roaring like a thunder-cloud, and the army of Râkshasas which had closed around on all sides overshadowed like masses of cloud, and the shower of weapons was like a downpour of rain. In the midst, S'rî Krishṇa and Balarâm, in fighting, were[3] as resplendent as lightning gleams in dense clouds. All the gods, seated in their respective cars, looking on from the sky, were celebrating the glories of the Lord, and were invoking victory on him; and the Yadubañsîs, along with Ugrasen, in great anxiety were regretting in their hearts, thus, "What is this we have done, that we have allowed S'rî Krishṇa and Balarâm to go into the army of the Asuras?"

Having related the story thus far, S'rî S'ukadev Jî said:—Lord of the Earth! when in the course of the fighting the greater portion of the Asuras[4] was cut to pieces, Baladev Jî descended from his chariot and bound Jurâsindhu. Hereupon, S'rî Krishṇa Chand Jî went and said to Balarâm, "Brother! release him alive; don't kill him; for he will go if living, and come again with

[1] For *dîtatâ* read *dînatâ*.
[2] Equivalent to "A barking dog never bites."
[3] For *lagne* read *lagte*.
[4] For *Asutoñ* read *Asuroñ*.

Asuras, and having killed them we shall remove the burden from the earth. But if we should not release him alive, the Râkshasas who have escaped will not come into our power." Having thus advised Baladev Jî, the Lord had Jurâsindhu released.[1] He went among those of his people who had fled, and escaped from the battle.

Looking all around, he says regretfully, "The whole army is vanished and gone;
My grief has become excessive; how can I live?[2] Now let me abandon my home and become an ascetic!"
Then his minister, advising, said, "Why should a wise person like you despair?
Sometimes defeat, and again there is victory; no one abandons government and country.

What matters it that you are defeated in the present conflict? Having collected our army afresh, we will come and send Krishṇa and Balarâm, with all the Yadubañsîs, to heaven. Do not be anxious on any point." Mahârâj! having thus advised and instructed, the minister conducted home Jurâsindhu and the Asuras who had fled and escaped from the battle, and there he began again to organize the army. On this side, S'rî Krishṇa and Balarâm, what are they seeing on the battle-field? A river of blood is flowing forth, in which chariots without charioteers are floating about, like boats. In various places dead elephants are seen lying like mountains; from their wounds blood spurts forth like fountains. There Mahâdev Jî, with ghosts and goblins, in extreme delight, is dancing and singing away, and forming and wearing chaplets of skulls. Female ghosts, goblins, and ascetics, keep on filling skulls and drinking the blood. Vultures, jackals, and crows, seated on the corpses, are feasting on the flesh, and fighting among themselves.

Having related the story thus far, S'rî S'ukadev Jî said:—Mahârâj! the Wind collected together as many chariots, elephants, horses, and Râkshasas as remained on the field, and Fire, in an instant, consuming the whole, reduced them to ashes. The five elements mingled with the five elements.[3] On their coming everyone beheld them; but on their going no one saw whither they had gone. Having thus destroyed the Asuras and removed the burden of the earth, S'rî Krishṇa and Balarâm, the benefactors of worshippers, came to Ugrasen, and prostrating themselves, and joining their hands, said, "Mahârâj! by your merit and power the army of the Asuras has been slain and driven back;

[1] This is an intensive compound. See *Hindî Manual* (ed. 1890), p. 190.

[2] *jîje* is for *jî,iye*, "it should be lived," and *kaise jî,iye* here means "How should I live?" The form *jî,iye* is parallel with the well-known *châhiye*.

[3] According to Hindû belief visible creation is formed from the five elements—earth, air, fire, water, and ether. These elements exist either free, or combined in specific forms. Death or destruction, therefore, means merely release from the compacting bond, allowing the elements to resume their free state.

now reign fearlessly, and give happiness to the subjects." As soon as this speech had issued from their mouths, Râjâ Ugrasen, feeling extreme delight, made great rejoicings, and began to rule righteously. In the meanwhile, after a certain time, Jurâsindhu, with as many troops as before, came again to attack; and S'rî Krishṇa and Balarâm Jî, just as before, again routed and slew them. In this way, Jurâsindhu came to attack seventeen times, each time with twenty-three complete armies; and the Lord again and again slew and drove them back.

Having related the story thus far, S'rî S'ukadev, the saint, said to King Parîkshit:—Mahârâj! while this was taking place, when some idea came into the mind of Nârad, the saint, then he suddenly arose and went to Kâlayaman's abode. On seeing him, he (Kâlayaman) arose, with the assembly, and stood up, and prostrating himself, and joining his hands, he asked, "Mahârâj! what has occasioned your coming here?"

> Having heard this, Nârad, reflecting, said, "In Mathurâ are Balabhadra and Murâri;
> Except thee, no one can kill them; nothing can result from Jurâsindhu;
> Thou art deathless and very powerful; Baladev and Hari are children."

Having said this, Nârad Jî added, "He whom thou seest cloud-coloured, lotus-eyed, with beautiful body, dressed in silk, and wearing a yellow scarf, his pursuit thou wilt not abandon without killing him." Having said this, Nârad, the saint, went away; and Kâlayaman began to organize his army. Meanwhile, in the course of a certain time, he collected together thirty millions of great and exceedingly frightful barbarians, such that their arms and necks were thick, their teeth large, their garb filthy, their hair brown, their eyes red like *ghũñghchî* seeds;[1] taking these with him, and with beating drums, he came to attack the city of Mathurâ, and surrounded it on all sides. Then S'rî Krishṇa Chand Jî, viewing his proceedings, reflected within himself, thus, "Now it is not good to stay here; for to-day this one has come to attack, and to-morrow Jurâsindhu also may attack, then the subjects will suffer affliction; therefore this is better that I should not stay here, but go with all of them and reside elsewhere." Mahârâj! Hari, having reflected thus, summoned Viśwakarmâ,[2] and instructing him, said, "Do thou go immediately and build a city in the midst of the sea, such that all the Yadubañsîs may remain happily in it, but may not know

[1] The *Abrus precatorius*, a bright red seed with a black patch on it, much like the eye of a crab.

[2] *Viśwakarmâ*, the Nominative sing. masc. of the Sanskrit *Viśwakarman*, means "the universal fabricator," or "all-maker." He is accounted the son of Brahmâ, and was the architect of the gods. His functions seem to have changed greatly between Vedic and modern times.

this secret, that they are not in their own houses. And, in an instant, convey them all there."

On hearing these words, having gone, Viśwakarmâ, having constructed in a single night a city of twelve *yojanas*[1] extent, in the midst of the sea, on the discus of Vishṇu,[2] as S'rî Krishṇa had told him, and giving it the name Dwârakâ, came and told Hari. Then the Lord ordered him thus, "At once do thou convey[3] all the Yadubañsîs there, so that nobody should know the secret of where they are come or who conveyed them."

When this direction had issued from the mouth of the Lord, in the very middle of the night, Viśwakarmâ transported all the Yadubañsîs, together with Ugrasen and Vasudev; and S'rî Krishṇa and Baladev went there also. Hereupon, hearing the sound of the waves of the sea, all the Yadubañsîs woke up, and, being greatly astonished, began to say among themselves, "Whence has the sea come into Mathurâ? This mystery passes comprehension."

Having related the story thus far, S'rî S'ukadev Jî said to King Parîkshit:—Lord of the Earth! having thus settled all the Yadubañsîs in Dwârakâ, S'rî Krishṇa Chand Jî said to Baladev Jî, "Brother! now we should go, protect the subjects, and slay Kâlayaman." Having said this, both the brothers went thence, and came into the Braj district.

---

## CHAPTER LII.

Krishṇa lures Kâlayaman into a cave, where he is killed by a glance from the awakened Muchukund—Krishṇa chased by Jurâsindhu up a mountain, where he is supposed to be burnt up; but he miraculously returns to Dwârakâ—Jurâsindhu occupies Mathurâ.

S'RÎ S'UKADEV, the saint, said:—Mahârâj! on coming into the district of Braj, S'rî Krishṇa Chand left Balarâm Jî in Mathurâ, and himself, the ocean of beauty, the light of the world, dressed in silk, wearing a yellow scarf, adorned with all ornaments, going into the army of Kâlayaman, suddenly appeared before him.[4] He, upon seeing him, said within himself, "Surely this is Krishṇa. All the marks which Nârad, the saint, pointed out are found in

[1] *yojana* is a measure of distance, about nine miles.

[2] The word *sudarśana*, "good-looking," or "beautiful," is the name of the discus with which Vishṇu or Krishṇa is armed.

[3] *pahunchâ,e de* is another intensive compound similar to *chhuṛâ,e diyâ* on p. 100 of text. See *Hindî Manual* (ed. 1890), p. 190.

[4] *ho nikalnâ* means "to turn up" in a more or less unexpected way.

this one. This one has slain Kañs and the other Asuras, and has slaughtered all the armies of Jurâsindhu." Thus reflecting in his mind,—

> Jurâsindhu thus calling out, said, "Why, Murâri, are you fleeing away?
> Come near; now act with me; stand still and fight;
> I am not Jurâsindhu nor Kañs; I will annihilate the Yâdava family."

O King! having spoken thus, Kâlayaman, with exceeding conceit, leaving his whole army behind, pursued S'rî Krishṇa Chand alone; but that fool did not know the secret of the Lord. Hari fled on just before him, and at arm's length he hurried on close behind. At length, fleeing on and on, when they had advanced some distance, the Lord entered into the cave of a mountain. Having gone there, he sees a man lying asleep. Hastily covering him with his yellow robe, he himself remained apart concealed. Afterwards Kâlayaman also, galloping and driving, arrived in that dark cavern; and seeing that sleeping man covered with a yellow robe, thought within himself that it was Krishṇa deceitfully sleeping.

Mahârâj! reflecting thus within himself, angrily giving a kick to that sleeping one, Kâlayaman said, "O trickster! are you pretending to sleep tranquilly, like an honest man? Get up; I am about to kill thee immediately." Speaking thus, he snatched away the silk dress from off him. He awoke from sleep; and when he angrily looked towards this [Kâlayaman], the latter, being burnt up, was reduced to ashes. On hearing these words, King Parîkshit said:—

> "O S'ukadev! explain this and say, Who was he who had gone and stayed in the cave?
> Why did the other become ashes from his glance? Who gave him that great boon?"[1]

S'rî S'ukadev, the saint, said:—Lord of the Earth! Muchukund, the son of Khattrî Mânadhâtâ, of the Ikshwâku race, was exceedingly strong and very powerful, whose fame in breaking to pieces the armies of his enemies was spread through the nine regions of the earth. Once all the gods, harassed by the Asuras, greatly alarmed, came to Muchukund, and very submissively said, "Mahârâj! the Asuras have greatly increased; now we cannot escape from their hands; quickly protect us. This custom has come down traditionally, that whenever gods, saints, or rishis became weak, Kshatriyas assisted them."

On hearing these words, Muchukund accompanied them, and went and began to combat with the Asuras. In this contest several ages were passed in fighting. Then the gods said to Muchukund, "Mahârâj! you have undergone much fatigue on

[1] The boon is the power of consuming another with a glance.

our account; now sit down somewhere and rest yourself, and give the body ease.

> For a long time you have fought; your wealth, house, together with your family, are gone;
> No one of yours remains there; therefore now do not set out for home.

Go wherever else you are inclined." Hearing this, Muchukund said to the gods, "Lords of Compassion! please kindly point out to me some retired spot, where I may go and sleep tranquilly, and no one may wake me." On hearing these words, being pleased, the gods said to Muchukund, "Mahârâj! please go into a cave in the Dhawalâgiri mountain, and sleep; no one will wake you there; and if anyone, knowingly or unknowingly, shall go there and wake you, then, on seeing him, he shall be consumed to ashes by your glance."

Having related the story thus far, S'rî S'ukadev Jî said to the King:—Mahârâj! having thus obtained the boon from the gods, Muchukund remained in that cave; hence, as soon as his glance fell upon him, Kâlayaman was burnt to ashes. Afterwards, the abode of compassion, Kânh, the benefactor of worshippers, cloud-coloured, moon-faced, lotus-eyed, becoming four-armed, bearing the shell, discus, club, and lotus, peacock-crowned, with Makara-shaped earring,[1] wearing a floral wreath and yellow silken robes, revealed himself to Muchukund. On seeing the form of the Lord, he prostrated himself flat on the earth,[2] then rising up, with joined hands, said, "Lord of Compassion! as you, having entered this very dark cave, by causing light have dispelled darkness, so now, by kindly imparting the mystery of your name, remove the doubt of my mind also."

S'rî Krishṇa Chand said, "*My* births, actions, and qualities are manifold; they can, by no means, be reckoned, though anyone should reckon ever so much; but I will relate the mystery of this birth, hear it:—On the present occasion I took birth in the house of Vasudev; therefore my name became Vâsudev; and I alone, having killed Kañs, along with all the Asuras, have removed the burden of the earth. And seventeen times, Jurâsindhu, with forces of twenty-three complete armies each, advanced to make war; he also was defeated by me alone. And this Kâlayaman, bringing a crowd of three *karoṛs* of barbarians, came to fight: he, by your glance, is burnt to death." As soon as these words had issued from the mouth of the Lord, having heard them, Muchukund became wise; then he said, "Mahârâj! your illu-

[1] The Makara is a fabulous animal, regarded as an emblem of Kâma, the god of love. It is also one of the nine treasures of Kuvera, the god of riches.

[2] The word *ashṭâng* means "eight members," that is, the eight members of the human body. There are several enumerations, but, for the purpose of prostration, they are the forehead, both arms, the body, the knees, and the feet. This implies that the body is brought "flat on the earth."

sion is predominant; it has fascinated the whole world. By reason of it, no one keeps in balance any remembrance or understanding.

You perform acts for the happiness of all; therefore you endure great affliction;
As a bone pricks a dog's mouth; he sucks his own blood;
He thinks it oozes from that very bone; he esteems a misfortune happiness.

And, Mahârâj! he who has come into this world, without your kindness is not able to issue from this dark well in the form of an abode; therefore I also am anxious as to how I shall escape from the house-formed well." S'rî Krishṇa Jî said, "Listen, Muchukund! the matter is just as thou hast said; but I am pointing out the method of thy salvation,[1] do thou do it. Thou, having obtained sovereignty, for territory, wealth, and women, committed grievous injustice, that, unless penance be performed, will not leave you; therefore, having gone into the northern region, do thou perform austerity. Having abandoned this your body, then thou wilt take birth in the house of a Rishi; then thou wilt obtain deliverance." Mahârâj! when Muchukund heard these words, he thought thus, "Now the Kali Yug is come." Thinking this, he took leave from the Lord, and having prostrated himself, and perambulated round, Muchukund went to Badrînâth; and S'rî Krishṇa Chand Jî came into Mathurâ, and said to Balarâm,—

"I have extirpated Kàlayaman, and sent Muchukund to the district of Badrî;
The army of Kâlayaman is dense; that has encompassed our Mathurâ;
Come; let us slay the barbarians there, and remove the burden of the whole earth."

Having spoken thus, S'rî Krishṇa Chand, taking Haladhar with him, issued from the city of Mathurâ and came where Kâlayaman's army was drawn up; and, on coming, both began to fight with it. At length, when, by fighting on, the army of barbarians was all slain by the Lord, he said to Baladev Jî, "Brother! now we should take all the wealth of Mathurâ and send it to Dwârakâ." Balarâm Jî said, "Very well." Then S'rî Krishṇa Chand had all the wealth of Mathurâ brought out, and had it laden on buffaloes, carts, camels, and elephants, and sent it to Dwârakâ. In the meantime, Jurâsindhu, again taking twenty-three complete armies, advanced against the city of Mathurâ. Then S'rî Krishṇa and Balarâm, in great agitation, issued forth, and going in his presence, showed themselves, and fled away, in order to obliterate the distress of his mind. Then the minister said to Jurâsindhu, "Mahârâj! who is so strong as to stand before

[1] *Lit.*, "thy crossing" [the ocean of repeated existences].

your Majesty? See! these two brothers Krishṇa and Balarâm, having abandoned all wealth and home, taking their lives only, through fear of you, are fleeing away naked-footed."[1] Hearing these words from the adviser, Jurâsindhu also pursued them with his army, thus loudly exclaiming,—

> "Why are you fleeing away timidly? make a stand and do something;
> Why are you stumbling, recovering yourselves, and trembling so violently? Your death is come near."

Having related this much of the story, S'rî S'ukadev, the saint, said:—Lord of the Earth! when S'rî Krishṇa and Baladev Jî, having fled, showed the manner of mankind, then all the recent grief departed from the heart of Jurâsindhu, and he became greatly delighted, such that any description of it is impossible. Afterwards S'rî Krishṇa and Balarâm, fleeing on, ascended a mountain, named Gautam, which was eleven *yojanas* high,[2] and went and stood on its summit.

> Seeing that, Jurâsindhu loudly exclaimed, "Balabhadra and Murâri have ascended the peak;
> Now how will they escape from us? Set fire to this mountain."

As soon as this direction had issued from the mouth of Jurâsindhu, all the Asuras went and surrounded that mountain, and bringing wood and doors from every town and village, arranged them all around. Placing on that old clothes saturated with *ghî* and oil, they set fire to it. When that fire blazed up to the peak of the mountain, those two brothers took the road from there to Dwârakâ in such a way that no one ever saw them going. And the mountain was burnt to ashes. Then Jurâsindhu, thinking that S'rî Krishṇa and Balarâm were burnt to death along with the mountain, felt great delight, and came with his whole army into the city of Mathurâ; and assuming the government of the place, issued a proclamation in the town, and established his station there. He pulled down all the old palaces of Ugrasen and Vasudev, and he had fresh ones built for himself.

Having related thus much of the story, S'rî S'ukadev Jî said to the King:—Mahârâj! in this way, having deceived Jurâsindhu, S'rî Krishṇa and Balarâm went and dwelt in Dwârakâ; and Jurâsindhu also, going from the town of Mathurâ, taking all his army, making great rejoicings, being free from doubt, returned home.

[1] *prâṇ le bhâgnâ* means "to fly for one's life"; *nange pâ,oñ*, "naked feet," a necessary consequence of any attempt to run in Indian shoes.

[2] Notice the abrupt, but idiomatic, change in construction here. *Lit.*, "S'rî Krishṇa and Balarâm, fleeing on, there was a mountain named Gautam eleven *yojanas* high, they ascended that," &c.

## CHAPTER LIII.

**The marriage of Balarâm with Rewatî—The birth of Rukminî at Kuṇḍalpur—Her beauty—Her father discusses in council a suitable husband for her—Krishṇa is generally accepted—Rukma insists on the choice of S'iśupâl—Rukminî sends to Krishṇa to lay her heart at his feet.**

S'RÎ S'UKADEV, the saint, said :—Mahârâj ! now hear the continuation of the story. When S'rî Krishṇa Chand, the source of joy, having killed Kâlayaman, saved Muchukund, deceived Jurâsindhu, and taken Baladev Jî with him, he went into Dwârakâ, then life came into the souls of all the Yadubañsîs, and happiness was diffused in the whole town. All the citizens began to live in peace and happiness. Meanwhile, after a certain time, one day, several Yadubañsîs went to Râjâ Ugrasen and said, "Mahârâj ! Balarâm's marriage should now somehow be effected ; because he is become capable." On hearing these words Râjâ Ugrasen called a Brâhmaṇ, and instructing him carefully, said, "O god ! do you go somewhere, and having seen a good family and house, effect the betrothal of Balarâm Jî, and return." Having spoken thus, and having sent for *rolî*,[1] unbroken rice, a silver coin, and a cocoa-nut, Ugrasen Jî made the sectarial mark on the Brâhmaṇ,[2] gave him the coin and the cocoa-nut, and dismissed him. He, proceeding on, went to the abode of Râjâ Rewat, in the country of Arntâ ; and having betrothed Balarâm Jî to his daughter Rewatî, and fixed the auspicious moment, he caused the *ṭîkâ*[3] to be brought by his (Rewat's) Brâhmaṇ, and brought him to Râjâ Ugrasen in Dwârakâ ; and he related all that had occurred there. On hearing it, Râjâ Ugrasen, being exceedingly pleased, called for that Brâhmaṇ who had conveyed the *ṭîkâ*, caused a festivity to be prepared, and accepted the nuptial gifts ; and having presented him with much wealth, dismissed him. Afterwards, himself, accompanied by all the Yadubañsîs, with much pomp, going into the country of Arntâ, effected the marriage of Balarâm Jî.

Having related thus much of the story, S'rî S'ukadev, the saint, said to the King :—Lord of the Earth ! in this way all the Yadubañsîs effected the marriage of Baladev Jî ; and S'rî Krishṇa Chand Jî himself alone, taking his brother, went into Kuṇḍalpur, and having fought with Râkshasas, seized Rukminî, the daughter of Bhîshmak Nareś, the betrothed of S'iśupâl, and bringing her to his house, married her. Hearing this, King Parîkshit asked S'rî S'ukadev Jî :—Ocean of Compassion ! in what way did S'rî

[1] *rolî* is a mixture of rice, turmeric, alum, and some acid, used by Hindûs to make the sectarial mark on the forehead.

[2] The *-kar* of the Conjunctive Participle has here the force of *-ed* in English ; *lit.*, "He *tilak*-ed that Brâhmaṇ."

[3] The *ṭîkâ* are the nuptial gifts which the relatives of the bride have to send to the bridegroom.

Krishṇa Chand go into Kuṇḍalpur, slay the Asuras, and bring away Rukminî, the daughter of Bhîshmak? Explain that to me.

S'rî S'ukadev Jî said:—Mahârâj! please listen attentively, I will expound the whole mystery of that place. There is a city named Kuṇḍalpur in the country of Vidarbh; there is a king named Bhîshmak, whose fame is spread all around. In his house S'rî Sîtâ Jî[1] went, and took incarnate form. As soon as the daughter was born, Râjâ Bhîshmak sent for the astrologers. They came, fixed the auspicious moment, fixed on Rukminî as the name of the girl, and said, "Mahârâj! it is our opinion that this girl will be exceedingly well disposed, good-natured, a treasury of beauty, and in good qualities the equal of Lakshmî, and that she will be married to the Âdi-Purush."

As soon as this statement issued from the mouth of the astrologers, Râjâ Bhîshmak, feeling very happy, made great rejoicing, and gave a good deal to some Brâhmaṇs. Afterwards, that girl began to grow up day by day, like a digit of the moon, and sporting about in childish play, gave pleasure to her parents. Meanwhile she became somewhat older; then she began to play many different kinds of surprising games with her friends and companions. One day, that girl with eyes like a deer, voice like a cuckoo, with eye-lash like the Champak flower, and face like the moon, went to play blind man's buff with her friends. Then at the time of play all the companions began to say to her, "Rukminî! thou art come to spoil our fun; for where thou art hiding in the dark with us, there is light from thy moon-like face, therefore we cannot hide." Hearing this, she smiled and remained silent.

Having related the tale thus far, S'rî S'ukadev said:—Mahârâj! in this way she was sporting with her friends, and day by day her beauty was doubling, when unexpectedly[2] Nârad Jî came into Kuṇḍalpur, and, having seen Rukminî, went into Dwârakâ to S'rî Krishṇa Chand, and said to him, "Mahârâj! in Kuṇḍalpur, in the house of Râjâ Bhîshmak, there is born a daughter, a mine of beauty, excellence, and amiability, the rival of[3] Lakshmî; she is suitable for you." From the time when this secret was heard[4] from Nârad, the saint, Hari set his mind[5] upon her night and day. Mahârâj! by this process S'rî Krishṇa Chand heard of the name and qualities of Rukminî; and I will relate how Rukminî heard of the name and fame of the Lord. On one occasion, several mendicants from various countries went into Kuṇḍalpur, and celebrated the glories of S'rî Krishṇa Chand, recounting how the

[1] For *Sîtâ kî* read *Sîtâ Jî* in text. Sîtâ was the bride of the illustrious hero Râma.

[2] The *ki* marks transition of thought, and the phrase implies that the visit occurred in the midst of the circumstances related, in a somewhat unexpected manner.

[3] For *kâ* read *kî*.

[4] The verb *sun pânâ* means "to get to hear," "to come to know of"; but there is no Nominative in the sentence, and Lallû Lâl has treated it as a Passive.

[5] This may equally well be rendered by "fixed his heart."

Lord took birth in Mathurâ, and having gone into Gokul and Brindâban and joined the cowherd lads, indulged in childish sports, and having slain the Asuras, and removed the burden of the earth, had given happiness to the Yadubaṅsîs. On hearing of the actions of Hari, all the citizens with great astonishment began to say among themselves, "When shall we see with our eyes him of whose sports we have heard with our ears?" In the midst of this, by some means, the mendicants went into the court of Râjâ Bhîshmak and began to celebrate the exploits and virtues of the Lord. Then—

> The beautiful Rukminî ascended a balcony; the sound of Hari's actions fell on her ears;
> She is astonished, her mind is spell-bound; then, peeping, she wishes to see;
> Having heard, the Princess remained attentive; the creeping-plant of love sprang up in her bosom.
> The beautiful one was absorbed and agitated with emotion; Hari's virtues deprived her of consciousness and sense.

Having spoken thus, S'rî S'ukadev Jî said:—Lord of the Earth! in this way S'rî Rukminî Jî heard of the fame and name of the Lord. Then, from that very day, night and day, during the eight watches or sixty-four *gharîs*,[1] she continues thinking of him while sleeping, waking, sitting, standing, walking, moving about, eating, drinking, or playing; and is constantly celebrating his virtues. Continually she rises early in the morning, and having bathed and made an earthen image of Gaurî,[2] and having offered *rolî*, unbroken rice, and flowers, and propitiated her with incense, lamps, and consecrated food, with joined hands and bowed head, constantly says before her,—

> "Do you, O Gaurî! have pity on me; give the Lord of the Yadus for husband, and remove my affliction."

In this way Rukminî began to pass her time. One day she was playing with her companions, when Râjâ Bhîshmak, seeing her, thinking within himself, began to say, "This one is now become marriageable; should we not speedily give her somewhere, people will ridicule us. It is said that, 'In whose house there may be a grown-up daughter, his alms-giving, virtuous conduct, prayer, and penance, are useless; because, from what is done, no virtue accrues, until he be discharged from the debt due to his daughter.'"[3] Having reflected thus, Râjâ Bhîshmak

[1] These are alternative expressions for the whole day.

[2] Gaurî, "the brilliant," is a name of the goddess Pârvati, the wife of S'iva. But the word *Gaur* or *Gaurî* is here used because Rukminî being under the marriageable age, she herself was a *gaur*, and therefore turned to Pârvati under the form Gaur. The word also means "turmeric," a colour used in marriage ceremonies.

[3] A sacred obligation rests on every Hindû to see that his daughter is not unmarried when she attains puberty.

came into his court, and summoning all his councillors and family folk, said, "Brothers! my daughter is become marriageable, on this account we should search somewhere for a respectable, virtuous, handsome, and well-disposed husband."

On hearing these words, those people recounted the family, virtues, personal appearance, and prowess of the kings of various countries; but what anyone said made no impression on the mind of Râjâ Bhîshmak. Then his eldest son, whose name was Rukma, began to say, "Father! S'isupâl, the king of the city of Chanderî, is very powerful, and in every respect our equal. Let us betroth Rukminî to him there, and get reputation in the world." Mahârâj! when the king made as if he did not hear what he also said, then his younger son Rukmakeś said,—

"Father! let us give Rukminî to Krishṇa; let us betroth her to Vâsudev;"[1]
Hearing this, Bhîshmak says delightedly, "O son! thou hast said well;[2]
Thou, child! art much wiser than all; I approve of what you said.

It is said,—

By inquiring of small and great, make your resolve sure;
Accept the gist of the statement; this is the way of the world."

Having spoken thus, Râjâ Bhîshmak added, "This is good counsel uttered by Rukmakeś. Among the Yadubaṅsîs, Râjâ Sûrasen has become very famous and powerful; Vasudev Jî is *his* son. How great are they in whose house the Âdi-Purush, the indestructible, god of all gods, S'rî Krishṇa Chand Jî, took birth, and destroyed the very powerful Kaṅs and the other Râkshasas; and having removed the burden of the earth, gave splendour to the Yadu family; and gave happiness to the subjects as well as all the Yadubaṅsîs! So, if we give Rukminî to S'rî Krishṇa Chand Jî, Lord of Dwârakâ, then we shall acquire fame and greatness in the world." On hearing these words, all the members of the assembly, being greatly pleased, said, "Mahârâj! this has been thought out by you; such a husband and house will not be met with elsewhere. This is best, that we should marry Rukminî to S'rî Krishṇa Chand alone." Mahârâj! when all the members of the council had thus spoken, then Râjâ Bhîshmak's eldest son, whose name was Rukma, hearing it, petulantly said,—

"These great blockheads are talking without understanding; they do not know Krishṇa's circumstances;

[1] *Vasudev* is used for *Vâsudev* in text, on account of the metre.
[2] *teṅ* is for *taiṅ*, "by thee." This is made clear by Pandit Yogadhyân Miśra's punctuation: *kahî, pût! teṅ nîkî bât.*

He has remained sixteen years with Nand, then everyone called him a cowherd ;
Clothed in a blanket he grazed cows ; seated in the cow-field he ate his labourer's fare ;

He is a village cowherd. What is there stable about his genealogy? Whose son can we call him, the secret of whose very parents is unknown? One thinks him of Nand the cowherd ; another esteems him as [1] of Vasudev ; but up to the present time no one has yet discovered the secret as to whose son Krishṇa is ; therefore anyone says what comes in his mind. Mahârâj! everybody knows and respects us ; but when did the Yadubansîs become kings? What does it signify that, a short time since, by strength, they have acquired greatness ; the former stain will not now pass away. He is called the servant of Ugrasen ; shall we get any fame in the world by a betrothal with him? It is said, 'Marriage, enmity, and friendship should be made with equals, then lustre is obtained.' [2] If we give her to Krishṇa, people will say, 'The brother-in-law [3] of a cowherd!' From that all our name and fame will depart."

Mahârâj! having spoken thus, Rukma added, "S'iśupâl, the king of the city of Chanderî, is very strong and powerful ; from fear of him all tremble violently ; and royalty has come down in his house from antiquity ; therefore it is now best that Rukminî should be given to him, and Krishṇa's name even should not again be brought before me." On hearing these words, the people of the council, through fear, feeling deep regret in their hearts, remained silent ; and Râjâ Bhîshmak also said nothing. Hereupon, Rukma, summoning astrologers, fixed the propitious day and moment, and sent the nuptial gift to Râjâ S'iśupâl's place, by the hand of a Brâhmaṇ. That Brâhmaṇ, taking the nuptial gift, proceeded on, and going into the city of Chanderî, arrived in the court of Râjâ S'iśupâl. On seeing him, the king, making obeisance, asked the Brâhmaṇ, "Tell me, O Divinity! whence come you? and with what object are you come?" Then that Brâhmaṇ, giving a blessing, related all the circumstances of his going. On hearing him, being pleased, Râjâ S'iśupâl, summoning his Purohit, accepted the nuptial gifts, and giving something considerable to that Brâhmaṇ, dismissed him. Afterwards he invited Jurâsindhu and all other kings of the various countries. They, each bringing his army, came ; then this one also, taking his army, went forth to the marriage. That Brâhmaṇ came and told Râjâ Bhîshmak that he had taken the nuptial gift, saying, "Mahârâj! I, having given the present to Râjâ S'iśupâl, am

[1] This use of *kar* to express "as" is very idiomatic.

[2] Here we have two more Aoristic Passives parallel to *châhiye*, "it should be wished." In Panjâbî the Passive is regularly formed by the insertion of *î*. In both cases it is a survival of the Sanskrit Passive form.

[3] A grossly immoral innuendo is conveyed under this term.

returned ; he, with much pomp, leading the marriage procession is coming to the wedding ; do you do your duty."

Hearing this, Râjâ Bhîshmak, at first, was greatly dejected; afterwards, having reflected somewhat, he went into the palace and told his queen. She, having heard, inviting musicians and all the ladies of the family, had festivities prepared, and began to perform all the customary ceremonies of marriage. Then the king, coming out, ordered his chiefs and ministers to collect together all the things which they should have in the marriage of a girl. On receiving the king's order, the advisers and chiefs prepared and sent for everything immediately, and brought and laid them before him. The people saw and heard; then this rumour spread about the city, that the marriage of Rukminî with S'rî Krishṇa Chand was in progress; that the wicked Rukma did not allow to take place ; now it will be with S'iśupâl.

Having related the story thus far, S'rî S'ukadev Jî said to King Parîkshit :—Lord of the Earth ! in the city, then, this was the talk in each house, and in the palace the women, singing and playing music, were performing the customary ceremonies. The Brâhmaṇs, reciting and reciting the Vedas, were having the marriage ceremonies performed. In various places drums were being beaten. Again and again posts of sprouting plantain were being fixed in the ground ; golden vessels were being filled, and the people were placing them down ; and garlands and wreaths of flowers they were fastening ; and in one direction the citizens were sweeping and cleansing, quite separately, the markets, roads, and squares, and covering them with silk canopies. In this way both in and out of the house a bustle was going on, when, just then, two or three friends went and said to Rukminî,—

> " Rukma has given thee to S'iśupâl ; now, Rukminî ! thou hast become a queen."
>
> Thinking, and bowing her head, she said, " The Lord of the World is mine, by heart, acknowledgment, and vow ! "[1]

Having said this, Rukminî, in much anxiety, sent for a Brâhmaṇ, and joining her hands, supplicated and extolled him highly, and having explained to him all her desire, said, " Mahârâj ! take my message to Ḍwârakâ, and delivering it to the Lord of Dwârakâ, get him to come with you; then I shall be deeply grateful to you,[2] and shall know this, that you alone, compassionately, have given me S'rî Krishṇa as husband."

On hearing these words the Brâhmaṇ said, " Good ! tell me

[1] The absence of verb or inflexion, save the one word *mere*, "of me," renders the meaning very obscure. Eastwick is altogether wrong ; Hollings catches the import, and that is all. The *Sukha-Sâgar* gives the clue by the prose rendering, *Mere swâmî manasâ-vâchâ-karmanâ se S'yâmasundar Vaikunṭhanâth haiñ*, " My husband, by thought, word, and deed, is S'yâmasundar, the Lord of Vaikunṭh."

[2] *Lit.*, " I will acknowledge your great virtue."

the message and I will take it, and will repeat it to S'rî Krishṇa Chand. He is the Lord of Compassion; if he will condescend to come with me, I will bring him." When this declaration had issued from the mouth of the Brâhmaṇ, Rukminî, at once writing an affectionate letter, gave it into his possession, and said, "Give the letter to S'rî Krishṇa Chand, the source of joy, and tell him from me, that this servant, with joined hands and great humility, says that 'You are the Searcher of Hearts, and know the thoughts[1] of every mind; what more shall I say? I have taken refuge with you; now my modesty is your affair;[2] do that by which it may be preserved, and, coming to this servant, speedily reveal yourself.'"

Mahârâj! this having been said and heard, when Rukminî dismissed the Brâhmaṇ, he, meditating on the Lord and calling on his name, set out for Dwârakâ, and, through his desire for Hari, arrived there at the mere saying of a word.[3] Going there, he saw that the city is in the midst of the sea, and that all around it there are very great mountains, and woods and groves give their splendour, in which the cries of various animals and the notes of birds resound; and beautiful lakes filled with pure water, in which lotuses are blooming, upon which swarms on swarms of bees are humming; and, on the bank, geese and cranes are disporting themselves; gardens of fruits and flowers of various kinds extend for miles; on the borders of these betel gardens are flourishing. At the pits and wells, gardeners are standing, singing sweet melodies, working the water-wheels and buckets, and irrigating with water high and low objects; and crowds upon crowds of water-bearing women were at the landing-stairs.

Beholding this beauty, and being delighted, as that Brâhmaṇ advanced onwards, what does he see? All around the city is a very lofty rampart, in which are four gateways, in which are gold-inlaid and jewel-studded panels; and within the city are glittering gold, silver, and jewel-studded, five-storeyed and seven-storeyed palaces, so high that they conversed with the clouds, the spires and pinnacles of which are brilliant as lightning. Various coloured flags and standards are fluttering; from windows, casements, apertures, and lattice-work, fragrant odours are emanating; at each door are placed posts of sprouting plantain, and golden vessels filled; garlands and wreaths are suspended, and in every house joyful instruments are sounding; in various places, stories, legends, and conversations about Hari are going on; the eighteen castes are dwelling in ease and happiness; and the discus called Sudarśan protects the city.

Having related the story thus far, S'rî S'ukadev Jî said:—

[1] The word *bât* is here understood.

[2] Notice the Dative, "to you," meaning that the thing spoken of "relates to" or is "concerned with" the person addressed.

[3] Meaning, "in the time required for the utterance of a word," or "immediately."

Râjâ! looking on at such a beautiful and pleasing city of Dwârakâ, that Brâhmaṇ entered and stood in the court of Râjâ Ugrasen, and giving a benediction, he asked, "Where is S'rî Krishṇa Chand?" Then someone pointed out to him the palace of Hari. When he went and stood there, the door-porter, seeing him, prostrated himself and asked,—

"Who are you, and whence come? The letter of what country have you brought?"

He said, "I am a Brâhmaṇ, and a resident of Kuṇḍalpur. I am come to deliver the letter of Rukminî, the daughter of Râjâ Bhîshmak, to S'rî Krishṇa Chand." On hearing these words, the door-keeper said, "Mahârâj! Sir, be pleased to enter the palace. S'rî Krishṇa Chand is opposite, resplendent on a throne." Having heard that statement, the Brâhmaṇ went inside; then Hari, on seeing him, descended from the throne, prostrated himself, and showed great respect; and placing him on the throne, washed his feet, and drank his foot-water, and began to perform the service which one renders to a tutelary deity. At length, having applied fragrant unguents, and bathed and washed him, and caused him to partake of six-flavoured food; next, he gave betel, and perfumed him with saffron and sandal, placed on him a necklace of flowers, conducted him into a jewelled palace, and caused him to repose on a handsome jewel-studded couch. Mahârâj! he also fatigued by the journey was very tired indeed;[1] on lying down he obtained rest, and slept. S'rî Krishṇa Jî, for a certain time, then, sat there desirous of hearing what he had to say. He was constantly saying in his inmost heart, "Now he will get up, Now he will get up." At last, when he saw that he did not rise, seating himself at his feet, he began to rub his feet. Hereupon his sleep was broken, and he arose and sat up. Then Hari, inquiring after his welfare, asked,—

"Is your king and country well?[2] Tell us your commission;
What purpose are you come for, and by showing yourself have given us happiness?"

The Brâhmaṇ said, "Abode of Compassion! please give heed and listen; I am about to relate the cause of my coming. Mahârâj! the daughter of Râjâ Bhîshmak of Kuṇḍalpur, since she heard your name and excellence, has night and day continued meditating on you, and was desirous of serving the lotus-feet; and an opportunity even occurred, but the affair mis-

[1] Notice the structure of this most idiomatic sentence. The phrase *bâṭ kâ hârâ*, "defeated by the road," or "dead beat by the journey"; and *thakâ to thâ hî*, "tired, indeed, he was, very." Such forms are thoroughly colloquial.

[2] *tumtanauṅ* should be printed as one word; it is the Braj equivalent of *tumhârâ*. Both Hollings and Eastwick have understood *tanauṅ* to be a form of *tanu*, "the body," or "person," and have thus missed the meaning of the verse.

carried." The Lord said, "How was that?" The Brâhmaṇ replied, "Compassionate to the lowly! one day Râjâ Bhîshmak, having summoned all his family and the members of his council, said, 'Brothers! the daughter is become fit for marriage; now a husband for her should be settled upon.' As soon as this speech had issued from the mouth of the king, they recounted the family, the virtues, the reputation, and valour of several different kings; but they made no impression on his mind.[1] Then Rukmakeś mentioned your name; then, being pleased, the king approved of what he had said, and said to them all, 'Brothers! in my mind, what this has said has become a line of stone;[2] what do you say?' They said, 'Mahârâj! if the three worlds were to be searched, still such another house and bridegroom would not be found; therefore, it is now fitting that no delay should occur; Rukminî's marriage should speedily take place with S'rî Krishṇa Chand.' Mahârâj! this affair had been resolved on; whereupon Rukma interposed, and betrothed Rukminî to S'iśupâl. Now he, bringing with him the whole army of Asuras, has advanced to the marriage."

Having related the story thus far, S'rî S'ukadev Jî said:—Lord of the Earth! that Brâhmaṇ, having thus related all the news, gave the letter of Rukminî Jî into the possession of Hari. The Lord very affectionately took the letter, and clasped it to his bosom; and having read it, was pleased, and said to the Brâhmaṇ, "Divinity! be anxious on no point. I, having gone with you, and having destroyed the Asuras, will fulfil her wish." Having heard this, the Brâhmaṇ was comforted; but Hari, thinking of Rukminî, began to be anxious.

---

## CHAPTER LIV.

**Krishṇa hurries to Kuṇḍalpur to secure Rukminî—He is followed by Balarâm with an army—Rukminî's anxiety as to his timely arrival—Krishṇa, by arrangement, meets Rukminî at a temple of Devî, and carries her off.**

S'RÎ S'UKADEV JÎ said:—O King! S'rî Krishṇa Chand, having thus fortified the Brâhmaṇ, added,—

"As, by friction, having kindled, they draw forth fire from wood,
So I will bring the beautiful one, having destroyed the army of Asuras."

[1] That is, "they did not meet his inclination."
[2] That is, "is engraven on my mind."

Having said this, then putting on nice clothes and ornaments which were pleasing, and going to Râjâ Ugrasen, the Lord, having joined his hands, said, "Mahârâj! Bhîshmak, the king of Kuṇḍalpur, having written a letter about the giving away of his daughter, by means of his Purohit, has invited me alone. If you command me, I will go, and marry his daughter."

Having heard, Ugrasen says thus, "Why rests your heart on a distant country?
You are going there alone, Murâri! Let no discord arise with anyone!

Then who will convey to us here intelligence of you?" Having spoken thus, Ugrasen added, "Good! if you wish to go there, then do both you brothers go, with all your armies; and having effected the marriage, speedily set out back. Do not quarrel and wrangle with anyone there; because should you be long-lived, then many beautiful ones will come and remain with you." On receiving the order, S'rî Krishṇa Chand said, "Mahârâj! you have spoken truly; but I am going on ahead; you will please send Balarâm Jî, with the army, afterwards."

Having spoken thus, Hari, having taken leave of Ugrasen and Vasudev, came towards that Brâhmaṇ, and sent for his charioteer Dârak, and the chariot. He, on receiving the Lord's command, immediately yoked the four-horsed chariot. Then S'rî Krishṇa Chand ascended it, and placing the Brâhmaṇ beside him, set out from Dwârakâ towards Kuṇḍalpur. When they issued from the city, what do they see? Herds and herds of deer are running along on the right side, and, in front, a lion and lioness, with their prey, are approaching, roaring. Having seen this propitious omen, the Brâhmaṇ, having reflected in his mind, said, "Mahârâj! now, from seeing this omen, this occurs to me, that just as these, having accomplished their object, are approaching, just so you, also, having accomplished your object, will come." S'rî Krishṇa Chand said, "By your kindness." [1] Having said this, Hari advanced beyond that place, and visiting various new countries, cities, and villages, arrived in Kuṇḍalpur. Then he saw there that, in various places, from the objects provided for the marriage which were placed ready, the beauty of the city was much enhanced.[2]

The lanes are swept, the squares have awnings; they are sprinkled with perfume and sandal;
Spinach and betel were formed into bunches, and between each golden cocoa-nuts were inserted.

[1] A common method of saying "Thank you!" implying that what may have occurred has resulted "from the kindness" of the inquirer.

[2] The phrase *aur kî aur*, "other of other," is common colloquially. It implies that one condition has become another condition; the gender of the genitival sign changing with the idea alluded to. Here it is *chhabi*, "beauty," and, therefore, the feminine form is used. It is parallel to *din kî rât ho gaî*, "of day night became," that is, "day became night."

Green leaves, fruits, and flowers, in profusion; at every house, wreaths,
Flags, banners, and garlands, are stretched; and handsome vessels made of gold.

And in every house there was joy. Mahârâj! such, indeed, was the splendour of this city. And in the palace the festivities which were going on, how can anyone describe them? Only when seen is that possible. Afterwards, S'rî Krishṇa, having seen the whole city, came and encamped in an enclosure of Râjâ Bhîshmak; and having seated himself in the cool shade, and become cool, he said to that Brâhmaṇ, "Divinity! you first go and announce the news of my arrival to Rukminî Jî, that she may be comforted, and grief removed from her mind; afterwards come and let me know the private matters there, that I may then devise the remedy." The Brâhmaṇ said, "Lord of Compassion! to-day is the first day of the marriage; there is great bustle and pomp in the palace. I am going; but should I find Rukminî Jî alone, I will impart to her the secret of your coming." Having spoken thus, the Brâhmaṇ went thence. Mahârâj! on this side Hari, then, arrived quietly and alone; and, on the other side, S'iśupâl, bringing all the Asura army, with Jurâsindhu, came with such pomp that it had no bounds; and came with such a crowd that, by the weight, S'eshanâg[1] began to totter, and the earth to overturn. Having received notice of his coming, Râjâ Bhîshmak went forward to receive him, with his councillors and the members of his family; and having advanced very courteously to meet them, and having invested them in wedding garments, and presented them with jewel-studded weapons and ornaments, and elephants and horses, conducted them into the city; and gave them a reception-room;[2] then he respectfully provided them with food and drink.

Having related the story thus far, S'rî S'ukadev, the saint, said:—Mahârâj! I am now stating the intermediate story, please listen attentively. When S'rî Krishṇa Chand set out from Dwârakâ, then all the Yadubaṅsîs went and said to Râjâ Ugrasen, "Mahârâj! we have heard that Râjâ S'iśupâl, with the whole army of Asuras and Jurâsindhu, is come into Kuṇḍalpur to a marriage, and that Hari has gone there alone; therefore we know that there will be a combat there between him and S'rî Krishṇa Jî. Knowing this, even, how can we become indifferent, and abandoning Hari, stay here? our inclination does not agree to this. For the rest, let what you order be done."[3]

[1] S'eshanâg is the thousand-headed snake who is supposed to support the world.

[2] A *janwâsâ* is a place provided in a bride's house for the reception of the numerous train which accompanies the bridegroom.

[3] That is, "we are ready to carry out your instructions in anything necessary to give effect to our wishes."

On hearing this statement, Râjâ Ugrasen, being exceeding alarmed, and disquieted, called Balarâm Jî to him, and, explaining the matter, said, "Do you take all my army, and speedily go to Kuṇḍalpur before the arrival[1] of S'rî Krishṇa, and get him to come back with you." On receiving the king's command, Baladev Jî, having collected fifty-six *karoṛs* of Yâdavas, set out for Kuṇḍalpur. Then the army of elephants—black, white, and smoke-tinted—appeared like a mass of cloud; and their perfectly white teeth, like rows of cranes; the drum resounded like thunder, and the weapons were glittering like lightning; troops and troops of horse-soldiers, wearing red and yellow dresses, were seen hither and thither; rows upon rows of chariots were going along, glittering. Looking on upon the splendour of these, and being delighted, the gods, with much friendship, each seated in his car, kept raining down flowers from the sky, and were wishing victory to S'rî Krishṇa Chand, the root of joy. While this was going on, taking all the army, and proceeding on, just as Hari arrived in Kuṇḍalpur, Balarâm Jî also arrived there. Having related thus, S'rî S'ukadev Jî added:—Mahârâj! S'rî Krishṇa Chand, the ocean of beauty, the light of the world, had in this way reached Kuṇḍalpur; but Rukminî, not having heard the news of his coming,—

Dissatisfied, she looks all around; as the moon becomes dimmed at dawn;
Great anxiety increased in the heart of the beautiful one; she gazed, standing on a lofty balcony;
Ascending repeatedly she peeps through casement and door; from her eyes a stream of water is released;
Dissatisfied, with clouded mind; she draws deep sighs;
Agitated, with water raining from her eyes; reflecting sadly, she says,—

"Why has Hari not yet come? his name, indeed, is Searcher of Hearts. What fault has occurred through me, such that he has not yet thought of me? Has not the Brâhmaṇ arrived there? Or, thinking me ugly, has Hari no reliance or affection for me? Or, hearing of the coming of Jurâsindhu, has the Lord not come? To-morrow is the wedding-day, and the Asura has come. Should he to-morrow take my hand, then how shall this sinful soul survive without Hari? Prayer, penance, vows, and religious duty have not protected me;[2] now what shall I do, and where shall I go? S'iśupâl has come with his marriage-procession; why does the Lord, Compassionate to the Lowly, delay?"

When these words had issued from the mouth of Rukminî,

[1] The repetition of *na pahunchte* implies a continuation of the idea, meaning "in the course of his not arriving," that is, "before he arrives."

[2] *âṛe ânâ*, "to come into protection," "to act as protector," is a form parallel with the more common *kâm ânâ*, "to come into use," "to be useful."

then a friend said, "How will Hari come into a far country without the permission of his father and relatives?" And another said, "He whose name is Searcher of Hearts, and Compassionate to the Lowly, cannot live without coming. Rukminî! be comforted; be not distressed. My heart is filled with this assurance that someone will come immediately and say that Hari has come." Mahârâj! those two were chattering on thus between themselves, when, in the midst of it,[1] the Brâhmaṇ came, and pronouncing a blessing, said, "S'rî Krishṇa Chand Jî has come, and is encamped in the royal enclosure, and Baladev Jî, bringing all the army, is coming afterwards." Upon seeing the Brâhmaṇ and hearing these words, life came into the soul of Rukminî Jî, and she then felt such happiness as a devotee feels when he has attained the reward of his austerity.

Afterwards S'rî Rukminî Jî, joining her hands and inclining her head, said in the presence of that Brâhmaṇ, "To-day you having come and announced the arrival of Hari, have given me life; what shall I give in return? Were I to give the illusion[2] of the three worlds, I should still not be free from the obligation I owe you." Having spoken thus, she restrained herself, and remained abashed. Then that Brâhmaṇ, being highly gratified, pronouncing a benediction, rose from thence, and went to Râjâ Bhîshmak. And he explained everything, and told him of the circumstances of the arrival of S'rî Krishṇa. On hearing the authentic account, Râjâ Bhîshmak arose and hastened, and, proceeding on, came where S'rî Krishṇa and Balarâm, the abode of happiness, were staying in the enclosure. On coming, he prostrated with the eight members,[3] and standing in his presence, with hands joined, Râjâ Bhîshmak said,—

> "You, O Hari! are the word of my heart;[4] how shall I
> utter what the wicked have done?

Now my desire is fully accomplished, in that you have come and revealed yourself." Having thus spoken, and provided tents for the Lord, Râjâ Bhîshmak came to his own house, and anxiously began to say,—

[1] The phrase *waise meñ* refers to the manner of what was taking place, and implies that "while things were going on in the manner just described, the Brâhmaṇ came," &c. The more common *itne meñ* refers, of course, to quantity, and implies that on so much having taken place, something fresh occurs.

[2] The *mâyâ*, or "illusion," implies all those fancied realities which constitute the illusion of existence; and, therefore, it implies "wealth," "power," &c., in fact, "the whole universe."

[3] See note [3], p. 49.

[4] "The word of my heart," means, the word constantly thought of, or the name perpetually invoked. It is strange that, although Eastwick refers to this passage in the Vocabulary, and explains it properly, he yet follows Hollings in his translation, and renders *bach* by "root"; because, apparently, it is the name of orrice-root. It is not impossible that the expression in the Text may be an apocopated form of the common phrase *man-vach-karm*, "thought, word, and deed." In this case, the import would be similar, implying that Hari was the speaker's all-in-all.

"Everyone knows the exploits of Hari; who knows what will now take place?"

And all the citizens, both women and men, coming where S'rî Krishṇa and Baladev were, and bowing their heads, and singing the praises of the Lord, and eulogizing, were thus saying among themselves, "S'rî Krishṇa alone is the fitting husband of Rukminî. Vidhanâ[1] grant that this pair may be united, and may live long!" Meanwhile, from something which came into the mind of the two brothers, they went to see the city. Then in the markets, roads, and squares in which these two brothers were going along, crowds on crowds of men and women were close to them; and they, sprinkling over them perfume, sandal, and rose-water, and showering down flowers, and stretching out their hands, were speaking thus among themselves, and pointing out the Lord:—

"Balarâm is dressed in blue; Ghanaśyâm[2] is wearing yellow silk;
With earrings tremulous, and crown resting on head; the lotus-eyes wish to steal our hearts."

And these were going along looking about them. At length, having seen all the city and the army of Râjâ S'iśupâl, they returned to their own camp. And having heard the news of their arrival, Râjâ Bhîshmak's eldest son, being exceeding wrathful, went to his father, and began to say, "Tell me truly, at whose invitation has Krishṇa come here? I have not got at the mystery, how he came here uninvited. A marriage affair is a matter of happiness; what has this one to do with that? These two deceptive, perverse people go only where they stir up strife. If you wish your own welfare you will tell me the truth. At whose invitation are they come?"

Mahârâj! Rukma having thus threatened his father, rising up from there, went in a state of perplexity where Râjâs S'iśupâl and Jurâsindhu were seated in their assemblies, and said to them, "Râma and Krishṇa are come here; inform all your people of that, that they may be careful." On hearing the name of the two brothers, Râjâ S'iśupâl, looking back on the exploits of Hari's life, was dejected, and began to reflect deeply; and Jurâsindhu began to say, "Listen! wherever these two come they stir up some mischief or other.[3] They are very powerful and deceptive. In Braj they have slain quite easily Kañs and the other very great Râkshasas. Do not you think them children; they, fighting with anyone, have never been conquered. S'rî Krishṇa seventeen times destroyed my army; when I attacked the eighteenth time,

[1] See note [1], p. 140.
[2] *Ghanaśyâm*, "the dark blue cloud," a name of Krishṇa.
[3] Notice *âweñ haiñ* and *machâweñ haiñ*, the Aorist fortified with the Substantive verb. It is really a Present tense, here used in a continuative or habitual sense.

he fled and ascended a mountain; and when I set it on fire, he trickily went off to Dwârakâ.

> This one's secret no one has gained; now he has come here to do mischief;
> He is a trickster; he will practise trickery; by no one will he be understood.[1]

Therefore, now some plan should be devised by which all our reputations may be preserved." When Jurâsindhu had said thus much, Rukma spoke thus, "What things are they about which you are so apprehensive? I know them well; that they were wandering about various woods, singing, dancing, playing the flute, and grazing cows. What do these rustics know about the science of war? Have no anxiety in your mind about anything; I, in a moment, will slay and repulse Krishṇa and Balarâm, with all the Yadubañsîs."

S'rî S'ukadev Jî said:—Mahârâj! that day, Rukma, having counselled and encouraged Jurâsindhu and S'iśupâl, returned to his home; and they passed the night in uncertainty. As soon as it was dawn, on the one hand, Râjâ S'iśupâl and Jurâsindhu, thinking it the marriage-day, were engaged in the bustle of setting forth the marriage-procession; and, on the other hand, at Râjâ Bhîshmak's place also festivities began to take place. Hereupon, Rukminî Jî, on rising up, sent to inform S'rî Krishṇa Chand, through a Brâhmaṇ, thus, "Abode of Compassion! to-day is the wedding-day; when two *gharîs* of day remain, I shall go to worship at the temple of Devî, to the east of the city. My honour is yours; do that by which it may be preserved."

Afterwards, when about one watch of the day had passed, the friends, companions, and women of the family arrived. These, on coming, at first having filled a square place in the courtyard with large pearls, and arranged a golden bejewelled seat, seated Rukminî upon it, had her rubbed with oil by seven married women;[2] afterwards, having applied perfumed unguents, bathed and washed her, they adorned her with the sixteen decorations and dressed her in the twelve ornaments,[3] covered her with a red bodice, and seated her fully prepared. Meanwhile, about four *gharîs* of the day remained. Then Rukminî the young, taking with her all her friends and companions, went, with sounding music, to worship Devî; then Râjâ Bhîshmak made some of his people accompany her for protection.

[1] *jânyau paṛai* is the Braj form of *jânâ paṛe*. This phrase is equivalent to *kisî se nahîñ jânâ jâwe*.

[2] The husbands of the women who perform this office must be living at the time.

[3] The sixteen appliances for decoration are:—1, tooth-brush; 2, tooth-powder; 3, cosmetic; 4, minium; 5, saffron; 6, antimony; 7, spangles, 8, hair-oil; 9, comb; 10, perfume; 11, betel; 12, paint for teeth and lips; 13, indigo; 14, henna; 15, flowers; 16, red dye. The twelve ornaments are the bangles, anklets, nose-ring, &c.

Having got the news that the king's daughter was gone out of the city to worship Devî, Râjâ S'iśupâl also, from fear of S'rî Krishṇa Chand, summoned his greatest heroes, champions, braves, valiant men, and soldiers, and having given them most minute[1] instructions, sent them forth to watch over Rukminî Jî. They, also, going, with their several weapons elevated, accompanied the king's daughter. Then Rukminî Jî, adorned with every ornament, with troops on troops of friends and companions, in the shade of a screen, moving along in the environment of the blackest Râkshasas, was as beautiful as the moon with a cluster of stars in the midst of a dark cloud. At length, after a time, moving on, she arrived at the temple of Devî. Having gone there and washed her hands and feet, and rinsed her mouth, becoming purified, the king's daughter, at first, with sandal, unbroken rice, flowers, perfumes, lamps, and consecrated food, devoutly worshipped Devî, according to the Vedic ritual; afterwards, having caused female Brâhmaṇs to be fed with desirable food, and clothed them in nice garments, and drawn the sacred mark with *rolî*,[2] and applied rice thereto, she gave them a fee, and received from them a blessing.

Afterwards, having perambulated round Devî, that moon-faced one, of the colour of the Champak blossom, with eyes like a deer, voice like the cuckoo, gait like an elephant, taking her friends, being in anxiety about meeting Hari, as she was about to depart thence, having finished her devotions, S'rî Krishṇa Chand also, seated alone in his chariot, arrived where all the warriors attendant on Rukminî were standing armed with weapons.

Having related thus much, S'rî S'ukadev Jî said :—

> Having worshipped Gaur, as soon as she went forth, one says agitatedly,
> " Hark! beautiful one! Hari is come; see his pennon waving."

Hearing these words from the friend, and seeing the ensign of the chariot of the Lord, the king's daughter with extreme delight was unable to contain herself, and placing her hand on the hand of her companion, and assuming a fascinating appearance, hoping to join Hari, slightly smiling, she was so moving with slow pace amidst them all that her beauty cannot be described. Afterwards, upon seeing S'rî Krishṇa Chand all the guards stood as though deprived of sense, and the screen fell from their hands, whereupon they beheld the fascinating form of Rukminî Jî; then, becoming still more confounded, they became so feeble that they lost all consciousness of body and mind.

> Having strung her eyebrow-bow, and drawn the string of her darkened eyelashes,
> And discharged the arrows of her glances, she slays, but they remain living.

[1] *Sab bhāṅti ūnch nīch*, " every kind of up and down," or " all the ins and outs of the affair."

[2] See note [1], p. 152.

Mahârâj! then all the Râkshasas stood merely gazing, like painted pictures; and S'rî Krishṇa Chand, amidst them all, made the chariot advance to Rukminî, and stood there. On seeing the Lord of her life, she modestly stretched out her hand to meet him; then the Lord, raising her with the left hand, seated her on the chariot.

With trembling body, and exceedingly abashed mind; abandoning all, she set out with Hari;
As a Vairâgî abandons his house, and fixes his affection on the feet of Krishṇa.

Mahârâj! Rukminî Jî then obtained the reward of her prayers, penance, vows, and virtuous acts, and her recent sorrow was all dissipated. The enemies, with their weapons, stood looking at her face; the Lord, taking Rukminî from the midst of them, proceeded—

As a lion springs into the midst of many packs of jackals,
Seizing his prey, walks off fearless and roaring.

Afterwards, on S'rî Krishṇa Chand's going off, Balarâm Jî, also, sounding the drum, accompanied by all the army, went and rejoined him.

---

## CHAPTER LV.

S'iśupâl and Jurâsindhu pursue Krishṇa with an army, but are defeated—Rukma then attempts an attack, but is taken prisoner—Rukma is shaved and bound to Krishṇa's chariot—At the intercession of Rukminî he is released—Rukma then abandons Kuṇḍalpur, and founds the city of Bhojakaṭu—The marriage of Krishṇa at Dwârakâ.

S'RÎ SUKADEV JÎ said:—Mahârâj! having gone some distance, S'rî Krishṇa Chand, looking at the thoughtful and bashful Rukminî Jî, said, "Beautiful one! now be not anxious about anything; I, by the sound of my shell, will remove all the fear of your mind; and, having arrived in Dwârakâ, will marry you according to Vedic rites." Having spoken thus, the Lord, having placed his necklace on her, and seated her on the left side, sounded the shell, when all the attendants of S'iśupâl and Jurâsindhu started up. This affair spread throughout the whole city, that Hari had taken away Rukminî.

Meanwhile, hearing of the abduction of Rukminî from the mouths of those people who had gone with the king's daughter to watch over her, Râjâs S'iśupâl and Jurâsindhu, in great wrath, putting on coats of mail and helmets, fastening waist-belts, attached all their weapons, and each taking his army, hurried after Krishṇa to fight with him; and having gone near him, flourishing about their weapons, they challenged thus, "Ho! why are you fleeing away? Stop! take your arms and fight. Those who are Khatriyas, heroes and braves, do not turn their backs in the field." Mahârâj! on hearing these words the Yâdavas again faced them, and the weapons began to fly on both sides. Then the child Rukminî, greatly alarmed, concealing herself with her veil, was weeping much, and heaving deep sighs; and looking steadfastly at the face of her lover, reflecting in her inmost heart, was saying thus, "He, for me, is enduring this affliction." The Lord, the Searcher of Hearts, knowing the secret of Rukminî's mind, said, "Beautiful one! why art thou fearing? In thy very sight, having smitten the Asura army, I will remove the burden of the earth. Do not thou be anxious in thy mind on any point."

Having related thus much of the story, S'rî S'ukadev Jî said:—Râjâ! at that time, the gods, seated in their respective cars, are seeing what from the sky? that—

> The Yâdavas are warring with the Asuras; there is a great battle;
> Krishṇa stands looking on; Balarâm is fighting.

The kettle-drum is sounding; bards are singing war-songs; panegyrists are celebrating glories; horseman with horseman, elephant-rider with elephant-rider, charioteer with charioteer, foot-soldier with foot-soldier, are in close combat. Heroes and braves of this side and that, attacking each other, are striking blows; and cowards, abandoning the field, are fleeing with their lives. The wounded are standing up writhing; headless trunks, with swords in their hands, are moving around on all sides; and corpses on corpses are lying about. From them a river of blood has flowed; in that, here and there, elephants, who have fallen dead, appear like islands, and their trunks like alligators. Mahâdev, accompanied by ghosts, goblins, and spirits, choosing heads, were making and wearing skull-garlands; and vultures, jackals, and dogs, fighting among themselves, were dragging away at the corpses, and rending and devouring them. Crows, plucking out the eyes from the carcases, were carrying them off. At length, in the very sight of the gods, Balarâm Jî cut down the Asura army as an agriculturist cuts down his crop. Thereupon Jurâsindhu and S'iśupâl, on their whole army being destroyed, accompanied by a few of the wounded, fled, and went to a place, and halted. There S'iśupâl, with many regrets, shaking his head, said to Jurâsindhu, "Now that ignominy has been attained, and a stain put on the family, it is not right to live in the world; therefore, should you give leave, I will go into the battle and die fighting.

> Otherwise, I will make the woods my dwelling; I will take Yogî vows; I will abandon all hope;
> Honour and character are gone; now why should I live? why, by preserving life, should I accept disgrace?"

Having heard this speech, Jurâsindhu said, "Mahârâj! you are wise, and in all things intelligent;[1] how shall I counsel you? Those who are intelligent people do not grieve over what has occurred;[2] because the Creator of good and evil is quite another. Man has no power; this dependent one is subject to another. As a wooden image, when the juggler makes it dance, dances; just so man is subject to the Creator. He does what he pleases; therefore, in pleasure and pain no delight or grief should be felt; all should be regarded as a dream. I took twenty-three separate complete armies, seventeen times, and attacked the city of Mathurâ, and this very Krishṇa seventeen times defeated the whole of my army. I felt no grief; and, the eighteenth time, when the army of this one was destroyed, I felt no delight either. This one fled, and ascended a mountain; I burnt him just there; there is no knowing how this one lived; the conduct of this one is in no wise to be understood." Having said this, Jurâsindhu added, "Mahârâj! this is now fitting, that this circumstance should be set aside. It is said, that, if life be spared, then afterwards everything remains; as it happened to me; having been defeated seventeen times, I conquered the eighteenth time. Therefore, that should be done, in which your welfare may be, and perverseness should be abandoned."

Mahârâj! when Jurâsindhu had thus counselled and spoken, the other one was somewhat comforted, and taking with him as many wounded soldiers as were saved, with sorrow and regret, accompanied Jurâsindhu. These, then, having been thus defeated, went from here. But listen to the affairs of the place where the house of S'iśupâl was. Anticipating the return of her son, when the mother of S'iśupâl began to prepare festivities, a sneeze occurred before her, and her right eye began to throb. Having perceived this ill omen, her forehead throbbed; hereupon someone came and said, "Your son's entire army is cut up, and even the bride has not been obtained; now, fleeing thence, he comes with his bare life." On hearing these words, the mother of S'iśupâl was greatly troubled, and remained speechless.

Afterwards, having heard of the flight of S'iśupâl and Jurâsindhu, Rukma, in great anger, came and sat in his council, and began to declaim to all, thus, "Krishṇa can never escape from my hands to go anywhere.[3] I will go immediately, kill him, and bring back Rukminî; then my name is Rukma; otherwise, I will not again come into Kuṇḍalpur." Mahârâj! having thus vowed, taking one complete army, Rukma hastened forth to fight with S'rî Krishṇa Chand; and he went and surrounded the army of the Yâdavas. Then that one said to his people, "Do you slay

[1] *jân* here is for *jnânî*.

[2] *hu,î* is adjective to *bât*, meaning "the affair which has come to pass," or "existent circumstances."

[3] *Lit.*, "Krishṇa, having escaped from my hands, where is he able to go?" The interrogative is often used to imply the impossibility of an event.

the Yâdavas, and I will go forward, and capture Krishṇa living." On hearing these words, his companions began to fight with the Yadubañsîs, and he, driving his chariot forward, and going near S'rî Krishṇa Chand, challenged him and said, "O treacherous rustic! what dost thou know of royal practices? Just as in infancy thou didst steal milk and curds, so thou hast come here also and removed the beautiful one.

I am not a herdsman inhabiting Braj." Saying this he took arrows.
He selected those dipped in poison; drawing the bow he discharged three arrows.

Seeing those arrows coming, S'rî Krishṇa Chand cut them just in their flight.[1] Then Rukma discharged other arrows; the Lord cut and threw down them also, and preparing his own bow, discharged several arrows so that the charioteer, along with the horses of the chariot, were obliterated; and the bow being cut from his (Rukma's) hand, fell down. Then Hari cut and threw down as many weapons as he employed. Then he, exceedingly enraged, took up shield and sword, and leaping from the chariot, sprang towards S'rî Krishṇa Chand, as a foolish jackal comes at an elephant, or as a moth rushes at a lamp. At length, on coming up, he attacked the chariot of Hari with a club, whereupon the Lord at once seized and bound him, and was about to kill him, when Rukminî Jî said,—

"Kill him not; he is my brother; release, O Lord! your servant.
Fool and blind, what does he know? The very husband of Lakshmî he esteems mortal.
You are the Lord of devotion, first and eternal; for the sake of worshipper you manifest yourself, O Deity!
How could this stupid recognize you? or celebrate you? O Kind to the Lowly! O Compassionate One!"

Having said this, she pursued, "Good people take no notice of the faults of fools and children, as the lion bestows no thought on the barking of a dog. And if you should kill this one, there will be grief to my father; and to do this is not right of you. In whatever place your feet fall, all creatures there are in delight. It would be a very strange thing if, with a relation such as you,[2] Râjâ Bhîshmak should suffer grief for a son." Mahârâj! having spoken thus, Rukminî Jî once more said, "You have acted well

[1] *bîch hî*, "the very midst," that is, in the midst, or course, of their passage through the air. Eastwick translates "severed them in two"; but *bîch hî kâṭnâ* means "to ward off" any weapon thrown.

[2] *rahte* is elliptical, meaning "on the being," or "during the existence"; therefore the phrase is, "while a relation such as you exists;" the inference being that so powerful a son-in-law ought to protect his father-in-law from ill, and not himself be the source of misery.

towards a relative, in that you have seized and bound him, and with sword in hand, are ready to slay him." Then becoming extremely agitated, trembling, with eyes filled with tears, sobbing, and falling at his feet, she beseechingly[1] resumed :—

> "O Lord ! give to me my relative [as] an alms ; obtain thus much glory in the world."

From hearing this remark, and from looking towards Rukminî Jî, all the anger of S'rî Krishṇa Chand Jî was tranquillized ; then he did not slay him,[2] but beckoned to the charioteer. He quickly stripped off his turban, and tying his hands behind his back, and shaving his moustaches, beard, and head, leaving seven locks of hair, bound him behind the chariot.

Having related the story thus far, S'rî S'ukadev Jî said :—Mahârâj ! S'rî Krishṇa, in this direction, reduced Rukma to this condition, and, from yonder, Baladev, having cut up and defeated the whole army of Asuras, came to meet his brother as a white elephant, having broken off, eaten, and scattered the lotuses in a lotus-pool, wearying [of the sport] retires. At length, after a time, he came near the Lord, and perceiving Rukma bound, very testily said to S'rî Krishṇa Jî, "What is this you have done, that you have seized and bound your brother-in-law ? Your bad habits are not departing—

> In binding this one you have shown little sense ; by this, Krishṇa ! you have made a breach in the relationship ;
> And have fixed a stain on the Yadu family ; now who will form [matrimonial] alliance with us ?[3]

When this one came before you to fight, why did you not counsel him and send him back ?" Mahârâj ! having spoken thus, Balarâm Jî released and counselled Rukma, and very courteously dismissed him. Then joining his hands with great humility, Balarâm, the abode of happiness, said to Rukminî Jî, "O beauteous one ! this condition of your brother which has occurred involves no fault of ours ; this is the fruit of his actions done in a former birth. And it is, also, the duty of Kshatriyas, on account of territory, wealth, and women, to mutually equip armies, and to make war [on each other]. Do not be displeased at what has happened ; regard my statement as the very truth, [that] defeat and victory are associated intimately with him.[4] But this world is an ocean of misery ; having come here, where is happiness ?

[1] *god pasârnâ* means literally "to spread out the skirt," that is, to ask some gift ; hence, to beseech, beg, entreat.

[2] *Lit.*, "strike him from life."

[3] For *kari hai* read *karihai*, "will do." The *hai* is the sign of the Braj Future tense.

[4] *Hâr* and *jît* are both feminine, but the singular verb is used to agree with the nearer of the two. The *hî* is emphatic to indicate the intimacy of the connection ; the sense being that such changes of circumstances are unavoidably connected with the soldier's calling.

But men, being in the power of delusion, acknowledge from pure imagination,[1] [such things as] misery and happiness, good and bad, defeat and victory, association and separation; but in this [matter] there is no delight [or] grief to the soul. Do not be uneasy at your brother's being disfigured; for wise folk say the soul [is] immortal, destruction [is predicable] of the body, on this account, from the body's being dishonoured, nothing of the soul's is gone."

Having related the story thus far, S'rî S'ukadev Jî said to King Parîkshit:—Incarnation of virtue! when Balarâm Jî had thus counselled Rukminî,—

> Having heard, the beauteous one reflected in her mind, and was ashamed [in presence] of her husband's elder brother;
> With a sign[2] she says to her loved one, "Urge on the chariot, O King of Braj!"
> She screens her body with a veil, and utters the sweet speech to Hari;
> "Baladâ,û stands before us, O husband! drive the chariot quickly."

As soon as this speech had issued from the mouth of S'rî Rukminî Jî, on the one side S'rî Krishṇa Chand Jî drove the chariot towards Dwârakâ, and, on the other side, Rukma, going among his people, began, with deep concern, to say, "I came from Kuṇḍalpur having made this vow, that I will go at once and, having slain Krishṇa and Balarâm, along with all the Yadubaṅsîs, will bring back Rukminî. That vow of mine has not been fulfilled; but, on the contrary, I have lost my honour. Now I shall no longer live; having abandoned this country and the condition of a householder,[3] and having become a Vairâgî, I will go somewhere and die."

When Rukma had said this, someone among his people said, "Mahârâj! you are a great hero, and very powerful; in that[4] they escaped alive from your hand was their good fortune; they got out by force of their destiny;[5] otherwise, when can any enemy, opposing you, escape alive? You are sagacious; why contemplate such a course [as that which you have just expressed]? sometimes there is defeat, sometimes victory; but it is the duty of warriors and heroes not to abandon fortitude. Well, then! the enemy has escaped to-day, another time we

[1] *man hî man se*, "from nothing but the mind."

[2] *mâṅhiṅ* = *meṅ*; *sainoṅ meṅ*, or *sainoṅ se*, means "with signs, winks, gestures."

[3] *Gṛihasthâśrama* is the state or condition of a householder, involving all social duties and worldly cares.

[4] *Jo* is the equivalent of "in that," and the correlative is *so*; literally, "from your hand in that they escaped living, that same was their good time." The plural "good days" indicates "fortune," "luck."

[5] For *prârabdh* read *prârabdhi*.

shall slay him." Mahârâj! when this one had thus counselled Rukma, the latter began to say this, "Listen,—

> [I have been] defeated by them, and honour is gone; in my heart there is much shame;
> May I die[1] [if] I go to Kuṇḍalpur; rather let me found an altogether different town."
> Having said this, he founded a city, and sent for his son, wife, and property;
> It[2] was named Bhojakaṭu. In this way Rukma founded a town.

Mahârâj! on that side, Rukma, then, remained there at enmity with King Bhîshmak; and, on this side, S'rî Krishṇa Chand and Baladev Jî, proceeding on, drew near to Dwârakâ.

> When the dust flew about and overshadowed the sky, the citizens became aware [of his approach].
> As soon as they perceived Hari coming, they prepared the city;
> Its beauty became that of the three worlds;[3] by whom can it be uttered?[4]

Then there were festivities in every house; at every door posts of plantain were fixed; golden vessels with water and fresh sprouts were placed; flags and banners fluttered; garlands and wreaths were attached; and in every market, road, and square, troops upon troops of young maidens were standing bearing four-sided lamps;[5] and Râjâ Ugrasen also, along with all the Yadubañsîs, advancing triumphantly to meet them, with every customary ceremony,[6] conducted Balarâm, the abode of happiness, and S'rî Krishṇa Chand, the root of joy, into the city. The beauty of the preparation at that time is indescribable. In the hearts of all, both women and men, joy was diffused. Coming before the Lord, all of them respectively were welcoming him with presents; and the women, from their doors, gates, pavilions, and upper rooms, were singing songs of rejoicing, and lowering down *ârtîs*,[7] and raining down flowers; and S'rî Krishṇa Chand and

[1] *Janm na hoñ*, "let not births be," that is, future births. He imprecates *janm-maraṇ*, or "eternal death," on himself.

[2] For *tâkauñ* read *tâ kau;* it is the genitive inflexion, meaning, "its name was fixed as Bhojakaṭu."

[3] All the splendours of heaven, earth, and hell were concentrated in it.

[4] *kaun pai = kis se*, meaning that no one can describe the beauty of the city.

[5] A lamp divided into four compartments and having four wicks, emblematic of the four-faced Brahmâ, is used at every Hindû marriage ceremony.

[6] *rîti bhâñti kar*, "with customs and manners"; that is, all sorts of customary ceremonies.

[7] The *ârtâ* ceremony is performed at marriages. It consists of presenting the bridegroom, on his reaching the house of the bride, with a platter, divided into several compartments; in the midst of which there is a lamp made of flour filled with *ghî*, in which there are several lighted wicks. This object is waved round the head of the bridegroom.

Baladev Jî, as was fitting, kept on delighting the hearts of all. At length, proceeding on in this way, they reached and entered the royal palace. Some days afterwards, one day S'rî Krishṇa Jî went into the royal court, where Râjâ Ugrasen, Sûrasen, Vasudev, and all the other greatest Yadubañsîs were seated; and having saluted, he said before them, "When anyone, having conquered in battle, carries off a beauteous one, it is called a Râkshas marriage."

On hearing this statement, Sûrasen Jî summoned the Purohit, and, advising him, said, "Do you fix the day for S'rî Krishṇa's marriage." He immediately opened an almanac, and seeing a good month, day, time, and asterism, and reflecting on a propitious sun and moon, he fixed the wedding-day. Then Râjâ Ugrasen gave this order to his minister, "Do you get together all that is necessary for the marriage"; and, sitting down himself, and writing various letters, had them sent away, in the charge of Brâhmaṇs, to the Pâṇḍavas, Kauravas, and other kings of the country and foreign parts. Mahârâj! on receiving the letter, all the kings, respectively being pleased, arose and hastened, and they were accompanied by Brâhmaṇs, Paṇḍits, bards, and even beggars.

And on receiving the news, Râjâ Bhîshmak also, having consigned to a Brâhmaṇ much clothes, weapons, jewelled ornaments, and chariots, elephants, horses, slaves, and sedan chairs with female slaves, and in his very heart vowing the gift of his daughter, very humbly sent to Dwârakâ. From one direction, the kings of various countries came; and from this other direction, that Brâhmaṇ also came, bearing all the paraphernalia sent by Râjâ Bhîshmak. The splendour of Dwârakâ city at that time is indescribable. Afterwards the marriage-day arrived; then, with all the usual ceremonies, the husband and girl were taken beneath the marriage-structure and seated. And all the greatest chiefs of the Yadubañsî race also came and sat down. Then,—

> The Paṇḍits there are reciting the Vedas; Hari with Rukminî is circumambulating round;
> Drums, kettle-drums, and pipes are resounding; the delighted gods are raining down flowers;
> Mystics, saints, bards, and heavenly minstrels, being[1] in the sky, are all looking on;
> Seated in cars around they are bending their heads; the wives of the gods are all singing songs of rejoicing.
> The Lord hand in hand[2] [with Rukminî] finished the perambulation, and seated Rukminî on the left side;

[1] *baye* is here exceptionally used for *hokar*. It will be seen that the verbal forms here are all aoristic.

[2] *hâth gahyau* = "hand-taken"; part of the ceremony of a Hindû marriage being the perambulation seven times round the sacred fire, hand in hand, and tied together. The next line relates that the knots were unloosened.

The knot was undone, the sitting-board was returned; the family goddess was then worshipped;
Hari and the beauteous one unloose the bracelet; they sport with the prepared milk and rice;
Exceeding delight penetrated the Lord of the world; having looked on and being delighted, all give [1] blessings;
"May the pair Hari and Rukminî live long; whose nature has imbibed the water of immortality."
They gave gifts to the Brâhmaṇs who had come; they clothed the minstrels and panegyrists;
The kings who had come from various countries, they dismissed and escorted all back.[2]

Having related thus much of the story, S'rî S'ukadev Jî said:—Mahârâj! the person who shall read and hear the story of Hari and Rukminî, and having read and heard shall bear it in mind, shall obtain faith, salvation, and renown. Again, the fruit which results from the horse and other sacrifices,[3] the bestowal of cows and other creatures, bathing in the Ganges and other streams, the making of pilgrimages to Prayâg and other places, that fruit is obtained by relating and hearing the story of Hari.

---

## CHAPTER LVI.

The birth of Pradyumna—He is carried off by Sambar and cast into the sea—He is swallowed by a fish, and brought back to Sambar's kitchen—He is there nourished by Rati, by desire of Sambar—On attaining his majority he slays Sambar and carries off Rati.

S'RÎ S'UKADEV JÎ said:—Mahârâj! one day S'rî Mahâdev Jî [4] was seated in his own place in meditation, when [5] all at once Kâmadev [6] came and annoyed [him]. Then Hara's [7] meditation was broken, and, becoming deprived of knowledge, he began to sport with Pârvatî Jî.[8] Hereupon, after some time, when knowledge returned to S'iva Jî while he was continuing dallying, he became enraged and burnt Kâmadev to ashes.

[1] *deñhiñ* is the 3rd pers. pl. Pres. It is the Aorist *deñ* fortified by a termination, such forms being common colloquially.

[2] The allusions in these verses are to customs and ceremonies of Hindû marriage hich would require an essay to explain.

[3] For *aśwamedâdi* read *aśwamedhâdi*.

[4] Mahâdev is a name of S'iva.

[5] The particle *ki* here merely marks a transition of ideas, which I have expressed by "when."

[6] *Kâmadev*, "the god of desire," a name of the Indian Cupid.

[7] *Hara* is another name of S'iva.

[8] Pârvatî is the name of S'iva's wife.

When S'iva burnt up the powerful Kâmadev, Rati[1] lost all fortitude;
Without a husband the pure one is greatly agitated; her body agitated and restless.
Kâma's wife wanders about, writhing, and crying "Husband! husband!" embraces the earth.
Perceiving the woman greatly distressed without her husband, Gaurâ[2] thus addressed her,—

"O Rati! do not be anxious; hear the secret by which thou wilt meet with thy husband. I relate it [now]: First, then, he will be born in the house of S'rî Krishṇa Chand, and his name will be Pradyumna. Afterwards Sambar[3] will take him away and will set him adrift on the ocean. Then through being in the stomach of a fish,[4] he will come into the kitchen of that very Sambar. Do thou go and remain just there; when he comes thou wilt take and nourish[5] him. Then he, having slain Sambar, will take thee with him, and go into Dwârakâ and dwell there happily." Mahârâj!—

S'iva's queen thus counselled Rati. Then, recovering fortitude, she came to Sambar's house;
The beauteous one in the kitchen remains; night and day expecting her loved one.[6]

Having related the story thus far, S'rî S'ukadev Jî said:—Râjâ! there Rati, with the hope of meeting the loved one, began to stay thus; and here Rukminî became pregnant; and in ten months, in full time, a son was born. Having received this news, the astrologers came, settled the propitious moment, and said to Vasudev, "Mahârâj! having seen the lucky star of this child, it occurs to us that, in beauty, goodness, and bravery, he will be equal to S'rî Krishṇa Chand Jî himself; but during infancy he will remain in water; afterwards, having slain an enemy, he will come and meet you with his wife." Saying this, and fixing his name as Pradyumna, the astrologers took their fee, and were dismissed; and, in the house of Vasudev, the customary ceremonies and rejoicings began. Afterwards, S'rî Nârad, the saint, having gone and forthwith counselled Sambar, said, "In what [sort of] sleep art thou sleeping? Hast thou consciousness or

[1] *Rati*, "delight" or "pleasure," is the name of Kâmadev's wife, the Indian Psyche.

[2] Gaurâ is a name of Pârvatî, the wife of S'iva.

[3] *Sambar*, or properly S'ambara, is the name of a Daitya or demon of drought. His legend goes back to Vedic times.

[4] *peṭ meñ ho*, "having been in the stomach." This use of *ho* or *hokar* is equivalent to *viâ*.

[5] The Imperative in *-iyo* implies futurity. It differs from the form *-iye*, which is respectful.

[6] *Lit.*, "wishing for the loved one's path."

not?" He said, "What?" This one replied, "The incarnation of thy enemy Kâma, named Pradyumna, is born in the house of S'rî Krishṇa Chand."

Râjâ! Nârad Jî, having thus cautioned Sambar, departed; and Sambar, reflecting in his inmost heart, fixed upon this device, "In the form of wind, I will go there and fetch him away, and set him adrift on the ocean; then the anxiety of my mind will be obliterated, and I shall become void of fear." With this thought, Sambar arose from there, and becoming invisible, went on and came into the palace of S'rî Krishṇa Chand, where Rukminî Jî, in the lying-in chamber, pressing with her hand and fondling to her breast, was giving milk to the babe. And he silently stood in ambush. As soon as Rukminî Jî's hand became separated from the child, the Asura, disseminating his illusion, took him up and so conveyed him away that, among the women seated there, no one either saw or knew who had come, or in what form, or how he had taken [the child] up and carried it off. Afterwards, not seeing the child, Rukminî Jî was exceedingly agitated, and began to cry. Having heard the sound of her weeping, all the Yadubañsîs, both men and women, came around, and giving utterance to a variety of remarks, began to be anxious.

Hereupon Nârad Jî[1] having arrived, counselled them all, and said, "Do not be at all apprehensive at the departure of the child. He has nothing to fear. He may go anywhere, but death will not affect him. Childhood having passed, he will come and meet you along with a beautiful wife." Mahârâj! having thus imparted the secret to all the Yadubañsîs, and counselled them, when Nârad had taken leave, they also, having thought the matter over, became satisfied.

Now hear the tale further. Sambar, who had carried away Pradyumna, threw him into the ocean. There a fish swallowed him; that fish was swallowed by another big fish. Hereupon a fisherman having gone there, as soon as he threw his net, that fish entered it. The fisherman, having drawn the net, and seen the fish, being exceedingly pleased, took it, and came home. At length that fish was given by him to Râjâ Sambar. The Râjâ accepted it and sent it to his kitchen. When the cook cut that fish open, another fish came from within it. When the stomach of that one was split open, a dark-complexioned, very beautiful boy came from within it. On seeing that he was much astonished; and he took that boy and gave it to Rati. She accepted it with the greatest pleasure. Sambar heard of this affair, and sending for Rati, said, "Nourish this boy excellently with care." Hearing this remark of the king, Rati, taking that boy, came to her own house. Then Nârad Jî going there said,—

[1] For *na* read *ne*; and for *samjnâkar* read *samjhâkar*.

"Now do thou carefully nourish this one; then the husband Pradaman will come and manifest himself.
Having killed Sambar, he will take thee away; his infancy will be passed here."[1]

Having imparted this much of the secret, Nârad the saint departed, and Rati, very kindly and attentively, began to nourish [the child]. As the boy grew up the desire of meeting her husband grew upon Rati. Sometimes she looked upon his form and affectionately pressed him to her bosom; sometimes, kissing his eyes, mouth, and cheeks, she herself smilingly clung to his neck, and was saying thus,—

"The Lord has brought about this fortunate conjuncture; I have found my husband in a fish."

And, Mahârâj!

She brought milk affectionately, and kindly caused him to drink it;
Dandling him and singing his praises, she, loving, was calling him "husband."

Afterwards, when Pradyumna was five years old, Rati, dressing him in various kinds of clothes and ornaments, began to realise the desire[2] of her heart, and to give pleasure to her eyes. Then when that boy, taking hold of the hem of Rati's garment, began to say, "Mother! mother!" she, laughing, said, "O husband! what is this you are saying? I am your wife; do you reflect in your heart and look [into the matter]. Pârvatî said this to me, 'Do thou go and stay in Sambar's house; thy husband will be born in the house of S'rî Krishṇa Chand Jî; he will come to thee through the stomach of a fish.' And Nârad Jî also said, 'Do not thou be dejected; thy husband is coming to meet thee.'[3] Since then, cherishing the hope of meeting you, I have taken up my abode here. By your coming my hope is fulfilled."

Having said this, Rati then taught her husband the whole science of archery. When he became clever in archery, one day Rati said to her husband, "Husband! now it is no longer right to remain here; because your mother, S'rî Rukminî Jî, without you is as pained and distressed as a cow without a calf; hence this is proper that, having slain Sambar, you should take me with you, go into Dwârakâ, and show yourself to your mother and father, and give pleasure to those who are longing to see you."

S'rî S'ukadev Jî, having recounted this affair, said to the king:— Mahârâj! in this way hearing Rati's words again and again, when

[1] For *bitai hai* read *bitaihai*. The *hai* is only the termination of the Future tense.

[2] The word *sâd* is generally feminine; but is treated as masculine in all editions of the Prem-Sâgar.

[3] The Present tense is here used for the proximate Future, meaning "He will soon rejoin you."

N 2

Pradyumna Jî was grown up, one day, playing about, he went near to Râjâ Sambar. Upon seeing him, esteeming him as his own very son, he tenderly said, "I have brought this boy up as my own son." As soon as he heard this, Pradyumna Jî very angrily said, "I, a child, am thy enemy; now do thou fight and see my strength." Saying thus, he challenged [1] and confronted him. Then Sambar laughingly said, "Brother! whence has this second Pradyumna come on my account? What! have I fed with milk and developed a snake, that he is speaking thus?" Having said this, he continued, "Why art thou saying these words? Are the messengers of death come to take thee?"

Mahârâj! as soon as he heard these words from the mouth of Sambar, he said, "Pradyumna is my own name; do thou to-day fight with me. Thou, indeed, sent me adrift [2] on the ocean; but now I am come again to take my revenge. Thou thyself hast developed thine own death in thine own house. Who is whose son? and who is whose father?" [3]

Hearing this, Sambar seized a weapon; the temper of his heart was inflated with anger;
Like the foot placed in the dark on the tail of a snake.

Then Sambar sent for all his army, and taking Pradyumna outside, and angrily raising a club, and roaring like a thunder-cloud, said, "Let me see now who will save thee from death." Saying this, as he rushed forward and struck out with a club, Pradyumna easily cut it down. Then that one angrily hurled fiery arrows, and this one, letting go watery arrows, extinguished them. Then Sambar, with excessive anger, made [use of] all the weapons which were near him; but this one promptly cut them down one after the other.[4] When no weapon was left in his possession, Pradyumna angrily rushed forward and grappled [with him], and a wrestling match began between them. After a time, this one flew up to the sky with that one; having arrived there, he cut off his head with a sword, and threw it down; and came back and slaughtered the army of the Asuras.

Sambar being slain, Rati obtained happiness; and immediately a car came from heaven. Rati and her husband both mounted and seated themselves upon it, and went to Dwârakâ, as if a beautiful cloud were going accompanied by lightning. And proceeding onwards, they arrived where golden palaces were glittering, like the lofty Sumeru mountain.[5] Descending from

[1] *Lit.*, "to strike the arms," because wrestlers strike their hands on the arms before trying a fall.

[2] Notice this emphatic form of the Past tense, which is difficult to render exactly in English. It is produced by placing the auxiliary in the early part of a phrase; and is common colloquially. Here it also assists one of Lallû Lâl's jingling rhymes; for *bahâyâ* is intended to rhyme with *phir âyâ*.

[3] These interrogatives, as is often the case, imply a denial, meaning, "I am not your son; neither are you my father."

[4] "one after the other" is implied in the repetition of *kâṭ*.

[5] *Sumeru*, or, as it is more commonly written, *Meru*, is a fabulous moun tain of

the car, they both suddenly entered the female apartments. Having seen them, all the beauteous ones were startled, and, having supposed that S'rî Krishṇa was come accompanied by a beautiful woman, they were abashed. But no one knew this secret that it was Pradyumna; all were calling him nothing but Krishṇa.[1] Hereupon, when Pradyumna Jî said, "Where are our parents?" Rukminî Jî said to her friends, "O friends! who is this one in the likeness of Hari?" They said, "It occurs to us that this is undoubtedly[2] the son of Krishṇa alone." As soon as she heard these words, a stream of milk flowed forth from the breast of Rukminî Jî, and her left arm began to throb, and her heart was agitated to embrace him; but without her husband's permission she was unable to embrace him. Then Nârad Jî having come there, and having related the foregoing story, obliterated the doubt from all their minds. Then Rukminî Jî, running, kissed the head of her son, pressed him to her bosom; and having effected the marriage with the customary ceremonies, received her son and his wife into the house. Then all the Yadubañsis, both women and men, came, and made festivity, and were highly delighted. In every house songs of congratulation resounded; and happiness was diffused throughout the whole city of Dwârakâ.

Having related the story thus far, S'rî S'ukadev Jî said to King Parîkshit:—Mahârâj! in this way Pradyumna having been born, and having spent his youth elsewhere, and slain his enemy, came into the city of Dwârakâ accompanied by Rati. In every house joy and festivities took place.

---

## CHAPTER LVII.

The wondrous jewel Sumantakâ is obtained from the Sun by Satrâjit—It is lost by his brother Prasen, and falls into the possession of Jâmwant, a bear—Krishṇa recovers the jewel and returns it to Satrâjit, and receives Satibhâmâ in marriage as a recompense.

S'RÎ S'UKADEV JÎ said:—Mahârâj! Satrâjit[3] at first accused S'rî Krishṇa Chand of stealing a jewel; afterwards perceiving the

the Himâlayas, of stupendous proportions, on which the river Ganges falls, in its descent from heaven to earth. It is compared to the heart of a lotus, from which the several regions of the universe extend like the petals. Its four faces, fronting east, south, west, and north, are coloured white, yellow, black, and red, respectively; and the Regents of the four cardinal points occupy their appropriate sides of the mountain. The summit is the residence of Brahmâ, and it is a favourite resort of the subordinate divinities and saints.

[1] *Lit.*, "Krishṇa, only Krishṇa, they were saying."

[2] *samajh meñ ânâ*, "to come into comprehension," "to occur to one's apprehension." The phrase *ho na ho*, "be or not be," "whatever may be or not be," is used adverbially to express "undoubtedly," or "unquestionably."

[3] *Satrâjît* means "always conquering," and also "conqueror of the great."

falsity [of the charge], and becoming ashamed, he[1] gave his daughter Satibhâmâ in marriage to Hari.

Having heard this, King Parîkshit asked S'rî S'ukadev Jî, thus:—O abode of compassion! who was Satrâjît? where did he obtain the jewel? and how did he accuse Hari of theft? afterwards, how did he discover the falsity and give the girl in marriage? Do you expound and tell me this.

S'rî S'ukadev Jî said:—Mahârâj! please listen; I will explain all this.[2] Satrâjît was a Yâdava. For a long time he performed a very arduous austerity to the Sun; then the Sun-god, being pleased, called him near, and giving him a jewel, said, "The name of this jewel is Sumantakâ,[3] in it is the abiding-place of happiness and prosperity; always honour it, and esteem it my equal in power and glory. If thou shalt meditate upon it with prayer, penance, self-restraint, and vows, thou wilt obtain from this anything thou mayest ask.[4] In whatever country, city, or house this shall go, misery, poverty, and death will never come; good times will always be there; and so also will there be increase and success."

Mahârâj! having spoken thus, the Sun-god dismissed Satrâjît; and he, taking the jewel, came to his house. Afterwards, rising quite early, having performed his morning ablution and being released from his meditations and libations, he was ever in the habit of worshipping the jewel with sandal, whole rice, flowers, incense, lamps, and consecrated food; and taking the eight loads of gold which issued from that jewel, he remained happy. One day while worshipping, Satrâjît, having looked upon the beauty and splendour of the jewel, reflected within himself,[5] thus, "It would be well were this jewel taken and shown to S'rî Krishṇa Chand."

Having reflected thus, and having fastened the jewel on his neck, Satrâjit went into the assembly of the Yadubañsîs. Having perceived the brilliance of the jewel from a distance, all the Yadubañsîs rose up, and said to S'rî Krishṇa Jî, "Mahârâj! the Sun is advancing from a longing desire to see you. Brahmâ, Rudra, Indra, and all the other gods, are meditating on you; and fixing their thought on you the entire day they are celebrating your praises. You are the indestructible First Male; Kamalâ[6]

He was the son of Nighna and the father of Satyabhâmâ; and was killed by S'atadhanwan.

[1] For *us se* read *us ne*. [2] See note [3], p. 179.

[3] The proper name of this jewel is Syamantaka, as printed by Pandit Yogadhyân Miśra in his edition. Its potency was such that it yielded eight loads of gold daily. A long account of it is given in the Vishṇu-Purâṇa, Book iv. chap. 13.

[4] *muñh mâñgâ phal*, "the result asked by the mouth," that is, any reward that may be desired.

[5] The word *nij*, in the sense of "own," is commonly accompanied by a Genitive; here it stands for the Genitive *apne*.

[6] Kamalâ is a name of the goddess Lakshmî.

ever waits on you, and has become a bondmaid; you are the god of all gods; no one knows your nature; your attributes and exploits are limitless! why, O Lord! having come into the world, will you be concealed?" Mahârâj! when all the Yadubañsis having seen Satrâjit advancing, had spoken thus, then Hari spoke, "This is not the Sun; it is Satrâjit, a Yâdava. This one, by austerities performed for the Sun, obtained a jewel. Its brilliance is like that of the Sun. He is advancing with that jewel fastened on."

Mahârâj! while S'rî Krishṇa Jî was making this observation, he came and seated himself in the assembly, where the Yâdavas were playing at *chaupaṛ* and dice.[1] Having perceived the splendour of the jewel, the mind of all was fascinated; and S'rî Krishṇa Chand also kept on looking. Then Satrâjît, having thought of something in his inmost heart, then took leave and went home. Afterwards, fastening the jewel on his neck again and again, he came constantly. One day all the Yadubañsîs said to Hari, "Mahârâj! take the jewel from Satrâjît and give it to Râjâ Ugrasen, and acquire renown in the world. This jewel does not suit him; it is fit for a king."

On hearing this expression, S'rî Krishṇa Jî, laughing away, said to Satrâjît, "Give this jewel to the king, and acquire fame and greatness in the world." As soon as he heard the name of giving, he bowed, and silently rising from that place, went to his brother in deep cogitation, and said, "To-day S'rî Krishṇa Jî asked the jewel from me, and I did not give it." As this statement issued from the mouth of Satrâjît, his brother Prasen angrily took that jewel and placed it on his own neck; and arming himself, and mounting a horse, he went forth to hunt. Having gone into a great forest, he bent his bow, and began to slay elk, spotted deer, hogdeer, the white-footed antelope, and common deer. Hereupon, as a deer sprang from before him, this one also being vexed galloped after that one, and proceeding on, arrived alone where for ages[2] there had been a large, deep cave.

Catching the sound of a deer and a horse's feet, a lion came from within it. He killing all these three, took the jewel, and re-entered that cave. As soon as the jewel went in, there was such a brilliance in that great dark cavern that its rays reached to Pâtâla. There was a bear named Jâmawant, who had been with S'rî Râmachandra during the incarnation of Râma; he had remained there with his family since the Tretâ age.[3] Having seen the light in the cavern, he arose and hastened, and proceeding on he came near the lion. Then he having slain the lion,

[1] *chaupaṛ* is played with cowries or small shells; *sâr* is a "piece" or object with which the game of *chaupaṛ* is played.

[2] For *juganjug* read *jugûn jug*, as Lallû Lâl himself printed it, in his edition of 1825; or *jugânujug*, "age after age," as Pandit Yogadhyân Miśra prints it.

[3] *Tretâ* is the second of the four ages of the world. The four divisions are Satya, Tretâ, Dwâpara, and Kali.

took the jewel and went near his wife. She took the jewel and fastened it on her daughter's cradle. The [daughter], seeing that, kept on laughing and playing, and the whole place was, the whole day, illuminated.

Having related the tale thus far, S'rî S'ukadev Jî said:—Mahârâj! the jewel was thus gone, and this was the fate of Prasen. Then the people who had gone with Prasen, came and said to Satrâjît, "Mahârâj!—

> He left us and hurried away alone; we have found no trace of him where he went."
>
> Their statement not succeeding [in convincing], they searched [again], and returned; they did not find Prasen anywhere in the wood.

On hearing this statement, Satrâjît abandoned eating and drinking, and becoming greatly dejected, and anxious, began to say within himself, "This deed is S'rî Krishṇa's, who, having murdered my brother for the jewel, has taken the jewel and gone home. First he was asking it from me; I did not give it; now he has taken it thus." He is thus saying within himself, and night and day is in great anxiety. Once he, at night time, was seated on the bed near his wife, his body emaciated, his mind clouded, maintaining silence, pondering deeply something in his mind, when his wife said,—

> "Why, husband, are you pondering in your mind? tell me your secret."

Satrâjît said, "It is not right to tell the secret of a difficult matter to a wife; because a thing never stays in her stomach.[1] What she hears in the house, she publishes outside. She is without knowledge; she has no knowledge of anything, whether good or bad." As soon as she heard this remark, Satrâjît's wife testily said, "When did I hear anything in the house, and tell it outside, as you say? Are all women alike?" Having thus spoken, she resumed, "As long as you do not state before me what is in your mind, so long I will not take food or even water." Having heard this vow from his wife, Satrâjît said, "God knows what is true and false;[2] but one thing has come into my mind, that I [now] state before you; but thou shouldst not tell it to anyone."[3] His wife said, "Good! I will not tell."

Satrâjît began thus, "One day S'rî Krishṇa Jî asked me for the jewel, and I did not give it; hence it has occurred to me that *he*, having gone into the wood, has killed my brother, and appro-

[1] That is, "She cannot keep a secret."

[2] This is an asseveration, to assure his wife that he is uttering his real thought.

[3] Notice the difference between *par* and *parantu*; the first is connective, the second restrictive. Satrâjît says, "God knows the truth! but I really was revolving a matter in my mind, which I will tell you; only you must not tell anyone else."

priated the gem. This is his handiwork; no one else has the power to do such a thing."

Having related thus much, S'rî S'ukadev Jî said:—Mahârâj! on hearing this statement she was unable to sleep all night; and passed the night in restlessness.[1] As soon as it was dawn, she went and said to her friends, companions, and servants, "S'rî Krishṇa has slain Prasen, and taken the jewel; I heard this fact last night from my husband's mouth; but you must not mention it before anybody." They, saying "All right," went away from thence silent; but, being astonished, when seated in private they began to talk the matter over among themselves. At last one servant, having gone into the female apartments of S'rî Krishṇa Chand, related the affair. On hearing this, it occurred to them all that if Satrâjît's wife said it, it could not be false. Imagining this, and becoming dejected, the whole harem began to speak ill of S'rî Krishṇa. Hereupon someone came and said to S'rî Krishṇa, "Mahârâj! you have been accused of slaying Prasen, and of appropriating the jewel; why do you remain inactive? Adopt some remedy for this."

On hearing this statement, S'rî Krishṇa Jî was at first confounded; afterwards, having reflected somewhat, he went where Ugrasen, Vasudev, and Balarâm were seated in council, and said, "Mahârâj! all people are fixing this stain upon us, that 'Krishṇa has slain Prasen, and appropriated the jewel;' therefore, with your permission, we will go search for Prasen and the jewel, so that this infamy may be got rid of." Having spoken thus, S'rî Krishṇa came from thence, and accompanied by several Yadubañsîs and companions of Prasen, went to the forest. Having gone some distance and inspected, the marks of horses' feet were seen. By keeping these in view they reached the place where the lion had slain and eaten Prasen along with his horse. Seeing both their corpses, and the marks of a lion's feet, they all became aware that the lion had killed him.

Thinking this, and not finding the jewel, S'rî Krishṇa Chand took all of them along, and went where there was that deep, dark, and terrible cave. What do they see at its door! A dead lion is lying there; but the jewel is not there also. Seeing this marvel, all began to say to S'rî Krishṇa Jî, "Mahârâj! in this forest from whence came so strong a creature that slew the lion, and entered the cave with the jewel? Now, there is no remedy for this. You have searched as far as the obligation to search extended. The stain has passed from you; now the iniquity has fallen on the lion's head."

S'rî Krishṇa Jî said, "Come, let us enter the cave, and see who has killed the lion and taken away the jewel." They all said, "Mahârâj! how shall we enter that cave on seeing the mouth of which fear comes upon us? rather, we say humbly to you also,

[1] *sât pâñch karnâ*, "to make seven and five," is equivalent to being "at sixes and sevens," that is, in confusion, doubt, or uncertainty.

that you also should not go into this very terrific cavern. Now, please start for home. We unitedly shall say in the town that the lion, having killed Prasen, took the jewel; and that some creature, having slain the lion and taken the jewel, went into a frightful deep cavern. We come [back] having seen this with our own eyes." S'rî Krishṇa Chand said, "My mind is fixed on the jewel. I will go into the cavern alone. I will come [back] after ten days. You will stay here for ten days. Should any delay occur to me in this [matter], then go home and state the circumstances." Mahârâj! having said this, Hari entered that dark, frightful cavern, and, proceeding onwards, arrived where Jâmawant was sleeping, and his wife was standing rocking her child in a cradle.

She, having seen the Lord, being afraid, cried out, and Jâmawant woke up; then rushing, he came and clung to Hari, and a wrestling match began. When no stratagem nor force of his had any effect upon Hari,[1] he began to reflect within himself thus, "Lakshmaṇ and Râma are of my strength; but in this world who is so strong as to fight with me?" Mahârâj! Jâmawant, having thus wisely reflected within himself, and thought of the Lord,—

> Shrank back, with joined hands, and said, "Reveal [thyself], O Raghunâth!
> Searcher of hearts! I know you; by merely witnessing your sports I recognize you.
> You have done well to take incarnate form; you will remove[2] the burden of the earth.
> Since the Tretâ age I have remained in this place; Nàrad told me your mystery.
> 'In the matter of the jewel, the Lord will come here; then he will show himself to thee.'"[3]

Having related thus much, S'rî S'ukadev Jî said to King Parikshit:—Râjâ! when Jàmawant, having recognized the Lord, made this statement, then S'rî Murâri, the benefactor of devotees, perceiving the affection of Jâmawant, and being gratified, assumed the guise of Râma, and holding a bow and arrows, revealed himself. Thereupon Jâmawant, having abased himself to the earth,[4] rose up, joined his hands, and said, with exceeding humility, "O Ocean of Kindness! Friend of the Meek! should I receive your permission, I will make known my wish." The

[1] Notice this idiom, *us kâ bal Hari par na chalâ*. It is a form in common use colloquially.

[2] For *kari hau* read *karihau*, 2nd pers. pl. Fut.

[3] There are some unusual forms here; thus, *kâje* is the Locative of *kâjâ*, "work," "affair," "business"; *aihaiñ* and *daihaiñ* are, respectively, contractions of *â-ihaiñ* and *de-ihaiñ*, 3rd pers. pl. Fut.; and *to kauñ* is the Braj form of *tû ko*.

[4] *Lit.*, "having performed the eight-membered abasement." (See note [2], p. 149.)

Lord said, "Well, speak." Then Jâmawant said, "Purifier of the Guilty! Lord of the Poor! it is in my heart that I should give this girl Jâmawatî to you in marriage, and acquire fame and greatness in the world." Bhagwân said, "If such is thy wish, I also agree to it."[1] As soon as this promise issued from the mouth of the Lord, Jâmawant at first worshipped S'rî Krishṇa Chand with sandal, unbroken rice, flowers, perfume, lamps, and consecrated food, and afterwards gave his daughter in marriage, according to Vedic ritual; and he presented that jewel also in her dower.

Having related the story thus far, S'rî S'ukadev the saint said:—O King! S'rî Krishṇa Chand, the root of joy, taking Jâmawatî, along with the jewel, came out from the cavern; and now please hear the story of those Yâdavas, the companions of Prasen and S'rî Krishṇa, who were standing at the mouth of the cavern. When they had passed eighteen days[2] outside the cavern, and Hari had not come, they, in despair, troubled by a variety of anxieties, grieving bitterly, came from thence into Dwârakâ. Having got this news, all the Yadubañsîs were exceedingly disconcerted, and repeating S'rî Krishṇa's name, with great grief, began to bewail bitterly; and lamentation fell upon the entire female apartments. At last, all the queens, being greatly agitated, with emaciated bodies and disturbed minds, issued from the royal palace, and weeping bitterly came outside the city where, at the distance of a *kos*, there was the temple of Devî.

Having worshipped, and propitiated Gaur, and joined their hands and drooped their heads, they began to say, "O Devî! to thee, gods, men, and saints, all hasten, and what they ask from thee that they obtain. Thou knowest everything of the past, future, and present; say, when will S'rî Krishṇa Chand, the root of joy, come?" Mahârâj! all the queens then, sitting immovably[3] at the door of Devî, were propitiating thus, and Ugrasen, Vasudev, Baladev, and all the other Yâdavas, were seated in grave anxiety,—when, in the midst of this, S'rî Krishṇa, the indestructible dweller in Dwârakâ, laughing away, came and stood in the royal assembly, bringing Jâmawatî with him. Having seen the moon-face of the Lord, joy came to all of them; and having received this felicitous intelligence, all the queens also worshipped Devî, came home, and began to make rejoicings.

Having related thus much, S'rî S'ukadev Jî said:—Mahârâj! S'rî Krishṇa Jî, as soon as he was seated in the assembly, sent for Satrâjît, and having given him the jewel, said, "I did not take this jewel; you have falsely suspected me.

[1] *Lit.*, "If it has thus come into thy desire, then to us also is the sanction"
[2] Notice the idiom, "Eighteen days had elapsed to them."
[3] This is the famous process of "sitting *dharnâ*"; in which the complainant sits before the abode of one from whom he wishes to extort something, and refuses to eat, drink, or move away until his request be granted.

This jewel Jâmawant alone took; he gave it to me along with his daughter."
Taking the jewel, then, with bowed head, Satrâjît went; he went thinking [thus],
"I have done great wrong to Hari, unintentionally I have abused his family,
I have fixed a stain on the lord of the Yâdavas; and, in the matter of the jewel, have stirred up enmity;
Now let that be done which may remove the offence; let me give the Satibhâmâ jewel to Krishṇa."

Mahâraj! making such reflections in his heart of hearts, taking the jewel, grieved in mind, Satrâjît went to his house; and related to his wife all the thoughts of his soul. His wife said, "Husband! this affair you have well reflected on; let Satibhâmâ be given to S'rî Krishṇa, and get renown in the world." On hearing this expression, Satrâjît called a Brâhmaṇ, and having ascertained the felicitous time and moment, and having placed on a silver *rolî*, unbroken rice, silver, and a cocoanut, sent the marriage gift to the house of S'rî Krishṇa Chand by the hand of a priest. S'rî Krishṇa Jî, with much pomp, wearing the nuptial head-dress, came to the wedding. Then Satrâjît, with all customary ceremonies, gave his daughter according to Vedic ritual, and having given much wealth, in the wedding present conferred that jewel also.

On seeing the jewel, S'rî Krishṇa Jî took it out from that [present], and said, "This jewel is of no use to me, because you obtained it by performing austerity to Sûrya; in our family, with the exception of S'rî Bhagwân, we are not accepting things given by another deity. Put this in your own house." Mahârâj! as soon as these words had proceeded from the mouth of S'rî Krishṇa Chand Jî, Satrâjît took the jewel and remained ashamed; and S'rî Krishṇa Jî, taking Satibhâmâ, set out for his own house with a musical procession; and went and passed his time happily with Satibhâmâ in the royal palace.

Having heard the story thus far, Parîkshit asked S'rî S'ukadev Jî, thus, "Receptacle of kindness! why was the stain fastened on S'rî Krishṇa Jî? kindly tell me that." S'ukadev Jî said:—Râjâ!—

Mohan looked at the Moon on the fourth of the month Bhâdoṅ;
This stain clung to him; his heart was greatly dejected.

And listen:—

Should anyone look at the Moon, on the fourth of Bhâdon,
Let him hear this topic with his ears; no stain will attach to him.

## CHAPTER LVIII.

Duryodhan attempts to murder the Pâṇḍavas—Krishṇa and Balarâm hasten to Hastinâpur to protect them—Akrûr persuades Satadhanwâ to revenge himself on Satrâjît and to steal the wonderful jewel—Satadhanwâ does so, and gives the jewel to Akrûr—The latter carries the gem to Prayâg, and Balarâm goes in search of it—A pestilence rages in Dwârakâ; but Akrûr returns there with the jewel and gives it to Krishṇa, who presents it to Satibhâmâ.

S'RÎ S'UKADEV Jî said:—Mahârâj! I will now tell the story how Satadhanwâ, for the sake of the jewel, slew Satrâjît, took the gem, gave it to Akrûr, and fled from Dwârakâ; do you listen attentively. Once upon a time, someone came from Hastinâpur and delivered this message to Balarâm, the abode of happiness, and to S'ri Krishṇa Chand, the root of joy,—

The son of the blind one [1] invited the Pâṇḍavas; and caused them to sleep in his house;
At midnight, on all sides, he set fire to it.

On hearing this statement, both the brothers got very miserable and perplexed, and then called for their chariot from the charioteer Dârak, mounted it, and went to Hastinâpur, and having descended from the chariot, they went into the assembly of the Kauravas, and stood there. There they see that all, with emaciated bodies and disturbed minds, are seated. Duryodhan is pondering something in his heart; Bhîshma is shedding tears from his eyes; Dhritarâshṭra is experiencing much grief; tears are flowing from the eyes of Droṇâchârya [2] also; Vidûratha,[3] feeling remorse in his inmost soul, Gandhârî [4] came near him and sat down; others also who were wives of the Kauravas, as they repeatedly recalled the memory of the Pâṇḍavas, were weeping also; and the whole assembly was full of grief. Mahârâj! having witnessed the condition of that place, S'rî Krishṇa and Balarâm Jî also came near them and sat down; and they asked news of the Pâṇḍavas, but no one stated any of the secret, all remained silent.

Having related the story thus far, S'rî S'ukadev Jî said to King Parîkshit:—Mahârâj! S'rî Krishṇa and Balarâm Jî, then, having got the news of the burning of the Pâṇḍavas, went to Hastinâ-

[1] This means Duryodhana, the son of the blind king Dhritarâshṭra.

[2] Droṇâchârya was an *âchârya* or teacher, said to have been generated by the famous saint Bharadwâja in a bucket (*droṇa*). He was military adviser to both the Kauravas and the Pâṇḍavas, and afterwards became king of part of Pânchâla, and headed the Kuru troops in the great war against the sons of Pâṇḍu. He became the husband of Kripi, and the father of As'watthâman.

[3] Vidûratha was the son of Suratha, the son of Jahun, the son of Kuru, from whom the holy spot known as Kurukshetra was named.

[4] For *Gandhârî* read *Gândhârî*, the wife of Dhritarâshṭra, as Paṇḍit Yogadhyân Mis'ra prints it. The story here amplifies somewhat freely the statements of the Tenth Chapter of the Bhâgavata-Purâṇa.

pur.[1] But in Dwârakâ there was a Yâdava named Satadhanwâ, to whom formerly Satibhâmâ had been betrothed. Akrûr and Kritavarmâ went together to his place, and both of them said to him, "S'rî Krishṇa and Balarâm have gone to Hastinâpur; now has come thy opportunity; take thy revenge on Satrâjît; because he has committed a great fault towards thee, in that he has given thy betrothed to S'rî Krishṇa, and has raised up reproach against thee. Now here there is no one his helper." On hearing this speech, Satadhanwâ rose up angrily, and at night time went to the house of Satrâjît and challenged him. At length, by fraud and force, he slew him and returned with the jewel. Then Satadhanwâ, being seated alone in his house, reflected somewhat, and regretting in his heart, began to say,—

"I have committed this enmity towards Krishṇa; I listened to the advice of Akrûr;
Kritavarmâ and Akrûr came together and gave me advice. If a good person states a deceitful [thing], what can prevail against it?"[2]

Mahârâj! on this side Satadhanwâ, then, was in this way regretting and repeatedly saying, "Nothing can prevail against fate; the course of destiny no one can know;"[3] and, on the other side, having beheld Satrâjît dead, his wife, weeping grievously, cried out, "Husband! husband!" Having heard the sound of her weeping, all the people of the family, both women and men, making various kinds of remarks, began to weep violently; and lamentation fell upon the whole house. Having heard of the death of her father, Satibhâmâ immediately came, and having advised and counselled all, and caused her father's corpse to be placed in oil, she sent for her chariot, mounted it, and went to S'rî Krishṇa Chand, the root of joy, and in the course of a night and day arrived there.

As soon as he saw her, Hari arose and said, "O beauteous one! is the home prosperous?"
Satibhâmâ, joining her hands, said, "What prosperity [is there] without you, O Lord of the Yadus?
Satadhanwâ has caused us misfortune; he has killed my father, and taken the jewel.
Your father-in-law is placed in oil; remove all my griefs."

Having said this much, Satibhâmâ stood before S'rî Krishṇa and Baladev Jî, and began to cry out, "O Father! O Father!" and to weep bitterly. Having heard her grieving, S'rî Krishṇa and Balarâm Jî also, at first, being greatly dejected, cried and appeared like ordinary mortals; afterwards, giving hope and encouragement to Satibhâmâ, fortified her, and taking her with

[1] For *ho gaye* read *ko gaye*. This is a curious oversight.
[2] After *kapaṭ kî* the word *bât* is understood; *basnâ* means "to prevail against." It is possibly derived from *vaś*, "power."
[3] For *âe* read *jâe*.

them thence, came into Dwârakâ. S'rî S'ukadev Jî said:— Mahârâj! on coming into Dwârakâ, S'rî Krishṇa Chand,[1] seeing that Satibhâmâ was greatly pained, made this promise, and said, "Beauteous one! be firm in your heart, and be anxious about nothing. What was to be, that has taken place. But now I, having slain Satadhanwâ, will take revenge for your father, then I will do other work."[2]

Mahârâj! as soon as Râma and Krishṇa were come, Satadhanwâ, being greatly frightened, left his house, saying this within his heart, "At the suggestion of others I have acted inimically towards S'rî Krishṇa Jî; now whose refuge shall I seek?" He went to Kritavarmâ, and joining his hands, said with great humility, "Mahârâj! I did this thing at your suggestion, now S'rî Krishṇa and Balarâm are angry with me; therefore I have fled and have taken refuge with you; please point out some place where I can remain." Having heard this statement from Satadhanwâ, Kritavarmâ said, "Listen! I can do nothing for you.[3] The man who is at enmity with S'rî Krishṇa Chand, has gone from all. Wert thou not knowing that Murâri is exceedingly powerful, and that, on enmity being made with him, there will be defeat? What matters about anyone's suggestion? Why did you not reflect on your own strength and then act? It is the custom of the world that enmity, marriage, and friendship should be made with equals. Do not thou place hope on us; we are servants of S'rî Krishṇa Chand, the root of joy. It does not beseem us to act inimically towards him. Go where thou mayst find admittance."[4]

Mahârâj! having heard this speech, Satadhanwâ, becoming exceedingly dejected, went thence, and came to Akrûr. Closing his hands, drooping his head, humbly and beseechingly began to say, "Lord! you are the Yâdavas' chief and ruler, acknowledging you, all bow their heads. You are good, compassionate, and enduring; bearing pain yourself, you remove the pain of others. To you is the shame of the advice tendered; do you afford me your protection. I, paying deference to your advice alone, did this deed; now you alone should save me from the hand of S'rî Krishṇa."

On hearing this speech, Akrûr Jî said to Satadhanwâ, "Thou art a great fool, in that thou art saying such a speech to me. Dost thou not know that S'rî Krishṇa Chand is the creator and the remover of the ills of all? After acting antagonistically with him, who can ever remain in the world? What was injured by the adviser?[5] Now, indeed, on thy head the affair has fallen.[6]

[1] For *Krishṇa Chand se* read *Krishṇa Chand ne*.
[2] Meaning, that he will kill him before he attends to any other affair.
[3] *Lit.*, "From us nothing can be."
[4] *Lit.*, "Where thy horns may be contained, there go."
[5] This use of the Genitive with the Past Participle is very common in the sense of "by"; but both Hollings and Eastwick have missed the meaning here.
[6] The word *bât* is understood.

It is said that, this is the custom of gods, men, and saints, they make friendships for their own selfish ends; and in the world there are many kinds of people; they utter many different kinds of speeches for their own selfish purposes; therefore it is fitting for a man not to go upon the suggestion of anyone. Whatever act he would do, at first he should take thought on his own good and evil in the matter, afterwards he should enter on the task. Thou didst commit the act heedfully; now for thee there is nowhere in the world a place to remain in. Whoever has acted inimically towards S'rî Krishṇa has not afterwards lived: wherever he fled to and remained, there he has been killed. It is not for me to die that I should take thy part; in the world life is dear to all."

Mahârâj! when Akrûr Jî had thus made harsh, dry statements to Satadhanwâ, then he became hopeless, and giving up the hope of life, deposited the jewel with Akrûr Jî, ascended his chariot, and fled from the city; and after him, S'rî Krishṇa and Balarâm Jî also rose up, ascended their chariot, and pursued; and moving on and on, these, having gone a distance of a hundred *yojanas*, overtook him. Hearing the sound of their chariot, Satadhanwâ was exceedingly alarmed, got down from his chariot, and entered into the city of Mithilâpur.

The Lord, seeing him, angrily commanded his discus Sudarśan [thus], "Do thou at once cut off the head of Satadhanwâ." On receiving the command of the Lord, the discus Sudarśan went and cut off his head. Then S'rî Krishṇa Chand went to him and searched for the jewel, but found it not; then he said to Baladev Jî, "Brother! Satadhanwâ is killed, and the jewel not obtained." Balarâm Jî said, "That jewel some great man has obtained. He has not brought it and shown it to us. That jewel is not to be concealed near anybody. Do you take notice, at length it will manifest itself somewhere or other."

Having said this much, Baladev Jî said to S'rî Krishṇa Chand, "Brother! now do you set out for Dwârakâ city, and I am going to search for the jewel. Wherever I shall find it, I will bring it thence."

Having related the story thus far, S'rî S'ukadev Jî said to King Parîkshit:—Mahârâj! S'rî Krishṇa Chand, the root of joy, having slain Satadhanwâ, set out for Dwârakâ city, and Balarâm, the abode of happiness, proceeded to search for the jewel. Searching on in country after country, town after town, and village after village, Baladev Jî, proceeding onwards, arrived at the city of Ayodhyâ. Having obtained news of his arrival, Duryodhan, the King of Ayodhyâ, arose and hastened to him. Having advanced and met him, and made presents, spreading silken foot-cloths, he conducted the Lord, with a musical procession, into his own palace. Having seated him on a throne, and honoured him in various ways, and provided him with food, with great humility, downcast head, and joined hands, he stood before him, and said,

"Ocean of compassion! how is it that you have come hither? kindly let me know."

Mahârâj! Baladev Jî, perceiving the affection of his heart, and being pleased, related the whole secret of his coming. Having heard his statement, Râjâ Duryodhan said, "Lord! that jewel, by no means, will remain with anyone; at some time or other, it will spontaneously manifest itself." Having spoken thus, again joining his hands, he resumed, "Compassionate to the lowly! I am very fortunate in that I have obtained the sight of Your Honour while staying at home, and have got rid of birth after birth of sin. Now kindly fulfil the heart's desire of your servant, and having remained here some days, and made me your pupil, and taught me club-fighting, acquire fame in the world." Mahârâj! having heard this speech from Duryodhan, Balarâm Jî made him a pupil, and remaining there some time, taught him the whole science of club-fighting; but the jewel he searched for there also in the whole city, and found not. Subsequently, after the arrival of S'rî Krishṇa Jî, after some time Balarâm Jî also came into the city of Dwârakâ. Then S'rî Krishṇa Chand Jî, accompanied by all the Yâdavas, having taken Satrâjît from the oil, performed the rites of fire, and with his own hands ignited the pyre.[1]

When S'rî Krishṇa Jî was at leisure from these kindly duties, Akrûr and Kritavarmâ, having reflected somewhat among themselves, went to S'rî Krishṇa Jî, and taking him aside, and showing him the jewel, said, "Mahârâj! the Yâdavas are all become impious and are fascinated by delusion; abandoning remembrance and thought of you, they have become blinded by wealth. If these should now experience some hardship, then they would return into the service of the Lord; therefore we, leaving the town, and taking the jewel, will flee. When we shall have caused the adoration and recollection of you [to revive] among them, then we shall come back into the city of Dwârakâ." Having said this much, Akrûr and Kritavarmâ, with all their relatives, at midnight, S'rî Krishṇa Chand being privy to it, fled from the city of Dwârakâ, so that nobody knew whither they had gone. As soon as it was dawn, this gossip spread through the whole city, "It is not known whither Akrûr and Kritavarmâ, with their families, went in the dead of the night, and what has happened."

Having related the story thus far, S'rî S'ukadev Jî said:—Mahârâj! on this side, in the city of Dwârakâ, this began to be a constant topic of conversation in every house; and on the other side, Akrûr Jî first having gone to Prayâg, and having caused himself to be shaved, and having bathed at the Tribeṇî,[2]

[1] That is, he had the corpse burnt with the usual Hindû ceremonies. It is the right and privilege of the nearest in relationship to apply fire to the funeral pyre.

[2] The *Tribeṇî* means "the three braids" or locks of hair, and here alludes to the junction of the three rivers, Ganges, Jumnâ, and Saraswatî, at Allahabad.

and having given alms and done virtuous acts, and having constructed there a Hari-paiṛî,[1] he went to Gayâ. There, also, having seated himself on the banks of the river Phalgû he performed S'râddh[2] according to the S'âstras[3]; and having feasted the people of Gayâ, he gave bountiful alms. Then having seen the Mace-Bearer,[4] he went thence and came to the city of Kâśî. Having obtained news of his coming, all the kings thereabout came, met him, and began to make presents, and to remain there, performing sacrifice, alms-giving, austerity, and vows.

Hereupon, after some time had passed, S'rî Murâri, the benefactor of devotees, having resolved in his mind to recall Akrûr Jî, came to Balarâm Jî, and said, "Brother! now some affliction should be caused to the subjects, and Akrûr Jî should be recalled."[5] Baladev Jî said, "Mahârâj! do whatever enters your inclination, and give happiness to good people." As soon as these words issued from the mouth of Balarâm Jî, S'rî Krishṇa Chand Jî acted so that, in every house in the city of Dwârakâ, were spread fever, tertiary ague, epilepsy, consumption, ringworm, itch, hemicrania, leprosy, elephantiasis, dropsy, fistula, tympany, dysentery, tenesmus, gripes, cough, colic, hemiplegia, palsy, sun-stroke, morbid humours, and other diseases.

And for four months, also, no rain occurred, by which the streams, rivers, and lakes of the entire city were dried up; no grass or corn either sprang up; living creatures of the sky, water, and earth, birds and cattle, being distressed, began to wither up and die; and the inhabitants of the town, through famine, began to complain grievously. At length all the inhabitants of the town, being greatly distressed, were exceedingly dismayed. They came to S'rî Krishṇa Chand, the eradicator of misfortunes, and supplicatingly, and most submissively, with joined hands and bowed head, began to say,—

"*We* are in your protection; how [is it] we are now enduring great hardship?
A cloud has not rained; pain has occurred; why has Vidhâtâ decreed this?"

[1] A *Hari-paiṛî* is a landing-place on a river-bank, dedicated to Vishṇu.

[2] *S'râddha* are funeral rites performed in honour, and for the benefit of, deceased ancestors. They are of three kinds, which are called (1) *Nitya*, or constant, in honour of deceased ancestors collectively, when three balls of meal and water are offered; (2) *Naimittika*, or occasional, when offerings are made on behalf of a parent, or some recently deceased ancestor; (3) *Kâmya*, or voluntary, performed for the greater benefit of ancestors in general.

[3] The S'âstras are the treatises containing the general ordinances for the regulation of society.

[4] An epithet of Vishṇu.

[5] Here *dîjiye* and *lîjiye* are similar in construction to the common form *châhiye*, "it ought." Balarâm is not asked to do anything; therefore they are not respectful Imperatives, as has been supposed; he is told what should be done, and he replies that Krishṇa may do what seems good to him, and Krishṇa proceeds to act accordingly.

Having said this, they resumed, "O Lord of Dwârakâ, compassionate to the lowly! you are our creator and remover [of misfortunes]; except to you, where should we go, and to whom should we speak? Whence has this calamity unprovoked[1] come? and why has it occurred? Kindly tell us."

S'rî S'ukadev, the saint, said:—Mahârâj! on hearing this speech, S'rî Krishṇa Chand Jî said to them, "Listen! the city from which a good man departs, there spontaneously family, poverty, and misery come. Since Akrûr Jî went away from this town, this has been the state of things here. Wherever good people, the truthful, and the servants of Hari remain, there infelicity, famine, and misfortune are destroyed. Indra keeps friendly with the worshippers of Hari; hence, in that city, rain falls excellently."

On hearing this statement, all the Yâdavas cried out, "Mahârâj! you have spoken the truth. This thing came into our minds also; for the father of Akrûr is named Suphalak;[2] he also is very good, truthful, and virtuous. Wherever he remains, there is never misery, poverty, and famine; rain at all times falls there, and thence arises prosperity. And please hearken, Once a great famine fell on the city of Kâśî, then the King of Kâśî sent for Suphalak. Mahârâj! on Suphalak's going there, in that country rain fell as desired, [a good] time ensued, and the misery of all departed. Then the king of the city of Kâśî gave his daughter in marriage to Suphalak. They began to remain there happily. The name of that princess was Gâdinakâ; her son is Akrûr."

Having spoken thus, all the Yâdavas said, "Mahârâj! we were aware of this before; now what you may command we will do." S'ri Krishṇa Chand said, "Now do you, most courteously, conduct Akrûr Jî from wherever you may find him." As soon as that direction had issued from the mouth of the Lord, all the Yâdavas, unitedly, went forth to search for Akrûr; and, proceeding onwards, arrived in the city of Vârâṇasî.[3] Having met with Akrûr Jî, and made presents, with joined hands, and downcast heads, they stood before him, and said,—

"'Come, O Lord!' Bala and S'yâm[4] are saying; without you the inhabitants of the city are uneasy;
Wheresoever you [are], there is the abode of happiness; without you [there is] the dwelling of hardship and poverty;

[1] The phrase *baiṭhe biṭhâ,e meṅ* means "in a mere seated condition," that is, without any action or provocation. The simple and causal Past Participles are often thus coupled in similar significations. For examples, see the *Hindî Manual*, p. 191.

[2] *Suphalak* means "the causer of good results."

[3] *Vârâṇasî* is a name of the holy city Kâśî; and is the word whence the English term "Benares" originated. It took this name from a small stream running past the north of the city into the Ganges, which was anciently called *Varaṇâ*, "an enclosure," but is still known as the *Burnâ*.

[4] That is, Balarâm and Krishṇa.

Although S'rî Gopâl[1] is in the city, still famine, giving affliction, has fallen.
S'rî and her husband[2] are in the power of good people; from them, they obtain all happiness and prosperity."

Mahârâj! on hearing this statement, Akrûr Jî, being much affected,[3] rose up, and taking with him Kritavarmâ, and all the Yadubañsîs, along with his family, went with a musical procession, and, in the course of some time, arrived with them all in the city of Dwârakâ. Having received intelligence of their coming, S'rî Krishṇa Jî and Balarâm came forward, and, with exceeding honour and respect, had them conducted into the city. O King! immediately on the entrance of Akrûr Jî into the city, rain descended and [good] times came, and the misery and poverty of the entire city passed away. Akrûr's greatness was [manifested]; all the inhabitants of Dwârakâ began to live in happiness and rejoicing.

Afterwards, one day S'rî Krishṇa Chand, the root of joy, called Akrûr Jî to him, and taking him apart, said, "Having taken the jewel of Satrâjît, what have you done [with it]?" He said, "Mahârâj! it is in my possession." Then the Lord said, "Give it to whom the thing belongs;[4] and if he should not exist, then consign it to his son; and should there be no son, give it to his wife; should there be no wife, give it to his brother; should there be no brother, assign it to his family [generally]; should there even be no family, give it to the son of his religious preceptor; should there be no preceptor's son, give it to a Brâhmaṇ;[5] but do not yourself take the property of anyone. This is justice; therefore now it is fitting that you should give Satrâjît's jewel to his grandson, and acquire greatness in the world."

Mahârâj! as soon as these words had issued from the mouth of S'rî Krishṇa Chand, Akrûr Jî brought the jewel, placed it before the Lord, and with joined hands most humbly said, "Lord of the lowly![6] please accept this jewel yourself, and remove my transgression; because, the gold which issued from this jewel, I took and spent in pilgrimages to holy places." The Lord said, "Well done." Having said this, Hari took the jewel, and went and gave it to Satibhâmâ, and removed all the anxiety from his mind.

[1] That is, Krishṇa, the nourisher of kine.
[2] S'rî is a name of Lakshmî, and her husband is Vishṇu, the guardian deity.
[3] For *atur* read *âtur*.
[4] *Lit.*, "Of whom the thing [is], to that one give [it]."
[5] Notice the order of succession to property.
[6] For *dînâ* read *dîn*.

## CHAPTER LIX.

The adventures of Krishṇa and Balarâm at Hastinâpur—Krishṇa marries Kâlindi —He directs the element Fire to satisfy his hunger by consuming a forest—Krishṇa stops the conflagration at the abode of a demon Maya, who builds a golden house for Krishṇa in return for his kindness—Krishṇa carries off Mitrabindâ, Satyâ, and Bhadrâ.

S'RÎ S'UKADEV Jî said :—Mahârâj ! one day S'rî Krishṇa Chand, the friend of the world, the root of joy, thought thus, " I should now go and see if the Pâṇḍavas escaped alive from the conflagration and are alert." Having said this, Hari, taking with him some of the Yadubañsîs, set out from the city of Dwârakâ, and came to Hastinâpur. Having received intelligence of his coming, the five brothers Yudhishṭhira, Arjuna, Bhîma, Nakula, and Sahadeva,[1] being greatly delighted, rose and hastened [towards him] ; and having come outside the town, and met him, had him very courteously conducted to their house.

On going into the house, Kuntî and Draupadî[2] summoned seven auspicious women,[3] and filled a square place with pearls, upon which having spread a golden seat, caused Krishṇa to be seated upon it, and causing rejoicings to be made, with their own hands caused the *ârtâ* to pass round.[4] Afterwards causing the Lord's feet to be washed, and conducting him into the cooking place, they had prepared for him food of six flavours. Mahârâj ! when S'rî Krishṇa Chand had finished his repast and began to eat betel, then—

> Kauñtâ[5] sat near and conversed ; asking the welfare of father and relatives ;
> Are Surasen and Vasudev well ? my brother, and nephew Baladev ?
> In them is my soul ; except you, who destroys hardship and misery ?
> Whenever heavy affliction has fallen, then you have afforded me protection ;

[1] These are the names of the five Pâṇḍava princes.

[2] Kuntî was the daughter of a Yâdava prince named S'ûra, and was brought up by her father's cousin, Kunti-bhoja, the feminine form of whose name she took, having previously been known as Prithâ. She was the first wife of Pâṇḍu, the father of the five Pâṇḍava princes, three of whom, Yudhishṭhira, Bhîma, and Arjuna, were her sons. Draupadî was wife in common to the five princes. She was the daughter of Drupada, king of Pânchala, and had also borne the name of Krishṇâ, probably from her dark complexion. The cause of her becoming the wife of five brothers is given in the *Mahâbhârata*, Âdi-parvan, ch. 191 (Calc. ed.) ; but it is no doubt the traditional remembrance of ancient polyandry ; in fact ch. 196 plainly says that the practice " had become obsolete in consequence of being opposed to custom and the Vedas."

[3] That is, women whose husbands are living, the lot of one whose husband is dead being unenviable.

[4] See note [7], p. 174.

[5] *Kauñtâ* is intended for Kuntî.

O Krishṇa! you are the remover of the sorrows of others; the five brothers are in your asylum.[1]
As a doe dreads a pack of wolves, so do these [dread] residence with the sons of the blind one."

Mahârâj! when Kuntî had spoken thus—

Then Yudhishṭhira, with joined hands, [said], "You are the Lord, Chief of the Yâdavas, and Master,
The highest devotees ever meditate on you; a thought of S'iva and Viranch[3] comes not [to them].
You have revealed yourself to us in our very house; what corresponding[4] virtuous act have we done?
By staying four months you will give happiness; after the rainy season has passed, you will go home."[5]

Having related the story so far, S'rî S'ukadev Jî said:—Mahârâj! on hearing this speech, the benefactor of devotees, S'rî Bihârî, giving them all hope and encouragement, stayed there; and began to increase their joy and affection day by day. One day, along with Râjâ Yudhishṭhira, S'rî Krishṇa Chand took Arjuna, Bhîma, Nakula, and Sahadeva, holding in his hand a bow and arrows, having ascended his chariot, went into the wood to hunt. Having gone there, he descended from the chariot, fastened his belt, turned up his sleeves, arranged his arrows, and beat about the jungle; he began to slay lions, tigers, rhinoceroses, buffaloes, elk, hog-deer, deer, and antelopes, and to bring them and lay them before Râjâ Yudhishṭhira; and Râjâ Yudhishṭhira, laughing away, and being gratified, accepted them, and began to give them to those whose food they respectively were; and the deer, antelope, and elk, to send to the kitchen.

Then S'rî Krishṇa Chand and Arjuna, hunting on, having advanced some distance beyond all the others, stood beneath a tree; then, having gone to the bank of a stream, they both drank the water. Hereupon what does S'rî Krishṇa Jî see? On the bank of the stream an exceedingly beautiful young woman, moon-faced, of the complexion of the Champaka, eyes like a fawn, voice like a cuckoo, gait like an elephant, waist like a lion, ornamented from head to foot, intoxicated with the passion of Anang,[6] having great beauty, was wandering alone. On seeing her, Hari, being astonished and motionless, said,—

[1] That is, they have taken refuge with you, as suppliants.
[2] That is, Dhritarâshṭra.
[3] *Viranch* is a name of Brahmâ.
[4] *aisau* is here equivalent to "similar," or "corresponding"; for the doctrine of *Karma* teaches Hindûs that every action is the result of some correspondingly efficient cause.
[5] *daihau* and *jaihau* stand for *de-ihau* and *jâ-ihau* respectively, 2nd pers. pl. of the Future.
[6] *Anang*, "the bodiless one," a name of Kâma, the god of love. We saw in a former chapter that the body of Kâma was consumed by the god S'iva.

"Who [is] that beauty [of] pleasing form? no one [is] with her."[1]

Mahârâj! having heard this expression from the mouth of the Lord, and having seen her, Arjuna hastily ran, and went where that very beautiful one was taking pleasure along the bank of the river, and began to ask, thus, "Say, beautiful one! who art thou? and from whence art thou come? and why art thou wandering here alone? This secret of yours expound, and tell all to me." On hearing this speech,—

The beauteous one tells her tale. "I am a maiden, the daughter of the Sun;
My name is Kâlindî; my father assigned me an abiding place in water;
He came and built [for me] a palace in the water. My father counselled me and said,
'Keep on, daughter! wandering near the river; thy husband will come and meet thee here;
In the Yadu family Krishṇa will be incarnate; in quest of thee, to this place, he will proceed;
The Primal Male, the imperishable Hari; for his purpose, thou art incarnate.'
As soon as my father the Sun had spoken thus, since then I have longed for the footstep of Hari."

Mahârâj! on hearing this speech, Arjuna, being greatly delighted, said, "O beauteous one! he for whose sake thou art wandering here, that very Lord, the imperishable, Dwârakâ-resident, S'rî Krishṇa Chand, the root of joy, has arrived." Mahârâj! when these words issued from the mouth of Arjuna, the benefactor of devotees, S'rî Bihârî also, having urged on the chariot, arrived there. On seeing the Lord, when Arjuna had related all that [girl's] secret, then S'rî Krishṇa Chand Jî, laughing, quickly causing her to mount the chariot, took the road to the town. While S'rî Krishṇa Chand is coming from the wood into the town, Viśwakarmâ,[2] perceiving the desire of the Lord, constructed an exceedingly beautiful palace, apart from all the rest. Hari, on arriving, caused Kâlindî to dismount there, and himself also began to stay there.

Some days afterwards, on a certain time, S'rî Krishṇa Chand and Arjuna, at night time, were seated in a certain place, when Agni[3] having come, with joined hands, and downcast head, said to Hari, "Mahârâj! I, a-hungered for many days, have wandered through the entire world; but found food nowhere. Now there is [but] one hope from you. If I get your permission, I will go

[1] *tâsu ke* is a double Genitive; *tâsu* being a Braj genitival form in itself. The Genitive often becomes a base for other case signs, as *tere ko*, *mere par*, &c., but seldom is used as a base for itself.

[2] Viśwakarmâ is the Vulcan, or artificer, of the Hindû Pantheon.

[3] Agni is the god of fire, and an ancient Vedic deity. It is also fire itself.

and devour the woods and jungles." The Lord said, "Good! go and eat." The Agni said, "Lord of Compassion! I am not able to go alone into the woods. If I go, Indra will come and extinguish me." Having heard this remark, S'rî Krishṇa Jî said to Arjuna, "Brother! do you go, cause Agni to take food, and return [to me]; he has been starving to death for many days."

Mahârâj! as soon as these words had issued from the mouth of S'rî Krishṇa Chand Jî, Arjuna, taking his bow and arrows, accompanied Agni. And Agni, going into the wood, blazed up, and began to consume the mango, tamarind, the fig, the sacred fig, the citron-leaved fig, the palm, the *Xanthocymus pictorius*, the butter-tree, the rose-apple, the *Mimusops Kauki*, the *Bauhinia variegata*, the grape, the *Chironjia sapida*, the orange, the lime, the jujube, and all other trees; and—

> Grass and bamboo, with a loud noise, crackles; the creatures of the wood, losing their way, wander about.

Whithersover one might look, there, in the entire wood, fire, with a great roaring, is burning, and smoke circling round went to the sky. Having perceived that smoke, Indra, having summoned the Master of the clouds, said, "Do you go, and with violent rain, extinguish the fire, and save the beasts, birds, and living creatures of the wood. Having received that order, the Cloud-master, taking with him an army of clouds, having come there and thundered, just as he was about to rain Arjuna struck [him with] such wind-arrows that the clouds, becoming very small pieces, were dispersed as flocks of cotton are dispersed by gusts of wind. No one saw them coming or going. As they came, so they quite easily disappeared; and the fire, continuing to consume the forest and underwood, came where? Where there was the palace of an Asura named Maya.[1] Having perceived Agni approaching filled with extreme anger, Maya, being very fearful, naked-footed, with a cloth thrown on his neck, and his hands clasped, issued from the palace, and came and stood before [Agni], and prostrating himself, supplicatingly said, "O Lord! O Lord! save me from this fire, speedily preserve me.

> Agni has fed and has obtained satisfaction; now do not pay heed to any offence [which I may have committed];
> Bear in mind my submissiveness; save me from Baisandar."[2]

Mahârâj! as soon as these words had issued from the mouth of Maya, the Daitya, Baisandar laid [aside] the fire-arrows, and Arjuna also stopped astonished. At length both of them, taking Maya along with them, went to S'rî Krishṇa Chand, the root of joy, and said, "Mahârâj!—

[1] This is the answer to the exclamatory interrogation just before it.
[2] This is intended for Vais'wânara, a name of Agni, occurring in the Rig-Veda.

This Asura Maya is useful; for you he will construct an abode;
Do you immediately take thought of Maya; extinguish the fire, and make him fearless."

Having said this, Arjuna placed on the ground with his hand the bow Gâṇḍîva,[1] along with the arrows. Then the Lord made a sign by winking towards the fire, and it was immediately extinguished; and in the whole wood coolness supervened. Then S'rî Krishṇa Chand, accompanied by Arjuna, took Maya with him, and proceeded forwards. Having gone there, Maya, in a single moment, constructed and set up a jewel-studded golden palace, exceedingly beautiful, delightsome and pleasing to the mind, such that its beauty is indescribable. Whoever had come to see it, stood still with astonishment like a picture. Afterwards, S'rî Krishṇa Jî delayed there four months; then, moving thence, where did he come? but where Râjâ Yudhishṭhira was seated in his royal court. On coming, the Lord asked from the king permission to go to Dwârakâ. As soon as this speech issued from the mouth of S'rî Krishṇa Chand, Râjâ Yudhishṭhira, as well as his Court, were much dejected, and in the entire female apartments also, both women and men began to feel every anxiety. At length the Lord, appropriately advising and counselling them all, gave them hope and encouragement, and taking Arjuna with him, and bidding Yudhishṭhira farewell, and proceeding from Hastinâpur, laughing and sporting, after a certain time, arrived at the city of Dwârakâ. Having heard of his coming there was joy in all the city; and the pain of separation departed from all. His parents, having seen the face of their son, obtained happiness, and lost all distress of mind.

Afterwards, one day, S'rî Krishṇa Jî, having gone to Râjâ Ugrasen, and having fully imparted to him the secret of Kâlindî, said, "Mahârâj! I have brought Kâlindî, daughter of the Sun; do you marry me to her according to Vedic ritual. On hearing this, Ugrasen, at that very instant, summoning his Minister, gave order thus, "Do you immediately go, and bring all the requisites for a marriage." Having received the order, the Minister at once brought all the requisites for the marriage. Then Ugrasen and Vasudev, having summoned an astrologer, and having had a propitious day settled, married S'rî Krishṇa Jî to Kâlindî, according to Vedic ritual.

Having related the story thus far, S'rî S'ukadev Jî said:— O King! it was in this way that the marriage of Kâlindî happened. Now I am about to relate the story how Hari afterwards brought Mitrabindâ and married her; do you attentively listen. Sûrasen's daughter [was] S'rî Krishṇa Jî's aunt; her name [was]

[1] The bow Gâṇḍîva, so called because made of *gâṇḍî* wood, was a weapon of Arjuna. It was presented by the god Soma to Varuṇa, and he gave it to Agni, who in his turn presented it to Arjuna.

Râjadhi Devî; her daughter [was] Mitrabindâ.[1] When she became marriageable, she effected *Swayamvara*.[2] There were collected the kings of all the various countries, having good qualities, repositories of beauty, intelligent, strong, heroic, very resolute, dressed out, one outvying the other.[3] Having received this intelligence, S'rî Krishṇa Chand Jî also, taking Arjuna with him, went there; and having arrived, stood in the very midst of the *Swayamvara*.

> The beauteous one, having seen Murâri, was delighted;
> having thrown the garland [round his neck], she continued gazing on his face.

Mahârâj! having witnessed this action, all the kings of the various countries, being abashed, began to be fretful in their hearts. And Duryodhan went and said to her brother Mitrasen, "Brother! Hari is your maternal uncle's son; having seen him, the beauteous one is become fascinated; this is a practice opposed to custom;[4] on this taking place there will be ridicule in the world. Do you go and advise your sister not to choose Krishṇa, otherwise there will be ridicule among a crowd of kings." On hearing this speech, Mitrasen went, and spoke advisingly to his sister.

Mahârâj! having heard and understood her brother's statement, when Mitrabindâ, having retired from proximity to the Lord, and stood at a distance apart, then Arjuna, bending down, said in the ear of S'rî Krishṇa Chand, "Mahârâj! now what are you abashed at? the affair is a failure; do what should be done;[5] there should be no delay." On hearing the statement of Arjuna, S'rî Krishṇa Jî, quickly having seized her hand, raised Mitrabindâ up from the midst of the *Swayamvara*, seated her in his chariot, and took her off; and, at that very instant, in the sight of all, urged on the chariot. Then all the kings, each having seized his own weapon, mounted on horses, and wheeling round the front of the Lord, went and stood ready to fight. And the people dwelling in the city, ridiculing and clapping away with their hands, abusively began to speak thus,—

> "He came to marry his aunt's daughter; from this, Krishṇa
> has acquired excellent renown."

Having related the story thus far, S'rî S'ukadev Jî said:—Mahârâj! when S'rî Krishṇa Chand saw that the army of Asura which had surrounded him on all sides would not rest without being fought, he drew from the quiver several arrows, and stretch-

1 Notice the absence of verbs in this phrase. It is not unusual in the relation of genealogical details.

2 That is, she chose a husband (*vara*) for herself (*swayam*).

3 *ek se ek adhik kâ*, "one [trying to be] of superior [quality] to another."

4 *lokaviruddha* should be one word. Iti s a compound adjective to *rîti*.

5 The word *karnâ*, though in the form of the Infinitive, is here the representative of the Sanskrit Future Passive Participle. See *Hindi Manual*, p. 175.

ing his bow, discharged them so that the whole army of the Asuras, having become scattered, disappeared in that very spot; and the Lord reached Dwârakâ in undisturbed happiness.

S'rî S'ukadev Jî said:—Mahârâj! S'rî Krishṇa Jî, having thus taken possession of Mitrabindâ, married her in Dwârakâ. Now I will further relate the story how the Lord brought Satyâ; do you listen attentively. In the kingdom of Kauśala [there was] a king named Nagnajit; his daughter [was] Satyâ.[1] When she became marriageable, the king sent for seven very huge and terrible bulls, whose nostrils had not been pierced; and having made this vow, turned them loose in the country, "Whoever, at one time, shall nose-ring these seven bulls and bring them, to him I will marry my daughter." Mahârâj! these seven bulls, with heads down, tails erect, pawing the ground, wander about, bellowing. Whomsoever they meet, they kill.

Afterwards, having received this intelligence, S'rî Krishṇa Chand, taking Arjuna with him, went there; and having arrived, stood before King Nagnajit. On seeing them, the king descended from his throne, prostrated himself, and having caused them to be seated on the throne, and presented sandal, unbroken rice, and flowers, and employed incense and lamps, and placed consecrated food before them, with joined hands and bowed head, he very humbly said, "To-day my [good] fortune has awakened, in that the Creator of S'iva and Viranch has come into my house." Having said this, he resumed, "Mahârâj! I made a vow, the fulfilling of which was difficult; but now I am assured that, by your favour, it will speedily be accomplished." The Lord said, "What sort of vow was it that you made, the fulfilment of which is difficult? Tell me." The king said, "Lord of Compassion! I, having released seven un-nose-ringed bulls, made this vow: Whoever at one time shall nose-ring these seven bulls, to him I will marry my daughter."

S'rî S'ukadev Jî said:—Mahârâj!

> Having heard [this], Hari tightened [his] girdle [and] went there; [and] having assumed seven forms, stood [where the bulls were];
> No one saw [his] invisible operations; all seven [he] nose-ringed, at one and the same time.

Those bulls, at the time of the nose-ringing of their nostrils, stood still, as wooden bulls might stand. The Lord, having pierced the nostrils of the whole seven, and having strung them on a rope, led them into the royal court. Having witnessed this exploit, all the inhabitants of the city, both women and men, being astonished, began to applaud; and Râjâ Nagnajit, immediately summoning his priest, gave his daughter according to Vedic ritual. In her dowry having conferred ten thousand cows, nine hundred thousand elephants, ten hundred thousand horses,

[1] See note [1], p. 202.

and seven million three hundred thousand chariots, he gave unnumbered male and female slaves. S'rî Krishṇa Chand, having accepted all, when he went thence, then being irritated, all the kings gathered round the Lord in his path. There, with his arrows, Arjuna smote and put all to flight. Hari, with delight and rejoicing, arrived in the city of Dwârakâ with them all. Then all the inhabitants of Dwârakâ, having come forward, with a musical procession, spreading silken foot-cloths, conducted the Lord into his palace; and, having seen the dowry, all were astonished.

Celebrating the greatness of Nagnajit, the people were saying, "This is a great betrothal.
The Lord of Kauśala has effected a good marriage; he has given all this marriage-portion to Krishṇa."

Mahârâj! the inhabitants of the city were making remarks of this sort, when, at that very time, S'rî Krishṇa Chand and Balarâm Jî, having come there, presented to Arjuna the whole marriage-portion which King Nagnajit had given, and acquired fame in the world. Further, I will now tell the story how S'rî Krishṇa Jî brought home Bhadrâ [as wife]; do you listen attentively and free from distraction. Bhadrâ, the daughter of the king of the district of Kekaya, effected a *Swayamvara*, and letters were written to the kings of various countries. They went, and were assembled together.

There S'rî Krishṇa Chand also, taking Arjuna with him, went; and, during the *Swayamvara*, went and stood in the assembly. Then the princess, with the garland in her hand, gazing at all the kings, came near to S'rî Krishṇa Chand, the ocean of beauty, the light of the world. Then upon seeing him, she was fascinated, and she threw the garland on his neck. Seeing this, her parents, being pleased, married that girl to Hari, according to Vedic ritual. In her dowry very much was given, so that there were no bounds to it.

Having told the story thus far, S'rî S'ukadev Jî said:—Mahârâj! S'rî Krishṇa Chand in this way married Bhadrâ. I will now tell the story how the Lord afterwards married Lakshmaṇâ; do you listen The King of Bhadradeś was exceedingly powerful and very famous. When his daughter Lakshmaṇâ was marriageable, having arranged a *Swayamvara*, letters were written to the kings of surrounding countries, inviting them. They, with great pomp, preparing their several armies, came there, and during the *Swayamvara*, in a very orderly fashion, went and sat down in rows.

S'rî Krishṇa Chand Jî also, taking Arjuna with him, went there. And when he went and stood in the *Swayamvara*, Lakshmaṇâ, having looked upon all, came and placed the wreath on S'rî Krishṇa Jî's neck. Afterwards, her father, according to Vedic ritual, married Lakshmaṇâ to the Lord. The kings from all the various countries who had come there, being greatly abashed, began to say among themselves, "Look! while we are here, how Krishṇa is carrying off Lakshmaṇâ!"[1]

Having spoken thus, each preparing his own army, all went and stood to block the way. When S'rî Krishṇa Chand and Arjuna, along with Lakshmaṇâ, taking the chariot, advanced, then these came and stopped them, and began to fight. At length, after a certain time, with arrows, Arjuna and S'rî Krishṇa Jî smote and put all to flight; and himself, with great joy and rejoicing, arrived at the city of Dwârakâ. As soon as he arrived, in every house in the entire city,—

> There were songs of congratulation and festivities; and there were ceremonies in the manner of the Vedas.

Having told the tale thus far, S'rî S'ukadev Jî said:—Mahârâj! in this way S'rî Krishṇa Chand Jî effected five marriages. Then, in Dwârakâ, with all eight queens, he began to live happily; and the queens, during the entire day, began to attend upon him. The names of the queens are, Rukminî, Jâmawatî, Satyabhâmâ, Kâlindî, Mitrabindâ, Satyâ, Bhadrâ, and Lakshmaṇâ.

---

## CHAPTER LX.

**Bhaumâsur carries off and conceals sixteen thousand one hundred princesses—Krishṇa slays him and marries the girls.**

S'RÎ S'UKADEV Jî said:—O King! once the Earth, assuming the body of a man, began to perform a very difficult austerity. There Brahmâ, Vishṇu, Rudra, all these three deities, came and asked him, "Why art thou performing this severe austerity?" The Earth replied, "Ocean of Compassion! I have the desire for a son, therefore I am performing great austerity; compassionately give me a son very strong, exceedingly renowned, and most glorious, such that no one in the world shall confront him, nor shall he die by the hand of anyone."

Having heard this speech, and being pleased, the three gods granted the boon, and said to him, "Thy son, named Narakâsur, will be exceedingly strong and greatly renowned. No one will fight with him and live. He will conquer all the kings of creation, and make them submissive to him. Having gone into Swargalok,[2] and having smitten and put the gods to flight, and snatched away

[1] "While we are here" is equivalent to "before our very faces."
[2] The Paradise of the god Indra.

the earrings of Aditi,[1] he will wear them himself; and appropriating the umbrella of Indra, will place it over his own head; he will bring sixteen thousand one hundred girls of the kings of the world, and keep them enclosed unmarried. Then S'rî Krishṇa Chand, taking all his army, will attack him, and thou wilt say to him, 'Kill him.' Then he, having killed [him], will take all the princesses, and set out for the city of Dwârakâ."

Having related the story thus far, S'rî S'ukadev Jî said to King Parikshit:—Mahârâj! The three gods, having conferred the boon, when they had thus spoken, the Earth, having said thus much, remained silent, "How shall I say such a thing as 'Slay my son'?" Later on, after a certain time, the Earth's son Bhaumâsur was produced, whose name is also called Narakâsur.[2] He began to reside in Prâgjyotishpur. Having constructed all round that city a rampart of mountains, and forts of water, fire, and air, he kept on snatching away, by force, the daughters of the kings of the whole world, and bringing them along with their nurses, placed them there. Constantly arising [betimes], he is unremittingly attentive to the food, drink, and clothing of those sixteen thousand one hundred princesses, and has them brought up with great care.

One day, Bhaumâsur, in great wrath, having seated himself in a flowery car which[3] he had brought from Lankâ,[4] went into the city of the gods, and began to annoy the gods. Through his annoyance, the gods severally abandoning the place, escaping with their lives, fled hither and thither. Then he snatched away the earrings of Aditi and the umbrella of Indra. Afterwards, he began to cause great affliction to the gods and saints of all creation.[5] Having heard of all his proceedings, S'rî Krishṇa Chand, the friend of the world, said within himself,—

"Having slain him, I will bring all the beauties; I will convey the umbrella of the master of the gods just there [where it ought to be];
Having gone, I will give [back] the earrings of Aditi; I will render Râjâ Indra fearless."[6]

[1] Aditi is the mother of the gods, the daughter of Daksha, and wife of Kaśyapa. The Matsya-Purâṇa says that these earrings were one of the objects produced at the mythological churning of the ocean. In Book V. chap. ii. of the Vishṇu-Purâṇa, Aditi is identified with all that is great, and the source of all knowledge, order, and religion; the very cosmic egg of Brahmâ, the primal source of all creation, is attributed to her.

[2] Narakâsur means "the demon of hell," and Bhaumâsur, "the demon of earth."

[3] For *jâ* read *jo*.

[4] Lankâ is a name for Ceylon.

[5] In previous editions this phrase reads *sur nar muniyo*, "gods, men, and saints." Capt. Hollings inserts "men" in his translation; and so does Prof. Eastwick, affording another proof that Eastwick was not translating his own edition of the text.

[6] *dai haun̄* should be one word = *de-ihaun̄*; and so should *kai haun̄* be also, which = *karûn̄* or *karihaun̄*. They are all aoristic forms, having here the sense of the Future.

Having said thus much, S'rî Krishṇa Chand resumed to Satibhâmâ, "O wife! do thou come with me, then Bhaumâsur will be killed; because you are a portion of the earth, and on this account have become his mother. When the gods gave the boon of a son to the Earth they said this, "When thou shalt order [someone] to slay [him] then thy son will die; otherwise, slain by anyone anyhow, he will not die."[1] As soon as she heard this statement, Satibhâmâ Jî, having reflected somewhat in her heart, saying this much, remained dissatisfied, "Mahârâj! my son is your son; how will you slay him?"

The Lord, evading this remark, said, "About slaying him I have not much concern; but once I gave you a promise, and that I want to fulfil." Satibhâmâ said, "What is that?" The Lord resumed, "Once Nârad Jî, having come, gave me a flower of the Kalpa-tree;[2] accepting it, I sent it to Rukminî. Having heard of the affair thou wast angry; then I made this promise, 'Be not dejected; I will bring the Kalpa-tree itself, and give it to thee.' Therefore I am going to redeem my promise, and take thee with me to show Vaikuṇṭh to thee."

On hearing this statement, Satibhâmâ Jî, being pleased, was ready to go along with Hari. Then the Lord, having seated her behind him on Garuṛ,[3] took her with him, and departed. Having gone some distance, S'rî Krishṇa Chand Jî asked Satibhâmâ Jî, "Tell me truly, beauteous one! having heard this affair, what at first didst thou imagine that made thee displeased? Explain the secret of that to me, that the doubt of my mind may depart." Satibhâmâ said, "Mahârâj! you having killed Bhaumâsur, will bring sixteen thousand one hundred princesses; you will reckon me also among them; thinking this, I was dissatisfied."

S'rî Krishṇa Chand said, "Thou shouldst not be anxious on any matter. I will bring the Kalpa-tree, and will place it in thy house; and do thou present me, along with that, to Nârad, the saint; then buy me back, and place me near thee; I will ever remain subject to thee. Just in this way, Indraṇî gave Indra, along with the tree; and Aditi [gave] Kaśyapa. By making this present, no wife of mine will be equal to thee." Mahârâj! talking away in this fashion, S'rî Krishṇa Jî arrived near Prâgjyotishpur. Upon seeing the fort of mountains, and the rampart of fire, water, and wind, there,[4] the Lord ordered Garuṛ and the discus Sudarśan; and they in a moment, having battered down, extinguished, swept away, and fixed, made up a good road.

When Hari, advancing forwards, began to penetrate into the

[1] That is, "he will not anyhow be put to death by anyone."

[2] The *Kalpavriksh*, or *Kalpadruma*, is a miraculous tree of Paradise, which grants all wishes.

[3] *Garuṛ*, or, more usually, *Garuḍa*, is a miraculous bird, of stupendous power, on which Vishṇu rides about.

[4] In the preceding page the rampart was mountainous, and the forts were constructed of the elements.

city, the Daitya garrison of the fort advanced to fight [with them]. The Lord, with his club, quite easily struck them down. Having received news of their death, a five-headed Râkshas named Mur, who was the guardian of that fort, most angrily, taking a trident in his hand, attacked S'rî Krishṇa Jî; and, with eyes intensely red, and teeth grinding together, began to say,—

"Who else in the world is stronger than me? Let me see him here."[1]

Mahârâj! having said this, Mur, the Daitya, sprang upon S'rî Krishṇa Chand, as Garuḍa jumps on a snake. Then he hurled the trident, which the Lord with his discus cut down. Then, being irritated, whatever weapons Mur flung at Hari the Lord quite easily cut down. Then he, being aghast, rushed upon and clung to the Lord, and began a wrestling match. At length, after some time, while fighting away, S'rî Krishṇa Jî, perceiving that Satibhâmâ Jî was much frightened, cut off his five heads with the discus Sudarśana. On the heads falling from the trunk, hearing the thud, Bhaumâsur said, "Of what is this the great noise?" Hereupon someone came and stated, thus, "Mahârâj! S'rî Krishṇa, having come, has slain the Daitya Mur."

Upon hearing this statement, at first Bhaumâsur was exceedingly sorrowful; afterwards, he gave order, to the commander of his forces, to fight. He, having arranged the whole army, and having gone to the gate of the fort, stood ready to fight; and, behind him, having heard of the death of their father, the seven sons of Mur, who were very powerful and great warriors, they also, bearing different kinds of weapons and arms, going to fight, stood confronting S'rî Krishṇa Chand Jî. From the rear, Bhaumâsur sent to tell his General and the sons of Mur, thus, "Do you fight heedfully; I also am coming."

On receiving the order to fight, taking with him the whole army of Asuras, along with the sons of Mur, Bhaumâsur's General advanced to fight with S'rî Krishṇa Jî; and, all at once, the whole army of soldiers went and spread like a cloud all around the Lord. From all sides, the warriors of Bhaumâsur were hurling various kinds of weapons and arms upon S'rî Krishṇa Chand; and he, in a quite easy manner, was keeping on cutting them down and making them into heaps. At length, Hari, noticing that S'rî Satibhâmâ Jî was much frightened, with his discus Sudarśana, in an instant, cut down the Asura army, together with the seven sons of Mur, as a farmer cuts down a crop of millet.

Having related the story thus far, S'rî S'ukadev Jî said to King Parîkshit:—Mahârâj! having heard that the whole army, along with the sons of Mur, was cut up, at first Bhaumâsur was exceedingly anxious and greatly disconcerted, afterwards having reflected a little, and recovered confidence, taking with him several very

[1] *dekhihoṅ* should be one word; it is 1st pers. sing. Aorist.

powerful Râkshasas, his eyes intensely red with anger, his girdle bound tightly, his arrows prepared, he came talking incoherently, and was ready to fight with S'rî Krishṇa Jî. When Bhaumâsur saw the Lord, he with excessive rage flung whole handfuls of arrows at once; these Hari severally cut into three and brought down. Then—

Bhaumâsur drew out his sword, and, wrathfully shouting, presented it at Krishṇa's breast;[1]
He makes a noise, like a great thunder-cloud; "O villager! thou wilt not be allowed to go."
He is uttering there harsh speeches; Bhaumâsur makes fierce war.

Mahârâj! he, indeed, violently was striking at him with a club; and, on S'rî Krishṇa Jî's body, his blows were falling as a whip of flowers on the body of an elephant. Afterwards, taking various weapons and arms, he warred with the Lord; and the Lord cut them all down. Then he went home again, and fetched a trident; and stood ready to combat [once more].

Then Satibhâmâ cried aloud, "O King of the Yadus! why are you not killing this one?"
Hearing this speech, the Lord poised the discus, and, cutting off the head, killed Bhaumâsur;
The head fell, with the earrings and crown; as soon as the trunk fell, S'esh[2] quivered;
In the three worlds there was happiness; the grief and misery of all departed;
His brilliancy went into Hari's body; gods and sages raise shouts of "Victory! victory!"
Their cars gather round, they rain down flowers; the gods recite the Vedas and sing [his] glory.

Having related thus much of the story, S'rî S'ukadev, the saint, said:—Mahârâj! as soon as Bhaumâsur was dead, the Earth came, along with the wife and son of Bhaumâsur, and began, very meekly, with joined hands and downcast head, to say before the Lord, "O luminous form of Brahmâ! Bihârî, the Benefactor of Devotees! You, for the sake of good and virtuous people, are assuming endless forms; your greatness, actions, and illusions, are limitless; who knows it? and to whom is there so much power that, without your favour, he can extol it? You are the god of all gods; no one knows your nature."

Mahârâj! having spoken thus, the Earth having placed the umbrella and earrings before the Lord, he resumed, "Lord of the Lowly! Friend of the poor! Ocean of compassion! this Subhagdant, the son of Bhaumâsur, has come to take refuge

[1] Uotice this idiom, "to give on the body." It occurs again towards the bottom of the same page of the text; "to give the hand on the head"
[2] The great serpent S'eshanâga, who supports the world.

with you. Now, compassionately, place your soft lotus-like hand on his head, and make him fearless from [all] fear of you." As soon as he heard these words, the Treasury of Compassion, S'rî Kânh, tenderly placed his hand on the head of Subhagdant, and caused him to be free from [all] fear of him. Then Bhaumâvatî, the wife of Bhaumâsur, placed many presents before Hari, and with great humility, with joined hands and bowed head, stood and said,—

"O Kind to the Poor! Gracious Being! as you, by revealing yourself, have satisfied us all,[1] now come, and make my house holy." On hearing this remark, the Searcher of Hearts, the Benefactor of Devotees, S'rî Murâri, set out for the house of Bhaumâsur. Then both of them, mother and son, throwing silken foot-cloths for Hari, and conducting him into the house, seated him on a throne, and having presented an *argha*,[2] and accepted the nectar of his feet,[3] very humbly said, "O Lord of the Three Worlds! you have done well, in that you have slain this great Asura. Who, having acted antagonistically to Hari, obtained happiness in the world? Râvaṇ, Kumbhakarṇ, Kaṅs, &c., having acted inimically, lost their lives; and whosoever has acted maliciously, of them, in the world, no name-taker and water-offerer remains."[4]

Having said this, Bhaumâvatî resumed, "O Lord! now do thou regard my supplication; consider Subhagdant as your servant, and the sixteen thousand princesses which his father has kept in confinement unmarried, be pleased to accept." Mahârâj! having spoken thus, she brought out all the princesses, and stood them in rows upon rows before the Lord. They, on seeing the Light of the World, the Ocean of Beauty, S'rî Krishṇa Chand, the Root of Joy, becoming fascinated, with much supplication and entreaty, with joined hands, said, "Master! as you, having come, have taken us weak ones[5] from the confinement of this very wicked one, so now should you kindly take these servants with you, and keep them in your service, [it would be] well."

Having heard this, S'rî Krishṇa Chand told them this, "We are asking[6] for chariot and palanqueens, in order to take you with us," and looked towards Subhagdant. Subhagdant, understanding the cause of the Lord's inclination, went into his capital

[1] *Lit.*, "have caused us all to accomplish our work in life."

[2] An *argha* is a libation consisting of sesamum seed, flowers, barley, water, red sanders-wood, rice, and *dhurva*-grass.

[3] That is, "having drunk the water in which his feet were washed."

[4] That is to say no one is left who has taken the name of the deceased as an adopted son, and offers the libation of water to the manes.

[5] For *kâ* read *ko*.

[6] Notice this Aorist fortified by the substantive verb. It shows how completely this form is recognized as a Present tense. This combination is common colloquially, and sometimes, as here, crops up in books For several instances, see the Fables at the beginning of Dr. Hall's *Hindî Reader*.

city, had elephants and horses prepared, and had yoked splendid and glittering two-wheeled cars and chariots, and caused to be braced up and brought splendid easy chairs, palkîs, litters, sedans, and chaṇḍols. Hari, on seeing them, directed all the princesses to mount them, and taking Subhagdant with him, and going into the palace, seated him on the throne, and giving him the royal forehead-mark with his own hand, and having taken leave, when, accompanied by all the princesses, he went thence to Dwârakâ, no description of the splendour of that occasion is possible, inasmuch as [1] the splendour of the elephants and oxen, the brilliance of the Gangâ-Jamunî [2] housings, the glitter of the iron facings of the horses, and the lustre of the coverings of the easy-chairs, palkîs, litters, sedans, chaṇḍols, chariots, and two-wheeled carriages, the sheen of their pearl-fringes, joining into one with the light of the Sun, was shining.

Subsequently, S'rî Krishṇa Chand, taking all the princesses, proceeding on, in a certain time arrived at the city of Dwârakâ. Having gone there, and placed the princesses in the palace, he went to Râjâ Ugrasen, and saluting him, at first S'rî Krishṇa Jî related the whole secret of the killing of Bhaumâsur and the releasing and bringing of the princesses; afterwards, having taken leave of Râjâ Ugrasen, the Lord, taking Satibhâmâ with him, mounted on Garuḍa with the umbrella and earrings, and went to Vaikuṇṭh.[3] On arriving there,—

He gave the earrings to the husband of Aditi; and placed
the umbrella over the head of the Master of the gods.

Having received this news, Nârad came there. Hari said to him, "Do you go and say to Indra that Satibhâmâ asks of you the Kalpa-tree. See, now, what he says, and bring me back the answer to this; afterwards, [the answer] will be reflected on." Mahârâj! having heard this direction from the mouth of S'rî Krishṇa Chand Jî, Nârad Jî [4] said to the Master of the gods, "Your brother's wife asks from you the Kalpa-tree. What do you say [to that]? tell me. I will go and tell her that Indra says so-and-so." On hearing this, Indra at first, hesitatingly, reflected somewhat; afterwards he went and told Indrânî what Nârad had said.

Hearing this, Indrânî says, angrily, "Master of the Gods!
thy stupidity is not leaving thee;
Thou art a great fool, O blind husband! Who is Krishṇa?
Whose brother [is he]?

Dost thou remember this, or not, that he, having obliterated thy worship in Braj, and got the inhabitants of Braj to worship

[1] It is not uncommon to find *ki* in this sense.

[2] Gangâ-Jamunî means "light and dark"; those being the tints of the water of those rivers.

[3] Vaikuṇṭh is the heaven of Vishṇu.

[4] For *na* read *ne*.

a mountain, deceptively, himself ate all the food prepared for thy worship? Then, for seven days, having caused thee to rain upon the mountain, he abased thy pride, and dishonoured thee in all the world. Hast thou any shame about this affair, or not? He pays attention to what his wife says; why dost thou not listen to what I say?"

Mahârâj! when Indrânî had thus expressed herself to Indra, he, returning just as he came,[1] came to Nârad Jî, and said, "O King of Rishis! do you go to S'rî Krishṇa Chand, and say from me, that the Kalpa-tree shall not leave the Nandan wood and go elsewhere; and should it go, it shall not stay there under any circumstances. Having said thus much, then advising him, add, that he should not, as formerly, now injure me there, as in Braj, having deceived the inhabitants, and, under the pretence of a mountain, ate up all that had been prepared for my worship; otherwise there will be a great fight [between us]."

Having heard this, Nârad Jî came, and, having related to S'rî Krishṇa Chand what Indra had said, he added, "Mahârâj! Indra, for his part, was [for] giving the Kalpa-tree; but Indrânî did not allow him to give." As soon as he heard these words, S'rî Murâri, the destroyer of pride, went to the Nandan wood, and having smitten and put to flight the guardians, and taken up the Kalpa-tree, and placed it on Garuḍa, came away. Then those guardians who, having received blows from the hand of the Lord, had fled away, went to Indra and complained loudly. Having received the news of the taking away of the Kalpa-tree, O Mahârâj! Râjâ Indra, being exceedingly angry, taking his thunderbolt in his hand, and summoning all the gods, mounted the elephant Airâwat, and stood prepared to make war with S'rî Krishṇa Chand Jî.

Then Nârad Jî, the saint, went and said to Indra, "Râjâ! thou art a great fool, in that, at the dictation of a wife, thou art become ready to war with Bhagwân. On such a statement being made, art thou not ashamed? If thou didst [intend] fighting in reality, then why didst thou not fight when Bhaumâsur snatched away thy umbrella and the earrings of Aditi? Now that the Lord has slain Bhaumâsur and has brought back the earrings and umbrella, thou art ready to fight with him alone. If thou wast so very strong, why not have fought with Bhaumâsur? Thou hast forgotten that day when thou camest back after having gone into Braj, with great humility, and caused the Lord to forgive thy fault. Again art thou come to war with that very same one?" Mahârâj! on hearing this statement from the mouth of Nârad Jî, Râjâ Indra, as he was ready for battle,

[1] This idiom, *apnâ sâ muñh le*, has never been fully explained. It conveys the sense of "discomfited," as rendered by Eastwick; but its exact meaning is, "having taken away a face like his own [when he came]"; in other words, he went away as he came, without gaining what he wanted, or receiving any comfort.

lamenting and regretting, being ashamed, was troubled in mind.

Subsequently, S'rî Krishṇa Chand set out for Dwârakâ, and all the Yâdavas, having seen Hari, were delighted. The Lord, having conveyed the Kalpa-tree into the palace of Satibhâmâ, set it down; and Râjâ Ugrasen married to S'rî Krishṇa Chand, according to Vedic custom, the sixteen thousand one hundred princesses who were unmarried.

> There were rejoicings according to Vedic rites; thus was Krishṇa taking pleasure in the world;
> In his sixteen thousand one hundred houses Krishṇa abides with the greatest affection.
> The queens, who numbered eight, with them [he had] close and unceasing affection.

Having related the story thus far, S'rî S'ukadev Jî said:—O King! Hari in this way slaughtered Bhaumâsur, and gave back Aditi's earrings and Indra's umbrella, and having effected sixteen thousand eight hundred and eight marriages, S'rî Krishṇa Chand, in the city of Dwârakâ, began to sport happily with them all.

---

## CHAPTER LXI.

**Krishṇa's conversation with his wife Rukminî.**

S'RÎ S'UKADEV Jî said:—Mahârâj! once, in a gem-bespangled golden palace, there was spread a curtained bedstead studded with fine gold; on that foam-like beds, adorned with flowers, with bolsters and pillows for the cheek, were emitting a fragrant odour. Camphor, rose-water, perfume, sandal, compound-scent, all round the bed, was placed in vessels.[1] Various kinds of pictured representations were drawn on the walls around; in recesses, here and there, flowers, fruits, sweetmeats and confections were placed; and all the materials for enjoyments which should have been there were ready.

Wearing a splendid full petticoat, on which were stitched real pearls, a sparkling bodice, a shining wrapper, and a glittering veil; adorned from head to foot, with sectarial marks applied,[2] a nose-

[1] *Lit.*, "filled into vessels," that being the idiomatic use of *bharnâ*. The singular verb is used because, according to rule, the verb should agree with its nearest subject.

[2] *rolî kî âṛ* are transverse marks drawn across the forehead with a compound of rice, turmeric, alum, and acid, to proclaim the creed of the wearer.

ring of the largest pearls, head-flowers, and ear-flowers,[1] hair-parting mark, marks between the eyebrows, forehead pendant, moon-necklace, a string of gold and coral beads, a breast ornament, a five-rowed and a seven-rowed necklace, a pearl necklace, double and triple nine-gemmed[2] bracelets, and armlets, wristlets, bracelets, nine-stoned bracelets, bangles, body-marks, toe-rings, a bell-girdle, great toe-ring, toe ornaments, anklets, and wearing all the other jewel-studded ornaments,[3] the moon-faced, *champaka*-complexioned, gazelle-eyed, cuckoo-voiced, elephant-gaited, lion-waisted, S'rî Rukminî Jî; and the cloud-coloured, moon-faced, lotus-eyed, peacock-diademed, with wild-flower necklace on breast, wearing yellow silk robes, and with a yellow scarf on, the ocean of beauty, light of the three worlds, S'rî Krishṇa Chand, the root of joy, were [both] reclining there, and were, between themselves, mutually giving and receiving pleasure, when, all at once, while still lying there, S'rî Krishṇa Jî said to Rukminî Jî, "Listen, beauteous one! I am [about to] ask thee something; do thou give me its answer. It is this:[4] Thou, indeed, [art] very beautiful, endowed with every good quality, and the daughter of Râjâ Bhîshmak; and the most strong and very famous Râjâ S'iśupâl, King of Chanderî, such that, in his family, royalty has descended through seven generations, and I, from fear of him, fled and wandered about, and abandoning the city of Mathurâ, came to dwell in the sea, from fear of him alone;—to such a king your parents and brother were giving you, and he had actually come to the marriage also with the marriage procession; not choosing him, you, having abandoned family restrictions, shame of the world, and regard for parents and friends, sent for me through a Brâhmaṇ.

I am not in accomplishments worthy of you; I am not a king, and am destitute of beauty and good qualities;
Some mendicant [came] and praised [me]; which you, listening to, treasured in your heart.
A king prepared his army and came to marry you; then you sent to summon me.
I came, and serious commotion indeed resulted; how, indeed, [was it] that my reputation was preserved?[5]
In the sight of them [all] I took you away; Haladhar[6] scattered their army.

[1] These are metal ornaments bearing these names.
[2] The nine esteemed gems are—pearl, ruby, topaz, diamond, emerald, lapis-lazuli, coral, sapphire, and *gomedak* (? agate).
[3] Renderings of the terms used in this list of ornaments are offered to satisfy the natural curiosity of the student. It is, however, practically a list of proper names of specific articles, which can only be committed to memory, and associated with the particular objects when those objects are seen.
[4] The equivalent of *ki* in this phrase.
[5] Intimating that he escaped by a miracle.
[6] *Haladhar*, "the bearer of the plough," a name of Balarâm.

You wrote and sent, indeed, these words, 'Come and release me from S'iśupâl.'
That engagement was yours; it was no wish of mine.
At present you have lost nothing, [therefore] beauteous one! heed my words:—
Should there be any high-familied, virtuous, and powerful sovereign worthy of you, go and live with him."

Mahârâj! on hearing this speech, S'rî Rukminî Jî, being astounded, staggered, and fell down, and dropped on the earth; and, like a fish deprived of water, fluttered, became senseless, and began to heave deep sighs. Then,—

Here, the curls, on her beautiful face, were entangled together;
Like the Moon, in forgetfulness, fallen; or a snake drinking the water of life.

Having seen this action, S'rî Krishṇa Chand, saying this much, rose up in trepidation, "This one, indeed, is just abandoning life;"[1] and, having become four-armed, went up to her, and raising her up with two arms, and seating her on his lap, with one arm he began to fan her, and with another hand to arrange her curls. Mahârâj! then the beloved of Nand, become subject to love, began to make a variety of efforts. Sometimes he was wiping the moon-face of the beloved one with his silken robe, sometimes he was placing his soft lotus-like hand on her heart. At length, after some time, life came back into the soul of S'rî Rukminî Jî. Then Hari said,—

"Thou, indeed, O beauteous one! [hast] deep love; thou didst not retain any fortitude in thy heart;
Thou, in thy mind, thoughtest, '[I am] really abandoned.' I, jesting with love, was depressing [you].
Now, do thou, O beauteous one, be comforted; tranquillize thy spirits, and unclose thy eyes;
As long as thou art not speaking, O beloved one! so long I am experiencing heavy affliction."
The lady, hearing the words of her lover, became conscious; having opened her lotus-eyes, she looked.
On seeing that Krishṇa held her in his lap, she was ashamed, and greatly abashed in heart;
In confusion she arose and stood up, and joined hands, and fell at Hari's feet;
Krishṇa said, putting his hand on her back, "Good! good! in that [thou] from love [became] insensible!

I arranged a joke, and that you understood as the very truth. It is not fitting to be angry over a jesting matter. Arise; now put away anger, and remove grief from your heart."

[1] That is, "on the point of death."

Mahârâj! on hearing these words, S'rî Rukminî Jî arose, and, joining her hands and bowing her head, said, "Mahârâj! that which you said, to wit,[1] 'I am not suitable to you,' was truly said; because you are the husband of Lakshmî, and the Lord of S'iva and Viranch; who is your equal in the three worlds? O Lord of the Universe! the person who should leave you and hasten to another, he is as one who, neglecting the glory of Hari, should sing the praises of a vulture. Mahârâj! that which you said, to wit, 'Do you look out for some very powerful king'; [as to] that, who in the three worlds is more powerful and a greater king than you? Tell me that.

"Brahmâ, Rudra, Indra, and all the remaining boon-giving deities, are at your service; by your favour they give boons to and make very strong, renowned, famous, and glorious, those whom they please; and those people who, for a hundred years, perform some very difficult austerity for you, obtain royal dignity. Again, they who, forgetful of your service, meditation, prayer, and penance, abandon rectitude and act iniquitously, they themselves lose their all, and are depraved. Lord of Compassion! of you, indeed, there is ever this custom, that, for the sake of your devotees, having come into the world, you are again and again becoming incarnate, and destroying the wicked Râkshasas, and removing the burden of the earth, and giving happiness to your own people, make them successful.

"And, O Lord! on whomsoever is your great favour, and when he, having attained wealth, royalty, youth, beauty, and power, becoming blinded by conceit, forgets duty, destiny, penance, truth, compassion, worship, and service, then you cause him to become poor; because the poor ever continue to meditate and reflect on you; therefore a poor person is pleasing to you. Upon whom your great favour is to be, will ever remain destitute of wealth." Mahârâj! having said this, Rukminî resumed, "O Lord of Life! I will not do as Ambâ, daughter of Indradawan, the king of the city of Kâshî, did; she left her husband, and went to Râjâ Bhîshma; and when he did not keep her, then she went back to her husband; then her husband turned her out, and she sat on the bank of the Ganges, and performed great penance to Mahâdev. Bholânâth[2] came and gave her the boon she asked; by the power of this boon she went and took her revenge on Râjâ Bhîshma. That will not be [done] by me.[3]

And you, O Lord! have said this, 'Some mendicant extolled [me],
You paid heed to his statement, and sent a Brâhmaṇ to me.'
The mendicants were S'iva, Viranch, and S'âradâ;[4] Nârad at all times sings your praises.

[1] Notice this use of *ki*.
[2] Bholânâth is a name of S'iva or Mahâdev.
[3] Equivalent to, "I cannot do that."
[4] S'âradâ, "autumnal," or "perennial"; a name of both Durgâ and Saraswatî.

A Brâhmaṇ was sent, knowing you to be compassionate ; you came and effected the destruction of the wicked ;
Knowing my meekness, you brought this handmaid with you ; you, O Lord ! have given me greatness."
Having heard this, Krishṇa says, "Listen, beloved one ! you have experienced my knowledge, meditation, and procedure ;[1]
You were affectionately cognizant of service and devotion ; my heart honoured thee alone."

Mahârâj ! on hearing these words from the mouth of the Lord, becoming satisfied, Rukminî Jî again began to serve Hari.

---

## CHAPTER LXII.

Krishṇa's wives have ten sons and one daughter each—Pradyumna carries off Chârumatî, and has a son by her named Aniruddha—Balarâm plays dice with Rukma—He is cheated, and slays Rukma.

S'RÎ S'UKADEV Jî said :—Mahârâj ! having taken his sixteen thousand one hundred and eight wives, S'rî Krishṇa Chand began to sport with delight in the city of Dwârakâ ; and the eight queens remain in Hari's attendance during the eight watches of the day. Ever rising at the dawn, one would wash his face ; another would apply unguents, and cause him to bathe ; another prepare and cause him to eat six-flavoured food ; another would make and feed the beloved one with nice *pân*, prepared with cloves, cardamoms, mace, and nutmeg ; another, selecting clean clothes and jewel-studded ornaments, and having perfumed and prepared them, was causing the loved one to wear them ; and another was smoothing his feet [with her hands].

Mahârâj ! in this way, all the queens, in various manners, served the Lord continually, and Hari, in every way, gave them happiness.

Having related the story thus far, S'rî S'ukadev Jî said :—Mahârâj ! in the course of several years,—

Each of the queens of the Lord of the Yadus brought forth children ;
Each had a daughter [like] Lakshmî, and ten dutiful sons apiece.

[1] The "knowledge" here spoken of is that understanding emanating from Krishṇa which fits the recipient for final emancipation ; the "meditation" is that profound thought on Krishṇa which confers knowledge on the devotee ; and by "procedure" is meant the course of conduct regulating transcendental things.

One hundred and sixty-one thousand, such was the increase, one in essence.[1]
These were the sons of Krishṇa, infinite in good qualities, strength, and beauty.

All were cloud-coloured, moon-faced, lotus-eyed, and dressed in blue and yellow frocks; with knotted-string and wooden charms placed on their necks, and in every house, by their respective childish sports, were giving happiness to their parents; and their mothers, in a variety of ways cherishing them, were bringing them up. Mahârâj! having heard of the existence of the sons of S'rî Krishṇa Chand Jî, Rukma said to his wife, "Now I will not give my daughter Chârumatî to the son of Kritavarmâ, who has asked for her. I will hold a *Swayamvara*. Do you send someone, and invite my sister Rukminî with her son."

On hearing these words, Rukma's wife very humbly wrote a letter to her sister-in-law, and invited her with her son, by the assistance of a Brâhmaṇ;[2] and arranged the *Swayamvara*. On receiving the letter of her brother and sister-in-law, Rukminî Jî, receiving permission from S'rî Krishṇa Chand, and taking leave, proceeded on with her son, and reached, from Dwârakâ, her brother's house in Bhojakaṭ.

Having seen her, Rukma obtained great happiness; respectfully he bowed down his head.
Falling at her feet, the brother's wife said, "There was a carrying-off; since then now you are come [for the first time]."[3]

Having said this, she again said to Rukminî Jî, "Sister-in-law! since you have come, show kindness and sympathy to us, and please take this daughter Chârumatî for your son." On hearing these words, Rukminî Jî said, "Sister-in-law! you know your husband's course of action; do not cause a quarrel to arise with anyone. Nothing can be predicated of my brother's affairs. Who knows what he may do, or when [he may do it]? Therefore, on his saying or doing anything, there attaches apprehension." Rukma said, "Sister! now do you have no kind of fear; no misfortune will arise. It is a direction of the Veda that, in the southern country, the gift of a daughter should be conferred

[1] The arithmetic is a little wrong here; for if each of the wives, as stated, had eleven children, there should have been a rising family of 177,188 sons and daughters. The *Sukha-Sâgara* is also wrong, for that book specifically states that there were 121,080 sons and 16,108 daughters, or a total of 137,188 children. The *Vishṇu-Purâṇa* is nearer, and puts down the total as 180,000. The whole of these figures are, probably, astronomical. In Buddhist tradition 16,000 is spoken of as a desirable number of wives; and 108 is a number of felicitous import all over India to the present day.

[2] This phrase, *Brâhmaṇ ke hâth*, means "through *or* by means of a Brâhmaṇ."

[3] That is, "This is the first time you have paid us a visit since you were carried off."

on a sister's son; on this account, I will give my daughter Chârumatî to your son Pradyumna. Having abandoned an inimical disposition towards S'rî Krishṇa Jî, I will contract fresh relations [with him]."

Mahârâj! having said this much, when Rukma rose from that place and went into the Court, Pradyumna Jî also, receiving permission from his mother, having arrayed himself, went into the *Swayamvara*. Then what do they see! the kings of various countries, dressed in various kinds of garments, with weapons and ornaments fastened on, adorned, and having in their hearts the desire for marriage, were all standing; and the girl, with the wreath of victory in her hand, casting her eyes around, was walking round in the midst; but her eyesight was resting on no one. Hereupon, as soon as Pradyumna went into the midst of the *Swayamvara*, on seeing him, that girl, becoming fascinated, came [forward] and placed the wreath of victory on his neck. All the kings regretfully stood staring,[1] with disconcerted countenances; and began to say within themselves, "Let us see how he will take away this girl from before us. We will snatch [her from him] in the road."

Mahârâj! all the kings, then, were speaking thus, and Rukma conducted the husband and girl beneath the canopy, and having made vows according to Vedic ritual, gave the girl, and, in her dowry, gave very much wealth and objects, which were limitless. Subsequently, S'rî Rukminî Jî, having married her son, and taken leave of her brother and sister-in-law, taking the son and his wife, mounted the chariot, when she went to the city of Dwârakâ, all the kings came and blocked the way, so that they should fight with Pradyumna, and take away the girl.

Perceiving this evil intention of theirs, Pradyumna, also, taking his arms and weapons, was ready for the conflict. For some time they combated with each other;[2] at length Pradyumna Jî, having smitten and put them all to flight, arrived at the city of Dwârakâ with joy and rejoicing. Having obtained news of his arrival, all the members of the family, both women and men, came out of the city and, with customary ceremonies, spreading silken foot-cloths, conducted him, with the sound of music. There was rejoicing throughout the whole city, and they began to reside happily in the palace.

Having related thus much of the story, S'rî S'ukadev Jî said to King Parîkshit:—Mahârâj! after some years Pradyumna Jî, son of S'rî Krishṇa Chand, the root of joy, had a son. Then S'rî Krishṇa Jî, having summoned the astrologers, and caused all the members of the family to be seated, and provided an entertainment, named [the child] in the manner prescribed by the law-books. The astrologers having inspected the horoscope, and

[1] *muñh dekhte rah jânâ* means "to keep staring with astonishment."

[2] Notice that the idea of mutuality is here expressed by a repetition of the Ablative case.

settled the year, month, fortnight, solar day, lunar day, hour, the sign, and the lunar mansion, fixed upon Aniruddha[1] as the name of the boy. Then,—

[He] cannot contain himself;[2] the presenting of gifts and fees to the twice-born
Gives no satiety to Krishṇa; [for] a son is born to Pradyumna.[3]

Mahârâj! having received the news of the existence of the grandson, Rukma at first wrote this very kindly in a letter to his sister and his sister's husband, "Should your grandson be married to my granddaughter, it will be very pleasant;" and afterwards, summoning a Brâhmaṇ, and giving him *rolî*, unbroken rice, money, and a cocoa-nut, explained what he wanted thus: "Do you go into the city of Dwârakâ, and, on my part, very humbly, give the nuptial gifts to Aniruddha, the grandson of Krishṇa, who is also my daughter's son, and then return." On hearing these words, the Brâhmaṇ, taking the nuptial gift and the propitious forecast along with him, proceeded on, and went to S'rî Krishṇa Chand in the city of Dwârakâ. Having seen him, the Lord, with great courtesy and respect, asked, "Tell me, O god! to what is your visit due?" The Brâhmaṇ said, "Mahârâj! I am sent by Râjâ Bhishmak's son Rukma, and I am come with the nuptial present and propitious forecast for uniting your grandson and his granddaughter."

On hearing this statement, S'rî Krishṇa Jî, having summoned ten of the brotherhood, and accepted the nuptial present and forecast, gave a great deal to the Brâhmaṇ, and dismissed him; and going himself to Balarâm Jî, began to think of starting. Ultimately those two brothers, rising up and going to Râjâ Ugrasen, related all the intelligence, and having taken leave of him, came forth, and sending about for all the paraphernalia of a marriage procession, they began to have it collected together. When, after several days, all the arrangements were ready, the Lord, with great pomp and ceremony, taking the marriage procession, went from Dwârakâ to the city of Bhojakaṭ.

Then, on a glittering chariot, S'rî Rukminî Jî was going along seated with her son and grandson; and, seated in another chariot, S'rî Krishṇa Chand and Balarâm were proceeding. At length, after a certain time, the Lord arrived there with them all. Mahârâj! on the arrival of the marriage procession, Rukma, taking with him Kalinga and all the other kings of the various countries, went out of the city, met the party, clothed them all

[1] In the Temiya-Jâtaka, Aniruddha is spoken of as the nephew of Buddha; affording one of the many points of union between the two faiths.

[2] *phûlâ na samânâ*, "not to be contained puffed out," idiomatically expresses "to be overjoyed," "not to be able to contain oneself with joy."

[3] The sense is that Krishṇa was so overjoyed that no amount of extravagance could satiate his desire to make presents.

in robes of honour, and most respectfully had them conducted into the female apartments. Afterwards, having caused all to eat and drink, he had them led under the pavilion, and he gave the girl according to Vedic ordinances. The presents which were given in her dowry to what extent can I describe? It is unutterable.

Having related the story thus far, S'rî S'ukadev Jî said:—Mahârâj! as soon as the marriage was completed, Râjâ Bhishmak went into the female apartments, and with joined hands, and great humility, said secretly to S'rî Krishṇa Chand Jî, "Mahârâj! the marriage is completed, and harmony prevails; now please take thought for speedy departure, because,—

> The kings and relatives whom Rukma has invited, they are all wicked and mischievous;
> Let no strife arise with anyone; for this very reason I speak, O Murâri!"

As soon as Râjâ Bhîshmak, having said this, had gone, Rukma came to S'rî Rukminî Jî,—

> Rukminî says loudly, "How shall we reach home?
> The kings your guests, come here allied with you, are enemies.
> If you, brother! wish us well, speedily come and conduct us;

Otherwise, in the midst of pleasantness unpleasantness will be seen arising." On hearing this speech, Rukma said, "Sister! do not be anxious about anything. I, at first, will dismiss those kings who have come as guests from various countries; afterwards I will do what you tell me." Having said this much, Rukma rose up from that place, and went to the kings who had come as guests. They began to say altogether, "Rukma! you have bestowed all this property of your house upon Krishṇa and Baladev; and they, through pride, have not taken it in good part. This is one matter of chagrin to us; and another is, that the thorn of that affair does not leave our hearts that Balarâm disgraced you."

Mahârâj! on hearing these words Rukma became angry. Then Râjâ Kalinga said, "One thing has occurred to me. If you tell me to do so, I will state it." Rukma said, "Tell me." Then he said, "We have nothing to do with S'rî Krishṇa; but summon Balarâm, then we, having played dice with him, will win back all the wealth. As he is conceited, we will send him back empty-handed." As soon as Kalinga had said this, Rukma rose up from thence, and, reflecting somewhat, went to Balarâm Jî and said, "Mahârâj! all the kings have respectfully invited you to play dice."

> Having heard this, Balabhadra at once came there; the kings arose and bowed their heads.

Afterwards, all the kings, having acted courteously towards

Balarâm Jî, said, "You are well practised at dice-play; therefore we wish to play with you." Having said this, they sent for and spread the dice-cloth, and [*chaupaṛ*] began between Rukma and Balarâm. At first Rukma won ten times; then he began to say to Baladev Jî, "The wealth is all expended; now with what will you play?" Hereupon Râjâ Kalinga said it was a difficult matter, and laughed. Having remarked this action, Baladev Jî bent down his head, and began to reflect. Then Rukma staked at one time ten *karoṛâs* of rupees, which, when Balarâm having won had picked up, all of them wranglingly said,[1] "This throw fell to Rukma; why are you collecting the rupees?"

> Having heard that, Balarâm gave it all back; he staked a hundred million, and took up the dice.

Then Haladhar won and Rukma lost. Then, also, cheatingly all the kings made out that Rukma had won; and thus said,—

> "Gambling and dice and chess-play, what do you know of these, O villager!
> Kings understand gambling and the actions of war; herdsmen understand cows."

On hearing these words, Baladev Jî's wrath increased as the waves of the sea increase at the full moon. At length, somehow or other, Balarâm Jî restrained his anger, and counselled his mind, and then staked seven hundred million rupees, and began to play. Then, also, Baladev Jî won, and the whole of them cheatingly said that it was Rukma alone who had won. Immediately on the occurrence of this injustice, there was a voice from heaven, to this effect, "Haladhar won and Rukma lost. O kings! why have you uttered a false statement?" Mahârâj! when all the kings as well as Rukma pretended not to hear the celestial voice, Baladev Jî, getting into a violent rage, said,—

> "A betrothal has been effected, but enmity has not been abandoned; you have again stirred up contention with us;
> I will kill thee, O unjust one! let my brother's wife take it well or ill.
> Now I will listen to no one's [words]; to-day I will take the life of the cheat."[2]

Having related the story thus far, S'rî S'ukadev Jî said to King Parîkshit:—Mahârâj! at length Balarâm Jî, in the sight of all, slew Rukma; and flinging Kalinga down, with a blow of the fist knocked out his teeth, and said, "Thou, also, didst stretch open thy mouth and grin." Afterwards having slain and put to flight all the kings, Balarâm Jî came to S'rî Krishṇa Chand Jî in the female apartments, and related the whole episode there.

[1] For *bol* read *bole*.
[2] Here, also, *karihauñ* and *harihauñ* should not have been divided into two.

On hearing that, Hari, with all [his party], set out from thence, and proceeding on, arrived with joy and rejoicing in Dwârakâ. As soon as he came there, happiness was diffused throughout the entire city, and in every house festivities began to be held. S'rî Krishṇa Jî and Baladev Jî went before Râjâ Ugrasen, and with joined hands said, "Mahârâj! through your excellence and majesty we have celebrated the marriage of Aniruddha, and having slain the wicked Rukma, have returned."

---

## CHAPTER LXIII.

S'iva bestows a thousand arms on Vâṇâsur, who begins to tear up mountains and trees—He wishes to fight with S'iva, but is diverted from doing so by an artifice—Vâṇâsur's daughter falls in love with Aniruddha, and brings him secretly into her apartments—Vâṇâsur discovers the affair, and captures and imprisons Aniruddha.

S'RÎ S'UKADEV Jî said:—Now if I should receive the strength of S'rî Dwârakânâth,[1] I will relate all the story of the abduction of Ushâ. As she, at night time, saw Aniruddha in a dream, and, becoming attached[2] to him, fretted, and then as Chitrarekhâ brought Aniruddha and united him to Ushâ, in that way I am about to relate the whole subject; do you pay attention and listen. In the family of Brahmâ, at first there was Kaśyapa; his son was Hiraṇyakaśyapa,[3] who was very strong, exceedingly powerful, and deathless. His son Harijan became the worshipper of the Lord named Prahlâd;[4] his son was Râjâ Virochaṇ, and Virochaṇ's was Râjâ Bali, whose glory and virtue are still diffused through the world, and that the Lord, assuming the Vâmana incarnation, having tricked Râjâ Bali, sent him to Pâtâla.[5] His

[1] A name of Krishṇa.

[2] For *âśakta* read *âsakta*. This misreading has led Eastwick into a mistranslation.

[3] The more correct form of the name is *Hiraṇyakaśipu*. He was the son of Kaśyapa by Diti, and obtained a boon from Brahmâ that he should not be slain by god, or man, or animal. This immunity from death caused him to commit many enormities, until he was torn to pieces by Vishṇu in the form of Nara-siṁha, or "half-man half-lion" incarnation.

[4] The form *Pahalâd* is due to Lallû Lâl's limited knowledge of Sanskrit. It was Prahlâd's adoration of Vishṇu which brought about the Narasiṁha incarnation.

[5] *Bali* is the offering made to a deity as an act of worship, and is also the name of a Daitya, to humble whose pride Vishṇu assumed the form of a *Vâmana*, or "dwarf," and received as a reward for pleasing Bali as much territory as he could cover with three steps. He immediately expanded his limbs to a prodigious extent, and covered the earth with one step, the heavens with the second step, but generously allowed Bali to go to Pâtâla, or hell.

eldest son was the very heroic and most glorious Vâṇâsur. He dwelt in S'oṇitapur, and continually went to Kailâs[1] to worship S'iva, and to cherish sacred duties, speak the truth, and to keep his sensual organs in subjection. Mahârâj! one day Vâṇâsur, having gone to Kailâs and worshipped Hara,[2] passing into affection, he began, by devotion, to play away upon the drum, and to dance and sing. Having heard his singing and playing, S'rî Mahâdev, the Lord of the simple-hearted, was pleased, and began, along with Pârvatî Jî, to dance and to play the tabor.[3] At length, dancing and dancing on, S'ankar[4] attained great happiness, and, being gratified, called Vâṇâsur near him and said, "Son! I am gratified with you; ask a boon; the boon thou shalt ask I will give thee.

> Thou, [with thy] hand, hast played music excellently; [by my] ears hearing [it], my mind is gratified."

As soon as he had heard these words, O Mahârâj! Vâṇâsur, joining his hands and bowing his head, very humbly said, "Lord of Compassion! if you have had compassion on me,[5] then first make me immortal and confer upon me the dominion of the whole earth; afterwards make me so strong that no one may obtain conquest over me."[6] Mahâdev Jî said, "I have granted to thee this boon, and have made thee free from all fear; in the three worlds no one shall attain thy strength, and Vidhâtâ[7] even shall have no power over thee.[8]

> Having played music excellently, thou gavest supreme happiness to me;
> I, with greatly delighted heart, have given to thee a thousand arms.[9]

Now do thou go home, rest contented, and exercise immoveable power." Mahârâj! having heard this decree from the mouth of Bholânâth,[10] and having acquired a thousand arms, Vâṇâsur, having become exceedingly happy, and having circumambulated, bowed his head, took leave, and having received permission,

[1] *Kailâs* is a lofty mountain, supposed to be in the Himâlaya range, where Kuvera, the god of riches, had his residence, and where the paradise of S'iva was located.

[2] *Hara* is a name of S'iva, and *Hari* is a name of Vishṇu.

[3] The *ḍamarû* is a small double-headed drum with a narrow waist, which is held in the hand while the ends are tapped with the fingers. It is one of the attributes of S'iva.

[4] A name of S'iva. It means "the conferrer of happiness."

[5] Notice this *mere par*, in which the Genitive is used as a base. It is not uncommon in parts of Northern India, and constantly crops up in books.

[6] *Lit.*, "that no one may conquer from me."

[7] A name of Brahmâ.

[8] *Lit.*, "no power of Vidhâtâ even shall act upon thee." This is a very useful idiom.

[9] "Arms" are symbolical of power; therefore, "a thousand arms" means "unlimited power."

[10] A name of S'iva.

came to S'oṇitapur. Afterwards, having conquered the three worlds, and made all the gods subject, he constructed around the city a wide deep trench of water, and a fortress of fire and water, and, having become fearless, began to reign happily. After a certain time,—

Without fighting,[1] the arms, throbbing and irritating excessively, became powerful;
Says Vâṇa, "With whom shall I fight? now against whom shall I advance?
Through not fighting, a violent irritation has occurred; who will satisfy the desire of my heart?"

Having said this, Vâṇâsur went out from his house and began to tear up mountains, to break them up, and reduce them to powder, and he went from country to country. When he had finished breaking up all the mountains, and the irritation and annoyance of his arms had not ceased, then,—

Says Vâṇa, "With whom shall I fight?" What shall I do with so many arms?
How can I endure the burden of my strength? I will go again, and speak to Hari."

Mahârâj! having thus communed with himself, Vâṇâsur went before Mahâdev Jî, and with joined hands and downcast head, said, "O Bearer of the Trident![2] Lord of the Three Worlds! the thousand arms which you kindly gave me have become a burden to my body; now I cannot endure their strength. Devise some remedy for this; please point out to me some very powerful person for me to fight with. In the three worlds I do not see anyone so heroic that he can stand before me and fight. Yea! as you have compassionately made me very powerful, so now kindly fight with me, and let the desire of my heart be, perhaps, satisfied.[3] Otherwise, point out some other very powerful one with whom I may go and fight, and remove the distress of my mind."

Having related thus much of the story, S'rî S'ukadev Jî said:—Mahârâj! having heard this sort of language from Vâṇâsur, Mahâdev Jî felt a convulsion[4] and said this much within himself, "I, forsooth, thinking this one a worthy person, granted the boon, now he is ready to fight with me. The pride of strength has come to this fool; he shall not escape alive. He who has become self-conceited on coming into the world lives[5]

[1] *larwe* is the Braj inflected Infinitive = *laṛne*.
[2] This should be one word, and spelt with the lingual *ṇ*, as *paṇi*.
[3] This repetition of the verb with the particle *to* between, implies doubt or uncertainty. See the *Hindî Manual* (3rd edit.), p. 142.
[4] *Lit.*, "experienced a twist," from anger or arrogance.
[5] The Past tense *jiyâ* implies that he is as good as dead already. It is common colloquially to use the Past to express what is speedily to be accomplished.

not long." Communing thus within himself, Mahâdev Jî said, "Vâṇâsur! be not uneasy, one to fight with thee, in a short time, will be [born] in the incarnation of S'rî Krishṇa in the Yadu family. Except him,[1] in the three worlds, there is no one to confront thee." Having heard this statement, Vâṇâsur being greatly pleased, said, "Lord! when will that person become incarnate? and how shall I know when he is born?" O King! S'iva Jî, having given a flag to Vâṇâsur, said, "Take this banner and set it up over your palace. When this banner shall break and fall of its own accord, thou wilt[2] know that thy enemy is born."

Mahârâj! when S'ankar had advised and spoken to him[3] thus, Vâṇâsur took the flag, bowed his head, and went home; subsequently, having reached his house and mounted the flag on his palace, he was day by day thinking of this alone, "When will that person manifest himself? and when shall I fight with him?" Hereupon, after several years had elapsed, his chief queen, whose name was Vâṇâwatî, became pregnant, and in the fulness of time a girl was born. Then Vâṇâsur, having summoned the astrologers, said, "Reckon out and tell me the name and qualities of this girl." As soon as these words were uttered, the astrologers quickly determined the year, month, fortnight, lunar day, day [of the week], hour, lucky moment,[4] and having reflected on the propitious sign, and fixed upon Ushâ[5] as the girl's name, said, "This girl will be a mine of beauty, good qualities, and amiability, and will be very intelligent; her planets and signs have presented themselves just thus."

Having heard this, Vâṇâsur was greatly pleased, and, first, having given bountifully to the astrologers, dismissed them; and, afterwards, having summoned the musicians, caused festivities to be prepared. Then as the girl began to grow up Vâṇâsur began to love her exceedingly. When Ushâ was seven years old, her father, as S'oṇitapur was quite close to Kailâs, sent her there, with several friends and companions, to be instructed by S'iva and Pârvatî. Ushâ, having conciliated Gaṇeśa and Saraswatî,[6] went before S'iva and Pârvatî, and with joined hands and bowed head, meekly said, "O Ocean of Compassion! S'iva and Gaurî! kindly give to me your servant the gift of knowledge, and acquire glory in the world." Mahârâj! having heard

[1] Notice this method of expressing "except." In prose it is better to write *us ke binâ*.

[2] Notice this use of the form *-iyo* to imply futurity. See *Hindî Manual* (3rd edit.), pp. 149, 150.

[3] For this use of the Dative with *kahnâ* see *Hindî Manual* (3rd edit.), pp. 92, 93.

[4] The curious form *mahûrat* in the text should, of course, be *muhûrtt*.

[5] *Ushâ* is derived from *ushas*, "the dawn." The *u* should be short, not long as in the text.

[6] Gaṇeśa, the elephant-headed deity, or god of wisdom; and Saraswati, the goddess of speech.

the exceedingly humble speech of Ushâ, S'iva and Pârvatî Jî, being pleased, caused her to begin to be learned. She, constantly going, studied on. Hereupon, in the course of a certain time, having studied all the literary treatises, she became accomplished and wise, and began to play all instruments. One day, Ushâ, together with Pârvatî Jî, was playing on the lute and singing according to the method of song,[1] when S'iva Jî came and said to Pârvatî, "O beloved one! the Kâmadev whom I had consumed, S'rî Krishṇa Jî has now raised up." Having said this, S'rî Mahâdev Jî, taking Girijâ[2] with him, went to the banks of the Ganges, and having thoroughly bathed,[3] and desired happiness, very amorously began to adorn Pârvatî with clothes and ornaments, and to be affectionate to her. At length, becoming enraptured in excessive joy, and playing away on the tabor, danced violently the Tâṇḍav dance,[4] and sang away, according to the method of the treatises on song, began to gratify S'ivâ,[5] and to embrace her very affectionately. Then Ushâ, gazing upon the happiness and affection of S'iva and Gaurî, and desiring to get a husband, said within herself, "Should I have a husband, then I also would be able to sport with him in the manner of S'iva and Pârvatî. A desirous female without a husband is as destitute of lustre as the night without the moon."

Mahârâj! when Ushâ had said this within herself, S'rî Pârvatî Jî, the Searcher of Hearts, knowing the internal emotions[6] of Ushâ, called her near affectionately, and lovingly counselling her said, "Daughter! do not be anxious in thy heart about anything; thy husband will come and meet thee in a dream. Thou wilt have him searched for, and wilt enjoy happiness with that very one."[7] Having conferred this boon, S'iva's queen dismissed Ushâ; and she, having studied all learning, and obtained a boon, prostrating herself, went to her own father. The father gave her an exceedingly beautiful separate palace to live in; and she, taking several friends and companions, began to reside there, and day by day grew up.

Mahârâj! when that girl was twelve years of age, having per-

[1] For *sângît* read *sangît*. This may be intended for a proper noun, and should be rendered "according to the method of the Sangita." There are two well-known Sanskrit treatises on this subject, called respectively *Sangîta-Ratnâkara* and *Sangîta-Pârijâta*. The allusion may be to these treatises, for the first of them dates from a high antiquity. The word does not occur in the *Bhâgavata-Purâṇa*.

[2] *Girijâ* means "mountain-born." It is synonymous with *Pârvatî* (from *parvata*, "a mountain"), and the name arose from the tradition that she was the daughter of Himavat, king of the Snowy mountains. Another of her names is *Umâ*, around which name the earliest traditions of this goddess cluster.

[3] See *Hindî Manual* (3rd edit.), p. 191, for this idiom *nhâ,e nhilâ,e*.

[4] This is a frantic dance indulged in by the votaries of S'iva.

[5] S'ivâ is the feminine form of S'iva, and, of course, means Pârvatî.

[6] For *antara gati* read *antargati*.

[7] These forms in *-iyo* express directions or orders to be accomplished in the future.

ceived the brilliancy of her moon-face, the full moon became deprived of beauty; in comparison with the darkness of the child, the blackness of the new moon began to fade; having perceived the tapering of her hair, the female snake, casting her slough, slunk away; having looked upon the curvature of her eyebrows, the bow began to throb; having seen the largeness and coquetry of her eyes, the deer, fish, and wagtail, were abashed; gazing on the beauty of her nose, the sesamum flower withered away; viewing the red of her lips, the Bimba began to be restless; having glanced at her rows of teeth, the heart of the pomegranate was rent; looking at the softness of her cheeks, the rose abstained from blossoming; having inspected the roundness of her neck, pigeons began to flutter; having viewed the nipples of her breasts, the buds of the lotus fell into the lake; perceiving the slimness of whose [1] waist, the lioness retired to the forest; looking at the smoothness of her thighs, the plantain was vexed; [2] noticing the yellowness of her body, gold was ashamed, and the Champaka was abashed; compared with her hands and feet, the lotus retained no dignity. Such was that elephant-gaited, cuckoo-voiced, fresh maiden, resplendent from the excellence of her youthfulness, who took away the beauty from all these.

Subsequently, one day, that fresh maiden having applied sweet-scented unguents, and washed away with pure water every impurity, and combed her hair, and arranged the parting, and filled in the division with pearls, and had used collyrium and tooth-powder, and applied henna and cochineal, and eaten betel, and having sent for excellent jewel-studded golden ornaments, and arrayed herself in head-decorations, forehead pendants, forehead circlet, a forehead band, an ear-knot, earrings, four-pearl ear ornaments, pearl earrings, a nose-ring of large pearls, a gold patch on the nose-ring, with pendants, a neck-brooch threaded on a necklace of two rows of pearls, a moon-necklace, a gold and coral necklace, a five-stringed necklet, a seven-stringed necklet, a neck ornament on the throat itself, armlets, nine-gemmed bracelets, bangles, wristlets, bracelets, rings, signets, seals, toe-rings, girdles of bells, anklets of sorts, footlets, great-toe rings, and toe-ornaments; and arrayed herself in a clean glittering wide petticoat with a border of real pearls, and a brilliant dress with a border and a hem, and a splendid bodice, close-fitting, and over that a glittering veil, and having furthermore perfumed herself; with this adornment, like Lakshmî, she went out, smiling frequently, with her friends, to pay respects to her parents. When, having arrived in front of them, and prostrated herself, Ushâ stood up, Vâṇâsur, having perceived the splendour of her youth, saying this in his own heart, dismissed her, "She is now marriageable." Afterwards he sent some Râkshasas to guard

[1] This should, probably, be *wis*, not *jis*.

[2] *Lit.*, "ate camphor."

her palace, and despatched several Râkshasîs to watch over her. They went there, and began to remain on the alert day and night,[1] and the Râkshasîs began to serve her.

Mahârâj! that princess was constantly performing penance, giving alms, and keeping vows, for the sake of a husband, and continually worshipping S'rî Pârvatî Jî. One day, being at leisure from the constant discharge of religious duties, at night time seated alone on her bed, she was reflecting in her heart thus, "Let us see when father will effect my marriage, and in what manner I shall meet my husband." Having said this, she went to sleep thinking only of a husband; then, in a dream, what does she see?—A person of youthful age, dark complexion, moon-faced, lotus-eyed, very beautiful, in the form of Kâma,[2] of fascinating appearance, dressed in yellow silk robes, with a peacock crown on his head, in triple-bent beauty,[3] with jewel-studded ornaments, with alligator-shaped earrings, a wild-flower garland, and one of gunjâ-seed;[4] and covered with a yellow garment, very coquettishly came and stood before her.

She, on seeing him, was charmed, and abashed, and remained with head bent down. Then he, having uttered some words imbued with love, increased his affection, drew near, took her hand, embraced her, and made her forget the doubts of her heart, her diffidence and bashfulness. Then mutually having cast aside reserve and bashfulness, seated on the bed, they indulged in blandishments, ogling, embraces, and kisses, began to give and receive happiness, and being absorbed in delight they began to converse lovingly,—when, in the midst of this,[5] after a time, as Ushâ lovingly desired to embrace the husband and press him to her bosom, sleep passed from her eyes, and just as she was with arms outstretched for the embrace, she remained dejected and regretful.

> She awoke, sincerely sorrowing; supreme misery was upon her;
> "Where has gone, that lord of my life?" She looks all around wistfully.
> Ushâ reflects, "Whom shall I meet?[6] How may I see that one again?
> If I to-day had continued sleeping, my lover had never departed [from me].
> Why was I about to clasp him happily, when this slumber left my eyes?

[1] *Lit.*, "during the eight watches."

[2] See note [6], p. 176.

[3] That is, with legs, back, and neck bent; supposed to be a graceful attitude.

[4] The *Abrus precatorius*, a red seed with a black patch on it, not unlike a crab's eye.

[5] The *ki* indicates transition of ideas, the sense being akin to "all at once, while this was going on," &c.

[6] She asks this because she does not know who has been with her.

On his going, the night became clogged; now how will this fatality pass away?[1]
Without the beloved one my soul is exceedingly uneasy; while not seeing him my eyes are longing;
My ears are desirous to hear his voice; where has the happiness-giving loved one gone?
If, in a dream, I should again see my sweetheart, I will resign my life to him."[2]

Mahârâj! having said this, Ushâ became greatly dejected, meditated on her lover, went to bed, muffled up her face and laid down.[3] When night had gone and day was come, and one-and-a-half watch of the day had passed, her friends and companions, unitedly, began to say among themselves, "What has occurred to-day that Ushâ, when so much of the day has passed, still sleeping, has not risen?" Having heard this, Chitrarekhâ, the daughter of Vâṇâsur's minister Kûshabhâṇḍ,[4] having gone into the picture gallery, sees what?—that Ushâ, in the curtained bed, troubled in mind, dejected in spirits, lying motionless, was sobbing and heaving deep sighs. Having seen this her condition,—

Chitrarekhâ agitatedly said, "O Friend, do thou explain to me,
Truly, to-day why art thou, fallen into the ocean of utter separation, grieving?
Crying and crying, thou art heaving deep sighs, for what cause is thy body and mind disturbed?
I will remove the grief of thy heart; I will do every act thy heart has desired.
[There is] no other friend so close as I; thou hast confidence in me.

[1] There is a little word-play here. Yama (or Jam) is the president of the nether regions, who inspects the record, and regulates the future destiny of departed souls. It also means "restraint," "stoppage," "coagulation," and in this sense is the base of the Hindî verb *jamnâ*, "to be congealed." As a feminine noun the word *daî* means "destiny," "fate" (as in the phrases *daî lagnâ*, "to be unfortunate," and *daî mârâ*, "smitten by fate"), and also "the deity"; while *jaihai* is for *jâ-ihai*, 3rd pers. sing. Fut. of *jânauñ*, "to go." Thus we may extract the two meanings, "The night has become congealed, O God! how will it now move on [again]?" and, "The night is become Yama (the Regent of Fate), how will this destiny (or fatality) now proceed?" Such far-fetched alliances of ideas will often be met with in verse. Both Hollings and Eastwick translate *jaihai* as a Past tense in order to arrive at some meaning. Prof. Eastwick says in a note that *daî* yields no sense; a statement certainly incorrect.

[2] *Prâṇ* means the five vital airs, hence "life"; *kisî ke sâth kar denâ* is "to give up to anyone," "to transfer to anyone."

[3] Meaning that she took to her bed in grief and covered her head in a sulky manner.

[4] Here Lallû Lâl has, blunderingly, inserted *Kûshabhâṇḍ* for *Kûshmâṇḍ*, the name of a kind of spirit or imp; but even thus he is wrong, for the name of this minister was *Kumbhâṇḍa*, of *kumbha* + *aṇḍa*, as Pandit Yogadhyân Miśra properly prints it.

Throughout the whole world I will wander ; wherever I go I will effect [thy] purposes ;
Brahmâ has granted me a boon ; and has made everything subject to me ;
S'âradâ [1] keeps with me ; by her power I will do what [thou] mayest say ;
Understand [me to be] so highly enchanting [that I can] deceive and bring [here] Brahmâ, Rudra, and Indra ;
No one knows my mystery ; my own attributes myself explains ;
No one else can thus tell it, however good or bad he may be ; [2]
Now do thou tell all thy affair ; how has this night passed ?
Act not deceitfully towards me, O loved one ! I will accomplish all thy hopes."

Mahârâj ! on hearing these words, Ushâ, with great modesty and downcast head, came near to Chitrarekhâ, and, with a sweet voice, said, "Friend ! I, thinking thee my friend, will relate the whole affair of last night. Do thou keep it in thine own heart, and [if] thou canst devise some remedy, then do. Last night, in a dream, a man, of the colour of a cloud, and a face like the moon,[3] and eyes like lotuses, wearing a yellow silk robe, and covered with a yellow scarf, came and sat near me ; and he, displaying great affection, carried away my heart in his hand.[4] I also, abandoning reserve and bashfulness, began to converse with him. At length, while conversing on, as love came upon me, I stretched my hand to lay hold of him, and hereupon my sleep departed, and his fascinating form remained in my thoughts.

I never saw or heard of such a one ; how shall I describe [him] as [he was] ?
His beauty is indescribable ; he is gone, having stolen away my heart.

When I, in Kailâs, was studying learning at S'rî Mahâdev Jî's, S'rî Pârvatî Jî said to me, 'Thy husband will come and meet thee in a dream ; thou wilt have him searched for.' That husband last night met me in a dream ; where shall I find him ? and to whom shall I relate the agonies of my separation [from him] ? Where shall I go ? in what manner shall I seek him ? I neither know his name nor his residence." Mahârâj ! when, having said

[1] A name of Saraswatî.

[2] *kahihai* should be one word ; and *kin* stands for *kyoñ na*. In standard Hindî this last phrase would be *koî kaisâ bhalâ burâ kyoñ na ho*.

[3] These epithets are compounds, and should have been printed as single words. This one is *chandravadan*, not *chandra badan* ; this latter spelling induced Hollings to mistake the meaning of the phrase.

[4] That is, "he took my heart captive."

this, Ushâ, sighing deeply, sank dispiritedly, Chitrarekhâ said, "Friend! now do not thou be anxious about anything in thy heart. I will search for, and cause thy husband to join thee, wherever he may be. I have power to go throughout the three worlds. Wherever he may be, there I will go and do my best to bring him to you.[1] Do thou tell me his name, and give me leave to go."

Ushâ said, "Sister! that proverb is applicable to thee, to wit, 'She was dead because she did not breathe.' If I had known only his name and village, what would there have been to be miserable about? Some remedy or other would have been applied." Having heard this, Chitrarekhâ said, "Friend! do not thou grieve over this either. I will draw and show thee the men of the three worlds; seeing the captor of thy heart among them thou wilt point him out; then the bringing and uniting [him to thee] is my affair." Then, laughing, Ushâ said, "Very well." Mahârâj! as soon as this expression issued from the mouth of Ushâ, Chitrarekhâ called for all the drawing materials, and sat down on the ground; and having propitiated Gaṇeśa and S'âradâ, and meditated on her spiritual preceptor, began to draw. At first she drew and exhibited the three worlds, the fourteen subdivisions, the seven islands, the nine divisions of the earth, the sky, the seven oceans, all the eight [spiritual] worlds, along with Vaikuṇṭh.[2] Afterwards, all the gods, Dânavas,[3] Gandharvas,[4] Kinnaras,[5] Yakshas,[6] Rishis,[7] Munis,[8] Lokapâls,[9] Digpâls,[10] and the kings of all countries, Chitrarekhâ drew separately, and exhibited one by one; but Ushâ did not find the one she wished for among them. Then Chitrarekhâ began to draw severally and to show one at a time the forms of the Yadubaṅsîs; hereupon, on seeing the portrait of Aniruddha, Ushâ said,—

[1] *Lit.*, "As it will be effected, just so will I bring [him]."

[2] The heaven of Vishṇu.

[3] The Dânavas are Titanic giants, descended from Danu, one of the daughters of Daksha, the wife of Kaśyapa. Sometimes they are reckoned as forty; sometimes as a hundred or more.

[4] The Gandharvas here are probably only the heavenly musicians.

[5] The Kinnaras are human-bodied, horse-headed monsters, reckoned among the celestial choristers, and also as assistants of Kuvera, the god of wealth.

[6] Yakshas are demi-gods attendant on Kuvera, the god of riches. Various accounts of their origin are given; and they are sometimes regarded as benevolent, and sometimes as malevolent.

[7] Rishis are ancient saints, to whom the hymns of the Vedas are held to have been revealed direct from heaven. Seven Rishis is the orthodox number anciently spoken of; but the original declarer, or composer, of any of the hymns is considered as a Rishi; and ultimately the name was applied to any specially saintly person.

[8] A Muni is a saint, or holy man, inspired with divine knowledge; and this inspiration he can attain by self-mortification and mental abstraction.

[9] Lokapâls are deities appointed by Brahmâ at the creation of the world to act as guardians to the different orders of beings.

[10] Digpâls are guardians of the four quarters of space and the four intermediate points.

"Now I have found my heart-stealer, O Friend! This one came to me at night.
Now, O Friend! do thou devise some means; search out this one and bring him from somewhere."
Having heard, Chitrarekhâ spoke thus, "Now how shall this one escape from me?"

Having spoken thus, Chitrarekhâ resumed, thus, "Friend! thou dost not know this one; I recognize[1] him. This Yadubañsî is the grandson of S'rî Krishṇa Chand Jî, the son of Pradyumna Jî, and his name is Aniruddha. At the banks of the sea, in the water, there is a city named Dwârakâ, where this one dwells. By command of Hari, watch over that city is constantly maintained by the discus Sudarśan, so that no Daitya, Dânava, or wicked person, should come and annoy the Yadubañsîs; and if anyone should come to the city, then he should not gain admittance without the permission of Râjâs Ugrasen and Sûrasen." Mahârâj! on hearing this statement, Ushâ, having become greatly dejected, said, "Friend! if that is such a terrible place, how wilt thou go there and bring me my husband?" Chitrarekhâ said, "Companion! be free from anxiety on this point; by the power of Hari, I will bring the lord of thy life to thee."

Having said this, Chitrarekhâ, wearing clothes marked with the name of Râma, and having drawn the cowherdesses sectarial mark of upright lines[2] of sandal; and having placed marks on her breast, the upper part of the arm, and throat, and casting a very large garland of *tulsî* on her neck, and taking a rosary of the very large beads of *tulsî* in her hand, drawing over her a chequered blanket, under her arm a sitting-cloth folded up, and pressing [there also] the book of the *Bhagavadgîtâ*, assuming the guise of a chief worshipper of Vishṇu, speaking thus to Ushâ, with bowed head, taking leave, she started for Dwârakâ,—

"Now by the path of the sky, through[3] mid-air I will go;
I will bring thy husband; then is my name Chitrarekhâ."

Having related thus much of the story, S'rî S'ukadev Jî said:—Mahârâj! Chitrarekhâ, by her illusive power, mounting upon the undulations of the air, in a dark night, with a dark cloud, in an instant, went into the city of Dwârakâ, and shone like lightning; and entered into the palace of S'rî Krishṇa Chand, so that her going was unknown to anyone. Afterwards, she searching and searching about, went where Aniruddha, sleeping alone on a bed, was sporting in a dream with Ushâ. On

[1] Here we have another instance of the Aorist fortified by the Substantive verb. See *Hindî Manual* (3rd edit.), p. 139.
[2] This should be *ûrddhapuṇḍra*, the upright lines drawn on the forehead of worshippers of Vishṇu.
[3] *hwai* = *hokar*. See *Hindî Manual* (3rd edit.), p. 199.

seeing him, she quickly raised the couch of the sleeping one, and at once took her departure.

> While sleeping, along with the couch, she conveyed him away for the sake of Ushâ ;
> Taking Aniruddha, she went where Ushâ sat in anxiety.

Mahârâj ! as soon as she saw Aniruddha with the couch, Ushâ, at first, being a little shocked, went and fell at the feet of Chitrarekhâ ; afterwards she began to address her thus, " Blessed, blessed, be thy energy and courage ! in that thou wentest to so terrible a place, and, in a moment, took up and brought [him] with the couch ; and fulfilled your promise. Thou hast taken all this trouble for me ; I cannot recompense thee for it. I remain debtor to thy kindness."

Chitrarekhâ said, " Friend ! in the world this is a great happiness, that we may give happiness to others ; and this act also is worthy, viz. to be assistant. This body is of no use ; should it be able to be useful to anyone, that of itself is an excellent use [to put it to]. In this is both one's own good and the supreme good."[1] Mahârâj ! having made this statement, Chitrarekhâ again speaking thus, took leave, and went to her house, to wit, " Friend ! by the power of Bhagwân I[2] have brought thy husband and united him to thee ; now do thou awaken him and fulfil thy desire." As soon as Chitrarekhâ had departed, Ushâ, exceedingly pleased and ashamed, but having fear of the first meeting, began to say in her inmost heart,—

> " By saying what word shall I arouse the loved one ? and how shall I press him to my breast with embraces ? "

At length, having tuned her lute, she began to play the sweetest of sounds. On hearing the sound of the lute, Aniruddha Jî woke up, and looking about on all sides, began to say within himself, " What place is this ? whose palace ? how did I come here ? and who brought me, with the couch, while sleeping ? " Mahârâj ! then Aniruddha, giving expression to various kinds of remarks, was wondering ; and Ushâ, with reserve and bashfulness, fearing the first interview, standing aside in a corner, and inspecting[3] the moon-face of her lover, was giving happiness to her partridge-like eyes. While this was going on—

> Aniruddha, seeing her, said, with astonishment, " Tell me, beauteous one ! thy circumstances.

[1] *paramârth* is not " another's advantage," as both Hollings and Eastwick translate, but *parama*, " the chief," *arth*, " object." All Hindû philosophy was directed towards securing " the primary object " of existence, that is, to know God and to become identified with Him. The text states that, by assisting others, we not only further our selfish purposes, but also attain the chief end of our being.

[2] *mane* should, of course, be *maiñ ne*.

[3] Lallû Lâl and his Indian Editor repeat the word *nirakh* to express the many glances she gave.

Who art thou? why didst thou come to me? or didst thou bring me thyself?
Do not deem truth and falsehood as one. I behold [things] like a dream."

Mahârâj! Aniruddha Jî spoke these words; and Ushâ gave no reply; rather, being still more bashful, she shrank into the corner. Then he hastily seized her by the hand, led her to the couch and seated her there, and speaking words imbued with love, he removed entirely the reserve, bashfulness and fear of her heart. Afterwards they, both seated on the bed, with mutual blandishments, and ogling, began to give and receive happiness, and to recite their love-story. While this was going on, in the midst of the conversation, Aniruddha Jî asked Ushâ, "O beauteous one! how didst thou at first see me? and, afterwards, in what way send for me here? Explain this mystery to me, that the doubt of my mind may depart." On hearing these words, Ushâ, looking at her husband's countenance, delightedly said,—

"You came and met me in a dream, and stole away my heart and departed;
I awoke, and deep grief took possession of my heart. Then I told Chitrarekhâ,
She it was, O Lord! who brought you here; her actions are not to be comprehended."

Having said this, Ushâ resumed, "Mahâraj! I, for my part, have related all the particulars of the way in which I saw and obtained you; now do you, please, explain your affairs and tell me how you saw me, O King of the Yâdavas!" Having heard these words, Aniruddha, being highly delighted, smilingly said, "O beauteous one! I also was looking upon thee last night in a dream, when, in the sleep itself, somebody raised me up and brought me here. The secret of this I have not yet discovered, that is, who brought me. I awoke, then I saw thee alone."

Having related thus much of the story, S'rî S'ukadev Jî said:—Mahârâj! in this way those two, the lover and the loved, conversing between themselves, increased their affection, they began to indulge in various kinds of love-sports, and to banish the pain of [previous] separation. Afterwards, perceiving the insipidity of the betel, the coldness of the pearl-necklace, and the dimness of the light of the lamp, Ushâ, having gone out, saw that it was the time of dawn. The light of the moon had waned, the stars were deprived of light, the blush of dawn was diffused over the sky, on all sides birds warbled on the lake, the night-lotus had faded, and the day-lotus had blossomed, and the male and female ruddy-goose had united together.

Mahârâj! observing this state of things, at once shutting all the doors, Ushâ, greatly agitated, came into the house, and very affectionately embracing her husband, laid herself down; afterwards, having concealed her husband, and hidden him from her friends and companions, secretly began to serve her husband. At length the friends and companions were aware of Aniruddha's coming. Then she, day and night, began to enjoy happiness with her husband. One day Ushâ's mother came to inquire after her daughter; then she secretly saw that she was seated in a chamber with a very handsome young man, and was gaily playing dice with him. On seeing this, without uttering a word, softly, inwardly pleased, and blessing [her daughter], silently, she returned to her own house.

Subsequently, after some time, one day, Ushâ, seeing her husband asleep, thinking this in her mind, hesitatingly came from out the house, "Let it by no means be [1] that anyone, by not seeing me, should think in her heart that Ushâ does not go out of the house because of her husband." Mahârâj! Ushâ, having left her husband alone, went out, it is true, but could not stay away from him.[2] Having re-entered the house and shut the door, she began to disport [again]. Having noticed this action, the wardens said among themselves, "Brother! what is this to-day, that the princess, after many days, came out of the house, and then retracing her steps, went away?" On hearing these words, one among them said, "Brother! I have been noticing [3] for some time past that the door of Ushâ's palace has remained closed day and night, and within the house some man is sometimes laughing away and conversing, and sometimes is playing at dice." Another said, "If this is true, let us go to Vâṇâsur and tell him; why do we remain consciously inactive?"

> One said, "This is not to be uttered; do you all keep seated apart;
> Let it be good or bad as it likes,[4] no one can efface destiny,
> Say nothing about the maiden; look on silently, and remain quite inactive."

Mahârâj! the gate-keepers were in the act of making these remarks among themselves, when, accompanied by several soldiers, walking round and about, Vâṇâsur lighted on that spot,[5] and casting his eyes above the palace, and not seeing the flag

[1] When not translating in the direct form, *kahîñ aisâ na ho ki* may be rendered by "lest."

[2] This Passive form of the Neuter verb *rahnâ*, like similar constructions with Active verbs, implies the impossibility of the idea spoken of. This accounts for the masculine form. It is the remaining from him which could not be endured. Notice the expression *jâte to*; it is the emphatic Statical form. See *Hindî Manual* (3rd edit.), pp. 182, 183.

[3] The Present tense is used with the Ablative in sentences implying "since," or "for some time past."

[4] For *bhalâ* read *bhalî*, and for the idiom see *Hindî Manual* (3rd edit.), p. 142.

[5] The compound *â nikalnâ* implies the unexpectedness of the coming.

given by S'iva, said, "What is become of the flag from here?" The gate-keepers replied, "Mahâraj! as regards that, many days ago it broke and fell." On hearing that statement, recollecting the promise of S'iva Jî, becoming thoughtful, Vâṇâsur said,—

"When did the flag and flagstaff fall? My enemy Hari has become incarnate somewhere."

As soon as this direction had issued from the mouth of Vâṇâsur, a door-keeper, having come and stood before him, with joined hands and bowed head, said, "Mahârâj! there is one thing; but that I am unable to utter; if I receive your Honour's command, then somehow or other I will state it." Vâṇâsur commanded [thus], "Well! say it." Then the warden said, "Mahârâj! forgive the fault. For several days we have been seeing that, in the princess's palace some man has come. Day and night he continues conversing. We do not know the secret concerning him, as to who the man is, and when and where he came from, and what he is doing." On hearing this statement, and giving credence to it, Vâṇâsur, very angrily, raising a weapon, softly entering Ushâ's palace alone, and secretly, sees what?—why, a man, dark-complexioned, very beautiful. covered by a yellow scarf, negligently in sleep, laying down slumbering with Ushâ.

Vâṇâsur reflects thus in his heart, "On a sleeping one being killed, there will be sin."

Mahârâj! having thus reflected in his heart, Vâṇâsur, for his part, placing there several guards, told them this, "As soon as this one wakes up, you will go and tell me." Having gone home, convened an assembly, and summoned all the Râkshasas, he began to say, "My enemy has arrived; do you take the whole army and go surround the palace of Ushâ; later on, I also shall come." Subsequently, on the one hand, having received the command of Vâṇâsur, all the Râkshasas came and surrounded the house of Ushâ; and on the other hand, Aniruddha Jî and the princess, having awakened from sleep, began to play with chess-men and dice. Hereupon, while playing away at dice, what does Ushâ see?—why, on all sides, a dense, fearful cloud had come around, lightning began to flash; frogs, peacocks, and sparrow-hawks began to utter cries. Mahârâj! on hearing the voice of the sparrow-hawk, the princess, saying this, clung to the neck of her lover,—

"O sparrow-hawk! do not you make [this] *piya piya* [calling]; [1] desist from this language of separation."

Hereupon, someone, going, said to Vâṇâsur, "Mahârâj! your enemy is awake." On hearing the name of his enemy, Vâṇâsur

[1] This imitative noise of the sparrow-hawk also means "Lover! lover!" as though calling away the loved one.

rose up with exceeding wrath, and taking his weapons, went and stood at Ushâ's door, and began secretly to peep in. At length, while looking on,—

> Vâṇâsur thus conceitedly says, "O fellow! who art thou within the house,
> With cloud-coloured body, fascinating as Madan,[1] lotus-eyed, wearing yellow raiment?
> O thief! why art thou not coming out? Whence now wilt thou obtain life from me?"[2]

Mahârâj! when Vâṇâsur, bawling out, had thus uttered these words, Ushâ and Aniruddha, having heard and seen, became exceedingly uneasy. Then the princess, experiencing much anxiety, becoming frightened, sighed deeply, and said to her husband, "Mahârâj! my father, with the army of Asuras, has come to attack; now how will you escape from his hand?"

> Then, indeed, angrily Aniruddha says, "Do not thou fear, O wife!
> The jackal-herd of Râkshas and Asuras, in an instant, I will destroy."

Having spoken thus, Aniruddha Jî, having recited passages from the Veda, summoned a rock one hundred and eight cubits [in size], and taking it in his hand, he issued forth, and, going into the midst of the army, challenged Vâṇâsur. As soon as he came out, Vâṇâsur prepared his bow, and, taking the whole army, so burst upon Aniruddha Jî as a swarm of honey-bees rushes on anyone. When the Asuras began to hurl various kinds of weapons, then angrily Aniruddha Jî, by means of the rock, so struck at several of them that the Asura army was scattered like scum [on a stagnant pool]. Some were killed, some were wounded; the saved fled away. Then Vâṇâsur went, and got all together, and began to fight [again]. Mahârâj! as many weapons as the Asuras were hurling went only in this direction or that, and not even one was touching the body of Aniruddha Jî.

> The weapons which would have fallen on Aniruddha, were cut in two by the edge of the rock;
> The blows of the rock were unendurable; like the thunder-bolt-blows which the Regent of the gods makes;
> On its hitting, heads were split down the midst; thighs and arms were broken, and bodies severed.

At last, fighting on, when Vâṇâsur alone remained, and all the army was cut up, then he, astonished in his heart, having said this, caught and bound Aniruddha Jî in a noose, to wit, "How shall I conquer this invincible one?"

Having related thus much of the tale, S'rî S'ukadev Jî said to

[1] A name of Kâma, the god of love.
[2] That is, "How will you preserve your life from me?"

King Parîkshit:—Mahârâj! when Vâṇâsur, having bound Aniruddha Jî with a noose, took him into his assembly, then Aniruddha Jî, for his part, was thus meditating in his heart, "To me trouble may or may not befall, but it is not proper to make the promise of Brahmâ a falsity; because if I should forcibly escape from the noose, he will be dishonoured; therefore it is better simply to remain bound." And Vâṇâsur was saying this, "O boy! now I am about to kill thee. If anyone should be thy helper, then do thou summon [him]." While this was going on, Ushâ, hearing of this condition of her lover, said to Chitrarekhâ, "Friend! a curse is on my life if my husband should be in affliction, and I should eat and sleep happily!" Chitrarekhâ said, "Friend! do not thou be at all anxious; no one will be able to do anything against thy husband. Be tranquil; S'rî Krishṇa Chand and Balarâm Jî, accompanied by all the Yadubañsîs, will immediately come to the attack; and, smiting the Asura host, will release and carry off Aniruddha along with thee. They have this very custom that, whatever king's pretty daughter they hear of, by force or fraud, as best they can they carry her off. This is the grandson of him who, having fought with the very strong and most famous Râjâs S'iśupâl and Jurâsindhu, carried away Rukminî, the daughter of Râjâ Bhîshmak, from Kuṇḍalapur. Just so will he now take thee away; do not thou be apprehensive about anything." Ushâ said, "Friend! I cannot endure this affliction,—

My loved one is carried off[1] bound in a noose; a poison-charged flame consumes my body;
How can I lie down with ease? [2] how can my eyes behold the loved one's affliction?
The loved one has fallen into calamity, why should I live? I will neither eat food, nor drink water;
Now, Vâṇâsur, kill my husband, or give me the refuge of my husband;[3]
What is to be, will be; what will anyone say to that?
I regard not the shame of the world or the Vedas; with the loved one, I consider misery [as] happiness itself."

Mahârâj! when Ushâ had spoken thus to Chitrarekhâ, she went near her husband, and sat down fearless and unhesitating. Then someone went to Vâṇâsur, and said, "Mahârâj! the princess has come out of the house and has gone near that man." On hearing these words, Vâṇâsur, summoning his son Skandh, said, "Son! do you raise your sister up from the assembly, take her indoors, and confine her there, and do not let her go out."

On receiving the command of his father, Skandh went to his sister, and angrily said, "What is this thou hast done, sinner! that thou hast lost shame of the world, and for thine own

[1] *harî* is made feminine merely to rhyme with *bharî*.
[2] *senâ* = *se*, "with."
[3] That is, "either kill him or give him back to me."

modesty? O low creature! Shall I kill thee? It would be sin; and I fear [1] even ill-repute." Ushâ said, "Brother! what is pleasing to you, say and do. The husband which Parvatî Jî gave to me I have accepted. Should I abandon this one, and run after another, then I should raise reproach against myself. Women of low family abandon their husbands; this is the custom which has come down traditionally in the world. [If] she is disgraced with him with whom Vidhnâ[2] has allied her, then she is disgraced."[3] Mahârâj! on hearing these words, Skandh angrily seizing her hand, carried off Ushâ thence into[4] the palace, and did not let her go out again. Then removing Aniruddha Jî also from there, he conveyed him elsewhere, and confined him. Then, on the one hand, Aniruddha Jî, in the absence of his wife, was grieving greatly, and, on the other hand, the princess in the absence of her husband, abstaining from food and drink, began to perform severe penance.

While this was taking place, after a certain time, Nârad Muni Jî, at first, going to Aniruddha Jî, counselled him thus, "Do not be anxious about anything; S'rî Krishṇa Chand, the root of joy, and Balarâm, the abode of happiness, will immediately make war upon the Râkshasas, and release you, and take you away." Then, going to Vâṇâsur, he said, "Râjâ! he whom you have seized with a noose and bound is S'rî Krishṇa's grandson, and Pradyumna Jî's son; and Aniruddha is his name. You know the Yadubañsîs very well; what you know, that do. I came to make you careful on this point; having done that, I go."[5] Having heard this, saying this much to Nârad Jî, he dismissed him, to wit, "Nârad Jî! I know all about it."

---

## CHAPTER LXIV.

**Krishṇa hears of his grandson's imprisonment, overcomes Vâṇâsur, and releases Aniruddha.**

S'RÎ S'UKADEV Jî said:—Mahârâj! when Aniruddha Jî had been four months in bondage, Nârad Jî went into the city of Dwârakâ. Then what does he see there?—that all the Yâdavas are greatly

[1] Here, again, we have the Aorist with the Substantive verb.
[2] A name of Brahmâ.
[3] Meaning that there is no more to be said on the point.
[4] After *mandir* Lallû Lâl put *meñ*.
[5] Here, again, the Past tense is used to express the imminence of the departure; he is as good as gone.

dejected, disturbed in mind, and wasted in body; and S'rî Krishṇa Jî and Balarâm Jî, seated in their midst, were saying, with much anxiety, "Who has taken the lad, and conveyed him from here?" This kind of discourse was going on, and in the female apartments violent lamentation was maintained, such that no one was listening to what anyone was saying. As soon as Nârad Jî went, all the people, both women and men, rose and hastened to him; and in great agitation, with emaciated bodies, and disturbed minds, crying and lamenting, went and stood before him. Subsequently, submissively, with joined hands and bowed heads, and repeatedly beseeching, they began to inquire of Nârad Jî all the particulars.

"Speak the truth, O King of Rishis! with which, being comforted, we may preserve our lives.
How shall we obtain tidings of Aniruddha? Tell us, O holy one! let us rest on that."[1]

As soon as he had heard this much, S'rî Nârad Jî said, "Do not be anxious about anything; but remove the grief from your mind. Aniruddha is alive and well in S'oṇitapur; where, having gone, he has enjoyed himself with the daughter of Râjâ Vâṇâsur; therefore that [king] has seized and bound him with a noose. Without a fight he will, in no wise, release Aniruddha Jî. I have stated this secret matter to you; for the rest, give effect to any remedy you may be able to originate." Mahârâj! having related this intelligence, Nârad Muni Jî, for his part, departed. Afterwards all the Yadubañsîs went to Râjâ Ugrasen and said, "Mahârâj! we have received exact intelligence that Aniruddha Jî is in S'oṇitapur, in the palace of Vâṇâsur. He has enjoyed that [king's] daughter; therefore that [king] has kept him bound with a noose. Now what is the order for us?" On hearing this statement, Râjâ Ugrasen said, "Take the whole of my army, and, as best you can, release and bring back Aniruddha." As soon as this order had issued from the mouth of Ugrasen, O Mahârâj! all the Yâdavas, taking the army of Râjâ Ugrasen, were[2] accompanied by Balarâm Jî; and S'rî Krishṇa Chand and Pradyumna Jî, mounted on Garuḍa, went, in front of all, to S'oṇitapur.

Having related the story thus far, S'rî S'ukadev Jî said:—Mahârâj! when Balarâm, taking the whole army of Râjâ Ugrasen, and sounding the kettle-drum, proceeded from the city of Dwârakâ to S'oṇitapur, the splendour of that circumstance is indescribable, inasmuch as, in front of all there was a row of huge-

[1] The exact meaning of this phrase is not obvious. The words *tâ ke bal* mean "by force of that" or "by the aid of that," but what is alluded to can only be conjectured. Both Hollings and Eastwick suggestively translate "so that we may rely on your words," and probably the anticipated statement is what is meant by *tâ*.

[2] For *ha͂e* read *hu͂e*.

tusked furious elephants, on which the kettle-drum was being sounded, and flags and banners were fluttering; after them, another line of elephants with canopied howdahs, on which were seated the greatest Yâdava soldiers, warriors, heroes, and braves, wearing coats of mail and helmets and armed with every kind of weapon. After them, row upou row of chariots were seen; and in their rear troop after troop of cavalry were moving along, making their various coloured horses dressed in collars, harness, and tasselled strings and armour, pace, stop, dance, jump and leap; and in their very midst, panegyrists were celebrating their glory, and bards were singing war-songs. After them was proceeding the army of foot-soldiers, like an army of locusts, with shields, swords, knives, poignards, daggers, *dhops*,[1] darts, javelins, spears, lances, broad-swords, double-edged swords, bows, arrows, clubs, discuses, axes, pole-axes, iron-pointed staves, sword-sticks, curved and serpentine daggers, and various kinds of arms and weapons; and in their midst, the sound of kettle-drums, drums, tambourines, flutes, fifes, and horns, which arose, were exceedingly pleasing.

> The dust flew up and spread to the sky; the sun was concealed; it became like [2] night;
> The male and female *chakwa* [3] were separated; beautiful women enjoyed themselves with their husbands;
> The blue lotus bloomed, the white lotus drooped; nocturnal animals prowled about, thinking it was night.

Having related the tale thus far, S'rî S'ukadev Jî said:— Mahârâj! when Balarâm Jî, with twelve complete armies, demolishing, with much ostentation, the forts, strongholds, and fastnesses of that [king], and desolating the country, arrived at S'oṇitapur, and S'rî Krishṇa Chand and Pradyumna Jî also had joined him, someone, being greatly frightened and alarmed, with joined hands and bowed head, said to Vâṇâsur, "Mahârâj! Krishṇa and Balarâm, with all their army, have advanced to attack, and they have breached and thrown down our forts, strongholds, and defences, and have come and surrounded the city on all sides; now what is [your] command?"

As soon as he heard this, Vâṇâsur very angrily summoned his greatest Râkshasas and said, "Do you take all your forces, march out of the city, and halt in front of Krishṇa and Balarâm; afterwards I also will come." Mahârâj! on receiving the order, those Asuras, immediately taking the twelve complete armies, came, with arms and weapons, and stood before S'rî Krishṇa and Balarâm Jî to fight. Close after them came Vâṇâsur also, having meditated on S'rî Mahâdev and his service, ready

[1] *dhop* is the name of a long, straight sword.
[2] *bhẫt* is a form of the postposition *bhâve*, "like."
[3] These birds are supposed to separate from each other at night.

prepared. S'ukadev the saint said :—Mahârâj ! as soon as he meditated, the throne of S'iva Jî rocked, and his meditation was broken ; then he, by reflection, knew that trouble had happened to his worshipper, and that he should then go and dispel his anxiety.

Having reflected thus in his heart, and having divided his body with Pârvatî Jî, and bound up his matted locks, and applied ashes, and consumed a large quantity of hemp, swallow-wort, and thorn-apple, and put on a Brahmanical cord of white snakes, and covered himself with elephant hide, and put on a necklace of skulls and a garland of snakes, holding his trident, bow, hand-drum, and skull, mounted on Nândiyâ,[1] and taking an army of spirits, goblins, fiends, female demons, female imps, she-spirits, she-goblins, and female fiends, &c., Bholânâth went forth. The beauty of that pageantry is indescribable, inasmuch as in his ear was an earring of elephant-gem, on his forehead a moon, on his head he bears the Ganges, and makes his eyes intensely red, and with frightful aspect he assumes the form of the Destroyer. In this way playing and singing, and causing his army to dance, he was proceeding on ; insomuch that that appearance can be realized only on being seen ; it cannot be uttered.[2] At length, in a certain time, S'iva Jî, leading his army, arrived[3] where Vâṇâsur, with all the Asura army, was standing. On seeing Hara, Vâṇâsur delightedly said, "Ocean of mercy ! who but you would at this time remember me ?

Your glory will consume them ; now how will the Yâdava
family survive ?"

Having stated this, he proceeded to say, "Mahârâj ! let there be on this occasion a fair fight ; and let one oppose one, and fight in single combat." Mahârâj ! when this remark had issued from the mouth of Vâṇâsur, then, on the one side, the Asuras stood fronting for battle, and on the other side, the Yadubañsîs came and were ready. On both sides the instruments began to sound. The heroes, braves, soldiers, warriors, and the resolute began to prepare their weapons ; and the irresolute, timid, and cowardly began to fly from the field and to save their lives.

Then S'iva Jî, in the form of the Destroyer, was opposed to S'rî Krishṇa Chand ; and Vâṇâsur was opposite to Balarâm Jî ; Skandh encountered Pradyumna Jî ; and in this way one engaged with the other ; and from both sides the weapons began

[1] *Nândiyâ*, *Nânḍiyâ*, or *Nandin*, are names of the bull on which S'iva rides.

[2] This highly idiomatic sentence becomes simple when it is understood that *dekhe* is a past participle in the locative, used (as is frequently the case in Sanskrit) to express "on being" or "when" in connection with the idea of the base. The phrase is literally, "That form only on being seen comes into being ; it comes not into utterance."

[3] The presence of *ki* is here idiomatically correct, although it is untranslatable. The comma after it should, however, be removed, for it belongs to the word *jahâñ* which follows.

to fly. On that side, the bow Pinâk [was] in the hand of S'iva Jî; on this side [stood] the Lord of the Yadus with the bow Sârang. S'iva Jî discharged the Brahma arrow; S'rî Krishṇa Jî cut and brought down the Brahma weapon. Then Rudra sent forth a mighty wind; that Hari evaded by fiery energy. Then Mahâdev produced fire; Murâri caused rain and extinguished that, and created a fierce blaze, which ran into the army of Sadâśiva;[1] that, having burnt[2] the beards, moustachios, and hair, made all the Asuras frightful in aspect.

When the Asura army began to burn, and there was a great outcry for deliverance, Bholânâth caused rain to fall and cooled the burnt and half-burnt Rakshasas, sprites, and goblins; and himself very angrily took the Nârâyanî arrow in order to hurl it. Then reflecting somewhat in his heart, he did not hurl it, he put it down. Then it was that S'rî Krishṇa Jî, hurling the arrow Âlasya, stupefied them all, and began to cut up the Asura army, as a husbandman cuts his crop. Having seen this exploit, when Mahâdev, having reflected, said within himself, "Now without a cataclysmic war there is no success;" then Skandh, mounted on a peacock, rushed forward, and from the sky discharged an arrow on the army of S'rî Krishṇa Jî.

Then Pradyumna says to Hari, "[Someone] has mounted a peacock and is fighting from above;
Give the order, 'Let there be fierce fight'; I will slay [him]; he will at once fall to the earth."

As soon as this was said, the Lord gave the order, and Pradyumna Jî shot an arrow which hit the peacock, and Skandh fell down. As soon as Skandh fell, Vâṇâsur angrily bent five bows, and fixing two arrows apiece on each of the bows, began to pour them down like rain, and S'rî Krishṇa Chand began to cut them in the very midst. Mahârâj! then the kettle-drums, drums, and tambourines, of both sides, were playing; panegyrists were singing [a song] like the Dhamâl;[3] from wounds streams of blood were running as from syringes; here and there, in various places, the bright red blood looked like *gulâl*;[4] in the midst, sprites, goblins, and fiends, who having assumed various frightful forms were wandering about, were sporting like mimics, and the river of blood flowed forth like a stream of colour. How [call it] a battle? it was like the Holî festival going on on both sides. Hereupon, after the fighting had been going on for some time, S'rî Krishna Jî shot an arrow so that the charioteer of the chariot of that [other king] was swept away, and the horses were scared. At length, on the death of the charioteer, Vâṇâsur also left the battle-field and fled, and S'rî Krishṇa Jî pursued him.

[1] *Sadâśiva*, "the ever felicitous"; a name of S'iva.
[2] *jalâyke* should be one word; it is the Conjunctive Participle of *jalâna*.
[3] The Dhamâl is a song sung at the Holî festival: *sî* agrees with *gîti* understood.
[4] The bright red powder scattered about at the Holî festival.

Having related the story thus far, S'rî S'ukadev Jî said :— Mahârâj ! having received intelligence of the flight of Vâṇâsur, his mother, whose name was Kaṭrâ, then in fearsome guise, with dishevelled locks, came stark naked and stood before S'rî Krishṇa Chand Jî, and began to cry out.

On seeing her the Lord closed his eyes, and having heard her voice he turned his back ;
During which time Vâṇâsur fled, and his army was rallied.

Mahârâj ! until Vâṇâsur had organized a complete army and come there, Kaṭrâ did not retire from before S'rî Krishṇa Jî ; [but] having seen her son's army she went home. Afterwards Vâṇâsur came and fought valiantly, but could not stand before the Lord ; then he fled and went to Mahâdev Jî. Having seen Vâṇâsur afflicted with fear, S'iva Jî very angrily summoned a violent fever and sent it at the army of S'rî Krishṇa Jî. That very powerful and energetic one, whose energy was the equal of the sun's, with three heads, nine feet, six hands, three eyes, and fearsome guise, came and penetrated the army of S'rî Krishṇa Chand. Through his energy the Yadubaṅsîs began to burn, and to shake and tremble. At length, being greatly pained and agitated, the Yadubaṅsîs came and said to S'rî Krishṇa Jî, "Mahârâj ! the fever of S'iva Jî having come, has burnt up and killed the whole army, now save us from his hand, otherwise not even one Yadubaṅsî will escape alive." Mahârâj ! having heard this, and perceiving them to be distressed, Hari sent forth the ague. That rushed upon the fever of Mahâdev. On seeing it that fever timidly fled, and, continuing his retreat, came to Sadâsiva Jî.

Then the fever says to Mahâdev, "Grant an asylum ; Krishṇa's fever is burning [me]."

Hearing this statement, Mahâdev Jî said, "Except S'rî Krishṇa Chand, there is no one in the three worlds who can remove S'rî Krishṇa Chand Jî's fever ; therefore this is better that thou go to S'rî Murâri, the helper of devotees." Having heard the speech of S'iva, and reflected, the violent fever went before S'rî Krishṇa Chand, the root of joy, and with joined hands, humbly, submissively, and entreatingly said, "O Ocean of Compassion ! Friend of the Humble ! the Purifier of the Fallen ! the Compassionator of the Lowly ! forgive my fault, and save me from your fever.

You are the Lord, the God of Brahmâ and the others ; your power is incomprehensible, O Lord of the Universe !
You alone having created, arranged what was created ; O Krishṇa ! the universe is all your illusion ;
By your favour, I comprehend this ; knowledge was granted ; the Creator of the universe became visible."

On hearing this speech, Hari, the Compassionate, said, "Thou hast come to my protection; therefore thou art saved; otherwise thou hadst not escaped living. I have pardoned thy fault on the present occasion; do not again attack my worshippers and servants; this is *my* order to thee." The fever said, "Ocean of Compassion! whoever shall hear this story, ague, intermittent fever, and tertiary ague, will never attack." Then S'rî Krishṇa Chand resumed, "Now do thou go to Mahâdev; stay not here, otherwise my fever will give thee trouble." On receiving this command, taking leave and prostrating himself, the violent fever went to Sadâśiva Jî, and the pain of the fever was entirely subdued.

Having related the story thus far, S'rî S'ukadev Jî said:—Mâhâraj!

Whoever hears this conversation, will have no fear of fever.

Afterwards Vâṇâsur, very angrily, taking bows and arrows in all his hands, came before the Lord, and challenged him, and said,—

"I fought a severe combat with you; still our desire is not satisfied."

When, having said this, he began to discharge arrows with all his hands, S'rî Krishṇa Chand, releasing the discus Sudarśan, cut off all his arms except four, as anyone in a moment would lop off the branches of a tree. On the cutting off of his arms, Vâṇâsur, being stupefied, fell down. A river of blood flowed forth from the wounds; in that the arms appeared like alligators and fishes; the severed heads of elephants were sinking like crocodiles; in the midst, chariots, like rafts and barges, were floating about; and hither and thither in the battle-field dogs, jackals, vultures, and other beasts and birds, were dragging about the corpses, and quarrelling and wrangling with each other, were rending and devouring them, while crows, picking out the eyes from the heads, were taking and flying away with them.

S'rî S'ukadev Jî said:—Mahârâj! seeing this to be the condition of the battle-field, Vâṇâsur became exceedingly dejected, and began to regret. At length, becoming destitute of strength, he went to Sadâśiva. Then,—

Rudra, having reflected in his mind, says, "Now you should gratify Hari."

Having said this much, S'rî Mahâdev Jî, taking Vâṇâsur with him, and reading the Veda [as they went], came where S'rî Krishṇa Chand was standing in the field of battle. Having thrown Vâṇâsur at his feet, S'iva Jî with joined hands said, "O [thou who art] merciful [to those who] come for sanctuary! now this Vâṇâsur has come to thy asylum; compassionately look on him, and bear not his fault in mind. You are repeatedly becoming incarnate, to remove the burden of the earth, and to destroy the wicked and cause the world to cross [the ocean of existence]. You are the Lord, invisible, inseparable, eternal; for the sake of worshippers you came into the world and are manifesting Bhagwant,[1] otherwise you ever remain in the form of Virâṭ,[2] of whom this is the form: heaven is the head, the sky is the navel, the earth is the foot, the ocean is the belly, Indra is the arms, the hills are the nails, the clouds are the hair, trees are the down, the moon and sun are the eyes, Brahmâ is the mind, Rudra is the pride, the air is the breath, day and night are the shutting and opening of the eyes, thunder is the voice.

In such a form you ever abide; by no one are you comprehended.

And this world is an ocean of misery; it is filled with water in the form of anxiety and delusion. O Lord! without the help of the boat of your name, no one is able to go across this most difficult ocean; and thus many are sinking and floundering. The man who, having obtained a mortal body, shall not bear your worship in mind and offer up prayer, will forget religion and enhance his sin. He who having come into the world does not call upon your name, has abandoned nectar and drunk poison. He in whose heart you have come and dwelt, having celebrated your virtues, has obtained faith and salvation."

Having said this much, S'rî Mahâdev Jî resumed, "O Ocean of Compassion! Friend of the Lowly! your greatness is unbounded. Who has so much power that he can celebrate it, and understand your exploits? Now have compassion upon me, and pardon the fault of this Vâṇâsur, and give him faith in you. He also is entitled to your faith, since he is part of the family of the devotee Prahlâd." S'rî Krishṇa Chand said, "S'iva Jî! there is no difference between you and me, and whoever shall suppose there is difference will fall into a great hell, and will never obtain me. He who has meditated on you, has finally obtained me. This one has guilelessly invoked your name, therefore I have made him four-armed. To whomsoever you have granted, or shall grant, a boon, him I have protected and shall protect."

[1] A name of Krishṇa; therefore the phrase may be rendered "manifesting yourself."

[2] *Virâṭ* is the Nominative form of *virâj*, "the radiant." The exact mythological position of Virâj is not clear. Manu says (i. 32) that Brahmâ divided his substance into male and female, and from the female portion Virâj arose. This Virâj was male, and from him was produced the first Manu (also styled the Self-existent Manu), who created the ten Prâjapatis, or progenitors of human kind. The Purusha-sûkta of the Rig-veda states that Virâj was produced from Purusha (the primal male), and that Purusha was then produced from Virâj. The Purâṇas give somewhat conflicting accounts of this metaphysical conception, which is, not improbably, merely intended to express the creation of form from the formless. The Harivanśa states that Vishṇu created Virâj; and this connection would account for his association here with Krishṇa. The Vishṇu-Purâṇa also (i. 12) declares that Virâj sprang from Vishṇu; but immediately afterwards identifies Virâj with Vishṇu himself.

Mahârâj! as soon as this promise had issued from the mouth of the Lord, Sadâśiva Jî, prostrating himself and taking leave, went to Kailâs with his army, and S'rî Krishṇa Chand remained just where he was. Then Vâṇâsur, with joined hands, and bowed head, submissively said, "O Lord of the Lowly! as you have now compassionately caused me to cross [the ocean of existence], now come and purify your servant's house, and take Aniruddha Jî and Ûshâ Jî along with you." On hearing this statement, S'rî Bihârî, the benefactor of devotees, taking Pradyumna Jî with him, set out for the house of Vâṇâsur. Mahârâj! then Vâṇâsur, being greatly delighted, with great courtesy conducted the Lord, spreading silken carpets for his feet. Afterwards—

> Having washed his feet he took his foot-water, and, sipping it, placed it on his forehead.

He then resumed, "The foot-water which to all is difficult of attainment, I have obtained by the favour of Hari, and have lost the sin of various births. This foot-water purifies the three worlds; its name is Ganges. Brahmâ filled an ascetic's pot with it; S'iva Jî placed it on his head. Then gods, saints, and Rishis honoured it, and Bhâgîrath, having performed austerity to the three gods, brought it into the world; since then its name has been Bhâgîrathî. This is the remover of the stain of sin,[1] the purifier, the giver of happiness to the saintly, the ladder to Vaikuṇṭh; and he who has bathed in it has lost the sin of various births. He who has drunk the water of the Ganges has certainly attained beatitude; they who have seen Bhâgîrathî have subdued the whole world." Mahârâj! having said this much, Vâṇâsur, bringing Aniruddha Jî and Ûshâ, with hands joined, before the Lord, said,—

> "Pardon my fault, what was to be was; I have given this Ûshâ [as] a slave."

Having spoken thus, Vâṇâsur, according to Vedic prescription, gave his daughter; and in her dowry bestowed much of which there were no bounds.[2]

Having told so much of the story, S'rî S'ukadev Jî said:— Mahârâj! as soon as the marriage had taken place, S'rî Krishṇa Chand, having given to Vâṇâsur hope and encouragement, and seated him on the throne, took leave, accompanied by his grandson and grand-daughter, and causing the kettle-drums to play, set out thence to the city of Dwârakâ, with all the Yadubaṅsîs. Having received intelligence of their coming, all the inhabitants of Dwârakâ went out of the city, and escorted the Lord with a musical procession. Then the inhabitants of the town, singing

[1] Eastwick translates "crimes and stains," but *malaharanî* is one word, "stain-remover," as Paṇḍit Yogadhyân Miśra prints it. Eastwick entirely omits the next two phrases; and Hollings omits the entire passage, from one *janm janm kâ pâp gaṅwâyâ* to the other.

[2] That is, he gave boundless wealth.

songs of rejoicing, from markets, roads, squares, halls, and houses, were making festivity; and Rukminî and all the other beauteous ones were singing songs of congratulation in the royal palace, and were observing the usual ceremonies; and the gods, each seated in his own car, were raining down flowers, and uttering shouts of victory; and, in the house and out, throughout the whole city, joy was prevailing. Then [1] Balarâm, the abode of happiness, and S'rî Krishṇa Chand, the root of joy, dismissed all the Yadubañsîs, and went and resided in the palace with Aniruddha and Ûshâ.

Ûshâ was brought into the house; on seeing her Krishṇa's wives were delighted;
The mother-in-law gave blessings and embraced her; having seen her and being delighted, she dressed her in ornaments.

---

## CHAPTER LXV.

The story of Râjâ Nrig—He is changed into a lizard, and lives for ages in a dry well—He is released from this state by Krishṇa.

S'RÎ S'UKADEV Jî said:—Mahârâj! Râjâ Nrig,[2] of the Ikshwâku [3] race, was wise, liberal, virtuous, and brave. He gave unnumbered cows in alms. If the grains of sand of the Ganges, and the drops of rain in the month Bhâdauñ, and the stars of heaven could be counted, then the cows given in alms by Râjâ Nrig could also be counted. A king who was so wise, great, and liberal, having for a slight fault become a lizard, abode in a dried-up well; him S'rî Krishṇa Chand Jî delivered.

Having related the story thus far, King Parîkshit asked S'rî S'ukadev Jî:—Mahârâj! for what sin did so virtuous and liberal a king become a lizard and remain in a dried-up well, and how did S'rî Krishṇa Chand Jî cause him to cross [the ocean of existence]? Do you explain this story to me, that the doubt of my mind may be removed.

S'rî S'ukadev Jî said:—Mahârâj! do you pay heed, give atten-

[1] The *ki* marks transition from one line of thought to another.

[2] Some confusion exists about this personality. The Vishṇu-Purâṇa (iv. 1) speaks of him as the son of Manu Vaivaswata and brother of Ikshwâku; but the Bhâgavata-Purâṇa says he was of the Nâga or Serpent race. The tradition here given is alluded to in the Linga-Purâṇa; but is more fully told in the Mahâbhârata (Anuśâsana-parvan, 3452).

[3] Ikshwâku was the first king of the Solar dynasty at Ayodhya.

tion, and listen; I will explain the whole tale just as it occurred. Râjâ Nrig, then, was simply keeping on constantly giving cows in alms; but one day, having bathed quite early, and performed the twilight acts of worship, he sent for a thousand white, purple, black, yellow, brown, and grey cows, with silver hoofs, golden horns, and copper backs, and had them dressed in silk, and vowed [them in alms]; and in addition to them he gave to the Brâhmaṇs large quantities of food and wealth. They taking them, went to their own homes. Next day the king again, in that way, began to make a gift of cows. Then one cow of the former day's vow, unknown [to the king], came and joined [the others]; that one, also, the king gave away along with those cows. The Brâhmaṇ accepting them went to his house. Afterwards the other Brâhmaṇ recognized his cow, and stopped it in the road and said, "This cow is mine; I received it yesterday from the king's place. Brother! why art thou going with this?" The Brâhmaṇ said, "This, indeed, I am just coming along with from the king's place; how was it thine?" Mahârâj! both those Brâhmaṇs in this way, with [exclamations of] "Mine, mine," began to dispute. At length, wrangling on, they both went to the king. The king having heard both their statements, joined his hands, and submissively said,—

"Let one accept a lâkh of rupees, and let one give the other the cow."

On hearing this speech, both the wrangling Brâhmaṇs very angrily said, "Mahârâj! the cow which, after uttering a blessing, we have received, we will not give up even by receiving a *karoṛ* of rupees; this is [connected] with our souls." Mahârâj! again the king, falling repeatedly at the feet of those Brâhmaṇs, in various ways flattered and counselled them; but those vindictive Brâhmaṇs paid no heed to what the king said. At length very angrily saying this, both the Brâhmaṇs left the cow and departed, "Mahârâj! the cow which you vowed and gave to us, and which we blessed, stretched out our hands, and took, that cow is not to be given for money. Well! [if] it thus remains with you it does not signify."

Mahârâj! on the departure of the Brâhmaṇs, Râjâ Nrig was at first dejected and began to say within his heart, "This impiety occurred through me unconsciously; how shall it be removed?" and afterwards he began to be extremely liberal and pious. After some time had elapsed, Râjâ Nrig, in the course of time,[1] died. The emissaries of Yama took him to Dharmarâj.[2] Dharmarâj, on seeing the king, rose from his throne and stood up; then, having placed him courteously on the seat, said most affectionately, "Mahârâj! you have great merit, and few sins; tell me which will you first be requited for?"

[1] *Lit.*, "having become subject to Time," that is, Fate or Destiny.
[2] Dharmarâj and Yama are names for the judge of departed souls.

Having heard this, Nrig, with joined hands, says, "Let not my virtue pass away, O Lord!
First I will suffer for the sin; having assumed a body I will suffer[1] affliction."

On hearing this statement, Dharmarâj said to Râjâ Nrig, "Mahârâj! you unknowingly a second time gave in alms a cow which had already been given in alms; for this fault you will have to become a lizard and remain in a dried-up well in the midst of a forest on the banks of the Gomtî. When, at the end of the Dwâpara age,[2] S'rî Krishṇa Chand shall become incarnate, he will give you deliverance." Mahârâj! having said this, Dharmarâj remained silent, and Râjâ Nrig, immediately becoming a lizard, fell down into a dried-up well, and by feeding on living creatures began to live there.

Afterwards, on several ages having elapsed, at the end of the Dwâpara age, S'rî Krishṇa Chand Jî became incarnate; and, having sported in Braj, when he went to Dwârakâ, and had sons and grandsons, one day several of the sons and grandsons of S'rî Krishṇa Jî, joining together, went to hunt, and, while hunting in the wood, became thirsty. By chance, they, while hunting about for water in the wood, went to that dried-up well where Râjâ Nrig, having taken birth as a lizard, remained. On peering into the well, one of them cried aloud to them all, "O brothers! see, what a great lizard there is in this well."

On hearing this statement, all of them ran, and stood on the coping-stone of the well and began to unite their turbans and waist-bands together, to let them down, and to haul [him up], and to say among themselves, "Brothers! without getting this one out of the well we will not go from here." Mahârâj! when he did not come out with that rope of turbans and waist-bands, they sent for, from the village, very thick and powerful ropes of hemp, thread, *mûn̥ a*,[3] and leather, and attaching a noose to the lizard in the well, began forcibly to haul him; but he was not even moved from there. Then someone, going into Dwârakâ, said to S'rî Krishṇa Jî, "Mahârâj! there is a very large, heavy lizard within a dried-up well in the wood. All the Princes have dragged him [till] they are tired; but he does not come out."

On hearing these words, Hari arose and hastened, and, proceeding onwards, came where all the boys were pulling out the lizard. On seeing the Lord, all the boys said, "Father! see, what a big lizard this is! we, for a long time, have been getting it out, but it does not come out." Mahârâj! having heard this speech, as soon as S'rî Krishṇa Chand Jî, having descended into the well, had placed his foot on his body, at once he quitted that body, and became a very handsome man.

[1] *sahihauñ* should be one word, as being the 1st pers. sing. Future.
[2] See note [3], p. 183.
[3] *mûnja* is the name of a grass (*Saccharum munja*) from which ropes are made.

In the form of a king he remained holding the feet [of Krishṇa]; with joined hands and bowed head, he solicits [thus],—

"Ocean of Compassion! you have acted very mercifully in that you have come and remembered me in this great calamity." S'ukadev Jî said:—Râjâ! when he, having assumed human form, began to speak in this kind of way to Hari, the children of the Yâdavas, and the sons and grandsons of Hari, with astonishment began to ask S'rî Krishṇa Chand, thus, "Mahârâj! what is this? and for what offence did he become a lizard and stay here? Kindly tell us that, then the doubt in our minds will depart." Then the Lord himself, telling [them] nothing, said to the king,—

"Explain your secret, so that all, having paid attention, may hear;
Who are you? Whence did you come from? For what sin did you obtain this body?"
Having heard, the king said, with joined hands, "You know all, O Lord of the Yadus!

Nevertheless you are asking,[1] therefore I will tell [all]. My name is Râjâ Nrig; for your sake, I gave innumerable cows to Brâhmaṇs. It happened one day that I, having vowed several cows, gave them to Brâhmaṇs. Next day one of those cows came back; that one I, with other cows, unintentionally gave in alms to another Brâhmaṇ. As soon as he had accepted it and gone out, the first Brâhmaṇ, recognizing his cow, said to him, 'This cow is mine; I obtained it yesterday from the king's place. Why art thou taking it away?' The other said, 'I am coming with it straight from the king's place; how is it thine?' Mahârâj! those two Brâhmaṇs, while quarrelling on this point, came to me. I counselled them and said, 'In exchange for one cow, receive from me a hundred thousand cows, and let one of you give up this cow.'

"Mahârâj! those two obstinately did not agree to my proposal. At length, leaving the cow, they both angrily went away. I, deeply regretting [what had occurred], sat patiently. At last the messengers of Yama conducted me to Dharmarâj. Dharmarâj asked me, thus, 'Râjâ! thy virtue is great, and thy sin is small. Tell me, which will you first have the requital of?' I said, 'Sin.' On hearing this word, O Mahârâj! Dharmarâj said, 'Râjâ! thou gavest a second time to a Brâhmaṇ a cow already given; for this impiety do thou, having become a lizard, go on earth, and stay in a dried-up well in the midst of a wood on the banks of the Gomtî. When, at the end of the Dwâpara age, S'rî Krishṇa Chand, having become incarnate, shall go near thee, thy release shall be accomplished.' Mahârâj! since then I, in the form of a lizard,

[1] Here we have the 2nd pers. instead of the 3rd pers. pl. with *âp*.

have been lying in this dried-up well, meditating on your lotus-feet. Now, having come, you have delivered me from great affliction, and carried me across the ocean of existence."

Having related the story thus far, S'rî S'ukadev Jî said to King Parîkshit :—Mahârâj ! having said this much, Râjâ Nrig, being dismissed, sat in a car and went to Vaikunṭh ; and S'rî Krishṇa Chand counselled all the youths and cowherds, and said,—

"Let no one injure a Brâhmaṇ ; let no one take away the portion of a Brâhmaṇ ;
Hold not back what has been vowed in the heart; speak truthful words to Brâhmaṇs ;
He who takes back what he has given to a Brâhmaṇ, Yama gives him a punishment as great as this [of Nrig] ;
Remain the servants of Brâhmaṇs ; bear [patiently] all the faults of a Brâhmaṇ ;
He who reveres a Brâhmaṇ, reveres me ; let no one suppose there is a difference between a Brâhmaṇ and me.

He who shall think there is a difference between me and a Brâhmaṇ will fall into hell ; and he who shall revere a Brâhmaṇ will obtain me, and without doubt will enter the supreme abiding-place." Mahârâj ! having said these words, S'rî Krishṇa Jî conducted them all thence, and set out for the city of Dwârakâ.

---

## CHAPTER LXVI.

**Balarâm visits Nand and Jasodâ at Braj, and dances with the cowherdesses.**

S'RÎ SUKADEV Jî said :—Mahârâj ! once S'rî Krishṇa Chand, the root of joy, and Balarâm, the abode of happiness, were seated in their jewelled palace ; whereupon Baladev Jî said to the Lord, "Brother ! when Kañs sent to call us from Brindâban, and we started for Mathurâ, you and I promised the cowherdesses, and Nand and Jasodâ, that we should speedily go and meet them ; however, not going there, we have come and dwelt in Dwârakâ. They must be thinking about us ; if you permit it, we will go see our birthplace, and, having comforted them, will return." The Lord said, "Very well !" On hearing this, Balarâm Jî took leave of all, and taking his plough and club, mounted his chariot, and set out.

Mahârâj ! the kings of the towns, cities, and villages into

which Balarâm Jî was going, advanced to meet him, and with great courtesy conducted him; and he continued to give consolation to each of them. After a time, proceeding onwards, Balarâm Jî arrived at the city of Avantikâ.

> He paid respect to his instructor in knowledge; Balarâm stayed there ten days.

Afterwards, taking leave of the Guru, Baladev Jî, proceeding onwards, arrived in Gokul. Then what does he see! In the woods, in all directions, cows are wandering about, lowing and panting, with mouths gaping open, without eating grass, thinking about S'rî Krishṇa Chand, and paying heed to the tones of his flute. Close behind them, the cowherd lads were going along, imbued with love, singing the praises of Hari, and hither and thither the inhabitants of the city were celebrating the exploits and sports of the Lord. Mahârâj! having gone to the birthplace and witnessed this condition of the inhabitants of Braj and the cows, Balarâm Jî compassionately brought tears into his eyes. Then having seen the flag and banner of the chariot, and thinking that S'rî Krishṇa Chand and Balarâm Jî were come, all the cowherd lads came running. On their coming, the Lord,[1] having descended from the chariot, began to embrace each separately and very affectionately to ask their welfare. Hereupon someone went and said to Nand and Jasodâ, "Baladev Jî has come." On receiving this intelligence, Nand, Jasodâ, and the chief cowherds arose and hastened. Having perceived them coming from a distance, Balarâm Jî ran, and went and threw himself at the feet of Nand Râ,e. Then Nand Jî, greatly delighted, with eyes filled with tears, very affectionately raised up Balarâm Jî, and embraced him, and lost the pain of separation. Then the Lord—

> Went and clasped the feet of Yaśumatî.[2] She tenderly embraced him.
>
> She met, embraced, and kept holding him to her bosom; a stream of tears flowed from her eyes.

Having related the story thus far, S'rî S'ukadev Jî said to the King:—Mahârâj! having met thus, Nand Râ,e Jî conducted Balarâm Jî into the house, and began to ask about his welfare, thus, "Tell me; are Ugrasen, Vasudev, and all the other Yâdavas, and S'rî Krishṇa Chand, the root of joy, happy? and do they ever think of us?" Balarâm Jî said, "By your favour, all are in joy and happiness, and ever, at all times, continue to celebrate your virtues." Having heard this, Nand Râ,e was silent. Then Jasodâ the queen, remembering S'rî Krishṇa Jî, with eyes filled with tears, agitatedly said, "Baladev Jî! is our beloved S'rî Krishṇa Jî well, the star of our eyes?" Balarâm Jî said, "He is very well." Then Nand's queen resumed, "Baladev! since Hari set out from

[1] Notice that here Balarâm is called *Prabhu*, "the Lord."
[2] A name of Yaśodâ or Jasodâ.

hence, darkness has been before my eyes; I have continued day and night meditating on him, and he, forgetting all remembrance of me, has gone and ensconced himself in Dwârakâ. And see, my sisters Devakî and Rohinî also have given up all affection for me.

> [I] thought Gokul near Mathurâ; still it was considered that I lived at a distance;
> [I thought], Hari is coming to meet and rejoin [us]; he did not return; this they [1] have done."

Mahârâj! when Jasodâ Jî, having said this much, becoming greatly agitated, began to cry, Balarâm Jî counselled, encouraged, and gave her confidence. Then he having eaten and partaken of betel, went out of the house. Then what does he see! All the young women of Braj, with emaciated bodies, disordered minds, dishevelled hair, squalid appearance, desponding souls, oblivious of household affairs, imbued with love, intoxicated with youthfulness, singing Hari's praises, agitated in consequence of separation [from a loved one], were proceeding hither and thither like drunken creatures. Mahârâj! on seeing Balarâm Jî, they became exceedingly pleased, and rushed to him, and prostrating themselves, and standing on all sides with joined hands, they began to ask and to say, "Tell us, O Balarâm! abode of happiness! now where dwells our life, the beauteous S'yâm? Does Bihârî ever bear us in mind, or having attained power, has he altogether forgotten former affection? Since he went from here, he sent [only] once a message, through Ûdho, enjoining penance. Then he took no thought of anyone. Now he has gone and taken up his abode in the ocean; then why should he take thought of anyone?" On hearing these words, a cowherdess cried out, "Friend! who would regret the love of Hari, when this conduct of his is seen by all?

> He is not [2] desired of anyone, who has turned his back on his parents.
> He was not remaining an hour without Râdhâ; this is she who has stopped him.[3]

Again, what advantage have you and I got by abandoning household duties, sacrificing respect for our families, and the good opinion of the world, and leaving children and husband, for the love of Hari? At length, having embarked us on the

[1] That is, Devakî and Rohinî.

[2] *nâhiñ* should be one word; it is a dialectal form of *nahîñ*. The separation has caused Eastwick to introduce a second phrase in his translation which is not intended here.

[3] This phrase is not clear. There is no such word as *barsânâ*, in the sense of "stay," "stop," or "restrain;" but it may be intended for *birsânâ*, "to cause to remain"; *birsâne parî* would mean "she had to stop (him)"; but it might also imply "she happened to be stayed." Neither Lallû Lâl nor Eastwick give the word in their vocabularies; and Eastwick follows Hollings in translating "causes him to stop away." The phrase is ironical.

vessel of love, he has abandoned us in the midst of the ocean of separation. Now we are hearing that, having gone into Dwârakâ, the Lord has contracted many marriages, and that S'rî Krishṇa has removed and married sixteen thousand one hundred princesses which Bhaumâsur had kept in his house. Now from them there have been sons, grandsons, and granddaughters; why should he leave them and come here?" Hearing this, another cowherdess said, "Friend! do not expend any regret over the words of Hari; because Ûdho Jî came and related all *his* good qualities." Having said this much, she resumed, "Friends! should you heed my advice now,—

Let us touch the feet of Haladhar Jî, and continue to sing only his virtues;
He is fair, not dark bodied; he will not act deceptively."
Having heard, Sankarshan[1] replied, "For your sake I have made this journey;
When we went we said to you that we should come; therefore Krishṇa has sent me to Braj;
I will stay two months, and dance the circular dance; I will fulfil all your hopes."

Mahârâj! Balarâm Jî, having said this much, directed all the young women of Braj, thus, "To-day is the night of Madhumâs;[2] decorate yourselves and come into the wood; I will dance the circular dance with you." Having said this, Balarâm Jî, in the evening, set out for the wood. After him, all the young women of Braj also, wearing nice dresses and ornaments, and adorned from head to foot, came near to Baladev Jî,—

All stood with heads bent; the beauty of Haladhar cannot be described;
Golden-coloured, wearing blue robes; moon-faced, lotus-eyed, captivating the heart;
An earring in one ear shed its lustre, as though sun and moon together shone;
The other ear had imbibed the flavour of the glory of Hari; the ear did not bear a second earring;
On each member of his body were numerous ornaments; the splendour of which baffles description;
The beauteous ones fell at his feet, saying this,—"Engage in delightful sport and the circular dance [with us]."

Mahârâj! on hearing this remark Balarâm Jî made [the mystic sound] *hûṅ*.[3] On his making the sound *hûṅ*, all the things

[1] Sankarshan is a name of Balarâm.
[2] Madhumâs is a name of the month Chaitra (March-April); "the night," means the night of the full moon.
[3] This mysterious exclamation is the equivalent of *om*, which is considered a union of the three letters *a*, *u*, *m*, emblematical of Vishnu, S'iva, and Brahmâ, respectively; or of the three Vedas. It is used by both Buddhists and Hindus.

[needful] for the circular dance came and presented themselves. Then, indeed, all the cowherdesses, abandoning reflection and modesty, and taking lutes, tabors, cymbals, pipes, flutes, and all other instruments, began to play and sing, and, with merry-makings, dancing about and gesticulation, to gratify the Lord. Having heard and seen their playing, singing, and dancing, and being delighted, Baladev Jî also, having drunk *vâruṇî*,[1] mingled with them all, and began to sing, and dance, and to perform various kinds of sports, and to give and receive pleasure. Then the gods, the Gandharvas, the Kinnaras, the Yakshas, with their respective wives, came, seated in cars, and singing the virtues of the Lord, rained down flowers from the sky ; the Moon with its starry sphere, looking on at the happiness of the circle of the dance, was showering down nectar with its rays, and air and water also were stopped in their course.

Having related the story thus far, S'rî S'ukadev Jî said :—Mahârâj ! in this way Balarâm Jî stayed in Braj, and during the two months Chaitra and Baisâkh danced and sported at night with the young women of Braj, and in the day-time, gave Nand and Jasodâ happiness by relating the history of Hari. One day at night-time while engaged in these [festivities], Balarâm Jî went,—

And having reposed on the banks of the stream, Râm angrily said there,
"Yamunâ ! do thou flow here, and bathe me with a thousand streams ;
If thou shalt not obey my words, your waters shall be divided into several portions."

Mahârâj ! when Yamunâ conceitedly paid no attention to what Balarâm Jî said, he angrily with his plough drew her [towards himself], and[2] bathed. From that day to the present the Yamunâ has been bent there. Afterwards, having bathed and relieved his fatigue, Balarâm Jî, having given pleasure to all the cowherdesses, took them with him, and, going from the woods, came into the city. There,—

The cowherdesses said, "Hear, O Lord of Braj ! take us, too, with you."

Having heard these words, Balarâm Jî, giving hope and encouragement to the cowherdesses, inspired them with confidence, and dismissed them, and on their being dismissed he went to Nand and Jasodâ. Then having counselled them also, and strengthened them, and stayed several days, he took leave and went to Dwârakâ ; and, in the course of time, arrived there.

[1] *Vâruṇî* is a spirituous liquor made from hogweed distilled with the juice of the date or palm.
[2] For *jau* read *au* or *aur*.

## CHAPTER LXVII.

**Paunrik assumes the appearance of Vishṇu, and is worshipped as a god—He is accordingly slain by Krishṇa—His son gets power from S'iva to revenge his father's death—His emissaries set fire to Dwârakâ, but he is repulsed and slain by Krishṇa's discus.**

S'RÎ SUKADEV Jî said:—Mahârâj! there was a king in the city of Kâśî, named Paunrik;[1] he was strong and very famous. He assumed the guise of Vishṇu, and by force and fraud captivated the minds of all. He constantly wore a yellow dress, a five-gemmed necklace,[2] a pearl necklace, and a garland of various gems, and bearing the shell, discus, club, and lotus, and having made two wooden arms, and placed a Garuḍa made of mere wood on a horse, he went about mounted on it. He called himself Vâsudev Paunrik, and caused himself to be worshipped by all. The king who would not obey his commands he attacked; then having smitten him, he held him in subjection.

Having told the tale thus far, S'rî S'ukadev Jî said:—Râjâ! seeing and hearing this conduct of his, the people of various countries, cities, villages, and houses, began to talk about it thus, "One Vâsudev has been manifested in the family of Yadu in the land of Braj, that one is dwelling in the city of Dwârakâ. A second [Vâsudev] has now appeared in Kâśî; which of the two shall we recognize and acknowledge as the true one?" Mahârâj! in various countries this report was in circulation, when, having obtained some inkling of the affair, Vâsudev Paunrik one day came into his assembly and said,—

"Who is the Krishṇa who lives in Dwârakâ, whom the world calls Vâsudev?
For the sake of devotees, I am become incarnate on earth; he has there assumed my guise."

Having spoken thus, he summoned a messenger, and having explained the height and depth of the affair, sent him into Dwârakâ, to S'rî Krishṇa Chand with these words, "Thou who, having assumed my guise, art going about, either abandon that; otherwise reflect on war." On receiving the order, the messenger, taking leave, proceeded along from Kâśî, and arrived at the city of Dwârakâ; and going into the assembly of S'rî Krishṇa Chand Jî, presented himself. The Lord asked him thus, "Who art thou? and whence art thou come?" He replied, "I am the messenger of Vâsudev Paunrik of the city of Kâśî. I am sent by

[1] This should be Pauṇḍraka, a king of the Pauṇḍra country to the south of Bihâr and Bengal.

[2] The necklace of Vishṇu, composed of sapphire, pearl, ruby, topaz, and diamond.

my master,[1] and am come to you to deliver some message. [If you] tell [me to do so] I will state [it]." S'rî Krishṇa Chand said, "Good! tell me." As soon as this direction issued from the mouth of the Lord, the messenger stood up, and joining his hands, said, "Mahârâj! Vâsudev Paunrik said, 'I am indeed the Lord of the Three Worlds, and Creator of the Universe. Who art thou who, assuming my guise, and flying from fear of Jurâsindhu, hast gone to live in Dwârakâ? Either give up imitating me and speedily come and take refuge with me, otherwise I will come and destroy thee with all the Yadubañsîs, and having removed the burden of the earth, will cherish my worshippers. I alone am the invisible, the incomprehensible, the incorporeal; gods, saints, sages, and men continually pray to, worship, and give alms for me. I alone as Brahmâ create; as Vishṇu preserve; as S'iva destroy. I alone, in the form of a fish, rescued the sinking Vedas; in the form of a tortoise, I supported the mountain [on which the universe rests]; as a boar, I sustained the earth; having taken incarnate form as Narasiñha, I killed Hiraṇyakaśyapa; having become incarnate as a dwarf, I deceived Bali; and, having assumed the Râma-avatâr, I killed the very wicked Ravaṇa. This is my special work, that whenever the Asuras come and annoy my worshippers, then I take incarnate form and remove the burden of the earth.'"

Having told the story thus far, S'rî S'ukadev Jî said to King Parîkshit:—Mahârâj! the messenger of Vâsudev Paunrik was making these statements, and S'rî Krishṇa Chand, the root of joy, seated on his jewelled throne, in the assembly of the Yâdavas, was listening laughingly, when, in the midst of it, a certain Yâdava cried out,—

"Has Yama come to take thee, that thou speakest such words?
Shall we slay thee, wretch! Thou art come in the quarrel of a deceiver.

If thou hadst not been an emissary, we had not let thee go unkilled. It is not right to slay a messenger." Mahârâj! when the Yadubañsî had said this, S'rî Krishṇa Jî called the messenger near, and counselling him, said, "Do thou go, and say to thy Vâsudev thus, 'Krishṇa says, Having desisted from imitating thee, I am coming to thy refuge; be careful.'" On hearing these words, the messenger, prostrating himself, took leave; and S'rî Krishṇa Chand Jî also taking his army, set out for the city of Kâśî. The messenger went and said to Vâsudev Paunrik, "Mahârâj! I went into Dwârakâ and stated to S'rî Krishṇa all the message you told me. Having heard it, he said, 'Do thou go and tell thy master thus, Be careful; I having desisted from imitating thee, am coming to take refuge with thee.'"

[1] Notice the Past Participle with the Genitive to express "sent by"; and the omission of *ko* after *kahna*.

Mahârâj! just as the messenger was saying these words, someone came and said, "Mahârâj! why is your majesty sitting carelessly? S'rî Krishṇa with his army has come to the attack." On hearing this statement, Vâsudev Paunrik, in that very guise came hastily to the attack with his whole army, and, moving on, came and confronted S'rî Krishṇa Chand Jî. Along with him another king of Kâśî also hurried to the attack. On both sides the armies stood arrayed against each other. They began to sound the warlike instruments; and the heroes, braves, and soldiers began to fight, and the cowards to quit the field and to fly with their lives. Then while fighting on, directed by Fate, Vâsudev Paunrik, just in that fashion, came before S'rî Krishṇa Chand Jî, and challenged him. Seeing him in the guise of Vishṇu, all the Yadubañsîs asked S'rî Krishṇa Chand thus, "Mahârâj! how shall we kill him in this guise?" The Lord said, "There is no fault in killing a deceiver."

Having said this, Hari gave order to the discus S'udarśan. He, on going, tore up the two arms made of wood; with that the [wooden] Garuḍa was also broken, and the horse ran away. When Vâsudev Paunrik fell down, S'udarśan cut off his head and threw it away.

On the head being cut off, King Paunrik passed over [the ocean of existence]; the head went and fell in Kâśî,
Where was his female apartment; the beauteous ones seeing his head,
Cried and tore their hair, saying this, "Who is the doer of this action?
You, indeed, were undecaying and immortal; how is it that life is gone in a twinkling?"

Mahârâj! having heard the lamentation of the queens, a son of his named Sudaksh came there, and having seen the head of his father cut off, very angrily began to say, "Who has killed my father? I will not live without taking revenge for this."

Having told the tale thus far, S'rî S'ukadev Jî said:—Mahârâj! having slain Vâsudev Paunrik, S'rî Krishṇa Chand Jî, taking the whole of his army, set out for Dwârakâ. And the son of [Paunrik] began to practise severe austerity to Mahâdev Jî in order to obtain revenge for his father. Hereupon, after some time, one day, being pleased, Mahâdev Bholânâth came and said, "Ask a boon." This one replied, "Mahârâj! grant me this boon, that I may take revenge on S'rî Krishṇa for my father." S'iva Jî said, "Good! if thou desirest to take revenge do one thing." He said, "What?" [The other] replied, "Offer a sacrifice with the Vedic prayers backwards; by so doing a female Râkshas will issue from the fire; whatever thou wilt say to her she will do." Having heard this promise from the mouth of S'iva Jî, Mahârâj! he went and summoned Brâhmaṇs, prepared an altar, got together sesamum, barley, *ghî*, sugar, and all the other essentials for a burnt-offering, prepared a *S'âkala*,[1] and began to sacrifice by repeating Vedic prayers backwards. At length, while keeping on sacrificing, from the vessel of fire a female Râkshas named Krityâ came forth. She, burning away the cities, countries, and villages in the very rear of S'rî Krishṇa Jî, arrived in the city of Dwârakâ, and began to consume the city. Seeing the city in flames, all the Yadubaṅsîs being afraid, went to S'rî Krishṇa Chand Jî, and cried out, "Mahârâj! how shall we escape from this fire? It is coming on consuming the whole city." The Lord said, "Do not be anxious on any point. This female Râkshas, named Krityâ, has come from Kâśî. I will at once arrange about her."

Mahârâj! having said this much, S'rî Krishṇa Jî gave order to the discus S'udarśan, thus, "Smite and drive back this one, and immediately go, burn up the city of Kâśî, and return." On receiving the command of Hari, the discus S'udarśan smote and put to flight Krityâ, and, on the mere speaking of a word, went and burnt up Kâśî.

The subjects fled, wandering about in distress; they bitterly abused Sudaksh;
The discus returned, having consumed the city of S'iva; he came and told it to Krishṇa.

---

## CHAPTER LXVIII.

Contest between Balarâm and the monkey Dubid—The latter is slain.

S'RÎ S'UKADEV JÎ said:—Mahârâj! I am about to give an exact recital of the story, how Balarâm, the abode of happiness, the receptacle of beauty, killed the monkey Dubid;[2] do you listen attentively. One day Dubid, who was the minister of Sugrîv, and the brother of the monkey Mayandrî,[3] and the friend of Bhaumâsur, began to say, "There is a thorn in my mind which perpetually annoys me." Hearing this, someone asked him, thus, "Mahârâj! what is that?" He replied, "Should I slay him who has killed my friend Bhaumâsur, the pain of my mind would depart."

[1] A *S'âkala* is a mixture of the ingredients just mentioned, in order to offer sacrifice according to the prescription of the S'âkala school of Vedic teachers. This school seems to have superseded all others; for their text of the Rig-veda is the only one now extant.

[2] The name is properly Dwivid, "double-cunning." The story is told in the Vishṇu-Purâṇa, V. xxxvi.

[3] Properly *Mainda*.

Mahârâj! having said this, he immediately advanced in great anger against the city of Dwârakâ, laying waste the country of S'rî Krishṇa Chand and harassing the people. Some he washed away by pouring down water; some he consumed by raining down fire; some he dashed down from mountains; some he flung mountains upon; some he drowned in the ocean; some he seized, bound, and concealed in caverns; the bellies of some he ripped up; some he slew with uprooted trees. In this way he was keeping on injuring the people; and wherever he was finding saints, sages and gods seated, he was raining down ordure, urine, and blood. At length, in this way afflicting and oppressing the people, he arrived at the city of Dwârakâ, and, assuming a minute form, he went and sat on the palace of S'rî Krishṇa Chand. Having seen him, all the beauteous ones within the palace, shutting up the doors, fled away and hid themselves. Then he, having obtained news of Balarâm Jî, with this thought in his heart, went on to Mount Rewat,—

> "First I will slay Haladhar; afterwards I will take the life of Krishṇa."

Where Baladev Jî was sporting with his wives, O Mahârâj! what does he there covertly see? Balarâm, having drunk spirituous liquor, and having taken all his wives with him, is indulging in a variety of sports, singing away, bathing, and causing [the others] to bathe, in the midst of a tank. Having witnessed this scene, Dubid climbed up a tree, and chattering away and snarling, began to jump and skip about from branch to branch and to play tricks, and began to void ordure and to micturate where there was a vessel full of spirituous liquor, and where all their clothes had been placed. As soon as all the beauteous ones saw the monkey, they timidly cried out, "Mahârâj! whence has this monkey come, who keeps on terrifying us and voiding excrement and urine on our clothes?" On hearing these words, Baladev Jî, coming out of the tank, laughingly threw a clod of earth; thereupon the [monkey], thinking him intoxicated, snarling very angrily, came down. As soon as he came down he overturned the pitcher full of spirituous liquor, which had been placed at the side [of the tank], and tore up all the clothes into shreds. Then, indeed, Balarâm Jî angrily uplifted his plough and pestle; and the other one, becoming as big as a mountain, advancing to fight against the Lord, stood ready. From the one side, the one was wielding the plough and pestle, and, on the other, the other one [was hurling] trees and hills.

> Both together are fighting desperately; they are not giving back in the least from their position.

Mahârâj! these two powerful ones, then, were fighting fearlessly, practising various kinds of feints and stratagems; but the very life was passing away from the spectators through fear. At length, the Lord knowing that they were distressed, smote and overthrew Dubid. As soon as he was dead, gods, men, and saints, and the souls of all were rejoiced, and grief was dispelled.

> The gods, swelling out [with joy], are raining down flowers, and are hailing Haladhar with [shouts of] "Victory! victory!"

Having related the story thus far, S'rî S'ukadev Jî said:—Mahârâj! that very monkey had existed from the Tretâ age; him Baladev Jî smote and released [from existence]. Afterwards, Balarâm, the abode of happiness, having given happiness to all, taking [them] with [him] thence, came into the city of S'rî Dwârakâ, and related the news of the death of Dubid to all the Yadubañsîs.

---

## CHAPTER LXIX.

**Sambû endeavours to carry off Lakshmaṇâ, the daughter of Duryodhan—He is taken prisoner—Balarâm demands his release; and on refusal, drags the city of Hastinâpur, with his plough, to the bank of the Ganges, in order to drown the whole inhabitants—He forgives the offence, but leaves the city on the river's bank.**

S'RÎ S'UKADEV Jî said:—Râjâ! now I am about to relate the story of the marriage of Lakshmaṇâ, the daughter of Duryodhan, to wit, how Sambû[1] went to Hastinâpur and married her. Mahârâj! when Lakshmaṇâ, the daughter of Duryodhan, was marriageable, her father, writing various letters, summoned the kings of all different countries, and prepared a *Swayamvara*. On obtaining news of the *Swayamvara*, S'rî Krishṇa Chand's son, who was [produced] from Jâmavatî, and named Sambû, also arrived there. Having gone there, what does Sambû see?—the kings of various countries, strong, accomplished, receptacles of beauty, very intelligent, wearing excellent dresses and jewel-studded ornaments, armed with weapons, in profound silence, in the midst of the *Swayamvara*, were standing in rows, and behind them, in the same way, all the Kauravas also. Here and there outside musical instruments were sounding; within, merry-makers were carrying on rejoicings; in the midst of all, the princess, beloved by her parents, bearing a garland, was moving about, a delicate image

[1] Properly *S'âmba*, the son of Krishṇa by Jâmbavatî. He is often mentioned in Paurânic legends, and was a great advocate of sun-worship. The *Sûrya-stotra* is ascribed to him. The tradition here related is given also in the Vishṇu-Purâṇa, V. xxxv.

like that of the eyes,[1] and saying this in her heart, "Whom shall I choose?"

Mahârâj! when that beauteous one, amiable, the receptacle of beauty, bearing the garland, bashfully moving about came before Sambû, he, abandoning thought and reserve, fearlessly seized her hand, seated her in his chariot, and took the road [home]. All the kings remained standing, looking [at each other's] faces; and Karṇa, Droṇa, S'alya, Bhûriśravâ, Duryodhan, and all the other Kauravas also, at that time, said nothing. Then becoming angry, they began to say among themselves, "See! what has this one done, who, having come into harmony, has produced discord." Karṇa said, "This is always the way of the Yadubaṅsîs; wherever auspicious business is proceeding they cause nothing but mischief." S'alya said,—

"Destitute of caste, they have quite recently been exalted;
having attained royalty, they have become insolent."[2]

On hearing these words all the Kauravas, with great wrath, seizing each his weapon, and saying this, rushed to the attack, "Let us see how strong he is who, taking the girl from before us, shall go forth;" and went and surrounded Sambû in the middle of the path.[3] Afterwards, from both sides, the weapons began to fly. At length, after a certain time of fighting, when Sambû's charioteer was killed and he had alighted, they surrounded and seized him, bound and carried him away. Having stood him in the very centre of the assembly, they asked him, thus, "Now where is thy valour gone?" Having heard this, he remained abashed. Hereupon Nârad Jî came, and said to all the Kauravas as well as Râjâ Duryodhan, "This is the son of S'rî Krishṇa Chand, named Sambû; do not say anything to him; what was to be has occurred. Immediately they receive the intelligence about him, S'rî Krishṇa and Balarâm will fit out an army and come; whatever should be said or heard, please say and hear that with them. To taunt a boy is by no means becoming of you. He may or may not have acted with boyish indiscretion."[4] Mahârâj! having spoken thus, Nârad Jî took leave, and, proceeding on, went to the city of Dwârakâ, and, going into the assembly of Ugrasen Râjâ, stood there.

On seeing him all stood up, with heads bowed; a seat was
instantly brought and given to him.

[1] *Putlî* means a doll, puppet, or delicate creature, and also the pupil of the eye. The phrase means that she was a *putlî* (delicate, slim creature) like the *putlî* (pupil) of the eyes.

[2] *Lit.*, "mounted on the head."

[3] Prof. Eastwick omits this sentence.

[4] This idiom more commonly occurs with the Aorist, as in *us kî sudh lo to lo*, a few lines further on; because it implies "may or may not." Here it means literally "he did then he did," implying that it was unimportant whether he did or not. See *Hindî Manual*, p. 142.

On being seated, Nârad Jî said, "Mahârâj! the Kauravas, having bound Sambû, have given him, and are giving him, much trouble. If now you should go and take thought for him then do so; if not, the escape of Sambû afterwards will be difficult.

The Kauravas have become very proud; they have shown neither respect nor consideration for you;
They have bound the boy as one would bind an enemy."

On hearing these words, Râjâ Ugrasen, very angrily summoning the Yadubañsîs, said, "Do you immediately take the whole of our army and march against Hastinâpur, and having slain the Kauravas and released Sambû, bring him here." On receiving the order of the king, when the whole army was ready to start, Balarâm Jî, counselling Râjâ Ugrasen, said, "Mahârâj! please do not send an army against them; if you will permit me, I will go and complain to them, and will release and bring Sambû; let me see why they have seized and bound Sambû. Unless I go,[1] the mystery of this affair will not be cleared up."

As soon as these words were said, Râjâ Ugrasen gave permission to Balarâm Jî to go to Hastinâpur, and Baladev Jî, taking along with him several of the greatest scholars, Brâhmaṇs, and Nârad the saint, went forth from Dwârakâ, and proceeding onwards, arrived at Hastinâpur. Then the Lord, having pitched his tent in an enclosure outside the city, said to Nârad Jî, "Mahârâj! we have encamped here; please go and announce the news of our arrival to the Kauravas." Having received the command of the Lord, Nàrad Jî went into the city and announced the news of the coming of Balarâm Jî.

Having heard, all became attentive; having advanced, they went there to receive him;
Bhîshma, Karṇa, and Droṇa, went forth together; they took with them fine clothes and silk robes;
Duryodhan, saying this, hastened, "My preceptor Sankarshan has come."

Having related the story thus far, S'rî S'ukadev Jî said to the king:—Mahârâj! all the Kauravas, having gone into that enclosure, met Balarâm Jî, and made him presents, and falling at his feet, with joined hands, offered manifold praises. Afterwards, having applied perfume and sandal, and placed on him a garland of flowers, they spread foot-cloths of silk, and had him conducted with a musical procession into the city. Then, having him entertained with food of six flavours, they sat near, and made inquiries about the comfort and prosperity of all, and asked, "Mahârâj! what is the cause of your coming here?" As soon as this speech had issued from the mouth of the Kauravas, Balarâm

[1] Notice this useful idiom, *bin mere gaye,* "without my being gone," "unless I go."

Jî said, "We have been sent out by Râjâ Ugrasen, and are come to you to deliver a message." The Kauravas said, "Tell [us what it is]." Baladev Jî said, "The Râjâ Jî said, It is not right of you to act antagonistically towards us.

You were many, he but one boy; you fought [with him], having abandoned understanding and discrimination;
You intentionally committed great injustice; relinquishing respect for the world, you seized possession of a son[1] [of Krishṇa];
Now you have become so proud that you have designedly afflicted him."

Mahârâj! on hearing these words, the Kauravas very angrily said, "Balarâm Jî! enough! enough! do not magnify Ugrasen too much. Such things cannot be listened to by us. It is only four days since[2] nobody knew or respected Ugrasen. Since he made a betrothal in our family he obtained dignity, now he has sent you to deliver a haughty message to *us!* Is he not ashamed of himself, in that, having obtained dominion, sitting quietly in Dwâraka, and having entirely forgotten recent events, he says whatever he pleases? Is that day forgotten, in which he was associating and eating with cowherds and Gûjars[3] in Mathurâ? We have quickly reaped the fruit of conferring sovereignty upon him, by allowing him to eat with us, and by forming an alliance with him. Had we conferred favour on a perfect person, he would have recognized our kindness as long as he lived. Someone has truly said that the friendship of the mean is like a wall of sand."

Having related the story thus far, S'rî S'ukadev Jî said:—Mahârâj! having said several such kind of things, Karṇa, Droṇa, Bhîshma, Duryodhan, S'alya, and all the other Kauravas, proudly arose severally, and went to their homes; and Balaram Jî, listening to their statements, and laughing [over the affair], sat there repeating this within his heart, "They have become proud of sovereignty and power, in that they are uttering such-like things; otherwise would they offer these discourtesies to that Ugrasen, the Lord of Brahmâ, Rudra, and Indra, to whom [these three] bow the head? Then my name is not Baladev if I do not sink all the Kauravas, with their city, in the Ganges."

Mahârâj! having said this much, Baladev Jî, with great anger, dragged with his plough all the Kauravas, with their city, to the banks of the Ganges, and was about to immerse them, whereupon being greatly agitated and frightened, all the Kauravas came with joined hands and bowed heads, and beseechingly and submissively said, "Mahârâj! please forgive our offence; we have come to

[1] For *sur* read *sut*, as Lallû Lâl wrote.

[2] That is, "only a short time ago."

[3] A caste of Râjputs formerly notorious for robbery. They came from Gûjarât; hence their name.

your protection, now please save us; what you shall say we will do; we will ever remain in obedience to the orders of Râjâ Ugrasen." Râjâ! as soon as these words were uttered Balâram's anger was pacified, and the city, which, by drawing with his plough, he had brought to the bank of the Ganges, he placed just there. From that time Hastinâpur has been on the bank of the Ganges; formerly it was not there. Afterwards, they released Sambû, and Râjâ Duryodhan, having propitiated his uncle and nephews, conducted them to his house, provided entertainments, and gave his daughter to Sambû, according to Vedic ritual,[1] and in [the matter of] her dowry he devoted much property.

Having recited thus much of the story, S'rî S'ukadev Jî said:—Mahârâj! in this way Balarâm Jî went to Hastinâpur, removed the pride of the Kauravas, and released and had his nephew married Then there was delight in the whole city of Dwârakâ, and Baladev Jî went and explained to Râjâ Ugrasen all the circumstances connected with Hastinâpur.

---

## CHAPTER LXX.

**Nârad visits Krishṇa, and observes his manner of living with his many wives.**

S'RÎ S'UKADEV Jî said:—Mahârâj! once it occurred to Nârad Jî that it was desirable to go and see how S'rî Krishṇa Chand was practising the duties of a householder with sixteen thousand one hundred and eight wives. Having reflected thus much, he proceeded on and came to the city of Dwârakâ. Then what does he see outside the city? In some places, in orchards, were standing various kinds of exceedingly lofty trees, flourishing, loaded with fruits and flowers waving about; on these pigeons, parrots, cuckoos, peacocks, and other birds were seated, warbling heart-fascinating songs; in other places, lotuses were blooming in beautiful lakes, and on these swarms upon swarms of bees were buzzing; on the banks, birds, together with the goose and crane, were making a merry clattering; elsewhere, in flower-gardens, the gardeners were singing away with sweet melodies, throwing the water high and low, and drawing water on to the garden-beds; elsewhere, at the wells and water-pits, wheels and buckets were at work, and at the watering-quays crowds on crowds of female water-carriers were engaged. Their beauty is indescribable; only by being seen can it be realized.

Mahârâj! Nârad Jî having seen, and having been delighted

[1] For *Ved ko* read *Ved kî*.

with the beauty of the woods and groves, on going into the city, sees exceedingly beautiful golden and jewelled palaces glittering brilliantly; upon these flags and banners are fluttering; on each gateway garlands and wreaths are bound; at the doors are placed pillars of plantain and golden pots filled with sprouts; from the lattices, windows, and apertures of every house the smoke of incense issuing was circling round like a dark cloud, and in the midst of that, golden pinnacles and points were glittering like lightning; in every house worship, recitation, burnt-offering, sacrifice, and alms-giving was going on; in various places adoration, meditation, songs, stories, and conversation about the Purâṇas was going forward; and here and there the Yadubaṅsîs were seated, holding court like that of Indra; and happiness was diffused throughout the entire city.

Having related the story thus far, S'rî S'ukadev Jî said to King Parîkshit:—Mahârâj! as soon as Nârad Jî entered the city, he was delighted, and began to say, "In what palace shall I first of all go, in order that I may find S'rî Krishṇa Chand?" Maharaj! having said this in his heart, Nârad Jî at first went into the palace of S'rî Rukminî Jî. There S'rî Krishṇa Chand was residing: that one, on seeing him, rose and stood up. Rukminî Jî filled and brought a vessel of water. The Lord having washed [his] feet, placed [him] on a seat, and set perfume, lamps, and consecrated food [before him], and offered adoration, with joined hands said to Nârad Jî,—

"Happiness and prosperity follow those men in whose house the feet of good people fall;
You, having come to the house [of me], a householder, for the sake of passing me across [the ocean of existence], are revealing yourself to me."

Maharaj! on the issuing[1] of this statement from the mouth of the Lord, Nârad Jî, having given this blessing, went into the palace of Jambavatî, "Lord of the World! may you remain long the head[2] of S'rî Rukminî!" Then he saw Hari engaged in playing *chaupaṛ*. On seeing Nârad Jî, as soon as the Lord rose up, Nârad Jî gave a blessing and turned back again. Then he went to Satibhâmâ's place, and saw S'rî Krishṇa Chand seated and applying oil and perfume. Nârad Jî returned silently thence, because it is said in the S'âstras that at the time of applying oil,[3] a king should not salute nor a Brâhmaṇ bless. Afterwards, Nârad Jî went to the house of Kâlindî, and there he saw that Hari was sleeping. Mahârâj! Kâlindî, on seeing Nârad Jî, having pressed Hari's feet, woke him up. The Lord on awakening went near the sage, prostrated himself, and with joined hands said, "The feet of the good are like the water of a place of pilgrimage—

[1] For *nikalne* read *nikalte*.
[2] That is, "the protector" or "guardian."
[3] Oil applied to the body was deemed impure; see Manu, iv. 132.

wherever they fall they make the place pure." Having heard this, Nârad Jî having given a blessing, went thence and stopped, and [then] entered the residence of Mitrabindâ. There he saw that a Brâhmaṇ-feast was in progress, and S'rî Krishṇa playing the host. Having seen Nârad Jî, the Lord said, "Mahârâj! as you have done me the favour of coming, please partake of the offering also, and give me your leavings, and purify my house." Nârad Jî said, "Mahârâj! I am going about a little, [then] I shall return; please feast the Brâhmaṇs; I will come and receive the leavings of the Brâhmaṇs." Having spoken thus, Nârad Jî took leave, and set out for the house of Satyâ, and what does he see there? S'rî Bihârî, the benefactor of devotees, seated delightedly amusing himself. Having seen this episode, Nârad Jî turned back again. Then he went to Bhadrâ's place, and saw that Hari was [there] eating. Returning thence, he started for the house of Lakshmaṇâ, and there he saw that the Lord was bathing.

Having related the story thus far, S'rî S'ukadev Jî said:—Mahârâj! in this way Nârad Muni Jî went the rounds of the sixteen thousand one hundred and eight houses, and saw no house without S'rî Krishṇa; wherever he looked there he saw Hari engaged in the work of the duties of a householder. Having seen this marvel—

Astonishment came[1] into the mind of Nârad, "There is no house without Krishṇa;
In whatever house I go, there is Hari, the beloved; thus has the Lord spread out his pastimes;
In each of the sixteen thousand and eight plus one hundred houses there is the mountain-bearer with a beauteous one."
Being delighted, the sage, speaking [thus], reflected, "This is your Yogî-illusion, O Lord of the Yadus!
No one can comprehend it; who can escape from your illusive power?"

Mahârâj! when Nârad Jî, with astonishment, had said these words, the Lord, S'rî Krishṇa Chand, the bestower of happiness, said, "O Nârad! do not thou be distressed in thy mind; my illusive power is exceedingly powerful, and is diffused throughout the whole world. It fascinates even me, then what power can another have that he should escape from its reach, and, having come into the world, not be fashioned in it?"

Nârad, having heard this, humbly said, with bowed head,
"Have compassion on me, Yadu Râ,e;

that your worship may ever remain in my thoughts, and my heart remain subject to your illusion, and not desire sensual

[1] This word *eh* does not occur in the dictionaries. It is a form of the Sanskrit *e, etum*, "to come," to rhyme with *greh*, "house."

objects." Râjâ! having said this much, Nârad Jî took his leave from the Lord, prostrated himself, and playing on the lute and celebrating [the Lord's] qualities, went to his own place; and S'rî Krishṇa continued sporting in Dwârakâ.

---

## CHAPTER LXXI.

**Krishṇa is solicited to release twenty thousand kings from captivity; and, at the same time, called to a great sacrifice of the Pâṇḍavas.**

S'RÎ S'UKADEV Jî said:—Mahârâj! one day S'rî Krishṇa Chand, at night-time, was sporting with S'rî Rukminî Jî, and S'rî Rukminî Jî was seated absorbed in happiness. She was giving happiness to her eye-partridges[1] by looking on the moon-face of her beloved one. When, in the meantime, the night passed away; the birds chirruped, the dawn overspread the sky; the partridge suffered separation, and the male and female ruddy-goose were united; the lotus bloomed, the water-lilies drooped; the moon was deprived of beauty, and the sun's power increased; all people awoke, and began to engage themselves in their various domestic occupations.

Then Rukminî Jî, for her part, quitting Hari's side, with modesty and reserve, began to engage herself in domestic duties; and S'rî Krishṇa Chand Jî, having purified his body, washed his face and hands and bathed, and become free from[2] prayer, meditation, worship, and oblations, and having given various kinds of alms to the Brâhmaṇs, and being easy in mind about his daily duties, and having received the morning offering[3] and having eaten it with betel, cloves, cardamoms, mace, and nutmeg, and having sent for and dressed himself in elegant clothes and ornaments, and put on his weapons, he went to Râjâ Ugrasen. Then, having saluted [the king], he went into the centre of the assembly of Yadubañsîs, and sat on a jewelled throne.

Mahârâj! at that very time a Brâhmaṇ went and said to the door-porter, "Go to S'rî Krishṇa Chand Jî and say, 'A Brâhmaṇ desirous of seeing you stands at the door; should he receive the Lord's permission he will come in.'" Having heard

[1] The *chakor*, or partridge, is believed to be fascinated by looking at the moon.

[2] *Nichint* or *niśchint*, "free from care," because the duties have been properly performed; the same meaning attaches to *suchit*, "easy in mind," in the same line.

[3] *Bâlabhog* (or *Mohanabhog*) is the name of a morning offering made to Krishṇa; not "sport with children," as Eastwick renders it.

the words of the Brâhmaṇ, the door-porter went to Bhagwân and said, "Mahârâj! a Brâhmaṇ desirous of seeing you stands at the door; should he receive permission, he will come in." Hari said, "Bring him at once." On the words issuing from the mouth of the Lord, the door-porter immediately conducted the Brâhmaṇ before him. Upon seeing the Brâhmaṇ, S'rî Krishṇa Chand descended from his throne, prostrated himself, advanced, and taking him by the hand, conducted him into the palace, and seating him on a jewelled throne beside himself, began to ask, "Tell me, O Deity! whence has your Honour come, and for what purpose did you set forth?" The Brâhmaṇ said, "Ocean of Compassion! Friend of the Lowly! I am come from the country of Magadha, and I bring a message from twenty thousand kings." The Lord said, "What is that?" The Brâhmaṇ said, "Mahârâj! the twenty thousand kings whom Jurâsandha has forcibly seized and put in manacles and gyves, and confined, have most submissively sent this message to you through me:—Lord of the Lowly! this is ever and at all times your custom, that whenever the Asuras are annoying your worshippers, you, taking incarnate form, are protecting your devotees. O Lord! as you released Prahlâd from Hiraṇyakaśyapa, and the elephant from the alligator,[1] just so compassionately now kindly release us from the hand of this most wicked one. We are in great affliction; except you, no one has the power to rescue us from this great calamity, and effect our release."

Mahârâj! as soon as he heard these words, the Lord mercifully said, "O Divinity! now do not be anxious; their anxiety is mine."[2] On hearing these words, the Brâhmaṇ being gratified, began to bless S'rî Krishṇa Chand. In the meantime Nârad Jî came and presented himself. Having saluted him, S'rî Krishṇa Chand asked him, "Nârad Jî! you are going and coming everywhere, tell me how are, now-a-days, our brother Yudhishṭhira and the other five Pâṇḍavas? and what are they doing? For some time we have received no news of them; therefore my thought is fixed upon them." Nârad Jî said, "Mahârâj! I am just come from those very people; they are, indeed, well and prosperous,[3] but at the present time they are very anxious about the preparations for a *râjâsûya* sacrifice;[4] and hour after hour are saying that, without the assistance of S'rî Krishṇa Chand our sacrifice will not be complete; therefore, Mahârâj! be pleased to agree to my proposal,—

[1] Both Hollings and Eastwick translate this as "shark;" but the Hindûs, in their pictures of the incident, represent a crocodile or alligator.

[2] That is, "it is now my part to look after them."

[3] Notice this method of marking a little emphasis by placing *haiñ* first in the sentence.

[4] A *râjâsûya* was a great sacrifice performed at the coronation of a supreme or universal sovereign. The particular sacrifice here alluded to is described in the Sabhâ-parvan of the Mahâbhârata.

First arrange their sacrifice, afterwards direct your steps somewhere else."

Mahârâj! on hearing these words from the mouth of Nârad Jî, the Lord summoned Ûdho Jî, and said,—

"Ûdho! you are my friend; never absent from my mind and eyes;
Urgent affairs [call me] in both directions; where shall I go first? Tell me, O hero!
There there are kings in deep misfortune, placing hope on me they are experiencing distress;
Here the Pâṇḍavas together have prepared a sacrifice."
Thus speaking, the Lord addressed him.

---

## CHAPTER LXXII.

**Krishṇa goes to Hastinâpur, to consult with the Pâṇḍavas about the release of the twenty thousand kings.**

S'RÎ S'UKADEV Jî said:—Mahârâj! at first S'rî Krishṇa Chand Jî dismissed the Brâhmaṇ who had brought the message of the kings, with these words, "Divinity! do you go and say to the kings from us, 'Do not be anxious on any account, I am coming speedily, and will release you.'" Mahârâj! having said this, S'rî Krishṇa Chand dismissed the Brâhmaṇ, and taking Ûdho Jî with him, went into the court of kings Ugrasen and Sûrasen; and they laid before them all the circumstances. They, having heard, remained silent. Hereupon Ûdho Jî said, "Mahârâj! do both these things; first release the kings from Jurâsandha; afterwards go and prepare the sacrifice; because no one else but a king can perform the ceremonies of a Râjâsûya sacrifice, and there are twenty thousand kings congregated there. Should you cause them to be released, they would all, expressing gratitude,[1] without being invited, go and perform the duties of the sacrifice. Mahârâj! should anyone conquer the ten regions [of the world], still he would not find so many kings congregated together. Therefore, this is now best that you should go to Hastinâpur, meet and consult with the Pâṇḍavas, and then do what should be done."[2]

Mahârâj! having said this much, Ûdho Jî resumed, "Mahârâj!

[1] *Lit.*, "having acknowleged [your good] qualities."

[2] *chaliye* and *kariye* are respectful Aorists, not Imperatives (see *Hindî Manual*, p. 141); and *kâm karnâ* is the equivalent of the Sanskrit Future Passive Participle (see *Hindî Manual*, p. 175).

Râjâ Jarâsandha is very liberal, and a respecter and worshipper of cows and Brâhmaṇs. Whoever goes and asks anything from him receives it; a mendicant does not come disappointed from his place. He speaks not falsely; with whomsoever his word is pledged he keeps faith. And he has the strength of ten thousand elephants; his strength is equal to that of Bhîmasen. O Lord! if you go there, take Bhîmasen also along with you. It occurs to me that his death is [to be] through Bhîmasen."[1]

Having related the story thus far, S'rî S'ukadev Jî said to King Parîkshit:—Râjâ! when Ûdho Jî had said these words, S'rî Krishṇa Chand Jî took leave of Râjâs Ugrasen and Sûrasen, and said to all the Yadubañsîs, "Get ready our army; we will go to Hastinâpur." On hearing these words, all the Yadubañsîs prepared and led forth the army, and the Lord also accompanied them with his eight queens. Mahârâj! when S'rî Krishṇa Chand, with his family, led his army, with kettle-drumming, and went from the city of Dwârakâ to Hastinâpur, the splendour of the cavalcade was indescribable. In front was the stronghold of elephants; on the left and right was the protection of chariots and horses; in the centre was the seraglio; and behind, accompanied by the whole army, and protecting all, S'rî Krishṇa Chand Jî was coming along. Wherever the encampment was, there, for several *yojanas* in extent, a beautiful and pleasing city was formed. The kings of various countries, being afraid, severally came, met them, and made presents; and the Lord, perceiving them to be timid, consoled them in every way.

At length, moving on in pomp, Hari arrived with all [his followers] near Hastinâpur. Hereupon someone went to Râjâ Yudhishṭhira and said, "Mahârâj! some king, leading a great army, and a multitude [of followers], has advanced to your Honour's country. Your Honour should speedily look to it, otherwise you may deem him arrived here." Mahârâj! on hearing this statement, Râjâ Yudhishṭhira, being greatly alarmed, saying this to his two younger brothers Nakul and Sahadev, sent them before the Lord, "Do you go see what king is coming." On receiving the king's command,—

> Sahadev and Nakul saw and returned, and said these words to the king,
> "Lord of our lives! Hari has come." Having heard [that], the king put away [all] anxiety.

Afterwards, with great delight, Râjâ Yudhishṭhira summoned Bhîma and Arjuna, and said, "Brothers! do you four brothers advance and conduct S'rî Krishṇa Chand, the root of joy." Mahârâj! having received the order of the king, and having heard of the arrival of the Lord, those four brothers were greatly pleased, and taking all the essentials for the meeting and paying

[1] Prof. Eastwick omits this sentence.

respects, and accompanied by the greatest scholars, they went to conduct the Lord with a musical procession. At length, having met each other with great respect and consideration, and made presents and offered adoration, according to the prescriptions of the Veda, these four brothers, spreading silken foot-cloths and sprinkling perfume, sandal, and rose-water, and showering down silver and gold flowers, and offering incense, lamps, and consecrated food, conducted S'rî Krishṇa Jî, and all [his followers], with a musical procession, into the city. Râjâ Yudhishṭhira, having met the Lord, acknowledged great happiness, and esteemed his life's work fruitful. Afterwards, without and within, all met all, and showed suitable mutual respect, and gave pleasure to [each other's] eyes. In the houses and outside them, there was joy in the whole city; and S'rî Krishṇa Chand remained there, and began to give happiness to all.

---

## CHAPTER LXXIII.

Krishṇa, Bhîma, and Arjuna visit Jarâsandha in disguise—Krishṇa relates the stories of Hanśchandra, Râtidev, and Uddâl—Jarâsandha is challenged to fight—He fights with Bhîma, and after a twenty-seven days' combat, he is slain—Krishṇa performs his funeral obsequies, and instals his son Sahâdev in his place.

S'RÎ S'UKADEV JÎ said:—Mahârâj! one day S'rî Krishṇa Chand, the ocean of compassion, the friend of the lowly, the benefactor of worshippers, was seated in an assemblage of sages, saints, Brâhmaṇs, and Kshatriyas, when Râjâ Yudhishṭhira came, and beseechingly and humbly, with hands joined and head bowed, said, "O Lord of S'iva and Viranch![1] gods, saints, sages and chief *Yogîs* are ever meditating on you. You are invisible, incomprehensible, and indivisible; no one knows your mystery.

Saints and chief Yogîs worship[2] with undivided attention; you never enter their minds for an instant;
To us, in our very houses, you are revealing yourself; you feel love for your worshippers.
Such sports as you, O Mohan! engage in, are not to be comprehended by anyone;
The world is lost in illusion; with us you act in the way of the world;

[1] Viranch is a name of Brahmâ.
[2] For *ghâwat* read *dhâwat*.

Those who keep you in remembrance, O Lord of the World! you regard as your superiors;
You are far from the proud, [but are] the root of life to the truth-speaker."[1]

Mahârâj! having said this, Râjâ Yudhishṭhira resumed, "O Compassionate to the Lowly! through your kindness, all my desires have been accomplished; but only one desire remains." The Lord said, "What is that?" The Râjâ replied, "Mahârâj! I have this wish, Let me perform a *râjasûya* sacrifice and offer it to you; then I shall cross the ocean of existence." On hearing these words, S'rî Krishṇa Chand, being pleased, said, "Râjâ! this is a good wish which you have made; in this, gods, men, saints, and sages, will all be gratified. This suits everyone, and there will be no difficulty to you in doing this; because your four brothers, Arjuna, Bhîma, Nakul, and Sahadev, are very famous and exceedingly powerful. In the world there is now no such person who can withstand them. First send these that they may go and, having conquered the kings of the ten quarters [of the world], may bring them into subjection to you; afterwards you may tranquilly perform the sacrifice."

Râjâ! as soon as these words had issued from the mouth of the Lord, Râjâ Yudhishṭhira summoned his four brothers, gave them armies, and sent the four of them in the four directions. Sahadev Jî set out for the south, Nakul started for the west, Arjuna hurried to the north, and Bhîmasen Jî came to the east. Afterwards, within a certain time, O Mahârâj! those four, having, by the power of Hari, conquered the seven *dwîpas* and nine divisions [of the universe],[2] and having subjugated the kings of the ten quarters, brought them with them. Then Râjâ Yudhishṭhira, joining his hands, said to S'rî Krishṇa Chand Jî, "Mahârâj! by your Honour's assistance, this work has indeed been accomplished, now what are your orders?" Hereupon Ûdho Jî said, "Incarnation of Justice! the kings of all countries, for their part, are come; but now there is one, the king of the country of Magadha, Jarâsandha alone, who is not subject to you; until he shall become subject, the performance of even the sacrifice will not be effective. Mahârâj! Jarâsandha, the son of Râjâ Jaindrath, is very powerful and famous, exceedingly liberal and virtuous. No one has power to withstand him." As soon as Râjâ Yudhishṭhira, having heard

[1] These verses are intended to express the different treatment accorded to believers and unbelievers. Saints even, who rely on their own efforts, meet with no encouragement, but the pious are visited by the Lord; to the world everything is a delusion, but to the pious the Lord acts as an ordinary mortal; Ugrasen, Vasudev, and others, because of their devotion, are treated as superiors.

[2] *Dwîpa* means an "island." According to ancient Hindû notions of geography, the world was formed in the shape of seven concentric circles, the central point being Mount Meru. Each circle of earth was separated from the next by a circumambient ocean of water. The *dwîpas* are sometimes reckoned as four, nine, or thirteen. The "nine divisions" mean the divisions of India or Bhârata itself. They are named in *Vishṇu-Purâṇa*, II. iii.

T 2

this statement, had become dejected, S'rî Krishṇa Chand said, "Mahârâj ! do not be anxious about anything. Give the order to me, along with brothers Bhîma and Arjuna, and we will, either by force or stratagem, seize and bring him, or kill him." On hearing these words, Râjâ Yudhishṭhira gave order to both the brothers. Then Hari took the road to the country of Magadha, taking them both with him. Having advanced [some distance], S'rî Krishṇa Jî said to Arjuna and Bhîma in the way,

"Having assumed the form of Brâhmaṇs, let us step forward ;
let the enemy be slain by fraud or force."

Mahârâj ! having said this, S'rî Krishṇa Chand Jî assumed the guise of a Brâhmaṇ ; along with him Bhîma and Arjuna also took the guise of Brâhmaṇs. All three [of them] having made the *tripuṇḍ*,[1] and taken a book under their arms, arrayed in brilliant, handsome forms, they went along either as the three embodied qualities, truth, passion, and darkness, might be going along, or as the three times, [past, present, and future]. At length, in the course of a certain time, travelling on, they arrived in the country of Magadha ; and at mid-day stood at the gate of Râjâ Jarâsandha. Having seen their disguise, the door-keepers went and said to the king, "Mahârâj ! three Brâhmaṇ guests, very splendid, great scholars, exceedingly learned, are standing at the door in want of something ; what is the order for us [with respect to them] ?" Mahârâj ! on hearing these words, Râjâ Jarâsandha rose and came, and saluting the three, conducted them very courteously into the house. Afterwards, having seated them on a throne, he himself stood before them with joined hands, and, having looked upon them and reflected much, he said,—

"The mendicant who comes to the door, that guest is called a great king ;
You are not Brâhmaṇs, but powerful warriors ; nothing deceptive is worthy ;
The deceiver who comes in deceptive appearance may deceive and go away, [but] is not called honest ;
Your martial lustre is not concealed ; you appear to be mighty heroes and braves ;
You are three glorious brothers ; bestowers of boons, like S'iva, Viranch, and Hari ;
By mental inference I have comprehended [you] ; do you, O divinities ! relate particulars of yourselves.
I will do whatever you may wish ; I will not swerve from my word ;
A generous person never speaks falsely ; he does not keep back wealth, body, or all he possesses ;
Ask [what you please], that very gift I will give—son, wife, possessions, or life."

[1] The *tripuṇḍ* are the three horizontal marks drawn with the ashes of cow-dung, which are the distinguishing marks of a worshipper of S'iva.

Mahârâj! on hearing these words, S'rî Krishṇa Chand Jî said, "Mahârâj! once on a time Râjâ Hariśchandra,[1] whose fame is still spread throughout the world, became very munificent. Listen! at one time, in the country of Hariśchandra, a famine occurred, and, being without food, all the people began to die; then the king, selling all that he possessed, began to feed them all. When the wealth of country and city was gone, and the king was destitute, one day, at evening, he had sat down hungry with his family, in this plight, Viśvâmitra came, and in order to test his faithfulness, said these words, 'Mahârâj! give me wealth, and take the reward of giving a daughter.'[2] On hearing this speech, he brought all that was in the house and gave it. Again the Rishi said, 'Mahârâj! my object will not be effected with this amount.' Then the king sold his male and female servants, and brought the money and gave it; and having parted with wealth and attendants, without money and without servants, he remained with [only] wife and son. Again the Rishi said, 'Image of Justice! my purpose is not effected with this money. Now to whom shall I go and beg? No one in the world appears to me more wealthy, virtuous, and liberal than thou. Yes, there is a Chaṇḍâla,[3] named Supach, a receptacle of illusion;[4] tell me, then, shall I go ask wealth from him? But there is shame in this also, inasmuch as, having asked from so liberal a king [as you], what shall I beg from him?' Mahârâj! on hearing these words, Râjâ Hariśchandra, taking Viśvâmitra along with him, went to that Chaṇḍâla's house; and he said to him, 'Brother! do thou keep me in pledge for a year, and fulfil this one's desire.' Supach answered—

'How will you do my drudgery? How will you remove passion and darkness from the mind?
You are a king, very glorious and mighty; mine is merely low drudgery.

Mahârâj! my work is this, to go and watch in the graveyard, and should a corpse come, I levy a tax on it; beyond that I take care of my own household. If this can be [done] by you, I will give money and keep you in bond.' The king said, 'Good! I will serve you for a year; do you give this one the money.' Mahârâj! as soon as this statement had issued from the mouth of the king, Supach counted out the money and gave it to Viśvâmitra; who accepted it and went to his house; and the king remaining there, began to perform his service. After some

[1] The pathetic story of Hariśchandra is told in the *Aitareya-Brâhmaṇa*, and in numerous more modern forms. It is one of the oldest of Indian traditions, and dates beyond the Vedic period itself.

[2] That is, a reward equal to that of bestowing a daughter in marriage.

[3] A Chaṇḍâla is the lowest of the castes, produced from a S'ûdra father and a Brâhmaṇ mother.

[4] That is, one so wealthy that he may be called a very receptacle for worldly property, the whole of which is esteemed mere illusion.

time, becoming subject to Fate, Râjâ Hariśchandra's son Rohitâśwa died. The queen, taking the corpse, went to the burning-place, and as soon as she had constructed the pyre and was beginning to perform the ceremony of burning, the king came and demanded the tax.

The queen, being pained and distressed, said, 'Behold, and reflect in your heart, O king!

This is your son Rohitâśwa; and for paying the tax I have nothing else with me than this cloth which I stand here wearing.' The king said, 'I have no power in this matter. I am employed on my master's business. Should I not do my master's work, my truth would depart.' Mahârâj! on hearing this speech, when the queen placed her hand on the border to take off the cloth, the three worlds trembled. Immediately, Bhagwân, having seen the rectitude of the king and queen, first sent a chariot, and afterwards, having revealed himself, released all three [from further transmigration]. Mahârâj! when Vidhâtâ, having revivified Rohitâśwa, and seated the king and queen with their son on the chariot, gave the order to go to Vaikuṇṭh, then Râjâ Hariśchandra, joining his hands, said to Bhagwân, 'O Friend of the Lowly! Purifier of the Fallen! Compassionate to the Poor! how can I go and enjoy repose in the Vaikuṇṭh abode without Supach?' Having heard this speech, and knowing the design of the king's heart, S'rî Hari, the benefactor of worshippers, the ocean of compassion, caused Supach also, together with [his whole] city, to cross [the ocean of existence] along with the king, queen, and prince.

On that side, Hariśchandra obtained the immortality; on this side, for ages and ages his fame has descended."

Mahârâj! having imparted this matter to Jarâsandha, S'rî Krishṇa Chand Jî said, "Mahârâj! hear further that Râtidev performed such a penance that for forty-eight days he remained without drinking water, and just as he sat down to drink, a certain thirsty person came. He did not drink the water himself; he gave it to that thirsty man. By that gift of water he obtained salvation. Again, Râjâ Bali gave munificent alms; therefore he obtained the sovereignty of Pâtâl; and to the present time his fame has come down to us. Again, observe that Uddâl the saint was [accustomed to] eat at [intervals of] six months. Once, at his eating time, a certain guest came to his house; he did not eat his food himself, but fed the hungry one with it; and died of that very state of hunger [in which he was]. Finally, by conferring that alms of food, he mounted a chariot and went to Vaikuṇṭh.

"Again, on one occasion, Râjâ Indra, taking all the gods with him, went and said to Dadhîchi, 'Mahârâj! we cannot now escape from the hand of Vritâsur; if you should give us [one of] your bones, we shall escape from his hand, otherwise it will be difficult to escape; because without a weapon of your bone, he in no wise will be killed.' Mahârâj! on hearing these words, Dadhîchi, having caused his body to be licked by a cow, extracted his thigh bone and gave it. The gods took it, and formed a thunderbolt from that bone; and Dadhîchi having lost his life, obtained a dwelling in Vaikunṭh.

Such were the boundless givers, whose fame is celebrated in the world."

Râjâ! having spoken thus, S'rî Krishṇa Chand Jî said to Jarâsandha, "Mahârâj! as in other former ages there were magnanimous liberal sovereigns, so now, in these times, are you. As formerly they fulfilled the desires of suppliants, so do you now fulfil our hopes.

It has been said, What has not a suppliant asked? what would not a liberal man give?
He is not covetous of house, son, or wife; he gives body and head, and acquires renown."

As soon as these remarks issued from the mouth of the Lord, Jarâsandha said, "The suppliant feels not the pain of the giver, still the liberal and constant abandons not his nature; whether he obtains in it happiness or misery. Lo! Hari, deceitfully becoming a dwarf, went to Râjâ Bali and asked three paces of ground. Then S'ukra[1] cautioned Bali; still the king did not go from his promise.

He gave the earth, along with his body; he has become famous in the world;
What fame has the beggar Vishṇu acquired? Having taken all, he still acted perversely.

Hence do you first declare your name and purpose, then I will give what you shall ask. I am not speaking falsely." S'rî Krishṇa Chand said, "Râjâ! we are soldiers; my name is Vâsudev. You know me very well. These two are Arjuna and Bhîma, my paternal cousins. We are come to fight with you; please fight with us; we are come to ask this only; we ask nothing else." Mahârâj! having heard this from S'rî Krishṇa Chand Jî, Jarâsandha laughingly said, "Why should I fight with thee? thou hast already fled from before me; nor will I fight with Arjuna either, for he went to the Vidarbh country disguised as a female. There remains Bhîmasen; if you say so, I will fight with him; he is my equal; no shame attaches to me in fighting with him.

First do you all eat food; afterwards fight in the wrestling arena."
Having given them food, the king came forth, and sent to call Bhîmasen thither.

[1] S'ukra is the planet Venus.

He gave his own club to him, and took another club himself;
Where the circle of spectators was formed, Murâri went and sat;
There Jarâsandha and Bhîma stood up simultaneously;
With helmets on their heads and loin-cloths tucked in, their appearance was that of jugglers.[1]

Mahârâj! when those two heroes, striking their arms, extending their clubs, changing their attitudes, and swaying from side to side, confronted each other in the arena, then it appeared as though two furious elephants had rushed on each other. At first Jarâsandha said to Bhîmasen, "First do thou strike with the club, because thou, taking the guise of a Brâhmaṇ, came to my door; hence I will not strike the first blow at thee." Having heard this, Bhîmasen said, "Râjâ! between you and me there is a fair fight, wherefore this understanding is unnecessary; let who will strike first." Mahârâj! those two heroes having mutually made these remarks, struck with their clubs simultaneously, and began the fight.

Each watching his opportunity, striking blows left and right,
They protected their bodies and leaped, and stood firm; they fenced and fought club with club.
With a clashing of blows, the clubs dashed together; there arose a noise and great uproar.

Having related thus much of the story, S'rî S'ukadev Jî said to King Parîkshit:—Mahârâj! in this way those two powerful men were waging fair fight all day long, and at evening, coming home, they ate together and reposed. Thus constantly fighting on, twenty-seven days were consumed. Then, one day, at their fighting time, S'rî Krishṇa Chand Jî reflected in his heart, thus. "This one will not thus be killed; because when he was born then he was produced as two halves. At that time the female demon Jarâ came and closed the mouth and nose of Jarâsandha; then the two halves were united. Having heard this news, his father Jaindrath[2] summoned astrologers and asked them what the boy's name should be, and what he would become. The astrologers said, 'Mahârâj! his name is Jarâsandha, and he will become very famous, undecaying and immortal. As long as his junction shall not be rent apart, he will not be slain by anyone.' Having said this, the astrologers took leave and departed." Mahârâj! S'rî Krishṇa Jî having reflected within himself on this affair, and having imparted his strength, he split a straw and indicated to Bhîmasen by this sign that he should split him up in this way. On this hint of the Lord, Bhîmasen seized Jarâ-

[1] The verb *âchhnâ* is a local form of *honâ*, meaning "to be," or "remain"; *bane âchheñ* is equivalent to *bane raheñ*.

[2] The name is given as Bṛihadratha in all Sanskrit authorities.

sandha and flung him down, and placing a foot on one thigh, he seized the other foot with his hand, and tore him up as anyone would split up a tooth-cleansing stick. As soon as Jarâsandha was dead, gods, men and Gandharvas began to play drums, kettle-drums, and fifes, and to rain down flowers, and to raise cries of "Victory!" and misery and enmity having departed, joy was diffused throughout the whole city. Then Jarâsandha's queen came crying bitterly and stood before S'ri Krishṇa Chand Jî, and joining her hands said, "Happiness! happiness! to you, O Lord! who have done such an act! You have taken the life of him who gave you everything. Such is the friendship you are showing to the person who entrusted[1] to you his son, his wealth, and his body.

> Assuming a deceitful form you practised guile and violence; by coming into the world you have acquired this renown."

Mahârâj! When Jarâsandha's queen, having come before the Abode of Compassion, compassionately[2] with joined hands, had thus beseechingly spoken, the Lord, being pitiful, first performed Jarâsandha's obsequies, and afterwards summoned his son Sahadev, gave him the mark of sovereignty, placed him on the throne and said, "Son! rule with justice, and protect sages, saints, cows, Brâhmaṇs, and your subjects generally."

## CHAPTER LXXIV.

The twenty thousand kings are released by Krishṇa, and are directed to be present at the sacrifice of the Pâṇḍavas.

S'RÎ S'UKADEV JÎ said:—Mahârâj! having seated him on the throne, and counselled him, S'rî Krishṇa Chand Jî said to Sahadev, "Râjâ! now do you go and fetch those kings which your father kept shut up in the cave of a mountain." On hearing this direction from the mouth of the Lord, Sahadev, the son of Jarâsandha, willingly went to the cavern, raised the stone from its mouth, brought forth the twenty thousand eight hundred kings, and led them before Hari. On their coming, wearing manacles and gyves, with iron chains on their necks, nails and hair elongated, their bodies emaciated, minds disturbed, in filthy guise, all the kings, standing in rows before the Lord, with joined hands beseechingly said, "O Ocean of Compassion!

[1] For *samairpa* read *samarpai*.
[2] That is, compassionating her husband's fate.

Friend of the Lowly ! you, coming in good time, have borne us in remembrance ; otherwise all had died. We have obtained a sight of you ; life has come into our souls ; our late misery is all passed away."

Mahârâj ! on hearing these words, the Ocean of Compassion, S'rî Krishṇa Chand, had no sooner looked on them than Sahadev immediately led them away, and had the manacles, gyves, and fetters struck off, caused them to be shaved, washed, and bathed, fed them with food of six flavours, dressed them in clothes and ornaments, equipped them with weapons, and had them again conducted before Hari. Then S'rî Krishṇa Chand Jî, becoming four-armed, and bearing the shell, discus, club, and lotus, revealed himself to them. As soon as the kings saw the form of the Lord, they joined their hands and said, "Lord ! you free the soul from the hard bond of the world ; what was difficult to you in freeing[1] us from the bond of Jarâsandha ? As you kindly have released us from this difficult bond, so now, please, having taken us from the house-like well, free us from desire, anger, covetousness, and fascination, that we seated apart may meditate on you, and cross the ocean of existence."

S'rî S'ukadev Jî said :—Râjâ ! when all the kings had spoken words so imbued with knowledge and self-abnegation, S'rî Krishṇa Chand Jî, being pleased, said, "Listen ! those in whose mind is my service without doubt will obtain faith and salvation. The mind alone is the cause of bondage and release ; to him whose mind is steadfast, house and forest are alike. Be not anxious on any other point ; stay at home happily, and rule with justice ; cherish your subjects ; continue in the service of cows and Brâhmaṇs ; do not speak falsely ; abandon desire, anger, covetousness, and pride ; worship Hari with willing devotion ; then undoubtedly you will obtain the highest dignity. He who has come into the world and indulged in pride, has not lived long. Lo ! whom has not pride destroyed ?

> He[2] was celebrated as having a thousand arms and being extremely powerful ; but Paraśurâm destroyed his strength ;
> King Veṇu became Râvaṇa, he went [to destruction] with his pride ;
> Bhaumâsur, Vâṇâsur, and Kañs, were extirpated by pride.
> Let no one indulge the pride of wealth ; he who abandons pride becomes fearless."

Having said this much, S'rî Krishṇa Chand Jî said to all the kings, "Now do you go to your homes, rejoin your families, settle your royal affairs, and before our arrival there, come quickly into Hastinâpur, to a Râjasûya sacrifice at Râjâ Yudhishṭhira's place." Mahârâj ! as soon as this direction had issued

[1] For *chhuṛnâ* read *chhuṛânâ*.
[2] This alludes to Sahasrârjun, see Chap. LXXXII.

from the mouth of S'rî Krishṇa Chand Jî, Sahâdev immediately prepared all the articles necessary for the departure of all the kings. They accepting them, took leave of the Lord, and each went to his own country; and S'rî Krishṇa Chand Jî also, taking Sahadev with him, went thence with Bhîma and Arjuna, and, proceeding onwards, arrived with delight and good fortune at Hastinâpur. Afterwards the Lord went to Râjâ Yudhishṭhira, and related to him the news of the death of Jarâsandha, along with the circumstances of the release of all the kings.

Having related thus much of the story, S'rî S'ukadev Jî said to King Parîkshit :—Mahârâj ! just as S'rî Krishṇa Chand Jî, the root of joy, reached Hastinâpur, all those kings, bringing their armies with presents, arrived also; and having been presented to Râjâ Yudhishṭhira, and having given complimentary presents, by direction of S'rî Krishṇa Chand Jî, encamped around Hastinâpur, and came and assisted in the work of the sacrifice.

---

## CHAPTER LXXV.

**Yudhishṭhira's great sacrifice—S'iśupâl abuses Krishṇa, and is slain by the discus —Duryodhan is dissatisfied, but conceals the feeling.**

S'RÎ S'UKADEV Jî said :—Râjâ ! I am about to relate how Râjâ Yudhishṭhira offered sacrifice, and S'iśupâl was killed : do you listen attentively. As soon as the twenty thousand eight hundred kings went, then as many other surrounding kings as there were, whether Sûryabaṅsîs or Chandrabaṅsîs, all came and presented themselves in Hastinâpur. Then S'rî Krishṇa Chand and Râjâ Yudhishṭhira unitedly made arrangements for all the kings with all possible courtesy, and allotted a separate office in the sacrifice to each of them. Afterwards S'rî Krishṇa Chand Jî said to Râjâ Yudhishṭhira, "Mahârâj ! we five brothers—Bhîma, Arjuna, Nakul, Sahadev, and myself—taking with us all the kings, will do the extraneous work, and do you, please, summon sages, saints and Brâhmaṇs, and begin the sacrifice." Mahârâj ! on hearing these words, Râjâ Yudhishṭhira, having invited all the sages, saints, and Brâhmaṇs, said, "Mahârâjâs ! please order whatever things may be needful in the sacrifice." Mahârâj ! as soon as this was said, sages, saints, and Brâhmaṇs, earnestly consulting books, wrote down on a sheet [of paper] all that is required for a sacrifice; and the king that instant sent for it, and had it placed before them. The sages, saints, and Brâhmaṇs unitedly constructed the altar. All the sages, saints, and Brâhmaṇs of the four Vedas, having spread their seats in the midst of the altar-place, sat down. Then, having become purified, Râjâ Yudhishṭhira also came with his wife, the skirts of their garments being fastened together, and sat down; and Droṇâchârya, Kripâchârya, Dhṛitarâshtra, Duryodhan, S'iśupâl, and as many other warriors and great kings as there were, also came and sat down. The Brâhmaṇs having pronounced the benediction, and caused Gaṇeśa to be worshipped, offered a jar of water,[1] and invoked the [nine] planets. The king selected [for the ceremony] Bharadwâja, Gotama, Vaśishṭha, Viśvâmitra, Vâmadeva, Parâśara, Vyâsa, Kaśyapa, and other very great sages, saints, and Brâhmaṇs; and they recited Vedic texts and summoned all the gods, and having caused the king to take the vow of sacrifice,[2] began the burnt-offering.

Mahârâj! having recited the various texts, the sages, saints, and Brâhmaṇs began to offer the oblations, and the gods, manifestly extending severally their hands, began to receive them. Then the Brâhmaṇs were reading the Vedas, and all the kings were bringing and presenting the apparatus for the burnt-offering, and Râjâ Yudhishṭhira was making the offering; hereupon the sacrifice was peaceably completed, and the king gave the final oblation. Then gods, men, and saints all began to utter praises to the king; and Yakshas, Gandharvas, and Kinnaras, began to play severally on instruments, to sing praises, and to rain down flowers.

Having recited this much of the story, S'rî S'ukadev Jî said to King Parîkshit:—Mahârâj! having been freed from the sacrifice, Râjâ Yudhishṭhira summoned Sahadev Jî, and asked him,—

> "Who should first be worshipped? to whom should unbroken rice and forehead-marks be given?
> Who is the greatest of gods? Him we should worship bowing the head."

Sahadev Jî said, "Mahârâj! the god of all gods is Vâsudev; no one understands his nature, he is the Lord of Brahmâ, Rudra, and Indra; him we should first worship with bowed head. As by applying water to the root of a tree all the branches become flourishing, so by worshipping Hari all the gods are gratified. This one is the creator of the world; and this one creates, preserves, and destroys. His sports are endless; no one knows their end. This very one is the Lord, the invisible, incomprehensible, indestructible. At his lotus-feet continually serves Kamalâ,[3] who has become his servant. For the sake of worshippers he has again and again taken incarnate form; and having assumed bodily form acts in the manner of the world.

[1] This is an offering to the gods. Five twigs are placed in the vessel, one of each of the following trees:—*Ficus religiosa* (Peepul), *Ficus indica* (Banyan), *Ficus glomerata* (Fig), *Mimosa albida* (Acacia), and *Mangifera indica* (Mango).

[2] A vow comprising certain gifts in alms.

[3] Kamalâ is a name of the goddess Lakshmî.

He calls us 'brother,' and comes while we are seated at home; he causes us to lose ourselves in his illusion;
Great fascination and affection causes us to forget; we regard God as a brother;
No one appears greater than him; his worship should be the first."

Mahârâj! on hearing these words, all the sages, saints, and kings cried out, "Râjâ! Sahadev Jî has said the truth, Hari alone is worthy of our first adoration." Then, indeed, Râjâ Yudhishṭhira placed S'rî Krishṇa Chand Jî on the throne, with his eight queens, and worshipped him with sandal, rice, flowers, incense, lamps, and consecrated food; afterwards he worshipped all the gods, sages, saints, Brâhmaṇs, and kings. He dressed them in variously coloured garments; and made forehead-marks of sandal and saffron; he decorated them with floral garlands, and having applied perfumes, the king, as was fitting, gratified them all. S'rî S'ukadev Jî said:—Râjâ!

In worshipping Hari all were happy; [but] S'iśupâl's head was bent to the earth.

For some time, then, he, with head bent down, remained reflecting, meditating something in his heart. At length, under the domination of Fate, he angrily descended from the throne, into the middle of the assembly, and shamelessly and fearlessly said, "In this assembly there are Dhṛitarâshtra, Duryodhan, Bhîshma, Karṇa, Droṇâchârya, and others, all most wise and honourable, but, on the present occasion, the dignity and judgment of all has been destroyed. The very greatest of saints remain neglected,[1] and the son of the cowherd Nand has been worshipped; and no one has said anything. He who, having taken birth in Braj, ate the orts of the cowherd-lads, has received, in this assembly, greatness and lordship.

All are thoughtlessly calling him great; they are giving the power of Lord of the Gods to a crow.[2]

He who made friends with cowherdesses and cowherds, has been constituted by this assembly as the very holiest; he who stole from every house and ate milk, curds, butter-milk, and butter, his praise has been sung by all unitedly; he who received alms on roads and at landing-places, here has been honoured; he who, by force and fraud, has enjoyed others' wives, him all have unanimously accorded the first forehead-mark; he who abolished the worship of Indra in Braj and established that of a mountain, afterwards having caused all the materials for worship to be brought to the mountain, himself by a stratagem devoured them;

[1] The phrase *baiṭhe rahe*, "left seated," implies that no notice is taken of the saints.

[2] For *kâgahi* read *kâg hi*. Eastwick has been betrayed into a mistranslation here by a misprint. Paṇḍit Yogadhyân Miśra prints the word correctly.

yet he was not ashamed; he whose genealogy, parentage, family, and duties are unsettled, him all have honoured as the Invisible and Indestructible one."

Having related thus much of the story, S'rî S'ukadev Jî said to King Parîkshit :—Mahârâj! in this fashion, being in the power of Fate, Râjâ S'iśupâl was uttering various offensive remarks, with respect to S'rî Krishṇa Chand Jî; and S'rî Krishṇa Chand Jî was seated on the throne in the midst of the assembly, and was listening and drawing a line for every statement made. Hereupon Bhîshma, Karṇa, Droṇa, and the great kings, having heard the reproaches against Hari, very angrily said, "O fool! thou, seated in the assembly, art disparaging the Lord in our presence! O base-born! be silent; otherwise we shall immediately dash thee down and kill thee." Mahârâj! having said this, each took a weapon, and all the kings rose and hastened to slay S'iśupâl. Then S'rî Krishṇa Chand, the root of joy, restraining them all, said, "Do not use your weapons against him; stand still and behold; he is being destroyed by his very self. I will endure from him a hundred offences, because I have promised [to do so]; I will not endure more than a hundred, and therefore I am drawing these lines."

Mahârâj! on hearing these words, all of them, joining their hands, inquired thus of S'rî Krishṇa Chand, "Lord of Compassion! what is the secret of this, that you will be pleased to tolerate a hundred offences from him? Please kindly explain that to us, in order that the doubt of our hearts may depart." The Lord said, "When he was born he had three eyes and four arms. Having heard this intelligence, his father Râjâ Damaghosh summoned the astrologers and greatest Paṇḍits, and asked thus, 'What sort of boy is this? Reflect on this matter and answer me.' On hearing the words of the king, the Paṇḍits and astrologers, having pondered on the sacred works, said, 'Mahârâj! he will become very powerful and famous. And this also comes from our meditation, that he will be killed by him from meeting whom one of his eyes and two of his arms will fall down.' Having heard this, his mother Mahâdevî, the daughter of Sûrasen, and sister of Vasudev, my aunt, became greatly dejected, remained day and night in anxiety solely on account of her son.

"After some time, on one occasion, taking her son she came into Dwârakâ to her father's house, and presented him to all of them. When he was presented to me, and one eye and two arms fell down, my aunt, binding me by a promise, said, 'His death is [to be] through you; you will not slay him; I ask this alms from you.' I said, 'Well! I will not take note of a hundred of his offences; after that, [if] he shall commit a fault, I will kill him.' Having taken this promise from me, my aunt took leave of all, and saying this [to herself], went home with her child, 'How should he commit a hundred offences that he should die by the hand of Krishṇa!'"

Mahârâj ! having related this much of the story, S'rî Krishṇa Jî,[1] having effaced uncertainty from the minds of all the kings, counted the lines which he had drawn at each offence. On counting them they were exceeding a hundred. Then the Lord commanded the discus Sudarśan, and that immediately cut off the head of S'iśupâl. A light which issued from his carcase rushed for a time to the sky, then returning, in the sight of all, entered the mouth of S'rî Krishṇa Chand. Having seen this exploit, gods, men, and saints began to shout "Victory ! Victory !" and to rain down flowers. Then Murâri, the benefactor of worshippers, gave him a third deliverance, and performed his obsequies.[2]

Having heard thus much of the story, King Parîkshit asked S'rî S'ukadev Jî thus :—Mahârâj ! in what way did the Lord give him a third deliverance? Please explain that to me. S'ukadev Jî said :—Râjâ ! once he was Hiraṇyakaśyapa ; then the Lord, taking incarnate form as Narasiñha, caused him to cross [the ocean of existence] ; a second time, he was Râvaṇa ; then Hari, assuming the Râma-incarnation, released him ; now this is the third time, hence it is the third deliverance.

Having heard this much, the King said to the Saint :—Mahârâj ! now tell me the continuation of the story. S'rî S'ukadev Jî said :—Râjâ ! on the completion of the sacrifice, Râjâ Yudhishṭhira bestowed dresses on all the kings and their wives, and gave unnumbered gifts to the Brâhmaṇs. It was the work of Râjâ Duryodhan to distribute the presents at the sacrifice. He, from enmity, gave many instead of one ; thereby he obtained renown : still he was not satisfied.

Having related this much of the story, S'rî S'ukadev Jî said to King Parîkshit :—Mahârâj ! as soon as the sacrifice was completed, S'rî Krishṇa Jî took leave of Râjâ Yudhishṭhira, and with his whole army and family, proceeding on from Hastinâpur, went to the city of Dwârakâ. On the Lord's arrival, rejoicings began in every house, and joy was in the whole city.

---

## CHAPTER LXXVI.

Explanation of Duryodhan's vexation—He makes himself ridiculous, and retires in anger.

KING PARÎKSHIT said :—Mahârâj ! everybody was pleased with the Râjasûya sacrifice ; but one, Duryodhan, was displeased ; what was the cause of this ? Explain that to me in order that the

[1] For *Krishṇa Jî se* read *Krishṇa Jî ne.*

[2] This episode is fully related in the Mahâbhârata, Sabhâ-parvan, 1418-1627, where the particulars are more clearly stated. He represents the opposition which the establishment of the Krishṇa-cult encountered.

perplexity of my mind may depart. S'rî S'ukadev Jî said :—Râjâ! your paternal grandfather was very wise. He gave, in the sacrifice, duties of such a nature and to whom he saw [they were appropriate]. He made[1] Bhîma superintendent of the food-preparation; he placed Sahadev over the religious ceremonies; Nakul was to bring the money; Arjuna was appointed over the attendance; S'rî Krishṇa Chand Jî took the work of washing the feet and removing the orts and the platters; to Duryodhan he gave the work of distributing the wealth; and he allotted some separate office to all the kings who were there. Mahârâj! all of them were performing the labour of the sacrifice guilelessly; but one, Râjâ Duryodhan alone, was doing the work deceitfully; therefore he, instead of one was taking several; having fixed this idea in his own mind that "Should their treasury be exhausted, there will be dishonour." By the favour of Bhagwân there was no dishonour; there was, on the other hand, reputation. On this account he was displeased; and this also he was not knowing that there was [the auspicious mark of] a wheel on his hand, [by which] if he gave one rupee, four would be collected [in its place].

Having recounted this much of the story, S'rî S'ukadev Jî said :—Râjâ! now listen to the sequel of the story. On the departure of S'rî Krishṇa Chand Jî, Râjâ Yudhishṭhira, having entertained all the kings with food and drink, and given them dresses of honour], very courteously dismissed them. They severally arranging their armies, set out for their respective countries. Afterwards Râjâ Yudhishṭhira, taking the Pâṇḍavas and Kauravas with him, went with a musical procession to bathe in the Ganges. Having reached the bank, he prostrated himself, applied dust [to his body], sipped water, and entered the river with his wife. All bathed with them. Then having bathed and washed, and completed the twilight worship, and having put on clothes and ornaments, accompanied by all, where does Râjâ Yudhishṭhira come?—but to where Maya the Daitya had erected a very beautiful jewel-studded golden palace. Mahârâj! having gone there, Râjâ Yudhishṭhira reclined on a throne. At that time, Gandharvas sang his praises, and bards and panegyrists recounted his fame. In the midst of the assembly dancing-girls were dancing; outside and inside the house merry-makers were singing, playing instruments, and making festivities; and Râjâ Yudhishṭhira's court was like the court of Indra. Hereupon, on obtaining news of the arrival of Râjâ Yudhishṭhira, Râjâ Duryodhan also, pretending deceitful friendship, came there very ostentatiously to meet him.

Having rehearsed the story thus far, S'rî S'ukadev Jî said to King Parîkshit :—Mahârâj! in the midst of the square, Maya had so contrived affairs, that whoever was going there was fancying

[1] For *hiyâ* read *kiyâ*.

that dry land was water, and water was dry land. Mahârâj! when Râjâ Duryodhan entered the palace, having seen dry ground, he had the fancy that it was water. He drew together and raised up his clothes. Then advancing further, and perceiving water, he was under the deception that it was land. As he put forward his foot, his clothes were wetted. Having witnessed this action, all the people of the assembly burst out laughing. Râjâ Yudhishṭhira, having stopped the laughter, turned away his face. Mahârâj! on hearing the laughter of them all, Râjâ Duryodhan, being exceedingly ashamed, angrily turned and went back. Having sat down in [his own] court, he began to say, "Having acquired the might of Krishṇa, Yudhishṭhira has become exceedingly proud; to-day, seated in his court, he turned me into ridicule. I will be revenged on him, and will break his pride; then is my name Duryodhan, otherwise it is not."

---

## CHAPTER LXXVII.

S'âlwa obtains power from S'iva to revenge S'iśupâl's death—He assaults Dwârakâ, and commits great havoc—Krishṇa comes to the rescue, but falls under S'âlwa's illusive power—At last frees himself from it, and slays S'âlwa.

S'RÎ S'UKADEV JÎ said:—Mahârâj! when S'rî Krishṇa Chand and Balarâm Jî were in Hastinâpur, a Daitya named S'âlwa, a companion of S'iśupâl, who, at the marriage of Rukminî, had received a blow from the hand of S'rî Krishṇa Chand Jî, and fled, began to perform austerities to Mahâdev Jî, having said in his heart, "Now I will take my revenge on the Yadubaṅsîs."

He conquered his sensual organs, making all [of them] submissive; he endured hunger and thirst, and all seasons.
In this manner he began to perform austerity, keeping in remembrance the feet of Mahâdev;
Ever on rising he took a handful of sand and ate it; fixing his mind on S'iva, he performed dreadful austerity.
A year was passed in this way; then, indeed, Mahâdev conferred a boon [on him].

"From henceforth, thou art become undecaying and immortal, and a chariot of illusion will be made and given to thee by the Daitya Maya; that will convey thee wherever thou wishest to go; it will have power to go to all places in the three worlds, through my gift, like a vehicle [of the gods]."

Mahârâj! when Sadâśiva Jî had conferred the boon, a chariot came and stood before him. He, having bowed to S'iva Jî, mounted the chariot and rushed violently to the city of Dwârakâ.

Having gone there, he began to stir up against the inhabitants of the city various kinds of injuries. Sometimes he was raining down fire, sometimes water; at times he was tearing up trees and casting them on the city; at times [he flung] mountains. Through fear of him, all the inhabitants of the city, being exceedingly frightened, fled, and went and cried out to Râjâ Ugrasen, "Justice! O Mahârâj! a Daitya has come and has stirred up great turmoil in the city. If he shall [continue] this sort of violence, no one will remain alive." Mahârâj! on hearing these words, Râjâ Ugrasen summoned Pradyumna and Sambû, and said, "See! this Asura, watching the back of Hari, has come to give pain to my subjects; devise some remedy for this." Having received the command of the king, Pradyumna Jî, taking the whole army, and seating himself on a chariot, went out of the city, and stood ready to fight; and perceiving that Sambû was alarmed, he said, "Do not be anxious about anything; by the puissance of Hari I will overthrow in a moment this Asura." Having made this remark, Pradyumna Jî, having taken the army, seized his weapons, [but] as he confronted that [Asura], the latter exercised such illusive power that day became very dark night. Pradyumna Jî immediately discharged refulgent arrows, and removed the great darkness as the sun's refulgence removes a fog. Then he shot several arrows so that that [Asura's] chariot was knocked about, and he, confusedly, was sometimes fleeing away and sometimes returning, and raising up a variety of demoniacal illusions, was fighting and giving great annoyance to the subjects of the Lord.

Having related thus much of the story, S'rî S'ukadev Jî said to King Parîkshit:—Mahârâj! there was indeed a fierce fight on both sides, when, in the midst of it, all at once Dubid, the minister of the Daitya S'âlwa, came and so struck Pradyumna Jî on the chest with a club that he fell down senseless. On seeing him fall, that [Dubid] shrieked out, "I have slain Pradyumna, the son of S'rî Krishṇa!" Mahârâj! the Yâdavas, for their part, continued the great battle with the Râkshasas. Then Dâruk, the charioteer's son, seeing that Pradyumna Jî had fainted, placed him on a chariot, and fled with him from the battle, and brought him into the city. On regaining consciousness, Pradyumna Jî angrily said to the charioteer,—

"It was not right of you, knowing me to be senseless, to make me flee [from the field];
Quitting the field, thou hast brought me home; this is not the act of a hero;
There is no one in the Yadu family who would abandon the field and flee.

Didst thou see me flying anywhere that thou to-day hast brought me flying from the battle? Whoever hears of this affair will ridicule and despise me. Thou hast not performed this act well, in that needlessly thou hast fixed [on me] the mark of disgrace." Mahârâj! on hearing these words, the charioteer descended from the chariot, and standing before him, with joined hands and bowed head, said, "O Lord! you are conversant with all polity; there is no duty in the whole world with which you are unfamiliar. It is said,—

'The hero in a chariot who falls wounded, him let the charioteer take out [of the battle];
The charioteer who, being wounded, falls, the chariot-rider should save and bear away.'
An exceedingly heavy club struck you violently; you fainted, and consciousness left your body;
Then I took you out of the conflict; I feared the injury and dishonour of my master;
You have taken rest for an hour, now go and fight again;
You know what is right and proper; the ridicule of the world should not enter the mind;
Now you will slaughter the whole of them; you will remove the illusion of the Dânava Maya."

Mahârâj! having spoken thus, the charioteer took Pradyumna Jî to the water, and having gone there, the latter washed his face, hands, and feet, recovered himself, put on coat of mail and helmet, and grasping his bow and arrows, said to the charioteer, "Well! what has been has been; but now do thou take me where Dubid is fighting with the Yadubansîs." On hearing these words, the charioteer immediately took the chariot where he was fighting. On going there, this one challenging, said, "Why art thou fighting indiscriminately? come and confront me, that I may send thee to S'iśupâl." On hearing this speech, when he rushed upon Pradyumna Jî, the latter, discharging several arrows, struck him down; and Sambû also, cutting up the army of Asuras, filled up the ocean [with them].

Having related this much of the story, S'rî S'ukadev Jî said:— Mahârâj! when all the Yadubansîs in Dwârakâ had spent twenty-seven days in fighting with the Asura army, then the Searcher of Hearts, S'rî Krishṇa Chand Jî, while seated in Hastinâpur, perceived the condition of Dwârakâ, and said to Râjâ Yudhishṭhira, "Mahârâj! I have seen in a dream at night that, in Dwârakâ, a great commotion is going on; and all the Yadubansîs are exceedingly afflicted; therefore, should you now give the order, I will set out for Dwârakâ." Having heard these words, Râjâ Yudhishṭhira, having joined his hands, said, "Let what is the Lord's wish [be carried out]." As soon as this statement had issued from the mouth of Râjâ Yudhishṭhira, S'rî Krishṇa and Balarâm, having taken leave from all, as soon as they got outside the city were surprised to see,[1] on the left side, a doe running towards them, and, in front, a dog standing and shaking his head.

[1] Surprise is implied by the interrogative form of the sentence.

Having seen these bad omens, Hari said to Balarâm Jî, "Brother! do you come on after with all the rest, I will go on in front." Râjâ! having spoken thus to his brother, S'rî Krishṇa Chand Jî went forward, [but] what does he see on the field of battle?—that the Asuras, on all sides, are striking great blows on the Yadubaṅsîs, and that these [latter], severally in extreme agitation, are hurling their weapons. As Hari, having seen this state of affairs, was standing there somewhat apprehensive, Baladev Jî also afterwards came up. Then S'rî Krishṇa Jî said to Balarâm Jî, "Brother! do you go and protect the city and the subjects; I will smite these and come on." Having received the command of the Lord, Baladev Jî, for his part, went on into the city; and Hari himself went into the battle where Pradyumna Jî was fighting with S'âlwa. On the coming of the Lord of the Yadus, there was the sound of the conch-shell, and everybody knew that S'rî Krishṇa Chand was come. Mahârâj! on the Lord's going there, S'âlwa caused his chariot to mount up into the sky, and thence began to rain down arrows like fire. Then S'rî Krishṇa Chand Jî, having counted out sixteen arrows, shot them so that his chariot and charioteer flew away, and he fell crashing down. As soon as he fell, he righted himself, and shot an arrow into the left arm of Hari, and shouted thus, "O Krishṇa! stand still; I will discover thy strength by fighting; thou, indeed, by fraud and force, hast killed S'ankhâsur, Bhaumâsur, S'iśupâl, and other most powerful ones; but now thy escape from my hands is difficult.

> Now the affair has fallen between you[1] and me; desist from trickery, and fight;
> The powerful Vâṇâsur and Bhaumâsur are expecting thee, O Hari!
> I will send thee where thou wilt not come back; shouldst thou flee, thou wilt not obtain greatness."

Having heard these words, as S'rî Krishṇa Jî said this, viz., "O fool! conceited, cowardly, cruel! those who are dignified, firm, and heroic soldiers, do not at first talk large words to anyone;" then he, rushing on, with violent anger, hurled a club at Hari; but the Lord most easily cut it down. Then S'rî Krishṇa Chand Jî struck a club at him. Having received that club [blow], he passed into the protection of his illusive power, and remained senseless for two hours. Afterwards he assumed a deceptive form, and, coming before the Lord, said,—

> "Your mother Devakî, in great agitation, has sent me;
> Your enemy S'âlwa has seized and carried off Vasudev."

Mahârâj! that Asura, having related this statement, went thence, and having produced an illusive Vasudev, bound and

[1] Both Eastwick and Hollings treat *tohi* as a Genitive, quite exceptionally. I regard it as an Ablative; for which there is some poetic authority.

brought it, and coming before S'rî Krishṇa Chand, said, "O Krishṇa! see; I have bound and brought thy father; and now, having cut off his head, and smitten all the Yadubañsîs, I will fill up the ocean; afterwards, having slain thee, I will establish undivided rule."[1] Mahârâj! having said this, he dragged down the head of the illusive Vasudev, and cut it off in the sight of S'rî Krishṇa Jî, and, having placed it on the point of a spear, showed it to all. Having witnessed this illusive action, at first the Lord fainted; afterwards, recovering himself, he began to say in his heart, "How was this, that this one has seized and brought Vasudev Jî from Dwârakâ, while Balarâm Jî is there? What! is this one more powerful than him, that, from before his face, he has taken and brought away Vasudev Jî?"

Mahârâj! the Lord having come into the Asura's illusive power, formed many various suggestions such as these, for some time, and was very apprehensive. At length, by thinking, Hari perceived and got at the whole secret of the contrivance of the Asura's illusion. Then S'ri Krishṇa Chand challenged him. Having heard the challenge of the Lord, he went to the sky, and began to hurl down thence weapons upon the Lord. Hereupon S'rî Krishṇa Chand Jî shot several arrows so that he, with his chariot, fell into the ocean. As soon as he fell, he recovered himself, and taking a club, he sprang upon the Lord. Then Hari, with exceeding anger, struck him down with the discus Sudarśan just as the Lord of the gods had struck down the Asura Vritra. Mahârâj! on his falling down, the jewel of his head came out and fell on the earth, and the refulgence entered into the mouth of S'rî Krishṇa Chand.

---

## CHAPTER LXXVIII.

**Krishṇa slays Vrikadant and Vidûrath—He then goes to Hastinâpur to assist the Pâṇḍavas against the Kauravas—Balarâm proceeds on pilgrimage, and slays Sût Jî, the relater of the Mahâbhârata, for a slight discourtesy.**

S'RÎ S'UKADEV Jî said:—Râjâ! now I am about to relate the story of Vrikadant and Vidûrath, the brothers of S'iśupâl, that is, how they were slain. Since S'iśupâl had been killed, these two had continued to reflect on taking revenge on S'rî Krishṇa Chand Jî for their brother. At last, on the death of S'âlwa and Dubid, they took all their forces and advanced to attack the city of Dwârakâ, and having surrounded it on all sides, began to hurl against it many various kinds of machines and weapons.

[1] *Lit.*, "the rule of one umbrella," the umbrella being a symbol of royal dignity.

A mighty uproar happened in the city; having heard the
outcry, Murâri mounted his chariot.

Afterwards S'rî Krishṇa Chand Jî, having gone outside the city, stood where those two Asuras, armed and in great anger, were ready for battle. On seeing the Lord, Vrikadant very conceitedly said, "O Krishṇa! do thou first hurl thy weapon; afterwards I will slay thee. I have said this to thee, so that, when dying, this desire may not linger in thy mind, that thou hast not struck a blow at Vrikadant. Thou hast slain the most powerful ones; but now thou wilt not escape living from my hand." Mahârâj! having uttered several such malignant words as these, Vrikadant hurled a club at the Lord, that Hari quite easily cut down. Then, having taken a second club, he began to wage a fierce fight with Hari. Then the Lord struck him down; and his soul came forth and entered into the mouth of the Lord.

Afterwards, having witnessed the death of Vrikadant, just as Vidûrath advanced to give battle, S'rî Krishṇa Jî hurled the discus Sudarśan, and that cut off Vidûrath's head and brought it down, together with the crown and earrings. Then he smote and put to flight the whole army of Asuras. At that time—

The delighted gods rained down flowers; Kinnaras and
bards sang the glories of Hari;
All the demi-gods, the sanctified, and the magicians, ascended
their cars and shouted "Victory! victory!"

Then all said, "Mahârâj! thy sports are infinite; no one understands the mystery of it. First there was Hiraṇyakaśyapa and Hiranâkus; afterwards there was Ravaṇa and Kumbhakarṇa; now these Dantavakra and S'iśupâl have come. You have slain these three times, and have given them the highest release; therefore, your procedure is not in the least understood by anyone." Mahârâj! having said this much, the gods, for their part, made obeisance to the Lord and went away, and Hari began to say to Balarâm Jî, "Brother! there is war between the Kauravas and the Pâṇḍavas; now what shall we do?" Baladev Jî said, "Abode of Compassion! be good enough to set off yourself for Hastinâpur; having performed pilgrimage, I also will come."

Having related this much of the story, S'rî S'ukadev Jî said:— Mahârâj! having heard these words, S'rî Krishṇa Chand Jî, for his part, set out for where, in Kurukshetra,[1] the Kauravas and the Pâṇḍavas were waging the war of the Mahâbhârata, and Balarâm Jî went out to perform pilgrimage. Afterwards, in the course of visiting all holy places, Baladev Jî arrived in Nîmashâr.[2]

[1] *Lit.*, "the field of the Kuru," a great battle-field in the neighbourhood of Delhi.

[2] The proper name of the place is *Naimishâraṇya*, a forest in which some celebrated saints resided, and where the Mahâbhârata was recited by Sauti. It was a famous place of pilgrimage.

Then what does he see there? On one side sages and saints are preparing a sacrifice, and, on the other side, in an assembly of sages and saints, Sût Jî,[1] seated on a throne, is reciting stories! On seeing him, S'aunaka[2] and all the other saints and sages rose up and made obeisance; but Sût, reclining on a cushion on the throne, continued looking on, seated.

Mahârâj! on Sût's not rising, Balarâm Jî said to S'aunaka and all the other sages and saints, "Who has made this fool the speaker, and has given him the seat of Vyâsa? A speaker should be religious, discriminating, and wise; this one is destitute of good qualities, avaricious, and exceedingly conceited. Again, [such a one] should be free from covetousness and desirous of the chief good; this one is very covetous and desirous of his own advantage. This seat of Vyâsa does not suit one who is destitute of knowledge and who is indiscriminating. Should we kill him, it would not matter much;[3] but he should be put out from here." On hearing these words, S'aunaka and the other very great saints and sages very meekly said, "Mahârâj! you are a hero, resolute, and acquainted with all that is right and politic; this one is a coward, irresolute, indiscriminating, conceited, and ignorant. Please forgive his fault, because he is seated on the throne of Vyâsa, and Brahmâ has placed him here for the purpose of the sacrifice.

> The fool has placed in his heart the pride of [his] seat;
> [therefore] he did not rise and salute you.
> This, O Lord! is his fault; he has fallen into error, but he is
> a good man;
> Should one kill Sût, it would be sin; no one in the world
> would call it good;
> Your remarks will not be fruitless; reflect on this in your
> own mind."

Mahârâj! on hearing these words, Balarâm Jî picked up a single blade of *kuśa* grass, and struck Sût gently with it. On its touching him, he died. Having witnessed this exploit, S'aunaka and the other sages and saints, raising lamentations and being greatly dejected, said, "Mahârâj! what was to be has come to pass; but now kindly remove our anxiety." The Lord said, "What is your desire? Tell me that, and I will satisfy it." The saints replied, "Mahârâj! let there be no obstruction in any matter in our sacrifices; this is our desire; please accomplish that and gain reputation in the world." As soon as these words issued from the mouth of the saints, the Searcher of Hearts, Balarâm Jî, summoned the son of Sût, and seating him on the

[1] The name properly is Sauti.

[2] S'aunaka is a saint of great reputation, the author of the earliest grammatical and ceremonial treatises, and the reputed originator of the system of the four castes.

[3] *Lit.*, "Should we kill him, what then?"

throne of Vyâsa, said, "This one will be more eloquent than his father; and I, having imparted deathlessness to him, have conferred long life [on him]. Now you can sacrifice free from anxiety."

## CHAPTER LXXIX.

**Balarâm slays Jâlav—He converses with Krishṇa about the war of the Mahâbhârata—He is purified from the crime of killing Sût Jî.**

S'RÎ S'UKADEV Jî said:—Mahârâj! having received the command of Balarâm Jî, when S'aunaka and all the other sages and saints, being greatly pleased, began to offer sacrifice, a Daitya named Jâlav, the son of Lav, came, and having raised dense clouds, and caused thunder, he sent forth a very fearful and exceedingly black storm, and began to rain down from the sky blood, excrement, and urine, and to commit various acts of violence.

Mahârâj! having witnessed this tyranny of the Daitya, Baladev Jî called his plough and pestle; they came and presented themselves. Then being exceedingly angry, the Lord dragged Jâlav with the plough, and struck him such a blow on the head with the pestle that—

The head was split open; the life escaped; there was a stream of blood on that spot;
The terrible hands and arms fell down; his eyes came from [the sockets], his hair was [blood]-stained.

On the death of Jâlav, all the saints were greatly pleased, and offered adoration to Baladev, and praising him greatly, made offerings. Next Balarâm, the abode of happiness, taking leave thence, went forth on pilgrimage. Then, O Mahârâj! while making the circuit of the earth by visiting all places of pilgrimage, he arrived where Duryodhan and Bhîmasen were carrying on a great conflict in Kurukshetra, and S'rî Krishṇa, with the Pâṇḍavas and very great kings, were standing looking on. On the going of Balarâm Jî, both the heroes made obeisance; one recognizing him as preceptor, the other esteeming him as a brother. Mahârâj! having seen those two fighting, Baladev Jî said,—

"O ye two mighty heroes, equal warriors! now do you resolute ones desist from strife;
Preserve the race of Kuru and Pâṇḍu; relatives and friends have all been destroyed."
Both heard, bowed their heads, and said, "Now we, having gone [into it], cannot quit the battle-field."

Then Duryodhan said, "Divine Preceptor! I do not speak falsely before you; please give heed to my words and listen. This Mahâbhârata war which is going on, and [in which] people have been, are being, and will be killed, [is being carried on] by advice of your brother S'rî Krishṇa Chand Jî. The Pâṇḍavas are fighting solely by the strength of S'rî Krishṇa Jî, otherwise what power had they that they should fight with the Kauravas? These helpless ones are as much in the power of Hari as wooden puppets are in the power of a juggler. Wherever he makes them go, there they go. It was not right of him to do such enmity to us by helping the Pâṇḍavas. He caused Duhśâsan's arm to be torn out by Bhîma; and caused me a blow on the thigh with the club. What more shall we say to you on the present occasion?

What Hari does is now occurring; this everybody knows."

As soon as this speech issued from the mouth of Duryodhan, Balarâm Jî, having said this, came near to S'rî Krishṇa Chand, "You also have abated nothing in doing mischief!" and said, "Brother! what is this you have done? that you have caused war, and caused Duhśâsan's arm to be torn out, and Duryodhan's thigh to be wounded? This is not the method of fair fight, that any strong person should pull out another's arm, or that one should aim a weapon below the belt! Yea! this is fair fight, that one should challenge one and use his weapons before his face." S'rî Krishṇa Chand said, "Brother! you do not know. These Kauravas are very irreligious and unjust; their tyranny is beyond description. First, they, at the instigation of Duhśâsan, S'akun, and Bhagadant, played dice, and, having cheated, won from Râjâ Yudhishṭhira all that he possessed. Duhśâsan dragged Draupadî with his hand; therefore Bhîmasen tore out his arm. Duryodhan ordered Draupadî to sit on his thigh; therefore his thigh was broken."

Having said this much, S'rî Krishṇa Chand resumed, "Brother! you do not know. However shall I relate the various acts of injustice of this kind which the Kauravas have done to the Pâṇḍavas? For this reason this fire of Bhârata will now by no means be extinguished. Make no attempt to remedy it." Mahârâj! as soon as this statement had issued from the mouth of the Lord, Balarâm Jî departed from Kurukshetra and came into the city of Dwârakâ, and having met Râjâs Ugrasen and S'ûrasen, with joined hands began to say, "Mahârâjâs! by your virtue and glory I have accomplished all the pilgrimages; but one fault occurred through me." Râjâ Ugrasen said, "What was that?" Balarâm Jî said, "Mahârâj! having gone into Nîmashâr, I killed Sût. His slaughter is fixed on me. Now, should you permit, I will go again to Nîmashâr, and having seen the sacrifice, bathed at the place of pilgrimage, and effaced the sin of that slaughter, I will return; afterwards I will cause Brâhmaṇs to be fed, and entertain my caste-folk, by which I shall gain fame in the world."

Râjâ Ugrasen said, "Good! let it be so forthwith." Mahârâj! having obtained the king's permission, Balarâm Jî, taking several Yadubansîs with him, went to Nîmashâr, bathed and gave alms, and became purified. Then having summoned a Purohit, caused a burnt-offering to be made, and entertained Brâhmaṇs, and feasted his caste-folk, he became purified according to the usage of the world. Having related this much of the story, S'rî S'ukadev Jî said :—Mahârâj!

He who attentively listens to this story destroys all his sins.

---

## CHAPTER LXXX.

**The story of Sudâmâ—He seeks relief in his poverty from Krishṇa.**

S'RÎ S'UKADEV Jî said :—Mahârâj! now I am about to relate the story of Sudâmâ, how he went to the Lord, and his poverty was terminated; do you hear it attentively. Towards the southern region there is the country of Drâviḍa; there Brâhmaṇs and traders live as kings; in whose government there is, in every house, adoration, and remembrance, and meditation on Hari; also, all are there performing penance, sacrifice, acting religiously, and giving alms; and virtuous and holy people, cows, and Brâhmaṇs are reverenced.

In that place all are dwelling in this way; [no one] knows anything else but Hari.

In that country there was a Brâhmaṇ named Sudâmâ, brought up under the same preceptor [1] with S'rî Krishṇa Chand, exceedingly humble, emaciated in body, and very poor, such that there was no thatch on his house, nor anything remaining there to eat. One day Sudâmâ's wife, being distracted by poverty, and suffering much misery, went to her husband, feeling alarm, and fearing and trembling, said, "Mahârâj! now we are suffering much misery through this poverty; if you should desire to get rid of it, I can point out a means." The Brâhmaṇ said, "What is that?" She replied, "Your great friend is the Lord of the three worlds, S'rî Krishṇa Chand, the root of joy, dwelling in Dwârakâ. Should you go to him this [poverty] will depart; because he is the giver of wealth, virtue, happiness, and salvation."

Mahâraj! when the female Brâhmaṇ had thus elucidatively spoken, Sudâmâ said, "O loved one! unless something be given, even S'rî Krishṇa Chand gives nothing to anyone. I am very well aware that, in my whole life, I have never given anybody

[1] *Lit.*, "A Guru-brother."

anything. Without something being given, whence shall I get anything? Yes! according to thy suggestion, I will go; then, having seen Krishṇa, I will return." On hearing these words, the Brâhmaṇ's wife, having tied up a little rice in a very old white vestment, brought and gave [the grains of rice] as a present for the Lord; and brought a string, a brass pot, and a staff, and placed them before him. Then Sudâmâ, placing the string and pot on his shoulder, and holding the packet of rice under his arm, and taking the staff in his hand, propitiated Ganeśa, meditated on S'rî Krishṇa Chand Jî, and set out for the city of Dwârakâ.

Mahârâj! while proceeding on his way, Sudâmâ began to say within himself, "Well! wealth, for that matter, is not in my destiny; but, by going to Dwârakâ, I shall certainly see S'rî Krishṇa Chand, the root of joy." Sudâmâ, making thoughts and reflections of this kind, in the course of three watches, arrived in the city of Dwârakâ. Then what does he see?—that the sea is all round the city, and the town is in its midst. What a [beautiful] city it is, around which there are woods, groves, flowers and fruits; at the ponds, pools, and masonry wells, wheels and buckets are in motion; in various places troops upon troops of cows are grazing, with each of which cowherd-lads, quite apart, are engaged in sports.

Having related this much of the story, S'rî S'ukadev Jî said:—Mahârâj! Sudâmâ having inspected the beauty of the woods and groves, went and viewed the interior of the city. There were glittering very beautiful golden jewel-studded palaces; at the various meeting-places the Yadubaṅsîs were seated, forming courts like that of Indra; in the markets, roads, and squares, various kinds of articles were being sold; in every house, in all directions, song-singing, alms-giving, the worship of Hari, and the praises of the Lord, were going on; and the inhabitants of the entire city were in happiness. Mahârâj! continuing to gaze at this marvel, and to ask his way to the palace of S'rî Krishṇa Chand, Sudâmâ went and stood at the lion-portal[1] of the Lord. He still timidly asked someone, "Where is S'rî Krishṇa Chand reclining?" The other replied, "Divinity! enter the palace; just opposite you S'rî Krishṇa Chand Jî is seated on a jewelled throne."

Mahârâj! having heard this statement, when Sudâmâ entered, as soon as S'rî Krishṇa Chand saw him, he descended from the throne, advanced forward, met him, and very affectionately taking him by the hand, led him on. Then having seated him on the throne, washed his feet, and accepted his foot-water, the Lord next smeared him with sandal, applied unbroken rice [to his forehead], decorated him with flowers, and offered adoration to Sudâmâ with incense and lamps.

[1] That is, the principal entrance.

Having done this much, the Lord of the Yadus joined his hands, and asked about his health and prosperity.

Having related the story thus far, S'rî S'ukadev Jî said to the king:—Mahârâj! having seen this action, the eight queens, together with S'rî Rukminî Jî, and the sixteen thousand eight hundred wives, and all the Yadubañsîs who were at that time there present, began to say within themselves, "What has this poor, weak, dirty Brâhmaṇ, destitute of raiment, done in a former birth of such a nature that the Lord of the Three Worlds has shown him so much honour?" Mahârâj! the Searcher of Hearts, S'rî Krishṇa Chand, then comprehending the matter in all their hearts, began to converse with Sudâmâ about the preceptor's house, in order to efface their doubt, thus, "Brother! do you remember that one day the preceptor's wife sent you and me to fetch fuel, and when we had got the fuel from the wood, and tied it into bundles, and placed it on our heads, we went home; then a storm and rain came on, and it began to rain violently. Water covered the earth all around; you and I, being soaked, were very miserable, and felt cold, and remained all night under a tree. At dawn, the preceptor came to search in the wood, and very kindly bestowing a benediction, conducted you and me and brought us home?"

Having said this much, S'rî Krishṇa Chand resumed, "Brother! since you left the preceptor's house I have received no news of you, as to where you were and what you were doing. Now you have come and shown yourself, you have given me great happiness, and purified my house." Sudâmâ said, "O Ocean of Compassion! Friend of the Needy! the Lord, the Searcher of Hearts! you know all things; there is no such thing in the world that is hidden from you."

---

## CHAPTER LXXXI.

**Sudâmâ's self-abnegation is rewarded with riches.**

S'RÎ S'UKADEV Jî said:—Mahârâj! the Searcher of Hearts, S'rî Krishṇa Jî, having heard the remark of Sudâmâ, and comprehending his many desires, jestingly said, "Brother! what present has thy wife sent to me? Why do you not give it? Why do you hold it under the arm?" Mahârâj! having heard these words, Sudâmâ was ashamed and dejected; and the Lord at once took from under his arm the parcel of rice; then, opening it, he ate from it with great avidity two handfuls of the rice; but when the third handful was ready, S'rî Rukminî Jî seized Hari's hand and said, "Mahârâj! you have given him two worlds; now will you preserve some mere abiding-place for yourself or not? This Brâhmaṇ appears to be well-disposed, of good family, impassive, and unworldly; because he experienced no delight at obtaining wealth; hence I perceived that he thinks gain and loss to be the same; he delights not at getting, and grieves not at losing."

As soon as these words had issued from the mouth of Rukminî Jî, S'rî Krishṇa Chand Jî said, "O loved one! this is my best friend; how can I express his worth? He is ever and at all times immersed in my love, and in comparison with that, he esteems the pleasure of the world like grass."

Having related the story thus far, S'rî S'ukadev Jî said to King Parîkshit:—Mahârâj! with various matters of this kind, the Lord, having instructed Rukminî Jî, caused Sudâmâ to be conducted into the palace. Afterwards, having caused him to be fed with food of six flavours, and with betel, Hari conducted Sudâmâ to a couch soft as foam, and placed him thereon. He was indeed quite fatigued by the toil of the journey;[1] he went on the couch, obtained happiness, and slept. The Lord then summoned Viśvakarmâ and said, "Do you go at once, and having built for Sudâmâ an exceedingly beautiful golden and jewelled palace, place in it the eight *siddhis*,[2] and the nine *nidhis*,[3] and return, so that he may have no object of desire." As soon as this direction had issued from the mouth of the Lord, Viśvakarmâ went there, and immediately built it and returned, and having told Hari, went back to his place.

As soon as it was dawn, Sudâmâ arose, and when he was at leisure from bathing, meditating, adoring, and worshipping, he went to the Lord to take leave. Then S'rî Krishṇa Chand Jî was not able to utter anything with his mouth, but, being immersed in love, with eyes filled with tears, in a state of stupefaction, he remained looking at him. Sudâmâ, having taken leave and made obeisance, went to his own house; and going along the road, he began to reflect within himself, "It was well that I asked nothing from the Lord. Had I asked something from him he would surely have given it; but he would have thought me avaricious and covetous. It does not matter; I shall explain [the matter] to my wife. S'rî Krishṇa Chand Jî showed me great honour and respect; and knew me to be free from covetousness; this to me is [equal to] a *lâkh* [of rupees]." Mahârâj! continuing to make such reflections, Sudâmâ came near his village; but what does he see? There is neither that place, nor that broken-down hut; there is a populous city like that of

[1] Notice the method of marking great emphasis in this sentence.

[2] The eight *siddhis* are eight supernatural faculties for the acquisition of magical power. They are named *aṇiman*, *mahiman*, *laghiman*, *gariman*, *prâpti*, *prâkâmya*, *îśitwa*, and *vaśitwa*.

[3] The nine *nidhis* are nine treasures belonging to Kuvera, the god of riches. Their names are *padma*, *mahâpadma*, *śankha*, *makara*, *kachchhapa*, *mukunda*, *nanda*, *nîla*, and *kharba*. They are, probably, the names of precious jewels.

Indra. On seeing that, Sudâmâ became exceedingly pained, and began to say, "O Lord! what hast thou done? Truly I had indeed one misfortune, thou hast given me an additional one! What is become of my cottage from here? and where is my wife gone? Whom shall I ask, and whither shall I search?"

Having said this, and gone to the door, Sudâmâ asked the hall-porter, "Whose is this very beautiful palace?" The hall-porter replied, "It belongs to Sudâmâ, the friend of S'rî Krishṇa Chand Jî." On hearing these words, when Sudâmâ was on the point of saying something, his wife, seeing him from within, came near her husband, wearing fine clothes and ornaments, adorned from head to foot, eating betel, perfumed, and accompanied by attendants.

She spread silken cloths at his feet, and joining her hands, uttered these words,
"Why are you standing [there]? enter the palace; put away all sadness from your heart;
After you went, Viśvakarmâ came; he in an instant erected this palace."

Mahârâj! having heard these words from the mouth of his wife, Sudâmâ went into the palace, and perceiving exceeding riches, was much dejected. The wife said, "Husband! having acquired wealth, people become happy; you have become sad, what is the cause of this? Kindly tell me, that the doubt of my mind may depart." Sudâmâ said, "O loved one! this [wealth] is a great deceiver. It has deceived all the world; it [now] deceives it, and will [continue to] deceive it. The Lord has given me that, and has not had confidence in my love. When did I ask anything from him? My heart is sad about what he has given me." The wife said, "Husband! you, indeed, asked nothing from S'rî Krishṇa Chand Jî; but the Searcher of Hearts knows the desires of every individual. There was a desire for wealth in my heart, and this the Lord has satisfied. Do not imagine anything further in your mind [on the matter]." Having related the story thus far, S'rî S'ukadev Jî said to King Parîkshit:—Mahârâj! whoever shall hear and recite this topic, that person shall never suffer misery on coming into the world; and ultimately shall go to a dwelling in Vaikuṇṭh.

## CHAPTER LXXXII.

**Krishṇa and Balarâm go to Hastinâpur to bathe during an eclipse—Cause of the sanctity of the place—Paraśurâm avenges Jamadagni's death—The inhabitants of Braj visit Krishṇa.**

S'RÎ S'UKADEV Jî said:—Râjâ! now I am about to relate the story of the Lord's going to Kurukshetra; do you listen attentively, how S'rî Krishṇa Chand and Balarâm Jî, accompanied by all the Yadubañsîs from Dwârakâ, went to Kurukshetra to bathe, at an eclipse of the sun. The king said :—Mahârâj ! be pleased to relate it ; I am listening attentively.

Then S'rî S'ukadev Jî said :—Mahârâj ! once having gained intelligence of an eclipse of the sun, S'rî Krishṇa Chand and Baladev Jî went to Râjâ Ugrasen and said, "Mahârâj ! after a long interval an eclipse of the sun has come about ; if on this occasion, you should go into Kurukshetra and do [what is usual], it will be very meritorious ; because it is written in the sacred books, "Whatever alms shall be given or virtuous act done in Kurukshetra, will be multiplied a thousand-fold." On hearing these words, the Yadubañsîs inquired of S'rî Krishṇa Chand, "Mahârâj ! how did Kurukshetra become such a place of pilgrimage ? Be kind enough to expound that to us."

S'rî Krishṇa Jî said, "Listen. The sage Jamadagni was very wise, meditative, austere, and glorious. He had three sons ; the eldest of them was Paraśurâm ; he, becoming a Vairâgî, left his home, and went to live in Chitrakûṭ, and began to perform austerity to Sadâśiva. On the birth of his sons, the sage, Jamadagni, giving up the condition of a housekeeper, became a Vairâgî, and went into the woods with his wife, and began to do penance. His wife's name was Reṇukâ ; she went one day to invite her sister ; her sister was Râjâ Sahasrârjun's wife. On the invitation being given, through conceit Râjâ Sahasrârjun's queen, the sister of Reṇukâ, laughing, said, 'Sister ! if you should be able to provide for us and our army, then give the invitation ; otherwise do not give it.'

"Mahârâj ! having heard these words, Reṇukâ, disappointed, silently rose from that place and came to her house. Perceiving her dejected, the sage Jamadagni inquired, 'What is the matter to-day, that thou art disconcerted ?' Mahârâj ! on hearing these words, Reṇukâ, crying, told him the affair just as it happened. On hearing it, the sage Jamadagni said to his wife, 'Do thou go, and at once invite thy sister, together with her retinue.' On receiving the instructions of her husband, Reṇukâ went to her sister's house and invited her. Her sister said to her husband, 'To-morrow you and I have to go,[1] with the army, to eat at the sage Jamadagni's place.' Hearing his wife's words, and saying, 'All right,' he laughed and remained silent. As soon as it was dawn, Jamadagni arose, and went to Râjâ Indra, and asked for Kâmadhenu.[2] Then he went, and invited and brought Râjâ Sahasrârjun. He came with the army, and Jamadagni entertained him with food as desired.

"Having feasted with the army, Râjâ Sahasrârjun became greatly ashamed, and began to say in his heart, 'Whence did

[1] Notice this expression in the form of the infinitive, with the force of the Sanskrit future passive participle. See *Hindî Manual* (3rd edit.), p. 175.

[2] This is a wonderful cow which yields everything that its possessor desires.

this one obtain, in a single night, the necessaries for the entertainment of so many people? and how has he prepared them? This secret is not to be understood.' Having said this, and taken leave, he went to his own house, and sent a Brâhmaṇ, telling him this, 'Divinity! do you go to the house of Jamadagni, and bring the secret of this matter, by whose power he, in the course of a single day, invited and entertained me and my army.' On hearing these words, the Brâhmaṇ quickly went, saw, and returned, and said to Sahasrârjun, 'Mahârâj! Kâmadhenu is in his house; by her power he in a single day invited and entertained you.' Having heard this news, Sahasrârjun said to that Brâhmaṇ, 'Divinity! do you go and say from me to Jamadagni, that Sahasrârjun has asked for Kâmadhenu.'

"On hearing the words, that Brâhmaṇ took the message and went to the sage, and told him what Sahasrârjun had said. The sage replied, 'The cow is not mine that I should give it; this is the property of Râjâ Indra; I am unable to give it to him; do you go and tell your king so.' On these words being said, the Brâhmaṇ came and said to Râjâ Sahasrârjun, 'Mahârâj! the sage has said, that Kâmadhenu is not his; that it belongs to Râjâ Indra, and that he is unable to give it.' As soon as these words had issued from the mouth of the Brâhmaṇ, Sahasrârjun summoned several of his warriors, and said to them, 'Do you go at once, and release Kâmadhenu from the house of Jamadagni and bring it.'

"Having received the command of their master, the warriors went to the place of the sage, and when they, having released Dhenu, in the presence of Jamadagni, took it away, the sage ran, and going into the path, stopped Kâmadhenu. On receiving this intelligence, Sahasrârjun angrily came, and cut off the sage's head. Kâmadhenu fled, and went to Indra's abode. Reṇukâ came and stood near her husband.

> She tore the hair of her head, and rolled about; holding his feet, she gave way to despair;
> Crying aloud, she beat her breast; calling out 'Husband! husband!' she lamented.

"Then having heard the lamentation and weeping of Reṇukâ, the guardians of the ten regions trembled, and the seat on which Paraśurâm was performing penance shook, and his meditation was disturbed. On the interruption of the meditation, Paraśurâm Jî bethought him, took his axe, and came to the spot where his father's corpse was lying, and his mother was standing beating [her breast]. On seeing this, Paraśurâm Jî became very angry; hereupon Reṇukâ, weeping continuously, related to her son all the secret of the slaughter of his father. On hearing this matter, Paraśurâm Jî, saying this to his mother, went where Sahasrârjun was seated in his assembly, 'Mother! first I will go kill my father's enemy, then I will come and take up my father.' On seeing that [enemy], Paraśurâm Jî angrily said,—

'O cruel, cowardly enemy of my family! you have slain my father and given me suffering.'

"Having said this, when Paraśurâm Jî took his axe and in great anger advanced, the [king] also took his bow and arrow and stood confronting him. Both the strong ones began a fierce fight. At length, fighting on, Paraśurâm, in the course of four hours, slew Sahasrârjun, and overthrew him. Then his army advanced to the attack; this also he cut to pieces near that [king's body]. Then he came thence, and performed his father's obsequies, and, having comforted his mother, then, on that very spot, Paraśurâm offered sacrifice to Rudra. Thenceforward that place has been known as Kshetra. Whoever goes there and during an eclipse gives alms, bathes, performs austerity and sacrifice, has a thousand-fold reward."

Having related this much of the story, S'rî S'ukadev Jî said to King Parîkshit:—Mahârâj! on hearing this narrative, all the Yadubansîs were pleased, and said to S'rî Krishṇa Chand Jî, "Mahârâj! let us go to Kurukshetra speedily; now make no delay; because we should arrive at the festival." On hearing these words, S'rî Krishṇa Chand and Balarâm Jî inquired thus of Râjâ Ugrasen, "Mahârâj! should everybody go to Kurukshetra, who will stay here to guard the city?" Râjâ Ugrasen said, "Leave Aniruddha, and go." Having received the king's command, the Lord summoned Aniruddha, counselled him, and said, "Son! do you stay here and protect cows and Brâhmaṇs, and cherish the people. I, with the Râjâ Jî, and all the Yadubansîs, will bathe at Kurukshetra and return." Aniruddha Jî said, "That order [shall be obeyed]." Mahârâj! having left Aniruddha alone in the guardianship of the city, Sûrasen, Vasudev, Ûdho, Akrûr, Kritavramâ, and the rest, and the Yadubansîs, small and great, along with their wives, were ready to start to Kurukshetra with Râjâ Ugrasen. When Râjâ Ugrasen with his army encamped outside the city, then the whole party assembled together. After these, S'rî Krishṇa Chand Jî joined them, accompanied by his brother, his brother's wife, all his eight queens and sixteen thousand eight hundred[1] wives, together with their sons and grandsons. On the arrival of the Lord, Râjâ Ugrasen broke up his encampment from there, and, like Râjâ Indra, advanced forwards with great pomp and ceremony.

Having related this much of the story, S'rî S'ukadev Jî said:—Mahârâj! proceeding on for some time, S'rî Krishṇa Chand, with all the Yadubansîs, with joy and happiness arrived in Kurukshetra. Having gone there, all bathed during the festival; and to the extent of his power, everyone gave alms, elephants, horses,

[1] Hitherto they have been reckoned as 16,100 [or 16,108, pp. 267, 269, 217, 218 note [1], and Chap. XC.]. The above is no doubt a slip on the part of Lallû Lâl.

chariots, pâlkîs, dresses, weapons, jewels, ornaments, food, and money; afterwards they all encamped there. Mahârâj! having obtained news of the going to Kurukshetra of S'rî Krishṇa Chand and Balarâm Jî, all the neighbouring kings, with their families, each bringing the whole of his particular army, came there and met S'rî Krishṇa and Balarâm Jî. Then all the Kauravas and Pâṇḍavas also, each bringing his own army, with his family, went there and met them. Then Kuntî and Draupadî, going into the female apartments of the Yadubañsîs, had interviews with all. Afterwards Kuntî, going before her brother, said, "Brother! I am very unfortunate! from the day I was betrothed I have been suffering affliction. Since you gave me in marriage, you have taken no thought of me; and Râma and Krishṇa, who are givers of happiness to all, they also have shown me no kindness." Mahârâj! on hearing these words, Vasudev Jî, feeling compassion, with eyes full of tears, said, "Sister! what art thou saying to me? I have no power in this matter. The course of fate is incomprehensible. The will of Hari is predominant. See! what a variety of miseries I endured through Kañs!

> All the world is become subject to the Lord; whatsoever may be the misery suffered, behold! the world revolves."[1]

Mahârâj! having said this much, and counselled and advised his sister, Vasudev Jî went where all the kings were seated in the court of Râjâ Ugrasen. And Râjâ Duryodhan, and the other very great kings, and the Pâṇḍavas, were extolling Râjâ Ugrasen alone, thus, "O king! you are very fortunate, in that you are always obtaining the sight of S'rî Krishṇa Chand, and are losing the sin of birth after birth. He whom S'iva and Viranch, and all the other gods, are seeking about for, that same Lord is ever protecting you; he whose mystery the supernaturally powerful, the self-restrained, saints, and sages, cannot gain, that very Hari receives your commands; he who is Lord of the whole world, that very one bows his head to you."

Having related this much of the story, S'rî S'ukadev Jî said:— Mahârâj! all these kinds of kings having severally come, are praising Râjâ Ugrasen, and he suitably gratifies them all. Hereupon, having heard of the arrival of S'rî Krishṇa and Balarâm Jî, Nand and Upanand also arrived, with their families, together with all the cowherdesses, cowherds, and cowherd-lads. When they were at leisure from bathing and almsgiving, Nand Jî went where Vasudev and Devakî, with their son, were residing. On seeing them, Vasudev Jî rose and met them, and both of them, with mutual affection, experienced such happiness as anyone feels who has found a thing which was lost. Afterwards Vasudev Jî related to Nand Râ,e Jî all the recent affairs of Braj; as, [for

[1] **Meaning that the course of nature proceeds regardless of individual suffering.**

example,] that Nand Râ,e Jî had brought up S'rî Krishṇa and Balarâm Jî. Mahârâj! on hearing these words, Nand Râ,e Jî's eyes filled with tears, and he kept looking at the face of Vasudev Jî. At that time, S'rî Krishṇa and Baladev Jî, in the first place, as is proper, prostrated themselves and made obeisance to Nand and Jasodâ Jî; afterwards, they went and met the cowherd-lads. There the cowherdesses came, and looking upon the moon-face of Hari, gave happiness to their chakora-eyes,[1] and received the reward of their lives.

Having said this much, S'rî S'ukadev Jî said :—Mahârâj! the love displayed by Nand, Upanand, Jasodâ, the cowherdesses, cowherds, and cowherd-lads, on meeting with Vasudev, Devakî, Rohinî, S'rî Krishṇa and Balarâm, is indescribable by me; that, only by being seen, is to be realized. At length, perceiving that all were greatly agitated by their affection, S'rî Krishṇa Chand Jî said, "Listen,—

The mortal who worships me, shall cross fearlessly the ocean of existence;
You have dedicated body, mind, and wealth; and have regarded me with never-ending affection;
No one is so fortunate as you; Brahmâ, Rudra, Indra—whoever he may be;
I have not come into the meditation of the chief practisers of Yoga; but have remained with you, and have constantly increased my love;[2]
I am dwelling in each body of the whole of you; the words which I say are incomprehensible and unfathomable.

As light,[3] water, fire, earth, and ether dwell in the body, so also is my splendour in every mortal frame." S'rî S'ukadev Jî said :—Mahârâj! when S'rî Krishṇa Chand had related the whole of this mystery, all the inhabitants of Braj were comforted.

---

## CHAPTER LXXXIII.

**The wives of Krishṇa relate to Draupadî the process of their respective marriages.**

S'RÎ S'UKADEV Jî said :—Mahârâj! I will give an account of such mutual conversations as took place between Draupadî and the

[1] The Chakora is a bird of the partridge species, said to be fond of gazing at the moon.

[2] Meaning, that the intense meditation of those who habitually practise meditation has not been rewarded by a revelation of his presence; but the cowherds have got his presence and increased affection without effort.

[3] The word *tej*, "splendour," is here substituted for the usual *vâyu*, "air"; the elements being ether, fire, air, water, and earth.

X 2

wives of S'rî Krishṇa Chand Jî; do you listen. One day the wives of the Kauravas and Pâṇḍavas were seated near the wives of S'rî Krishṇa Chand Jî, and were celebrating the virtues and exploits of the Lord. Hereupon, when some conversation was going on, Draupadî said to S'rî Rukminî Jî, "O beauteous one! say, how didst thou obtain S'rî Krishṇa Chand Jî?" S'rî Rukminî Jî replied,—

"Do you listen heedfully, O Draupadî! how the Lord effected his purpose.

It was my father's wish that his daughter should be given to S'rî Krishṇa Chand; but my brother set his heart on giving me to Râjâ S'iśupâl. The latter came to the marriage with a marriage procession, and I sent a Brâhmaṇ and summoned S'rî Krishṇa Chand Jî. On the marriage day, as I, having worshipped Gaurî, went home, S'rî Krishṇa Chand Jî took me from the midst of the whole Asura army, placed me in a chariot, and took his way home. After that, having obtained intelligence [of what had occurred], the whole Asura army came and fell upon the Lord, but they were quite easily smitten and put to flight by Hari. Then, taking me, he set out for Dwârakâ. On going there, Râjâ Ugrasen, Sûrasen, and Vasudev Jî married me to S'rî Krishṇa Chand Jî according to Vedic ritual. On gaining intelligence of the marriage, my father had a very bountiful dowry sent to me."

Having related the story thus far, S'rî S'ukadev Jî said to King Parîkshit:—Mahârâj! as Draupadî Jî had questioned S'rî Rukminî Jî, and she had answered, just so Draupadî Jî questioned Satyabhâmâ, Jambâvatî, Kâlindî, Bhadrâ, Satyâ, Mitrabindâ, Lakshmaṇâ, and the other sixteen thousand eight hundred[1] queens of S'rî Krishṇa Chand, and each of them gave a detailed account of the particulars of their respective marriages.

---

## CHAPTER LXXXIV.

Vasudev, the father of Krishṇa, performs a sacrifice.

S'RÎ S'UKADEV Jî said:—Mahârâj! now I am about to relate the coming of all the sages, and the sacrifice of Vasudev; do you listen attentively. Mahârâj! one day Râjâ Ugrasen, Sûrasen, Vasudev, S'rî Krishṇa, Balarâm, together with all the Yadubaṅsîs, were seated holding a court, and the kings of all the various countries were present there, when, in the midst of this, with the desire of seeing S'rî Krishṇa Chand, the root of joy, Vyâsa, Vaśishha,

[1] Here the author of the *Sukha-Sâgar* puts 16,100, thus showing that Lallû Lâl is merely careless, as before. See note [1], p. 305, and p. 218, note [1].

Viśvâmitra, Vâmadeva, Parâśara, Bhrigu, Pulasti, Bharadwâja, Markaṇḍeya,[1] and the other eighty-eight thousand sages, came there, and along with them Nârad Jî also. On seeing them, the entire assembly all rose and stood up. Then all prostrating themselves, spread silken foot-cloths, and conducted them all into the assembly. Afterwards, S'rî Krishṇa Chand, having placed them all on seats, washed their feet, drank the ambrosia of their foot-water, and sprinkled it upon the entire assembly. Then, having offered worship to them with sandal, unbroken rice, flowers, incense, lamps, and consecrated food, he circumambulated them. Next, joining his hands, he stood before them, and said, "Felicitous is our fate, that your honours have come and have revealed yourselves as we were seated in our house. The sight of holy people is equal to bathing in the Ganges. He who obtains a sight of the holy, loses the sin of birth after birth." Having related this much of the story, S'rî S'ukadev Jî said:—Mahârâj!

When S'rî Bhagwân uttered these words, all the sages remained reflecting,—

thus, "He who is the Lord, whose form is light, and who is the creator of all creation, when he has said these words, who has broached any other subject [to deserve our attention]?" When all the saints had said this in their hearts, Nârad Jî said,—

"Listen, O assembly! all of you, attentively. The illusive power of Hari is incomprehensible.

This one himself, as Brahmâ, creates, as Vishṇu preserves, as S'iva destroys; his actions are infinite; in this matter no one's intellect is of any avail; but we know this much by his favour, that the Lord has repeatedly taken incarnate form, and come [upon earth] to give happiness to holy people, to stay the wicked, and to make religion hold on its eternal course." Mahârâj! as soon as he had said these words, and Nârad Jî was about to rise up from the assembly, then Vasudev Jî, coming before him, with joined hands, meekly said, "O king of sages! how can man, having come into the world, escape from fate? Kindly tell me that." Mahârâj! as soon as these words had issued from the mouth of Vasudev Jî, all the saints and sages kept looking at the face of Nârad Jî. Then Nârad Jî, having comprehended the object in the hearts of the saints, said, "O Divinities! do not be surprised at this affair; the illusion of S'rî Krishṇa is predominant. This [illusion] has held in subjection the entire world; by this very thing Vasudev Jî has said these words; and another one has said this also, that whatever person remains near anyone, he becomes subject to the illusion of that person's qualities, power, and energy without knowing it. As,—

[1] These are the names of the principal authors or sages of the hymns of the Rig-Veda.

A dweller on the Ganges, goes elsewhere, and abandoning the Ganges, bathes in well-water;
Just so, the Yâdavas have become simpletons, and know nothing of the actions of Krishṇa."

Having said this, Nârad Jî, having effaced doubt from the mind of the saints, said to Vasudev Jî, "Mahârâj! it is said in the Scriptures, the man who performs pilgrimage, almsgiving, penance, vows, and sacrifice, is released from the bonds of the world, and attains the supreme state." On hearing these words, and being pleased, Vasudev Jî immediately sent for all the essentials of a sacrifice, and prepared them, and said to the sages and saints, "Kindly begin the sacrifice." Mahârâj! as soon as this remark had issued from the mouth of Vasudev Jî, all the Brâhmaṇs made and prepared the place of sacrifice. Hereupon Vasudev Jî, along with his wives, came and sat in the altar-place; and all the kings and Yâdavas prepared to assist in the work of the sacrifice.

Having related this much of the story, S'rî S'ukadev Jî said to the king:—Mahârâj! when Vasudev Jî came and sat in the altar-place, the saints began the sacrifice, according to the ritual of the Veda; and began to recite the texts and to offer burnt sacrifice; and the gods, hurrying severally, in bodily form,[1] began to receive [the offerings]. Mahârâj! when the sacrifice commenced, on the one side, Kinnaras and Gandharvas, playing away on pipes and kettle-drums, were singing praises, and bards and panegyrists were recounting glories; Urvasî and other *apsarases*[2] were dancing; and gods, seated in their respective celestial cars, were raining down flowers; and, on the other side, all the festive people were singing, playing on instruments, and making merry, and mendicants shouted "Victory! victory!" Meanwhile the sacrifice was completed, and Vasudev Jî gave the final offering, dressed Brâhmaṇs in silken robes, adorned them, and gave jewels and much wealth; and they, reciting severally Vedic texts, gave blessings. Afterwards Vasudev Jî presented dresses and entertained the kings of all the various countries also; then they respectively offered the sacrificial presents, took leave, and pursued their various roads home. Mahârâj! on the departure of all the kings, all the sages and saints also, along with Nârad Jî, took leave. Then when Nand Râ,e Jî, with the cowherdesses, cowherds, and cowherd-lads, began to take leave of Vasudev, the circumstances of the occasion are indescribable. On the one side, the Yadubañsîs were making various kinds of affectionate speeches; and, on the other side, all the Braj-dwellers [were doing the same]. A description of the scene is not to be made;

[1] For *sandeh*, "doubt," read *sadeh*, "with a body."

[2] An *apsaras* is a kind of fairy or female divinity, residing in the sky. They are the wives of the Gandharvas, and are prone to change their shapes, and are fond of bathing and dancing.

the happiness, only by being seen, can be realized. At length Vasudev Jî and S'rî Krishṇa and Balarâm Jî, instructed, comforted, and dressed [in robes of honour] Nand Râ,e Jî, with all the others, and gave them much wealth, and dismissed them.

Having related this much of the story, S'rî S'ukadev Jî said :—Mahârâj ! when, in this way, S'rî Krishṇa Chand and Balarâm Jî, having attended the festival, bathed, and sacrificed, had returned into the city of Dwârakâ with them all, then in every house there was joy and festivity, and songs of congratulation.

---

## CHAPTER LXXXV.

Krishṇa, to please his mother, brings from Yama his six elder brothers, who had been slain by Kaṅs.

S'RÎ S'UKADEV Jî said :—Mahârâj ! one day, within the city of Dwârakâ, when S'rî Krishṇa Chand and Balarâm Jî went to Vasudev Jî, he, having seen the two brothers, reflecting on this matter in his mind, rose and stood up, viz. In Kurukshetra Nârad Jî said that S'rî Krishṇa Chand is the creator of the world ; and having joined his hands, he said, "O Lord ! invisible, incomprehensible, indestructible ! always serving you, Kamalâ [1] has become a bond-woman ; you are the god of all gods ; no one comprehends your nature ; from you alone is there light in the moon, the sun, the earth, and the sky ; you alone are causing light in all places ; your illusive power is predominant, it has kept the whole world in forgetfulness [of verities] ; in the three worlds there is no such god, man, or saint, who may have escaped from its power." Mahârâj ! having said this much, Vasudev Jî resumed, "Lord !—

No one knows your mystery ; in the Vedas it is described as unfathomable ;
No one is your enemy [or] friend ; nor [have you] son, father, [or] beloved whole brother ;
You have descended [from heaven] to remove the burden of the earth ; for the sake of men, many disguises you have assumed."

Mahârâj ! having spoken thus, Vasudev Jî said, "O Ocean of Compassion ! Friend of the Lowly ! as you have saved various sinners, mercifully cause me also to be saved, so that, having crossed the ocean of existence, I may celebrate your [2] virtues."

[1] See note [3], p. 284.  [2] For *â,e ke* read *âp ke*.

S'rî Krishṇa Chand said, "O father! you are a wise person; why are you exalting your sons? Reflect yourself a little in your mind, that the sports of Bhagwat are infinite; their limit no one up to this day has ascertained. Behold! he—

> Resides as light in every human frame; for this very reason the world speaks of him as void of qualities;
> He also creates; he alone removes; he is mingled [with earthly things], he never can be bound [to them];
> Earth, ether, air, water, and fire, whatever body is [produced] from these five elements,
> The power of the Lord abides in them all. In the Veda, the precepts say thus."

Mahârâj! on hearing these words from the mouth of S'rî Krishṇa Chand Jî, Vasudev Jî, being under the influence of fascination, silently continued to gaze on the countenance of Hari. Then the Lord, proceeding thence, went near his mother; then, on seeing the face of her son, Devakî Jî said, "O S'rî Krishṇa Chand! the root of joy! one grief at times pierces me." The Lord said, "What is that?" Devakî Jî said, "Son! grief for your six elder brothers, whom Kañs killed, does not depart from my mind."

S'rî S'ukadev Jî said:—Mahârâj! on these words being said, S'rî Krishṇa Chand Jî went to Pâtâl, after saying this, "Mother! do not now grieve; I will go at once and bring back my brothers." On the departure of the Lord, Râjâ Bali, having received intelligence of it, came, and with much pomp and ceremony spread foot-cloths of silk, and caused him to be conducted into his own palace. Afterwards, having seated him on a throne, Râjâ Bali offered sandal, unbroken rice, and flowers, and placed before him incense, lamps, and consecrated food, and performed worship to S'rî Krishṇa Chand. Then, standing before him with joined hands, he glorified him greatly, and said, "Mahârâj! what is the cause of your honour's coming here?" Hari said, "Râjâ! in the Satya age there was a sage named Marîchi,[1] a great religious student, wise, truthful, and a worshipper of Hari. His wife's name was Ûrṇâ; she had six sons. One day these six brothers, in their youthful state, went into the presence of Prajâpati[2] and laughed. Having seen them laugh, Prajâpati very angrily pronounced this curse, 'Do you go, take incarnate form, and become Asuras.' Mahârâj! on hearing these words, the sons of the sage, being greatly frightened, went and fell at the feet of Prajâpati, and very beseechingly and humbly said, 'Ocean of Compassion! you have cursed us; but now kindly say when we shall obtain deliverance from this curse.' Having heard their humble words, Prajâpati,

[1] Marîchi was one of the great primitive sages; but his genesis is variously described.

[2] *Prajâpati*, "lord of creatures," a title applied to the chief divinities of the Veda, but subsequently converted into a separate deity presiding over procreation.

being compassionate, said, 'You, having seen S'rî Krishṇa Chand, shall be liberated.' Mahârâj !—

Saying this, their souls departed ; they became the sons which Hariṇâkus had ;
Then they were born to Vasudev ; Kañs came and slew them ;
On their being killed, Illusion, the giver of happiness, brought them to this place, placed them here, and departed.

Their mother Devakî grieves for them, therefore I have come here that I may take away my brothers and give them to mother, and remove the anxiety of her mind." S'rî S'ukadev Jî said :—Râjâ ! as soon as this statement had issued from the mouth of Hari, Râjâ Bali brought the six boys and gave them, and placed many presents before him. Then the Lord came thence to his mother, accompanied by the brothers. The mother having seen her sons, became greatly pleased. Having heard this affair, joy was in the whole city, and they were released from the curse.

---

## CHAPTER LXXXVI.

**The marriage of Subhadrâ, and wrath of Balarâm thereat.**

S'RÎ S'UKADEV Jî said :—Râjâ ! I am about to relate how Arjuna carried off S'rî Krishṇa Chand's sister Subhadrâ from Dwârakâ, and how S'rî Krishṇa Chand went to reside in Mithilâ ; do you listen attentively. When Devakî's daughter, who was younger than S'rî Krishṇa Jî, and whose name was Subhadrâ, was ready for marriage, Vasudev Jî summoned several Yadubañsîs, and S'rî Krishṇa and Balarâm Jî, and said, "Now the maiden is marriageable ; say, to whom shall we give her ?" Balarâm Jî said, "It is said that marriage, enmity, and friendship, should be contracted with equals. One thing occurs to me, that this girl should be given to Duryodhan, and that we [thereby] acquire renown and greatness in the world." S'rî Krishṇa Chand said, "It is my opinion that we should give the girl to Arjuna, and gain reputation in the world."

S'rî S'ukadev Jî said :—Mahârâj ! no one said anything as to the proposal of Balarâm Jî ; but as soon as these words issued from the mouth of S'rî Krishṇa Chand Jî, all cried out, "It is much the best to give the girl to Arjuna." On hearing this, Balarâm Jî, being offended, rose up and went thence, and all the folk, perceiving his ill-humour, were silent. Afterwards, gaining intelligence of this, Arjuna, making up the disguise of a Sannyâsî,[1] and taking a staff and a water-pot, went to Dwârakâ, and having seen a suitable spot, spread a deer-skin, and sat down on his hams.

He remained there during the four months of the rainy season; no one got at his secret;
Thinking him a guest, all served him; for Vishṇu's sake they were kind to him;
Krishṇa knew all his secret; but told it to no one.

Mahârâj! one day Baladev Jî also, taking Arjuna with him to entertain him, had him conducted home. As Arjuna was seated at food, the moon-bodied, deer-eyed Subhadrâ came in sight. On seeing her, on the one side, Arjuna, becoming fascinated, avoiding the gaze of all, began to look again and again, and to pass this reflection through his mind, "Behold! when will Vidhâtâ cause me to meet with what is prescribed in my horoscope?" and, on the other side, Subhadrâ Jî, beholding the brilliance of his beauty, being pleased, was saying thus in her heart,—

"It is some king; not a Sannyâsî. For what cause has he become an Udâsî?"[2]

Mahârâj! having said this, on the one hand, Subhadrâ Jî, going into the house, began to be uneasy about obtaining a husband, and, on the other hand, after eating, Arjuna, coming to his seat, began to form many various conceptions relative to obtaining his beloved one. While they were in this condition, after some time, on one occasion, at the festival of S'ivarâtra, all the inhabitants of the city, whether women or men, went out of the city to worship S'iva. There Subhadrâ Jî went with her friends and companions. Having gained intelligence of her going, Arjuna also mounted a chariot, and taking a bow and arrows, went and presented himself there. Mahârâj! when, having worshipped S'iva, Subhadrâ returned, accompanied by her friends, on seeing her, Arjuna abandoned all shame and modesty, seized her hand, lifted her up, and seating Subhadrâ in his chariot, took his road homewards.

Having heard this, Râma was exceedingly angry; taking his plough and pestle, he placed them on his shoulder;
He made his eyes bloodshot; he spoke in a voice like thunder;
"I will go immediately and produce a cataclysm; I will pick up the world and place it on my forehead;

[1] A Sannyâsî is a devotee who lays down worldly concerns, and even the ceremonial portions of his religion. He reads only the abstruse metaphysical treatises, and ceases to perform sacrifice; he wanders from place to place, and may mix with society, but still form no part of it.

[2] Udâsîs are religious mendicants who profess freedom from passion and affection. They are a kind of Stoics.

My sister, my beloved Subhadrâ, how shall a beggar carry her off!
Now wherever I shall find a Sannyâsî I will search them out and exterminate the whole fraternity."

Mahârâj! Balarâm Jî, for his part, in great anger, was simply chattering and fuming, when, having received intelligence of the affair, Pradyumna, Aniruddha, Sambû, and the greatest of the Yâdavas, coming before Baladev Jî, and severally joining their hands, said, "Mahârâj! should you order us, then we will go, seize, and bring the enemy."

Having related the story thus far, S'rî S'ukadev Jî said:—Mahârâj! when Balarâm Jî, accompanied by all the Yadubañsis, was ready to go after Arjuna, S'rî Krishṇa Chand Jî went and imparted to Baladev Jî all the secret of the abduction of Subhadrâ, and with great meekness said, "Brother! Arjuna, for one thing, is the son of our aunt; and, for another, he is an excellent friend. He may or may not have done this act, heedfully or heedlessly, considerately or inconsiderately, but for us to fight with him is by no means proper; this is contrary to religion, and contrary to worldly custom. Those who hear of this affair will say that the friendship of the Yadubañsîs is like a wall of sand." On hearing these words, Balarâm Jî, beating his head, angrily said, "Brother! this is just your work, to raise a fire and run with water; otherwise, what power had Arjuna that he should take away our sister?" Having said this, grieved at heart and hot with anger, Balarâm Jî, looking at his brother's face, dashed down the plough and pestle, and sat still; and with him all the Yadubañsîs also.

S'rî S'ukadev Jî said:—Râjâ! on this side, S'rî Krishṇa Chand Jî detained all of them with expostulation; and on the other side, Arjuna, going home, married Subhadrâ, according to Vedic ritual. On receiving intelligence of the marriage, S'rî Krishṇa and Balarâm Jî dedicated [as dowry] and sent off to Hastinâpur, by means of a Brâhmaṇ, clothes, ornaments, male and female slaves, elephants, horses, chariots, and a large sum of money. Afterwards, S'rî Murârî, the benefactor of devotees, having seated himself on a chariot, proceeded to Mithilâ, where there were two worshippers of his, named Sutadev and Bahulâs, one a king, the other a Brâhmaṇ. Mahârâj! on the departure of the Lord, Nârad, Vâmadev, Vyâsa, Atri, Paraśurâm, and several other saints, came and joined [the party], and accompanied S'rî Krishṇa Chand Jî. Then, whatever country it might be that the Lord was passing through, the king of each place advanced, and having offered adoration, was placing presents before him. At length, proceeding onwards, in the course of a certain time, the Lord arrived there. Having received intelligence of the coming of Hari, those two, just as they happened to be then seated, rose up and hurried with presents, and came to S'rî

Krishṇa Chand. On meeting with the Lord, they both laid their presents before him, prostrated themselves, joined their hands, stood up in his presence, and most meekly said, "O Ocean of Compassion! Friend of the Lowly! you have shown great mercy, in that you have revealed yourself to such sinners as we are, and purified us, and put an end to our being born and dying."

Having related this much of the story, S'rî S'ukadev Jî said :— Mahârâj! the Searcher of Hearts, S'rî Krishṇa Chand, having perceived the adoration of the hearts of those two worshippers, assuming two forms, went and resided in both their houses. They entertained him in every agreeable manner, and Hari, remaining there for some time, gave them additional pleasure. Afterwards, when the Lord had fulfilled the desire of their hearts, and had strengthened their knowledge, and proceeded to Dwârakâ, the sages and saints took leave by the way, and Hari went and resided in Dwârakâ.

---

## CHAPTER LXXXVII.

The manner in which the Veda glorifies the Deity.

HAVING heard thus much of the story, King Parîkshit asked S'rî S'ukadev Jî :—Mahârâj! with regard to what you formerly said, that the Veda extolled the Supreme Lord, how did the Veda extol Brahma void of qualities? Expound this to me, that the doubt of my mind may depart.

S'rî S'ukadev Jî said :—Mahârâj! listen! he who formed intellect, the senses, mind, soul, virtue, wealth, desire, and beatitude, that Lord ever remains in a form void of qualities; but when he creates Brahmâṇḍa,[1] he becomes a form possessed of qualities;[2] hence that same single Lord is both with and without qualities.

Having said this, S'ukadev the saint resumed :—Râjâ! the very question which you have asked was once asked of Naranârâyaṇ[3] by Nârad Jî. King Parîkshit said :—Mahârâj! please relate this, that the doubt of my mind may depart. S'ukadev Jî said :— Râjâ! in the Satya age, once Nârad Jî went into the World of Truth, where Naranârâyaṇ was seated with many other saints engaged in performing austerities, and asked, "Mahârâj! in what way does the Veda glorify the formless Brahma? Kindly tell me that." Naranârâyaṇ said, "Listen, Nârad! the very problem which you have asked of me, once was presented in the world of men, where Sanâtan and other sages were seated performing penance. Then the saint Sanandan, by relating a story,

[1] This is the cosmic egg whence all tangible creation proceeds.
[2] For *saragun* read *saguṇ*.
[3] Naranârâyaṇ is an epithet of Krishṇa.

effaced the doubt of all." Nârad Jî said, "Mahârâj! I also am staying just there; had this subject been broached, I also would have heard it." Naranârâyaṇ replied, "Nârad Jî! when you had gone to see Bhagwat in Setadip,[1] then the subject was broached; hence you did not hear."

Having heard this, Nârad Jî asked, "Mahârâj! please kindly tell me what was the subject there discussed." Naranârâyaṇ said, "Listen, Nârad! When the saints asked this question, Sanandan the saint began to say, 'Listen! when the great cataclysm occurred, the fourteen cosmic eggs become of the consistence of water; then the perfect Brahma remains slumbering alone. When Bhagwân has the wish to create, then the Vedas issue from his breath, and with joined hands praise him, just as a king who may be sleeping in his own house, and panegyrists, at early dawn, severally singing his glory, wake him up, so that he may become conscious and speedily engage in his duties.'"

Having related the matter thus far, Naranârâyaṇ said, "Listen, Nârad! when the Vedas have issued from the Lord's mouth they say this: O Lord! quickly become conscious, and create the universe, and remove your illusion from the minds of living beings, in order that they may recognize your form. Your illusion is predominant; it keeps all living creatures in ignorance; when released from this, living creatures have the knowledge to understand you. O Lord! except you, no one can exercise power over this. In whose heart you are dwelling in the form of knowledge, he alone conquers this illusion; otherwise who has the power to escape from the hand of Illusion? You are the creator of all; all creatures having arisen from you alone, are contained in you alone; just as many objects arise from the earth, and again mingle with it. Anyone may glorify and worship any god, but he glorifies and worships you alone. Just as anyone, having constructed various golden ornaments, may give them different names, but they are only gold; just in this way you have many forms; but regard them intelligently, then none of them are anything; wherever one may look there nothing but you appears. O Lord! your illusion is infinite! This it is which, having become the three qualities, truth, passion, and darkness, assumes three forms, and creates, preserves, and destroys the universe. The secret of this no one has discovered, and no one will discover; hence it is fitting for creatures to abandon all desire and meditate on you; in this alone does his advantage lie." Mahârâj! having related this much of the subject, Naranârâyaṇ said to Nârad, "O Nârad! when Sanandan the sage, having related this ancient history, had removed doubt from the minds of all, then Sanak[2] and the other saints worshipped Sanandan, according to the precepts of the Veda."

[1] Properly *S'wetadwîpa.*

[2] Sanak is one of the four sons of Brahmâ, and was a councillor and companion of Vishṇu.

Having related this much of the story, S'rî S'ukadev Jî said :—O Râjâ! whoever shall hear this conversation between Nârâyaṇ and Nârad will undoubtedly obtain the object of faith, and will attain salvation. The very story of the perfect Brahma which the Vedas sang, was recounted by Sanandan the saint to Sanak and the other saints; then that very story Naranârâyaṇ celebrated before Nârad, and Vyâsa obtained it from Nârad. Vyâsa recited it to me; and I now have recounted it to you. Whatever person shall hear and relate this story will obtain the reward he desires. The virtue there is in performing penance, sacrifice, almsgiving, and vows, that very virtue resides in telling and hearing this story.

---

## CHAPTER LXXXVIII.

The story of Vrikâsur—S'iva allows him to turn into ashes anyone on whose head he lays his hand—He attempts, by this means, to destroy S'iva—Krishṇa relieves S'iva from his danger by inducing Vrikâsur to destroy himself.

S'RÎ S'UKADEV Jî said :—Mahârâj! Bhagwat has surprising sports; this everyone knows. Whoever worships Hari will be poor, and by other gods being reverenced [he becomes] rich.[1] Behold! what is the characteristic peculiarity of Hari and Hara? The one is the husband of Lakshmî, the other is the husband of Gaurî; the one wears a garland of wild flowers, the other a garland of skulls; the one has a discus in his hand, the other holds a trident; the one supports the earth, the other sustains the Ganges; the one plays on a flute, the other a horn; the one is the Lord of Vaikuṇṭh, the other is a dweller in Kailâs; the one preserves, the other destroys; the one smears with sandal, the other applies ashes; the one wears woven fabric, the other a tiger's skin; the one reads the Veda, the other the Âgama;[2] the vehicle of one is Garuḍa, of the other [the bull] Nandî; the one resides with cowherd-lads, the other with ghouls and ghosts.

Both Lords have opposite peculiarities; make friends with which you please.

[1] For *mâne se* one is inclined to read *mânne se;* but the careful Paṇḍit Yogadhyân Misra preserves the same reading. Hollings translates it "by serving" (*mânne se*); and Eastwick evades the difficulty by the phrase "he who reverences other deities." I treat it as the Past Participle which it appears to be. There is warrant for such a use; but it is not common.

[2] Âgama is a general name for the Tântrika books on the mystic and obscene worship of S'iva and his S'akti, or female emanation.

Having related thus much of the story, S'rî S'ukadev Jî said:—Mahârâj! S'rî Krishṇa Chand said to Râjâ Yudhishṭhira, "O Yudhishṭhira! I gradually destroy all the wealth of those to whom I show favour; because brother, relation, wife, son, and all other members of the family, abandon one who is destitute of wealth, then impassibility springs up in him. From becoming impassible, he abandons the illusion of wealth and kindred, and becoming free from fascination, worships me with wrapt attention. By the potency of worshipping me, he attains the state of unchangeable Nirvâṇa."[1] Having said this, S'ukadev Jî resumed:—Mahârâj! by worshipping other deities, the heart's desires are fulfilled; but emancipation is not obtained.

Having related this subject, the saint again spoke to King Parîkshit thus:—Mahârâj! on one occasion, when Vrikâsur, the son of Kaśyapa, had gone out of his house, with the desire of performing austerity, he met in the way Nârad the saint. On seeing Nârad Jî, he prostrated himself, joined his hands, stood up before him, and with great humility said, "Mahârâj! among the three deities, Brahmâ, Vishṇu, and Mahâdev, which is the readiest granter of boons? Kindly tell me that, and then I will perform austerity to him." Nârad Jî said, "Listen, Vrikâsur! among these three deities, Mahâdev Jî is the greatest granter of boons. He delays not in being gratified, or in being vexed. Behold! S'iva Jî, by the performance of very little austerity, being pleased, gave to Sahasrârjun a thousand arms; and for a very little fault, being angry, he destroyed him." Mahârâj! having said this, Nârad the saint went away, and Vrikâsur, having come to his own place, began to perform great austerity and sacrifice to Mahâdev. In the course of seven days, he cut off all the flesh from his body, and gave it as a burnt-offering. On the eighth day, when he had made up his mind to cut off his head, Bholânâth came, and seizing his hand, said, "I am pleased with thee; whatever thou mayest wish, ask; I will give it to thee at once." As soon as these words issued from the mouth of S'iva Jî, Vrikâsur, having joined his hands, said,—

"Grant me now such a boon, that on whose head I may place my hand,
He may, in a twinkling, become ashes. O Lord! show me this favour."

Mahârâj! as soon as these words were uttered, Mahâdev Jî granted him the boon he had asked. On receiving the boon, he went to place his hand on the head of S'iva himself. Then, being frightened, Mahâdev Jî left his seat and fled; and the Asura ran

[1] *Nirvâṇa* has many explanations; literally it means "blown out," like a lamp, and has been held to express annihilation; but it is frequently taken to mean reabsorption into the Divine, but whether with, or without, the retention of consciousness is a moot point. Buddhists and Hindûs differ in their expositions of this term.

after him. Mahârâj! wherever Sadâśiva turned, he also came close behind him. At length, being greatly agitated, Mahâdev Jî went into Vaikuṇṭh. Perceiving him to be greatly distressed, the Benefactor of Devotees, the Lord of Vaikuṇṭh, S'rî Murârî, the Abode of Compassion, feeling compunction, assumed the guise of a Brâhmaṇ, and went before Vrikâsur and said, "O king of Asuras! why are you toiling after this one? Expound this matter to me." On hearing these words, Vrikâsur related the whole secret. Then Bhagwân said, "O king of Asuras! It is a very surprising thing that so intelligent a person as you are should be deceived. Who believes any statement to be true of this naked, mad, bhang and thorn-apple eating ascetic? This one, with [body] ever smeared with ashes, entwined with snakes, in frightful guise, accompanied by ghouls and ghosts, resides in a cemetery. Into whose mind do his words come as truth?" Mahârâj! having said this, S'rî Nârâyan continued, "O king of Asuras! if you esteem what I say to be false, place your hand on your own head and see [the result]."

Mahârâj! on hearing these words from the mouth of the Lord, when Vrikâsur, having become foolish through the power of illusion, placed his hand on his own head, he was consumed and became a heap of ashes. On the death of the Asura, instruments of delight began to sound in the city of the gods, and the divinities, shouting "Victory! victory!" began to rain down flowers, and Vidyâdhars, Gandharvas, and Kinnaras began to sing Hari's praises. Then Hari greatly glorified Hara and dismissed him, and granted to Vrikâsur the object of emancipation. S'rî S'ukadev Jî said:—Mahârâj! whoever hears and recites this topic will undoubtedly attain the most exalted state, by the favour of Hari and Hara.

---

## CHAPTER LXXXIX.

Bhrigu tests the gods and proves that Vishṇu, in the form of Hari, is the most excellent of the gods—Arjuna undertakes to preserve the children of a Brâhmaṇ, but fails to do so—Krishṇa redeems his promise for him.

S'UKADEV Jî said:—Mahârâj! on one occasion, on the banks of the Saraswatî, all the sages and saints were seated performing austerity and sacrifice, when someone among them asked, "Among the three gods, Brahmâ, Vishṇu, Maheś, which is the greatest? Kindly tell me that." Hereupon someone said "S'iva," another said "Vishṇu," and another said "Brahmâ"; but all of them together did not indicate any one as the greatest. Then several of the greatest saints and sages said, "We do not accept the dictum of anyone in this way; but, in truth, if anyone should go and make trial of the three gods, and pronounce [one to be] Religion personified, then we will accept his word as true."

Mahârâj! having heard these words, all of them assented, and directed Bhrigu, the son of Brahmâ, to test the three gods, and return to them. On receiving the command, Bhrigu the saint at first went to the world of Brahmâ, and preserving silence, went and sat in the court of Brahmâ; he neither prostrated, nor praised, nor circumambulated. Râjâ! having noticed the discourtesy of his son, Brahmâ was very angry, and was on the point of cursing him, but abstained from doing so by reason of his son's consanguinity.[1] Then Bhrigu, perceiving that Brahmâ was under the influence of passion, rose up from there, and went to Kailâs, and he went and stood where S'iva was residing with Pârvatî. Having seen him, S'iva Jî rose up, and when he was on the point of stretching forth his hand to meet him, the latter sat down. On his seating himself, S'iva Jî was exceedingly enraged, and took his trident in his hand to slay him. Then S'rî Pârvatî, very meekly, falling at his feet, counselled Mahâdev Jî and said, "This is your younger brother; please forgive his offence. It is said,—

> Whatever offence occurs through a child, a holy person never takes note of."

Mahârâj! when Pârvatî Jî had cooled S'iva Jî by counsel, Bhrigu, perceiving that Mahâdev Jî was absorbed in darkness, rose up and departed. Then he went into Vaikuṇṭh, where Bhagwân was sleeping with Lakshmî on a couch of flowers on a jewel-bespangled, golden, and curtained bedstead. On arriving, Bhrigu gave Bhagwân such a kick on the chest that he started up from sleep. Having seen the saint, Hari left Lakshmî, descended from the bedstead, and having placed the foot of Bhrigu Jî to his head and eyes, he began to press them, and to speak thus, "O king of sages! please excuse my fault; the blow of my hard chest was unintentionally given to your lotus-foot. Do not retain this offence in your mind." As soon as these words had issued from the mouth of the Lord, Bhrigu Jî, being greatly pleased, gave praises, took his leave, and came where, on the banks of the Saraswatî, all the sages and saints were seated. On his coming, Bhrigu Jî related the whole secret of the three gods, just as it occurred, thus—

> "Brahmâ is involved in passion; Mahâdev is immersed in darkness;
> Vishṇu, who is chief among the virtuous, no other god is greater than he."

[1] *Lit.*, "my-ness," that is, the son was his own.

On hearing this, the doubt of the sages disappeared, and delight was in the mind of all ;
All praised Vishṇu ; immovable faith was fixed in their hearts.

Having related this much of the story, S'rî Ŝ'ukadev Jî said to King Parîkshit :—Mahârâj ! I am about to relate an intermediate story ; do you listen attentively. In the city of Dwârakâ, Râjâ Ugrasen, for his part, was reigning virtuously, and S'rî Krishṇa and Balarâm were obedient to him. By the rule of the king, all the people were attentive to their respective duties, and were intelligent in business affairs, and enjoyed happiness and ease. There was also a very amiable and virtuous Brâhmaṇ residing there. On one occasion, having a son, he died. He took that dead son and went to the gate of Râjâ Ugrasen, and began to say what came uppermost. "You are very impious, wicked, and sinful ; from the acts and regulations of you alone the subjects are experiencing affliction, and my son also, through your sin alone, is dead."

Mahârâj ! having uttered many various expressions of this kind, the Brâhmaṇ placed the dead boy at the royal portal, and came to his own home. Afterwards he had eight sons, and all eight he deposited in this same fashion at the king's door. When the ninth son was about to be born, that Brâhmaṇ again went into Râjâ Ugrasen's court, and standing in the presence of S'rî Krishṇa Chand Jî, calling to mind the repeated pain of the death of his sons, and weeping greatly, began to speak thus, "Cursed be the king and his government too ! again, cursed be those people who serve this unrighteous one ! and cursed be me, in that I am abiding in this city ! Had I not remained in the country of these sinners my sons had been saved ! By the unrighteousness of these my sons have died, and no one has protected them."

Mahârâj ! standing in the midst of the court, the Brâhmaṇ, weeping greatly, uttered many expressions of this kind, but no one said anything. At last, Arjuna, seated near to S'rî Krishṇa Chand, keeping on hearing this and being disconcerted, said, "O divinity ! before whom art thou making this statement ? and why art thou grieving so much ? [1] In this court there is no archer who can remove thy affliction. Kings of the present day are selfish ; they are not removing the ills of others, that they may give happiness to their subjects, and that they may protect cows and Brâhmaṇs." Having spoken thus, Arjuna again addressed the Brâhmaṇ thus, "Divinity ! now do you go, and stay in your own house free from anxiety ; when the time for your having a son arrives, please come to me ; I will go with you, and will not allow the boy to die." Mahârâj ! on hearing

[1] **Notice here, also, the Aorist fortified with the Substantive Verb, in the sense of the Present tense.**

these words, the Brâhmaṇ angrily said, "Within this assembly, except S'rî Krishṇa, Balarâm, Pradyumna, and Aniruddha, I see no one strong enough to rescue my son from the hand of Death." Arjuna said, "Brâhmaṇ! thou dost not know me; my name is Dhananjay. I promise thee that if I do not save thy son from the hand of Death, I will bring thy dead sons, wherever I may find them, and show them to thee; and should they also not be found, then I will burn myself in fire along with the bow Gâṇdív."[1] Mahârâj! when Arjuna had thus bound himself by a covenant, the Brâhmaṇ, being satisfied, went home. Then, at the time of the son's birth, the Brâhmaṇ came to Arjuna. Then Arjuna, taking up his bow and arrows, arose and hastened with him. Afterwards, having gone there, Arjuna so thatched his house with arrows, that even air could not enter therein, and himself, bearing his bow and arrows, peregrinated around it.

Having related thus much of the story, S'rî S'ukadev Jî said to King Parîkshit:—Mahârâj! Arjuna resorted to many contrivances to save the child, but it was not saved; and the day was weeping at the time of the birth of the child. On that day, it did not even breathe; but came forth dead from the womb itself. Having heard of the birth of a dead boy, Arjuna, abashed, came to S'rî Krishṇa Chand, and after him came the Brâhmaṇ also. Mahârâj! on his coming, crying greatly, the Brâhmaṇ began to say, "O Arjuna! a curse is to thee and to thy life! in that, having spoken falsely, thou art showing thy face to people in the world! O eunuch! if thou couldst not save my son from death, why didst thou make the promise, that thou wouldst save my son, and if thou couldst not save him thou wouldst bring and give to me all my dead sons?"

Mahârâj! on hearing these words, Arjuna, taking his bow and arrows, rose from that place, and proceeding onwards, went to Dharmarâj,[2] in the city of Sanjamanî.[3] Having seen him, Dharmarâj arose and stood up; and joining his hands, and giving praises, said, "Mahârâj! what is the cause of your coming here?" Arjuna said, "I am come to take the sons of a certain Brâhmaṇ." Dharmarâj said, "Those children have not come here." Mahârâj! as soon as these words issued from the mouth of Dharmarâj, Arjuna, taking leave, thence wandered about everywhere; but he found the Brâhmaṇ's sons nowhere. At length, grieving and regretting, he came into the city of Dwârakâ, and having prepared a funeral pile, he prepared to burn himself along with his bow and arrow. Then having ignited the fire, as Arjuna was

[1] The celebrated bow Gâṇḍîva, the wonderful powers of which are so often alluded to in the Mahâbhârata, is supposed to have belonged to Prajâpati, Brahmâ, and S'iva. It was presented to Varuṇa by Soma, or Lunar influence; and Varuṇa gave it to Agni, or Fire, thereby symbolizing the union of Lunar, Atmospheric, and Solar powers. Agni gave the bow to Arjuna, and thus imparted this combined influence to humanity.

[2] A name of Yama, regent of the dead.

[3] The name of Yama's chief city.

about to place himself on the funeral pile, S'rî Murâri, the destroyer of pride, came and took him by the hand, and smiling, said, "O Arjuna! do not burn thyself; I will fulfil thy promise; I will bring that Brâhmaṇ's sons from wherever they may be, and give them to him." Mahârâj! having said this, the Lord of the Three Worlds, having seated himself on his chariot, taking Arjuna with him, he proceeded towards the eastern quarter; and having crossed the seven oceans,[1] arrived near the mountain Lokâlok.[2] Having gone there and descended from the chariot, he entered an exceedingly dark cavern. Then S'rî Krishṇa Chand Jî issued a command to the discus Sudarśan; that weapon, producing the effulgence of myriads of suns, proceeded onwards before the Lord dispelling the dense darkness.

Having left the darkness, they advanced a little,
Into its great waves they slid,[3] with closed eyes they entered into it;
Krishṇa and Arjuna arrived where S'esh Jî was reposing.

On going there, they opened their eyes and saw a large, long, broad, and high, and very beautiful golden and jewel-bespangled palace. There, on the head of S'esh Jî was placed a jewel-studded throne; on that, in the form of a dark blue cloud, handsome in figure, with face like the moon, eyes like the lotus, wearing a diadem and earrings, clothed in yellow raiment, with silken loin-cloth, with a garland of wild flowers and a necklace of pearls placed on him, the Lord[4] himself, in fascinating form, was reclining, and Brahmâ, Rudra, Indra, and all the other gods, were standing before and glorifying him. Mahârâj! having seen such a form, Arjuna and S'rî Krishṇa Chand Jî went before the Lord, and prostrating themselves, with joined hands, stated the whole cause of their coming. On hearing the affair, the Lord sent for all the sons of the Brâhmaṇ and gave them, and Arjuna, having looked upon them, was pleased, and accepted them. Then the Lord said,—

"Since you two are portions of me, Hari and Arjuna, look [upon me] as much as you please;
You went upon earth to bear its burden; you have given much happiness to virtuous and good people;

[1] See note [2], p. 275.
[2] This is a mountainous belt surrounding the world, at the furthest limit, beyond the seven circumambient oceans.
[3] The rendering of this word is conjectural. Hollings renders it by "there were" without regarding the fact that *tarang* is feminine. Eastwick translates "they entered," but in his Vocabulary he says the word in this very place means "to encircle." For none of these renderings is there any known warrant in the language. The verb *lasnâ* means "to be fitting" or "suitable," also "to shine," "be sticky" or "clammy." In this latter sense I conjecture that the phrase implies "slid" into the waves.
[4] The Supreme Lord is here meant.

You have destroyed all the Asuras and Daityas, and have adjusted the affairs of gods, men, and saints ;
Since two shares of me are in you, they will accomplish your purposes."

Having said this much, Bhagwân dismissed Arjuna and S'rî Krishṇa Jî. They, taking the children, came into their city ; the Brâhmaṇ obtained the Brâhmaṇ's sons ; in every house there was joy, festivity, and songs of congratulation. Having related thus much of the story, S'rî S'ukadev Jî said to King Parîkshit :—Mahârâj !—

Those who hear and meditate on this story, will have sons and prosperity.

---

## CHAPTER XC.

Description of Krishṇa's happy life with his numerous wives—His vast offspring, and the schools established for their instruction.

S'RÎ SUKADEV Jî said :—Mahârâj ! in Dwârakâ city S'rî Krishṇa Chand ever abides ; increase and prosperity shine in every house of the Yadubañsîs ; men and women are ever forming fresh designs with dresses and ornaments ; rubbing on scent and sandal, they apply perfume ; the traders have the markets, roads, and squares, sprinkled, swept, and cleaned ; there traders, from various countries are bringing many different articles to sell ; here and there the citizens are amusing themselves ; in different places Brâhmaṇs are reciting the Veda ; in every house people are listening to and repeating stories from the Purâṇas ; good and virtuous people are, night and day, singing the glories of Hari ; charioteers are continually yoking chariots and cars and bringing them to the royal portal ; chariot riders, chief charioteers, elephant riders, cavalrymen, heroes, braves, soldiers, and warriors, are coming to salute the king of the Yâdavas ; skilful people are dancing, singing, playing, and delighting ; and bards and panegyrists are again and again celebrating glories, and are receiving [as rewards] elephants, horses, vestments, arms, food, money, and golden jewel-studded ornaments.

Having related this much of the story, S'rî S'ukadev Jî said to the King :—Mahârâj ! on the one hand, in Râjâ Ugrasen's capital, there were going on, in this way, a variety of entertainments, and, on the other hand, S'rî Krishṇa Chand, the root of joy, was ever disporting himself with his sixteen thousand one hundred and eight young women. At times, the young women, engrossed in love, were making themselves up like the Lord ; at times,

Hari, being [1] [similarly] engrossed, is adorning the young women; and the mutual sports and frolics they indulge in are unutterable; they are not describable by me; only by being seen can it be realized.

Having said this, S'ukadev Jî said:—Mahârâj! one day, at night time, S'rî Krishṇa Chand was disporting with all the young women, and, having witnessed the various actions of the Lord, Kinnaras and Gandharvas, playing away on lutes, timbrels, pipes, and kettle-drums, were celebrating praise, and all was in accord, when in the midst of this, while disporting themselves, something occurred to the Lord, he went to the bank of a lake, taking them all with him, and entering the water began to indulge in water-play. Afterwards, while engaged in water-play, all the wives, being absorbed in the love of S'rî Krishṇa Chand, losing all regard for body and mind, having seen a *chakwâ* and *chakwî* seated on opposite sides of the lake calling to each other, said,—

> "O *Chakwî!* why art thou concealing grief? through separation from thy lover thou art not sleeping at night; [2]
> Having become greatly agitated, thou art calling thy lover! thou art ever reminding us of the lover;
> We, for our part, have become his slave-girls." Having spoken thus, they went onwards.

Then they began to say to the ocean, "O ocean! thou who are heaving deep sighs, and art keeping away night and day, why is that? Art thou separated from anyone? or is it grief for the lost fourteen jewels?" Having said this, then, looking at the moon, they said, "O Moon! why art thou emaciated in body and disturbed in mind? Hast thou consumption that thou wanest and waxest daily? or, having looked upon S'rî Krishṇa Chand Jî, are thy actions and thoughts disconcerted also, as ours are being disconcerted?"

Having related thus much of the story, S'rî S'ukadev Jî said to the King:—Mahârâj! in this way all the young women said a variety of things to the air, the clouds, the cuckoo, the mountains, the river, and the swan; those can be imagined. Afterwards all the women are disporting themselves with S'rî Krishṇa Chand, and remain constant in attendance; they are celebrating the virtues of the Lord, and receiving the reward which their hearts desired; and the Lord was carrying out the duties of the householder state in a conscientious way. Mahârâj! the sixteen thousand one hundred and eight queens, which have been previously described, had each of them ten sons and one daughter apiece, and their offspring was innumerable. I have not the power to describe them; but I know this much, that there were thirty millions eighty-eight thousand one hundred schools for the instruction of S'rî Krishṇa Chand Jî's offspring, and just the

[1] For *âsakta ko* read *âsakta ho*. [2] See note [1], p. 237.

same number of teachers. Furthermore, whatever sons, sons' sons, and daughters' sons, which S'rî Krishṇa Chand Jî had, none were deficient in beauty, strength, bravery, wealth, or virtue. Each one excelled the other ; how shall I attempt to describe them ? Having related this much, the sage said :—Mahârâj ! I have celebrated the sports of Braj and Dwârakâ ; this is felicitous all. Whoever shall recite it with affection will undoubtedly obtain faith and salvation. By hearing [1] the story of Hari, he will meet with the reward which arises from penance, sacrifice, almsgiving, vows, pilgrimage, and bathing.

[1] Lallû Lâl, and previous editions, put here *sunne sunâne se*, "by hearing and reciting."

HERE IS THE END.